WJEC/Eduqas

Religious Studies
for A Level Year 1 & AS

Philosophy of Religion
and Religion and Ethics

Richard Gray

Karl Lawson

Edited by Richard Gray

Illuminate
Publishing

Published in 2016 by Illuminate Publishing Limited, an imprint of
Hodder Education, an Hachette UK Company, Carmelite House,
50 Victoria Embankment, London EC4Y 0DZ

Orders: Please visit www.illuminatepublishing.com
or email sales@illuminatepublishing.com

© Richard Gray and Karl Lawson

The moral rights of the authors have been asserted.

British Library Cataloguing-in-Publication Data

A catalogue record for this book is available from the British Library

ISBN 978-1-908682-99-4

Printed in Wales by Cambrian Printers Ltd

08.21

The publisher's policy is to use papers that are natural, renewable and
recyclable products made from wood grown in sustainable forests. The
logging and manufacturing processes are expected to conform to the
environmental regulations of the country of origin.

Every effort has been made to contact copyright holders of material
reproduced in this book. If notified, the publishers will be pleased to rectify
any errors or omissions at the earliest opportunity.

This material has been endorsed by WJEC/Eduqas and offers high
quality support for the delivery of WJEC/Eduqas qualifications. While this
material has been through a WJEC/Eduqas quality assurance process, all
responsibility for the content remains with the publisher.

WJEC/Eduqas examination questions are reproduced by permission from
WJEC/Eduqas

Series editor: Richard Gray
Editor: Geoff Tuttle
Design and Layout: EMC Design Ltd, Bedford

Acknowledgements

Cover Image: © Skarie20/iStock

Image credits:

p. 1 Skarie20/iStock; **pp. 4 & 6** Rod Savely; **p. 7** (left) Ssavotije; (middle & right) Olaf Speier; **p. 9** Oliver Hoffmann; **p. 11** dslaven; **p. 16** Joe Gough; **p. 17** MikeCardUK; **pp. 18 & 19** MSSA; **p. 27** (left) Yeti Crab; (right) Steve Allen; **p. 32** Vladimir Wrangel; **p. 33** Unknown, English [Public domain], via Wikimedia Commons; **p. 34** SunnySideUp; **p. 35** GongTo; **p. 40** Everett – Art; **p. 41** Pearl Bucknall; **p. 42** GongTo; **p. 50** Patryk Kosmider; **p. 51** Nicku; **p. 56** (top left) mTaira; (top middle left) Lucky Team Studio; (top middle right) AC Rider; (top right) Zoran Ras; (bottom left) Peter Schulzek; (bottom middle left) Roland IJdema; (bottom middle right) Jim Valee; (bottom right) Niran Phonruang; **p. 59** Africa Studio; **p. 65** npine; **p. 66** VladisChern; **p. 73** Morphart Creation; **p. 75** Everett Historical; **p. 81** UMB-O; **p. 83** jcpgraphic; **p. 84** David Carillet; **p. 85** mehmetcan; **p. 86** Baciu; **p. 87** Zvonimir Alletic; **p. 93** Public domain; **p. 94** CHOATphotographer; **p. 100** Graphics RF; **p. 101** Everett – Art; **p. 104** By Shane Pope from Austin, United States (Richard Dawkins, original resolution) [CC BY 2.0 (http://creativecommons.org/licenses/by/2.0)], via Wikimedia Commons; **p. 106** Ziel (Own work) [CC BY-SA 3.0 (http://creativecommons.org/licenses/by-sa/3.0) or GFDL (http://www.gnu.org/copyleft/fdl.html)], via Wikimedia Commons; **p. 110** Sting [CC BY-SA 2.5 (http://creativecommons.org/licenses/by-sa/2.5)], via Wikimedia Commons; **p. 111** By Kaihsu Tai (own work, Kaihsu Tai) [GFDL (http://www.gnu.org/copyleft/fdl.html), CC-BY-SA-3.0 (http://creativecommons.org/licenses/by-sa/3.0/), via Wikimedia Commons; **p. 119** After Lysippos [Public domain], via Wikimedia Commons; **p. 120** Phonlamai Photo; **p. 121** The original uploader was Galilea at German Wikipedia [GFDL (http://www.gnu.org/copyleft/fdl.html) or CC-BY-SA-3.0 (http://creativecommons.org/licenses/by-sa/3.0/)], via Wikimedia Commons; **p. 123** From Carl Heinrich Bloch [Public domain], via Wikimedia Commons; **p. 124** Pavel L Photo and Video; **p. 130** SpeedKingz; **p. 131** By Friedrich Engels [Public domain], via Wikimedia Commons; **p. 140** Panos Karas; **p. 141** Nheyob (Own work) [CC BY-SA 4.0 (http://creativecommons.org/licenses/by-sa/4.0)], via Wikimedia Commons; **p. 142** Creative Commons Attribution-Share Alike 2.0 Generic license; **p. 148** Bartolomeo Montagna [Public domain], via Wikimedia Commons; **p. 151** Ema Woo; **p. 158** Aris Suwanmalee; **p. 159** Gagliarilmages; **p. 160** By Flickr user Steve Punter (You don't want me on Flickr) [CC BY 2.0 (http://creativecommons.org/licenses/by/2.0)], via Wikimedia Commons; **p. 162** Public domain; **p. 163** Public domain; **p. 166** Umit Erdem; **p. 176** Renata Sedmakova; **p. 177** Renata Sedmakova; **p. 192** Public domain; **p. 193** Bikeworldtravel; **p. 201** Georgios Kollidas; **p. 203** kulyk; **p. 207** skyearth; **p. 209** Public domain; **p. 210** bikeriderlondon; **p. 216** (top) Bernard Gagnon (Own work) [GFDL (http://www.gnu.org/copyleft/fdl.html) or CC BY-SA 3.0 (http://creativecommons.org/licenses/by-sa/3.0)], via Wikimedia Commons; (bottom) Daniel Mytens [Public domain], via Wikimedia Commons; **p. 219** anyaivanova; **p. 222** Michael Warwick

Contents

About this book

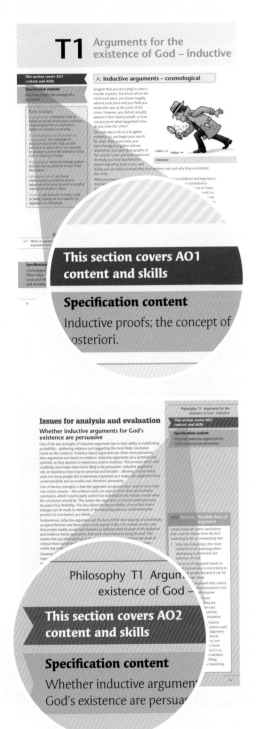

With the new A Level in Religious Studies, there is a lot to cover and a lot to do in preparation for the examinations at the end of AS or the full A Level. The aim of these books is to provide enough support for you to achieve success at AS and A Level, whether as a teacher or a learner.

This series of books is skills-based in its approach to learning, which means it aims to combine covering the content of the Specification with examination preparation from the start. In other words, it aims to help you get through the course whilst at the same time developing some important skills needed for the examinations.

To help you study, there are clearly defined sections for each of the AO1 and AO2 areas of the Specification. These are arranged according to the Specification Themes and use, as far as is possible, Specification headings to help you see that the content has been covered, for both AS and A Level.

The AO1 content is detailed, but precise, with the benefit of providing you with references to both religious/philosophical works and to the views of scholars. The AO2 responds to the issues raised in the Specification and provides you with ideas for further debate, to help you develop your own evaluation skills.

Ways to use this book

In considering the different ways in which you may teach or learn, it was decided that the books needed to have an inbuilt flexibility to adapt. As a result, they can be used for classroom learning, for independent work by individuals, as homework, and, they are even suitable for the purposes of 'flip learning' if your school or college does this.

You may be well aware that learning time is so valuable at A Level and so we have also taken this into consideration by creating flexible features and activities, again to save you the time of painstaking research and preparation, either as teacher or learner.

Features of the books

The books all contain the following features that appear in the margins, or are highlighted in the main body of the text, in order to support teaching and learning.

Key terms of technical, religious and philosophical words or phrases

> ### Key terms
> Efficient cause: the 'third party' that moves potentiality to actuality

Quickfire questions simple, straightforward questions to help consolidate key facts about what is being digested in reading through the information

quickfire

> 1.2 Who was the Unmoved Mover according to Aquinas'?

Key quotes either from religious and philosophical works and/or the works of scholars

Key quote

Nature therefore which has been corrupted, is called evil, for assuredly when incorrupt it is good; but even when corrupt, so far as it is nature it is good, so far as it is corrupted it is evil. (Augustine)

Study tips advice on how to study, prepare for the examination and answer questions

Study tip

Whilst you do not need to be able go into great detail regarding Craig's concepts of infinity, you should be able to show that you understand how his Kalam argument is put together, along with the basic differences (as explained in key terms) of potential and actual infinities.

AO1 Activities that serve the purpose of focusing on identification, presentation and explanation, and developing the skills of knowledge and understanding required for the examination

AO1 Activity *Thinking point*

Why do you think the idea of an 'efficient cause' is so important to the arguments of both Aristotle and Aquinas? Explain your answer using evidence and examples from what you have read.

AO2 Activities that serve the purpose of focusing on conclusions, as a basis for thinking about the issues, developing critical analysis and the evaluation skills required for the examination

AO2 Activity *Possible lines of argument*

Listed below are some conclusions that could be drawn from the AO2 reasoning in the accompanying text:

Glossary of all the key terms for quick reference.

Specific feature: Developing skills

This section is very much a focus on 'what to do' with the content and the issues that are raised. They occur at the end of each section, giving 12 AO1 examples and 12 AO2 examination-focused activities.

The Developing skills are arranged progressively, so as to provide initial support for you at first, and then gradually encourage you to have more independence.

AO1 and AO2 answers and commentaries

The final section has a selection of answers and commentaries as a framework for judging what an effective and ineffective response may be. The comments highlight some common mistakes and also examples of good practice so that all involved in teaching and learning can reflect upon how to approach examination answers.

Richard Gray
Series Editor
2016

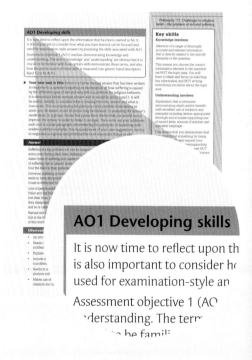

AO1 Developing skills

It is now time to reflect upon th is also important to consider he used for examination-style an

Assessment objective 1 (AO
derstanding. The term
be famili

T1 Arguments for the existence of God – inductive

Specification content

Inductive proofs; the concept of a posteriori.

Key terms

A posteriori: a statement that is based on actual observation, evidence, experimental data or experience – relates to inductive reasoning

Cosmological and teleological arguments: two examples of inductive arguments that use the evidence of, and within, the universe to attempt to prove the existence of the God of Classical Theism

Empirically: using knowledge gained through the experiences of any of the five senses

Inductive proof: argument constructed on evidence and/or experience that puts forward a possible conclusion based on these

Posit: to put forward, or state, a fact or belief, usually as the basis for an argument or conclusion

quickfire

1.1 What is needed for an inductive argument to make sense?

Specification content

Cosmological argument; Aquinas first Three Ways – (motion or change; cause and effect; contingency and necessity).

A: Inductive arguments – cosmological

Imagine that you are trying to solve a murder mystery. You know where the crime took place, you know roughly when it took place and you think you know who was at the scene of the crime. However, you did not actually witness it first-hand yourself, so how can you prove what happened? How do you solve the crime?

The only way to do so is to gather evidence. So, you begin your search for clues. After some time, you have managed to gather witness statements, you have photographs of the murder scene, you have examined the body, you have had forensics experts reporting back to you, and finally, you are ready to reveal who the murderer was and why they committed the crime.

Searching for clues

What you have just done is to induct a judgment, based on evidence and experience that has led to a possible conclusion. In philosophical terms your conclusion is reached via **inductive proof**. Such a proof is the only type available to us in many circumstances – particularly when we were not available to gather direct proof (i.e. we were not present at the time of the event to **empirically** witness it). Equally we cannot use pure logical reasoning to come up with a conclusion because neither the circumstances nor the events permit this to happen.

Inductive proofs are **a posteriori** because they require evidence and/or experience for them to make sense. In the philosophy of religion, any argument that is constructed upon evidence and/or experience is an a posteriori, inductive, argument. In the course of your study this applies to both the **cosmological and teleological arguments** for the existence of God. The former uses the evidence of the existing universe and asks the question 'Where did it come from?' as the basis for its argument. The latter looks at the structure and function of the universe and the things within it to suggest an order and purpose that could not have occurred by chance as the basis for its argument. In both cases, evidence is gathered and conclusions are **posited**.

Aquinas – First Way

Aquinas' First Way is often referred to as 'motion' or 'change'. Basically, Aquinas said that when we observe the universe, we notice that things tend to be in a state of change or motion. From this observation Aquinas noted that things do not do this of their own accord but are instead 'moved' (or 'changed') by something else (in this, Aquinas is restating what Aristotle said).

Key quote

It is certain, and evident to our senses, that in the world some things are in motion. Now whatever is in motion is put in motion by another, for nothing can be in motion except it is in potentiality to that towards which it is in motion; whereas a thing moves inasmuch as it is in act. For motion is nothing else than the reduction of something from potentiality to actuality. But nothing can be reduced from potentiality to actuality, except by something in a state of actuality. (Aquinas, *Summa Theologica*)

Aquinas said that if we looked back down this sequence of movements/changes, we would have to eventually come to something that started the whole sequence off. Now, as all things in the universe (that are observable) are either moving or movers, we need to find a point that started these things – and that means, necessarily, looking outside of the universe – i.e. to something which has not been moved by anything else and is in fact incapable of being moved/changed by anything else but is responsible for initiating the whole sequence of movement/change.

Aristotle named this the Prime Mover, and Aquinas developed this into the 'Unmoved Mover' – *'that which all men call God'*.

To illustrate this point further, Aquinas builds on Aristotle's examples and explanations. Aristotle speaks of things moving from a state of '**potentiality**' (i.e. something that it has a possibility of moving/changing into) towards a state of '**actuality**' (where it actually achieves or reaches its potential).

However, both Aristotle and Aquinas noted that this change could only happen if something that already possessed a state of actuality acted on that which was in its state of potentiality. This third party is known as the '**efficient cause**'.

Aristotle used the example of a block of marble (potential) becoming a statue (actual) but only when acted upon by the sculptor (efficient cause).

quickfire

1.2 Who was the Unmoved Mover according to Aquinas'?

Key terms

Actuality: when something is in its fully realised state

Efficient cause: the 'third party' that moves potentiality to actuality

Potentiality: the ability to be able to become something else

Potential

Efficient cause   *Actual*

quickfire

1.3 What example was given by:
i. Aristotle
ii. Aquinas
to explain how things with potential become actual?

quickfire

1.4 Where do we find an order of efficient causes?

Key quote

The second way is from the nature of the efficient cause. In the world of sense we find there is an order of efficient causes. There is no case known (neither is it, indeed, possible) in which a thing is found to be the efficient cause of itself; for so it would be prior to itself, which is impossible. (Aquinas)

Key quote

But if in efficient causes it is possible to go on to infinity, there will be no first efficient cause, neither will there be an ultimate effect, nor any intermediate efficient causes; all of which is plainly false. Therefore it is necessary to admit a first efficient cause, to which everyone gives the name of God. (Aquinas)

Aquinas uses the example of wood becoming hot in order to illustrate this point:

Key quote

Thus that which is actually hot, as fire, makes wood, which is potentially hot, to be actually hot, and thereby moves and changes it. Now it is not possible that the same thing should be at once in actuality and potentiality in the same respect, but only in different respects. For what is actually hot cannot simultaneously be potentially hot; but it is simultaneously potentially cold. It is therefore impossible that in the same respect and in the same way a thing should be both mover and moved, i.e. that it should move itself. (Aquinas)

In this, Aquinas is stating that the fire that makes wood hot must already have the property of hotness within itself in order, in turn, to make the wood hot. Were it to have any other state (e.g. coldness) within itself then it would be impossible to make the wood hot.

AO1 Activity

Why do you think the idea of an 'efficient cause' is so important to the arguments of both Aristotle and Aquinas? Explain your answer using evidence and examples from what you have read.

Study tip

When explaining the idea of motion in an essay it is worth remembering that the idea of motion does not necessarily mean movement in terms of velocity or direction; it can also mean the motion that an object has as it changes its state (e.g. H_2O molecules are in motion when heated and change from water to steam).

Aquinas – Second Way

Key quote

Now in efficient causes it is not possible to go on to infinity, because in all efficient causes following in order, the first is the cause of the intermediate cause, and the intermediate is the cause of the ultimate cause, whether the intermediate cause be several, or only one. Now to take away the cause is to take away the effect. Therefore, if there be no first cause among efficient causes, there will be no ultimate, nor any intermediate cause. (Aquinas)

Aquinas' second way deals with the concept of cause and effect. Everything observable in nature is subject to this law, according to Aquinas, although the idea that this chain of cause and effect could be traced back infinitely is seen as impossible by him. This then leads to the question: 'What was the first cause?' and, for Aquinas, the answer is 'God'.

Aquinas states here, not only the idea that cause and effect is a simple, undeniable, law of the universe but also that it is impossible for anything within the universe to cause itself. (It would be like you being your own parent – you cannot exist before you exist – you need something else to bring you into existence.)

If you imagine a line of dominoes, the first (efficient cause) is the one that causes the second (**intermediate cause**) one to fall, which in turn causes the third (**ultimate cause**) one to fall. However, the third one would not have fallen, had the first one not have hit the second one. Aquinas' idea of efficient cause followed by intermediate cause and ending at ultimate cause can seem confusing at first, but, by using the domino analogy (see diagram) it gives a suitable visual expression of the philosophical idea.

QUICKFIRE

1.5 Why does Aquinas claim that the first efficient cause is God?

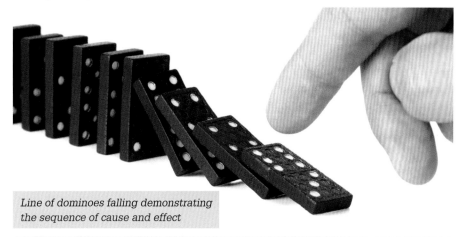

Line of dominoes falling demonstrating the sequence of cause and effect

Study tip

It is worth remembering that, as Ed Miller pointed out in his *Questions that Matter*, when Aquinas is arguing against an infinite series of causes and effects he is not thinking of a temporal series, or one that stretches infinitely backwards in time, but rather a hierarchical series, or one that extends infinitely upwards in being. This would therefore be based on an assumption that all things have their source in an ultimate cause (or, in Aquinas's words: 'God'). This idea also closely relates to the ideas of both Plato and Aristotle.

Aquinas – Third Way

Aquinas' third way deals with the concept of contingency and necessity. Again, Aquinas notes that everything that exists has the possibility of not existing (i.e. it is **contingent**) and draws the conclusion that if this was true of everything in existence then nothing would ever have come into existence. This is because in order for contingent beings to exist, there has to be a non-contingent (i.e. **necessary**) **being** that brought everything else into existence. For Aquinas, this necessary being is 'God'.

Key quote

The third way is taken from possibility and necessity, and runs thus. We find in nature things that are possible to be and not to be, since they are found to be generated, and to corrupt, and consequently, they are possible to be and not to be. But it is impossible for these always to exist, for that which is possible not to be at some time is not. Therefore, if everything is possible not to be, then at one time there could have been nothing in existence …. it would have been impossible for anything to have begun to exist; and thus even now nothing would be in existence … which is absurd. (**Aquinas**)

Aquinas states that all things in nature are limited in their existence. They all have beginnings and endings. Following this idea to its logical conclusion Aquinas notes that this means at one point in history nothing existed and that, even now, nothing would exist – which is plainly not the case.

Key terms

Contingent: anything that depends on something else (in the case of a contingent being – it is contingent upon another being for its existence, e.g. a child is contingent upon its parent)

Intermediate cause: this refers to a cause that relies on something else to have triggered it (remember the 2nd domino in the line!)

Necessary being: Aquinas' contention that a non-contingent being is necessary for contingent beings to exist. It is this necessary being that is the source of all existence for all other contingent beings

Ultimate cause: in the sense of Aquinas' writings, this is the end cause in the sequence that could not have occurred had there not been preceding efficient and intermediate causes (think about this as the penultimate domino in the line to fall)

QUICKFIRE

1.6 What has the possibility of not existing?

A way of thinking of this idea is to consider the relationship of the parent and the child. Without the existence of the parent, the child cannot come into existence. Or, to put it another way, the child is contingent on the parent for its existence.

Key quote

Therefore, not all beings are merely possible, but there must exist something the existence of which is necessary. But every necessary thing either has its necessity caused by another, or not. Now it is impossible to go on to infinity in necessary things which have their necessity caused by another, as has been already proved in regard to efficient causes. Therefore we cannot but postulate the existence of some being having of itself its own necessity, and not receiving it from another, but rather causing in others their necessity. This all men speak of as God. (Aquinas)

Aquinas states that the only possible solution to this dilemma is that something must exist that is unlike everything else in existence – in that it has no beginning and no end, in other words, it has necessary existence. This necessary existence is needed to bring about the existence of everything else. For Aquinas this being was 'God'.

quickfire

1.7 What is meant by necessary existence?

AO1 Activity

After reading the section on Aquinas' Three Ways, close the book and write down what you consider the main point of each way was.

Specification content

The Kalam cosmological argument with reference to William Lane Craig (rejection of actual infinities and concept of a personal creator).

quickfire

1.8 What did Craig state was true for everything that begins to exist?

Key terms

Actual infinite: something that is actually infinite in extent or in extent of the operations performed – it literally has no beginning and no end

Apologist: an individual who writes or speaks in defence of a particular cause or belief

Temporal: things relating to time

The Kalam cosmological argument

From the Arabic word 'to argue or discuss', the Kalam cosmological argument can trace its origins to the work of Islamic scholars in the 9th and 11th centuries of the Common Era. It has been modernised and championed by Christian apologist William Lane Craig.

In 1993 Craig stipulated his argument thus:

1. Everything that begins to exist has a cause of its existence.

2. The universe began to exist.

3. Therefore, the universe has a cause of its existence.

4. Since no scientific explanation (in terms of physical laws) can provide a causal account of the origin of the universe, the cause must be personal (explanation is given in terms of a personal agent).

This is a (relatively) straightforward and easy to follow argument. However, in order to answer challenges to the idea that the universe might be considered infinite, Craig developed the following defence to his second point:

i. An actual infinite cannot exist.

ii. A beginningless temporal series of events is an actual infinite

iii. Therefore, a beginningless temporal series of events cannot exist.

In order to explain this, an example of a library is often referred to: imagine a library with an actually infinite number of books. Suppose that the library also contains an infinite number of red and an infinite number of black books, so that for every red book there is a black book, and vice versa. It follows that the library contains as many red books as the total books in its collection, and as many red books as red and black books combined. But this is absurd; in reality the subset (i.e. red or black) cannot be equivalent to the entire set (i.e. red and black). Hence, actual infinites cannot exist in reality.

However, critics point out that this is ignoring the fact that there are two types of infinity recognised in standard mathematics – 'actual' and 'potential'. Craig only refers to the impossibility of the first, not the second in his initial argument. Craig responded by recognising that if an actual infinite was impossible, a **potential infinite** confirmed the fact that the universe had a beginning. This forms the second part of his argument.

Craig's Kalam argument is often seen as very confusing, not least because it depends on an understanding of the concepts of infinity that are, in themselves, difficult to grasp. However, in its simplest form it is straightforward and appealing – to such a degree that it has had significant influence in the rational theistic defence against atheistic arguments – especially in the fundamentalist Christian churches of America.

Is it possible to have an infinite number of red and black books?

AO1 Activity

Summary diagram to complete: select the five most important ideas as presented by Aquinas and Craig and explain why they are important to our understanding of the cosmological argument.

Summary

The Kalam cosmological argument bases itself on the impossibility of the universe being infinite. Once this is agreed, then it is reasonable to ask 'How did it start?' Craig's version posits the requirement for a personal creator.

Key quote

I think that it can be plausibly argued that the cause of the universe must be a personal Creator. For how else could a temporal effect arise from an eternal cause? If the cause were simply a mechanically operating set of necessary and sufficient conditions existing from eternity, then why would not the effect also exist from eternity? For example, if the cause of water's being frozen is the temperature's being below zero degrees, then if the temperature were below zero degrees from eternity, then any water present would be frozen from eternity. The only way to have an eternal cause but a temporal effect would seem to be if the cause is a personal agent who freely chooses to create an effect in time. For example, a man sitting from eternity may will to stand up; hence, a temporal effect may arise from an eternally existing agent. Indeed, the agent may will from eternity to create a temporal effect, so that no change in the agent need be conceived. Thus, we are brought not merely to the first cause of the universe, but to its personal Creator. **(Craig)**

Study tip

Whilst you do not need to be able go into great detail regarding Craig's concepts of infinity, you should be able to show that you understand how his Kalam argument is put together, along with the basic differences (as explained in key terms) of potential and actual infinities.

quickfire

1.9 What is meant by infinity?

quickfire

1.10 Which movement within Christianity has been particularly supportive of Craig's argument?

Key term

Potential infinite: the potential infinite is something that could continue on, were effort to be applied. E.g. it would be possible to always continue a number line if we wanted to, or we could always come up with a bigger number

Key skills

Knowledge involves:

Selection of a range of (thorough) accurate and relevant information that is directly related to the specific demands of the question.

This means you choose the correct information relevant to the question set NOT the topic area. You will have to think and focus on selecting key information and NOT writing everything you know about the topic area.

Understanding involves:

Explanation that is extensive, demonstrating depth and/or breadth with excellent use of evidence and examples including (where appropriate) thorough and accurate supporting use of sacred texts, sources of wisdom and specialist language.

This means that you demonstrate that you understand something by being able to illustrate and expand your points through examples/supporting evidence in a personal way and NOT repeat chunks from a text book (known as rote learning).

Further application of skills:

Go through the topic areas in this section and create some bullet lists of key points from key areas. For each one, provide further elaboration and explanation through the use of evidence and examples.

Study tip

One of the most common errors made in examinations is by candidates who see a key word in a title of an essay and write everything they know about it. Successful candidates avoid this and only use the information that is directly relevant to the question.

AO1 Developing skills

It is now time to reflect upon the information that has been covered so far. It is also important to consider how what you have learned can be focused and used for examination-style answers by practising the skills associated with AO1.

Assessment objective 1 (AO1) involves demonstrating knowledge and understanding. The terms 'knowledge' and 'understanding' are obvious but it is crucial to be familiar with how certain skills demonstrate these terms, and also, how the performance of these skills is measured (see generic band descriptors Band 5 for AS AO1).

Obviously, an answer is placed within an appropriate band descriptor depending upon how well the answer performs, ranging from excellent, good, satisfactory, basic/limited to very limited.

For starters, try using the framework / writing frame provided to help you in practising these skills to answer the question below.

As the units in each section of the book develop, the amount of support will be reduced gradually in order to encourage your independence and the perfecting of your AO1 skills.

EXAM PRACTICE: A WRITING FRAME

A focus on explaining how Aquinas demonstrates the need for a first cause of the universe.

Aquinas' first three of his Five Ways, form part of the cosmological argument for the existence of God.
The first of these ways was that of 'motion' or 'change' and is based on …

Aquinas developed the ideas of Aristotle who spoke of …

Aristotle's example to illustrate his ideas of potential moving to actual was …

Aquinas used his own example which was …

These ideas clearly show that the universe …

The Second Way deals with the chain of cause and effect which can be observed …

Aquinas stated that infinite regress was impossible because …

An example to explain this further could be …

Aquinas' Third Way dealt with …

This was important because it shows …

An example to illustrate this is …

In summary …

Issues for analysis and evaluation

Whether inductive arguments for God's existence are persuasive

One of the key strengths of inductive arguments lies in their ability in establishing probability – gathering evidence and suggesting the most likely conclusion based on this evidence. Evidence-based arguments are often more persuasive than arguments not based on evidence. Inductive arguments are *a posteriori* and synthetic (true in relation to how they relate to the world) as they depend on experience and/or evidence. This provides them with credibility and makes them more likely to be persuasive. Inductive arguments rely on experience that may be universal and testable – allowing it to be widely used. For many people this is extremely important as it makes the argument more understandable and accessible and, therefore, persuasive.

One of the key strengths is that the argument recognises there may be more than one correct answer – the evidence used can support more than one probable conclusion, which is particularly useful if an individual is not entirely certain what the conclusion should be. This means the argument can be persuasive precisely because it has flexibility. This also allows for the possibility of error that means changes can be made to elements of the reasoning without undermining the process (or conclusion) as a whole.

Furthermore, inductive arguments are the basis of the vast majority of scientifically accepted theories and these have a wide appeal in the 21st-century world, such that people readily accept such theories as valid precisely because of the inductive and evidence-based approaches that led to these theories being formed. This means that any philosophical or theological reasoning that mirrors the work of science must surely have a similar claim to both validity and persuasiveness – unlike any reasoning that has not been based on such foundations.

However, some may argue that they are not persuasive – often for the same reasons as others would claim them to be. For instance, one of the significant weaknesses of inductive arguments is that they can be accused of having limited effectiveness as 'undeniable proofs'. Their very flexibility means that they could be considered as weak arguments and, because of this, not persuasive.

It is also true to state that inductive arguments can be readily challenged if alternative evidence, that is equally as likely to be true, is provided – thereby undermining the persuasiveness of the argument. An extension to this is that it is also equally possible to accept all of the evidence but to deny the conclusion without contradiction. If this is accepted then it suggests that there can be no persuasiveness in the argument as this limits its effectiveness, particularly in terms of attempting to establish the existence of a divine being with specific characteristics (e.g. God of Classical Theism as the designer of the universe).

Perhaps most important to consider is that the premises, whilst supporting the conclusion, do not make it definite – for many, this means that inductive arguments are not persuasive enough to support a basis for religious belief.

This section covers AO2 content and skills

Specification content
Whether inductive arguments for God's existence are persuasive.

AO2 Activity *Possible lines of argument*

Listed below are some conclusions that could be drawn from the AO2 reasoning in the accompanying text:

1. Inductive reasoning is the most useful form of reasoning when attempting to determine the existence of God.

2. Any form of argument based on empirical evidence is more likely to persuade people because it can be seen to make sense.

3. Any form of argument that cannot provide a definite conclusion is too flimsy to persuade anyone.

4. Flexibility in arguments demonstrates that they are responsive to criticism and therefore strong arguments; making them more persuasive.

Consider each of the conclusions drawn above and collect evidence and examples to support each argument from the AO1 and AO2 material studied in this section. Select one conclusion that you think is most convincing and explain why it is so. Now contrast this with the weakest conclusion in the list, justifying your argument with clear reasoning and evidence.

Specification content

The extent to which the Kalam
cosmological argument is convincing.

The extent to which the Kalam cosmological argument is convincing

The Kalam cosmological argument as portrayed by William Lane Craig would seem to benefit from being written in the modern scientific age. Craig has the advantage over Aquinas et al., because he has access to contemporary scientific information about the universe: big bang theory, cosmological background radiation, etc. These all provide straightforward, scientifically valid evidence that the universe is finite and thus had a beginning. Indeed, the contemporary views of the universe all agree that there was a starting point – this provides an extremely useful groundswell of opinion for any argument attempting to demonstrate that a beginning of the universe is required.

In a sense, this renders the need for Craig to prove the universe as finite as meaningless. Why argue for something which is supported by the vast majority of the rational and scientific world. The fact that the universe had a point at which it began appears not be in dispute. In fact, not only is it not apparently in dispute, it is readily accepted, almost as scientific fact rather than theory. The concept that all things in our experience – including the universe itself, have beginnings, lends itself nicely to the first part of Craig's argument. Craig's work here, it would seem, is done – the Kalam cosmological argument for God's existence appears to be entirely convincing. However, things are not quite as simple as they at first seem!

Craig's argument moves from demonstrating that the universe had a beginning to the suggestion that this beginning had a cause, external to the universe – which Craig eventually asserts as being God. It is at this point of the argument that the empirical support thus far enjoyed, is no longer available. The question of how convincing the argument is now rests on how far the individual is willing to accept the next steps in Craig's argument.

Effectively, Craig suggests that the cause of the universe must be through the deliberate choice of a personal being as the physical laws of the universe that cause everything within the universe to work did not themselves exist until the universe did. This logically means that the cause of the universe could not be explained in terms of physical laws. The only viable other explanation for Craig is that the cause is personal. For Craig, the only viable personal agent capable of existing outside of the universe and having the will, power and ability to create the universe is God.

For the theist, there is much that is attractive about this argument. It involves modern cosmology, appears entirely rational and fits in with traditional theistic interpretations regarding creation. In this sense it is a convincing argument.

For those not predisposed to the position of the theist, however, the argument does not have the same power to convince. One of the key elements of the argument that is often cited is that Craig states, quite categorically, that infinity is impossible. Later in the argument he refers to a personal creator that is infinite. As an argument, this is self-contradictory and is one of the key reasons for non-theists to reject the Kalam cosmological argument for God's existence as unconvincing.

Listed below are some conclusions that could be drawn from the AO2 reasoning in the accompanying text:

1. Scientific points of view support the Kalam argument and strengthen it.

2. The Kalam argument is only as convincing as the individual's prior belief (or non-belief) in God.

3. The denial of infinity, if rejected, completely undermines the Kalam argument.

4. The conclusion of a personal creator is based on a false dichotomy.

Consider each of the conclusions drawn above and collect evidence and examples to support each argument from the AO1 and AO2 material studied in this section. Select one conclusion that you think is most convincing and explain why it is so. Now contrast this with the weakest conclusion in the list, justifying your argument with clear reasoning and evidence.

AO2 Developing skills

It is now time to reflect upon the information that has been covered so far. It is also important to consider how what you have learned can be focused and used for examination-style answers by practising the skills associated with AO2.

Assessment objective 2 (AO2) involves 'analysis' and 'evaluation'. The terms may be obvious but it is crucial to be familiar with how certain skills demonstrate these terms, and also, how the performance of these skills is measured (see generic band descriptors Band 5 for AS AO2).

Obviously, an answer is placed within an appropriate band descriptor depending upon how well the answer performs, ranging from excellent, good, satisfactory, basic/limited to very limited.

For starters, try using the framework / writing frame provided to help you in practising these skills to answer the question below.

As the units in each section of the book develop, the amount of support will be reduced gradually in order to encourage your independence and the perfecting of your AO2 skills.

Have a go at answering this question by using the writing frame below.

EXAM PRACTICE: A WRITING FRAME

A focus on evaluating how far the Kalam cosmological argument convinvingly demonstrates that God exists.

The issue for debate here is …

There are different ways of looking at this and many key questions to ask such as …

The Kalam cosmological argument is an inductive proof and as such has both strengths and shortcomings. In order to determine the extent to which this argument proves a convincing argument for God's existence, it is necessary to consider each of those strengths and shortcomings in turn …

In light of these considerations, it could be argued that …

Nevertheless, it is my view that …

and I base this argument on the following reasons …

Key skills

Analysis involves identifying issues raised by the materials in the AO1, together with those identified in the AO2 section, and presents sustained and clear views, either of scholars or from a personal perspective ready for evaluation.

This means that it picks out key things to debate and the lines of argument presented by others or a personal point of view.

Evaluation involves considering the various implications of the issues raised based upon the evidence gleaned from analysis and provides an extensive detailed argument with a clear conclusion.

This means that the answer weighs up the various and different lines of argument analysed through individual commentary and response and arrives at a conclusion through a clear process of reasoning.

Study tip

Always point out the relative strengths and weaknesses of the Kalam argument, as identified in your notes. Consider why these might be considered so, using relevant examples and/or evidence and then give your own reasoned opinion based upon what you have chosen to write about.

This section covers AO1
content and skills

Specification content

St Thomas Aquinas' Fifth Way –
concept of governance; archer and
arrow analogy.

quickfire

1.11 Why did Aquinas believe it was
necessary to suggest a guiding
intelligence behind the natural
workings of the universe?

Key quote

The Fifth Way is taken from the
governance of the world. We see that
things which lack knowledge, such
as natural bodies, act for an end,
and this is evident from their acting
always, or nearly always, in the
same way, so as to obtain the best
result. Hence it is plain that they
achieve their end, not fortuitously,
but designedly.

Now whatever lacks knowledge
cannot move towards an end,
unless it be directed by some
being endowed with knowledge and
intelligence; as the arrow is directed
by the archer. Therefore, some
intelligent being exists by whom all
natural things are directed to their
end; and this being we call God.
(Aquinas)

Specification content

Paley's watchmaker – analogy of
complex design.

Key term

Telos: the term can have a number
of meanings but generally refers to
the 'end' (as in final destination);
'goal' or 'purpose' of something – the
term is frequently found in Aristotle's
philosophy

B: Inductive arguments – teleological

Aquinas – Fifth Way

Aquinas teleological argument can be found in the fifth of his 'Five Ways' in the
Summa Theologica. Here Aquinas states that something that lacks intelligence
cannot move towards fulfilling a useful end, unless something with intelligence has
moved it.

Imagine, for example, that you need to
write your essay with a pen. The pen itself is
non-intelligent and cannot (however much
you may wish it!) write your essay for you.
The only way that it will do this is if you (as
an intelligent being) pick up the pen; hold it
in a way that is appropriate for writing and
then apply it to the paper, moving it to make
the shapes (i.e. writing) that are required to
communicate your ideas.

Aquinas' own example was that of the arrow
and the archer – archery was a frequent
pastime in his day, either as a sport or as
a way of killing other people in war, and
therefore his analogy would have made
sense to his audience.

Aquinas stated that the arrow, by itself,
cannot reach the target. It needs to be fired
by the archer in order for this to happen. He
relates this to the workings of the universe
stating that everything in the universe
follows natural laws, even if they possess no
intelligence (i.e. the regular movement of
the stars in the sky – for which in Aquinas'
time people had no rational 'scientific'
explanation).

The fact that these things also tend to follow
these laws and, in doing so, fulfil some
purpose or end goal (their '**telos**') yet don't
have the ability to 'think' for themselves,
suggests that (as with the arrow) they have
been 'directed' by something else. For Aquinas, the only possible explanation was
that this guiding intelligence was God.

*Aquinas' 5th Way uses the example
of the arrow and the archer*

Paley's watchmaker – analogy of complex design

William Paley, Archdeacon of Carlisle, is widely credited with proposing the design
argument in its popular modern form. He proposed his version in his *Natural
Theology* which was published at the beginning of the nineteenth century. His basic
argument follows that, were we to discover a stone whilst out walking, we may
enquire how it came to be and, through a consideration of natural events, might
come to a conclusion of how it was formed. However, were we to discover a watch,
we would not come to the same conclusions. Paley was interested in pointing out
why this was the case.

The watch in the 1800s would have comprised a watch-face with numerals on it, with 'hands' that pointed towards the time. The inner workings of the watch would reveal a very complicated system of cogs, springs and gears which enabled those hands to move in such a way as to measure the passage of time. The very complexity of these mechanisms would point towards the conclusion that this watch had been designed by a being of intelligence and was not the result of random chance. Paley states that we could draw this conclusion even if we were unaware of the purpose of the watch; if the watch went wrong or even if we didn't understand what some of the parts of the watch actually did. In summary, the watch, with all its complexities, needs an intelligent watchmaker, to explain how it came into being.

Workings of a watch

Paley then widens his argument and states that the universe in which we live (and using the natural world as evidence), is likewise complex and therefore too infers a designer, in much the same way as we inferred a designer for the watch. Paley spends a large amount of time detailing the workings of the eye – from the way that it perceives objects, to the function of the 'secretions' that keep the eyeball moving as well as the eyelids that protect the eye. He suggests that the incredible complexity of this unit within the human body alone is evidence for a designing intelligence. Again, as the watch needed the intelligent watchmaker, so too does the universe need an intelligent universe-'maker'.

Paley's account runs as follows:

'In crossing a heath, suppose I pitched my foot against a stone, and were asked how the stone came to be there, I might possibly answer, that, for any thing I knew to the contrary, it had lain there for ever: nor would it perhaps be very easy to shew the absurdity of this answer. But suppose I had found a watch upon the ground, and it should be enquired how the watch happened to be in that place, I should hardly think of the answer which I had before given, that, for any thing I knew, the watch might have always been there. Yet why should not this answer serve for the watch as well as for the stone? ...when we come to inspect the watch, we perceive (what we could not discover in the stone) that its several parts are framed and put together for a purpose, e.g. that they are so formed and adjusted as to produce motion, and that motion so regulated as to point out the hour of the day; that, if the several parts had been differently shaped from what they are, of a different size from what they are, or placed after any other manner, or in any other order, than that in which they are placed, either no motion at all would have been carried on in the machine, or none which would have answered the use that is now served by it ... the inference, we think, is inevitable, that the watch must have had a maker: that there must have existed, at some time and at some place or other, an artificer or artificers who formed it for the purpose which we find it actually to answer;

quickfire

1.12 How did Paley compare the stone and watch?

who comprehended its construction, and designed its use ... every manifestation of design, which existed in the watch, exists in the works of nature; with the difference, on the side of nature, of being greater and more, and that in a degree which exceeds all computation.'

AO1 Activity

Create a timeline flow chart that shows the order in which Aquinas, Paley and Tennant wrote. You should include key information about each of their arguments in this flow chart.

This will help in selecting the key, relevant information for an answer to a question that expects a knowledge and understanding of the development of the teleological argument.

Key terms

Anthropic: related to being human

Natural world: the world of nature, comprising of all objects, organic and inorganic

Study tip

Candidates frequently retell Paley's analogy without providing the final conclusion that the universe's designer (God) is analogous to the watchmaker. As this is the whole point of Paley's argument, ensure that you do not make the same mistake!

Specification content

Tennant's anthropic and aesthetic arguments – the universe specifically designed for intelligent human life.

quickfire

1.13 What were Tennant's three pieces of evidence to support his anthropic principle?

Key quote

The aesthetic argument for theism becomes more persuasive when it renounces all claims to proof and appeals to a logical probability. And it becomes stronger when it takes as the most significant fact ... the saturation of Nature with beauty ... God reveals himself in many ways; and some men enter His Temple by the Gate Beautiful. **(Tennant)**

Tennant's anthropic and aesthetic arguments

Whilst not using the specific term 'anthropic principle', in his 1928 work *Philosophical Theology*, Frederick Tennant developed a set of evidences that are widely recognised as **anthropic** principles today. The evidence included beliefs such as:

- The very fact that the **natural world** in which we live provides precisely the things that are necessary for life to be sustained.
- The fact that the natural world in which we live can not only be observed but holds itself up for rational analysis from which we can deduce its workings.
- The fact that the process of evolution, through natural selection, has led to the development of intelligent human life – to the degree that that intelligent life can observe and analyse the universe that it exists in.

Tennant stated that the theory of evolution supported the idea of an intelligent designer

Tennant's **aesthetic** argument relates to the natural appreciation that human beings have for things that are considered to be 'beautiful' and asks why we have such an appreciation as part of our nature. When looking at the rest of the natural world there appears to be no other species that reacts to its surroundings in this way. In fact, this can also be extended to the appreciation that humans have for music, art, poetry and other forms of literature as well as an appreciation for things like fashion, cosmetics and other such things that are said to enhance human beauty.

If a purely rational approach is taken towards human beings as a species, then only those things that are necessary for our survival are necessary for us to have in the world around us. Our understanding of the natural world informs us that living organisms operate on a 'survival of the fittest' mechanism and anything that does not aid evolution is quickly rejected by a species as it develops through time. Why then do we, as human beings, have an appreciation of beauty? Why are aesthetics so important to us?

Tennant's response was to claim that this appreciation was a direct result of a benevolent God. Having designed the world so that it led to the development of intelligent human life (*see anthropic principle*), God not only wanted his creation to live in the world, but also to enjoy living in it. Beauty and its appreciation were not necessary for humans to survive. For Tennant, the existence of beauty in the world was its own evidence for God's existence and led, by way of revelation, to the enquiring minds discovering the fact of God's existence for themselves.

AO1 Activity

Research further the ideas around Tennant's anthropic principle and aesthetic argument. This will help you to be aware of how he constructed his argument within the context of his *Philosophical Theology*. Specific knowledge and details gleaned from this will serve to fuel evidence and examples for both a demonstration of knowledge and understanding (AO1) but also to help sustain an argument (AO2).

Key term

Aesthetic: related to the concept and appreciation of beauty

quickfire

1.14 Why did Tennant consider that an appreciation of beauty led to the conclusion that the designer of the world was benevolent?

Key skills

Knowledge involves:

Selection of a range of (thorough) accurate and relevant information that is directly related to the specific demands of the question.

This means you choose the correct information relevant to the question set NOT the topic area. You will have to think and focus on selecting key information and NOT writing everything you know about the topic area.

Understanding involves:

Explanation that is extensive, demonstrating depth and/or breadth with excellent use of evidence and examples including (where appropriate) thorough and accurate supporting use of sacred texts, sources of wisdom and specialist language.

This means that you demonstrate that you understand something by being able to illustrate and expand your points through examples/supporting evidence in a personal way and NOT repeat chunks from a text book (known as rote learning).

Further application of skills:

Once you have made your choices and selected your information, compare them with another student. See if together you can decide on six and their correct order, this time, in sequence for answering a question.

AO1 Developing skills

It is now time to reflect upon the information that has been covered so far. It is also important to consider how what you have learned can be focused and used for examination-style answers by practising the skills associated with AO1.

Assessment objective 1 (AO1) involves demonstrating knowledge and understanding. The terms 'knowledge' and 'understanding' are obvious but it is crucial to be familiar with how certain skills demonstrate these terms, and also, how the performance of these skills is measured (see generic band descriptors Band 5 for AS AO1).

▶ **Your new task is this:** from the list of ten key points below, choose six that you feel are the most important in answering the question above the list. Put your points in order in priority explaining why they are the six most important aspects to mention from that topic. This skill of prioritising and selecting appropriate material will help you in answering examination questions for AO1.

A focus on explaining the teleological argument for God's existence.

1. The teleological argument was famously put forward by Aquinas, a medieval scholar who wanted to show how evidence in the world could point to God's existence.

2. The archer is needed to direct the arrow towards the target in the same way that a guiding intelligence is required to direct natural bodies to their end.

3. The existence of a complex universe seems to suggest that it did not occur by chance but was instead the result of deliberate design.

4. Design infers a designer and, by a process of inductive reasoning, it is possible to suggest that God is the designer of the universe.

5. William Paley was the Archdeacon of Carlisle who wrote *'Natural Theology'* to prove that God existed.

6. Paley's watchmaker analogy is a very well-known analogy that can be easily understood as an effective way of proving that the universe has a designer.

7. Paley explained that if you imagined walking across a heath, you may kick a stone but never question where it came from. However, if you kicked a watch whilst on the heath you might reasonably expect to ask where it had come from.

8. The anthropic principle is an effective way of demonstrating that modern understandings of the world, including the theory of evolution and the thickness of the ozone layer, are clear proofs for the existence of God.

9. Tennant's anthropic principle makes use of a series of evidences that point towards the idea that the universe has been deliberately designed for the development of intelligent human life.

10. The aesthetic argument is clear evidence that there exists a benevolent designer.

Issues for analysis and evaluation

Whether cosmological arguments for God's existence are persuasive in the 21st century

This section covers AO2 content and skills

Specification content

Whether cosmological arguments for God's existence are persuasive in the 21st century.

The 21st century is home to the modern scientific age. With computing technology and the communication of the Internet, human beings have been able to share information like never before. In doing so, we have access to all sorts of information about ourselves, and the universe in which we live. This includes ideas such as the big bang theory, oscillating universe, multi-verses and quantum mechanics. These ideas are fascinating and, for many, persuasive, in terms of providing an answer to the age old question of 'How did the universe begin?'.

Equally, detractors of traditional theistic arguments such as the cosmological argument, considerably undermine its claims to persuasiveness by pointing out that the arguments of Aquinas are flawed by an incorrect understanding of agreed scientific principle. Newton's First Law of Motion, for example, points out that the idea that nothing can move itself unless moved by another ignores the principle of inertia and is therefore wrong – things can move themselves – Anthony Kenny famously declared this observation as 'wrecking the First Way'.

With all this in mind, it would seem that the cosmological arguments, first put forward over two and a half thousand years ago by Ancient Greek philosophers, and then developed by medieval Christian monks, have little relevance in today's scientific world. As such, they would also be considered to lack any power to persuade people.

However, it should be borne in mind that the cosmological argument is based on the fact that there is a universe. This is an a posteriori observation – i.e. a scientific method. In which case, the fundamentals of the argument are based on the same assumptions as that of scientific theories. This would seem to suggest that the cosmological arguments are persuasive in the 21st century.

We should also consider the fact that, whilst science can quite effectively explain how the universe works, the way in which it does (and therefore how it started), what it can't do is answer the question of why the universe started. The cosmological argument can. In fact, Craig's Kalam argument convincingly demonstrates that the universe was the result of a deliberate choice from a personal creator.

The cosmological arguments are clearly based on cause and effect arguments; and so is science. For this reason alone, they should not be discounted. For the religious believer, the additional faith dimension provides the important element of hope and comfort, rather than just cold, hard scientific fact. The 21st century, with all of its modern-day wonders, still has room in it to accept that the cosmological arguments for God's existence are still persuasive.

AO2 Activity *Possible lines of argument*

Listed below are some conclusions that could be drawn from the AO2 reasoning in the accompanying text:

1. Arguments that were not formed in the scientific age have little value in the 21st century.

2. The use of scientific principles in constructing arguments makes them more persuasive.

3. People in the 21st century are more discerning in what they accept as truth than people who lived in the past.

4. 21st-century science has not answered all questions about the existence of the universe and therefore other points of view, such as the cosmological argument, should be considered equally valid.

Consider each of the conclusions drawn above and collect evidence and examples to support each argument from the AO1 and AO2 material studied in this section. Select one conclusion that you think is most convincing and explain why it is so. Now contrast this with the weakest conclusion in the list, justifying your argument with clear reasoning and evidence.

Specification content

The effectiveness of the teleological argument for God's existence.

The effectiveness of the teleological argument for God's existence

When Plato spoke of a 'craftsman' over two and half thousand years ago, it makes us wonder why he would come to such a conclusion when considering why the world in which we live is the way that it is. This guiding intelligence that fashioned pre-existent matter into the world of the senses laid the foundations for the development of the idea through Judeo-Christian thought, culminating in the religious assertion that the world in which we live is the result of a divine designer.

The effectiveness of the argument is said to be in its a posteriori, inductive form. Based on evidence of design obvious to the casual observer, the sheer complexity of our universe with its many life forms and complex, inter-connected systems that support life on the planet point clearly towards deliberate design from some almighty mind.

The analogical evidence provided by Paley is effective in pointing out that, just like a complex machine, our complex universe could not be the result of chance. It was down to an intelligent designing creator. These points all demonstrate how effective the teleological argument is for God's existence.

Furthermore, the contribution of Tennant, with both his anthropic and aesthetic arguments, surely proves beyond reasonable doubt that this is a universe deliberately designed for intelligent human life. We live in a world that provides everything we need – not only for our survival, but also for our enjoyment.

However, when the argument is looked at more closely, the superficial convenience of the points made by Aquinas, Paley and Tennant, all start to show signs of weakness.

The use of analogy is suspect at best as no human machine can ever adequately compare to the complex universe which we inhabit. Therefore how could we put forward the idea of an intelligent designer based purely on this? The similarities between the machine and the universe are too few.

Even if we did accept the analogy as valid – what about the times when things go wrong in the universe? Is the designer therefore inept? Or, as is the case for many machines, is it the case that there was more than one designer? Did they leave when they had finished putting our universe together? How do we even know that this is a good universe? What have we got to compare it to?

There are those that suggest it is an arrogant claim to make to assume that we are able to identify the cause of the complexities of the universe that we live in by asserting a divine designer that fits into the theistic model of religion. Proposing such an idea and asking others to accept it as a truism flies in the face of the evidence of the scientific age – modern-day evolutionary scientists such as Richard Dawkins point out that to hold such a view of a divine designer is 'unhelpful', 'childish' and 'superstitious nonsense' – in that it prevents people from properly engaging with a 'grown-up' view of the world as a place governed by the laws of nature not the laws of some god.

Despite the initial attractiveness of the teleological argument, the criticisms of it are simply too devastating and too wide ranging to ever accept that it is an effective argument for God's existence.

AO2 Developing skills

It is now time to reflect upon the information that has been covered so far. It is also important to consider how what you have learned can be focused and used for examination-style answers by practising the skills associated with AO2.

Assessment objective 2 (AO2) involves 'analysis' and 'evaluation'. The terms may be obvious but it is crucial to be familiar with how certain skills demonstrate these terms, and also, how the performance of these skills is measured (see generic band descriptors Band 5 for AS AO2).

Obviously an answer is placed within an appropriate band descriptor depending upon how well the answer performs, ranging from excellent, good, satisfactory, basic/limited to very limited.

▶ **Your task is this:** from the list of the 10 key points below, select six that are relevant to the evaluation task below. Put your selection into an order that you would use to address the task set. In explaining why you have chosen these six to answer the task, you will find that you are developing a process of reasoning within an answer.

A focus on evaluating the effectiveness of the teleological argument.

1. The teleological argument is an a posteriori, inductive proof.

2. Aquinas Fifth Way is based on the governance of the world

3. Paley's watchmaker analogy is too simplistic to be effective.

4. Inductive arguments only offer possibilities not conclusive proofs.

5. The watchmaker analogy was written after Hume's criticism of human analogies to describe things beyond our experience.

6. The anthropic principle is developed by contemporary scientists who use their scientific knowledge to offer an effective defence of the teleological argument.

7. It is our interpretation of patterns in the workings of the universe that makes us see design – in other words, design is only apparent not real.

8. The design argument is an ancient argument.

9. If a complex machine requires an intelligent designer then surely it is entirely rational to suggest that a complex universe also implies an intelligent designer.

10. The presence of beauty in the world is a subjective matter more aligned to natural selection than to the generosity of a benevolent designer.

Once you have made your choices, compare them with another student. See if together you can decide on the six key points that would be the most useful in constructing an evaluation to the question about the effectiveness of the teleological argument.

Key skills

Analysis involves identifying issues raised by the materials in the AO1, together with those identified in the AO2 section, and presents sustained and clear views, either of scholars or from a personal perspective ready for evaluation.

This means that it picks out key things to debate and the lines of argument presented by others or a personal point of view.

Evaluation involves considering the various implications of the issues raised based upon the evidence gleaned from analysis and provides an extensive detailed argument with a clear conclusion.

This means that the answer weighs up the various and different lines of argument analysed through individual commentary and response and arrives at a conclusion through a clear process of reasoning.

C: Challenges to inductive arguments

Introduction: Challenges to the cosmological argument

Having existed for over 2,500 years, the cosmological argument has attracted not only supporters but also those who wish to show its shortcomings. Scientific developments, particularly in the last 100 years, have taken our conventional understanding of a cause and effect universe and turned it upon its head. Quantum physics, chaos theory and similar radical progressions in our understanding of the workings of the universe have all had a role to play in diminishing the claims made by supporters of the cosmological argument, even though they are not always wholly successful. Indeed, some scientific theories, including most notably the big bang theory, have even been used to support parts of the cosmological argument – not least in demonstrating the concept that the universe had a starting point.

David Hume

The empirical philosopher David Hume was uncomfortable with the reasoning behind the cosmological argument, specifically in terms of the arguments it presented in relation to causes. Hume had four major challenges:

- Just because we observe cause and effect IN the universe does not mean that this rule applies to the universe itself! (Russell used the example 'Just because every human has a mother does not mean the whole of humanity has a mother'.) This is often called the 'fallacy of composition'.
- Whilst we can talk about things that we have experience of with some certainty, we have no experience of creating a universe and therefore cannot talk meaningfully about that.
- There is not enough evidence to say whether the universe had a cause and definitely not enough to make any conclusion as to what the cause might have been.
- Even if 'God' could be accepted as the cause of the universe, there is no way to determine what sort of God this would be and certainly no way of determining if it was the God of Classical Theism.

Introduction: Challenges to teleological argument

Tracing its origins to the earliest of Western civilisation's greatest thinkers, the design or teleological argument represents one of religious theists' most stalwart defences. The idea that the universe is far too complex, contains purpose for all things within it and has produced a life-form capable of observing, analysing and even philosophising about it and that none of these things seem likely to have happened by chance, all seems to point towards the existence of God; or so religious believers would like to claim. However, like the cosmological argument, this too has its detractors. The suggestions that we lack sufficient experience to make such claims about a grand design; that the analogies used do not hold up to scrutiny; that if the universe is designed why does it have so many flaws? As well as the alternative solutions proposed by scientific enquiry, all need serious consideration.

Specification content

David Hume – empirical objections and critique of causes (cosmological).

Key terms

Fallacy of composition: philosophical notion that what is true of the parts is not necessarily true of the whole (i.e. atoms are colourless but this does not mean that a cat, which is made of atoms, is colourless)

God of Classical Theism: the God that is generally associated with the Western monotheistic religions of Christianity, Islam and Judaism

Specification content

David Hume – problems with analogies; rejection of traditional theistic claims; designer not necessarily God of Classical Theism; apprentice god; plurality of gods; absent god (teleological).

Key person

David Hume (1711–1776): Scottish enlightenment philosopher who, as an empiricist, demonstrated a number of the flaws in the main theistic arguments for God's existence. Most significant work in relation to this is his 'Dialogues Concerning Natural Religion'.

Hume criticises the use of human analogies to demonstrate the fact that the universe is designed. He used the example of a house and an architect/builder and said that just because we know how a house is designed/built it does not mean that we can infer from this how the universe is designed/built. The house and the universe are just too different to draw that point of comparison, no matter the general resemblances that they may have in other ways. Analogies normally work on the following basis:

a. X and Y are similar.

b. X has the characteristic Z.

c. Therefore Y has the characteristic Z.

However, to claim what is true of Y based purely on a similarity to X is only as strong as the point at which X and Y are similar. If the similarity between them is weak, then, the conclusion drawn by the analogy is likewise weak. Hume concludes that, as the universe is unique, no analogy is sufficient to explain its origins. This would be used to devastating effect as a criticism when, years later, Paley constructed his analogy of the watchmaker.

Any analogy made by human beings is necessarily based on the experience that human beings have. If we lack experience of the thing that the analogy is being used to 'prove' then how can we be certain that the analogy is sound? As human beings have no experience of how the universe was designed, any analogy put forward to try to prove this matter is ultimately futile.

The suggestion that the universe is comparable to some artificial construct such as a house or a machine is also rejected. The universe demonstrates greater similarities to the living organisms within the natural world than it does to a static artificial construct. *'And does not a plant or animal, which springs from vegetation or generation, bear a stronger resemblance to the world, than does any artificial machine, which arises from reason and design?'* (Hume, *Dialogues*)

In his *Dialogues Concerning Natural Religion* Hume suggests there is fallacy in assuming that the universe is designed just because it seems so. He makes the distinction between authentic design and apparent design. In the first case, this would be the claim made by the classical theist – that God is responsible for the design of the universe. However, in the latter case, what we have is an appearance of design where none actually exists. Indeed, this is the point that Hume makes through Philo, the character in the *Dialogues* that most commentators associate with Hume's own view. Philo makes reference to the Epicurean hypothesis. This is a belief, stated by Epicurus, that the current so-called order in the universe that exists, is nothing more than the random association of atoms that had previously been in a chaotic state, but, through the principal nature of the universe, (which is change) these atoms re-organise themselves infinitely, and occasionally do so in a way that resembles order (and, thereby, design).

Even if we assume that the universe has a designer, as we have no universes to compare this one to, how do we know that it has been designed well? It may be, that were we able to make such a comparison, we would find that the designer of this one to be lacking in skill. Hume makes the comparison with a ship builder. If one saw for the first time a ship, one might assume that the shipbuilder was a genius to have made such a thing. However, if one were to investigate further they would find that the ship they are observing is nothing more than an imitation of other ships and, in comparison, it's not even that good. Neither does it take into account the various other ships that this shipbuilder may have tried to make along the way, in perfecting his art. Relating this to the work of a god in designing the universe, Hume observes that there may be better universes out there; that this

quicKpire

1.15 What is a fallacy of composition in relation to the cosmological argument?

Key quote

If we see a house, Cleanthes, we conclude, with the greatest certainty, that it had an architect or builder; because this is precisely that species of effect, which we have experienced to proceed from that species of cause. But surely you will not affirm, that the universe bears such a resemblance to a house, that we can with the same certainty infer a similar cause, or that the analogy is here entire and perfect. The dissimilitude is so striking, that the utmost you can here pretend to is a guess, a conjecture, a presumption concerning a similar cause; and how that pretension will be received in the world, I leave you to consider. (Hume)

quicKpire

1.16 Why does Hume reject the use of analogy to prove the existence of a divine designer?

Key quote

Specification content

Alternative scientific explanations including big bang theory and Darwin's theory of evolution by natural selection.

designing god is a poor designer in comparison in relation to others and that, in practising his art, he has produced a series of worlds and universes that have been *'botched and bungled, throughout an eternity, ere this system was struck out.'* (Hume, *Dialogues*)

After referring to the ship/shipbuilder analogy, Philo suggests that, as a house or ship has many builders, surely it makes sense to say that there were many builders likewise involved in constructing the universe. In making this assertion, Hume is demonstrating that the use of human analogies is a double-edged sword for those theists who rely on them to show the likelihood of the existence of a designing creator God.

Furthermore, after a ship or house builder has completed their task they move on. Perhaps this is also true of the supposed designer of the universe? He may well have left the universe to its own devices (this is very similar to the Deist position), or perhaps may even have died. There is no necessity for such a designer to have to exist for eternity, just because that which he has designed does.

AO1 Activity

Create a one-minute news round presentation that summarises the key points of Hume's criticisms.

This helps with the ability to select and present the key relevant features of the material you have read.

Study tip

Remember that Hume lived before Paley. Some candidates mistakenly state that Hume was criticising Paley but this was not the case. Make certain you are aware of the chronological order in which the main philosophers lived so that you do not make the same mistake!

Study tip

Referring to criticisms of the design argument is NOT the same as evaluating it. It is important to recognise that evaluations arise from the strengths and the weaknesses. Criticisms **on their own** are AO1 material – and belong only in part 'a' of your essay.

Big bang theory

The big bang theory is often used as a 'proof' that it was a random action that caused the beginning of the universe, not God. (However, many theists suggest that this action was not random but caused by God.) The big bang theory can be summarised by referring to an event that happened nearly 14 billion years ago, when a singularity appeared. A singularity is a scientific concept referring to a point in space-time that defies our current understanding of the laws of physics but where infinity exists. This singularity inflated, expanded and cooled to give us the universe we have today.

Charles Darwin's theory of evolution by natural selection

In his *Origin of Species*, Darwin notes that it was random chance that organises life in the universe, according to the principles of evolution and natural selection. Natural selection works on a principle of 'survival of the fittest' where only the strongest of a particular species survives long enough to pass on its genes to the next generation. In this way weak characteristics are 'bred out' of a species and it becomes stronger and more capable of surviving in its environment.

In other words, the reason for species being so well suited to their environment, was not as had been previously thought, due to a benevolent designer but was because of their ability to adapt to their surroundings and to pass on the favourable characteristics that allowed this adaptation to be successful.

This was anathema to the majority of people in the nineteenth century, who believed that God was the Prime Mover of the universe – not chance. However, in referring to the principle of natural selection, Darwin is stating that his notion of chance was not a reference to things 'just happening' but rather that they were happening according to a specific principle – however unpredictable it may be.

Darwin admitted that he did not know what mechanism caused these useful traits to be passed from one generation to another but, with the discovery of DNA in the 20th century, this problem has been largely overcome.

Key person

Charles Darwin: English naturalist who revolutionised the western world's understanding of how life developed. His most famous work, '*On the Origin of Species*' published in 1859, set forward the idea that life on Earth had developed through processes of natural selection and evolution. The theory made no mention of life developing as part of the work of a divine creator and was met with varying degrees of opposition from the religious establishment upon its publication.

AO1 Activity

Why do you think the challenges to the arguments are so wide-ranging? Explain your answer using evidence and examples from what you have read.

quickfire

1.17 What was the main idea behind Darwin's theory of natural selection?

Charles Darwin (1809–1882)

Key skills

Knowledge involves:

Selection of a range of (thorough) accurate and relevant information that is directly related to the specific demands of the question.

This means you choose the correct information relevant to the question set NOT the topic area. You will have to think and focus on selecting key information and NOT writing everything you know about the topic area.

Understanding involves:

Explanation that is extensive, demonstrating depth and/or breadth with excellent use of evidence and examples including (where appropriate) thorough and accurate supporting use of sacred texts, sources of wisdom and specialist language.

This means that you demonstrate that you understand something by being able to illustrate and expand your points through examples/supporting evidence in a personal way and NOT repeat chunks from a text book (known as rote learning).

Further application of skills:

Go through the topic areas in this section and create some bullet lists of key points from key areas. For each one, provide further elaboration and explanation through the use of evidence and examples.

AO1 Developing skills

It is now time to reflect upon the information that has been covered so far. It is also important to consider how what you have learned can be focused and used for examination-style answers by practising the skills associated with AO1.

Assessment objective 1 (AO1) involves demonstrating knowledge and understanding. The terms 'knowledge' and 'understanding' are obvious but it is crucial to be familiar with how certain skills demonstrate these terms, and also, how the performance of these skills is measured (see generic band descriptors Band 5 for AS AO1).

▶ **Your new task is this:** you need to develop each of the key points below by adding evidence and examples to fully explain each point. The first one is done for you. This will help you in answering examination questions for AO1 by being able to 'demonstrate extensive depth and/or breadth' with 'excellent use of evidence and examples' (Level 5 AO1 band descriptor).

Question focus on challenges to inductive arguments.

1. Anthony Kenny stated that the Physical principle highlighted in Newton's First Law of Motion 'wrecks the argument of the First Way'.

DEVELOPMENT: *This is because the principle of inertia can be used to show how animals have the capacity to move themselves without being moved by another.*

2. Even if 'God' could be accepted as the cause of the universe, there is no way to determine what sort of God this would be and certainly no way of determining if it was the God of Classical Theism.

3. The physical principle highlighted in Newton's First law of Motion 'wrecks the argument of the First Way'.

4. Hume criticises the use of human analogies to demonstrate the fact that the universe is designed.

5. If we lack experience of the thing that the analogy is being used to 'prove' then how can we be certain that the analogy is sound?

6. The current so-called order in the universe that exists is nothing more than the random association of atoms that had previously been in a chaotic state.

7. Hume makes the comparison with a ship builder. If one saw for the first time a ship, one might assume that the shipbuilder was a genius to have made such a thing.

8. Hume demonstrates that the use of human analogies is a double-edged sword for theists.

9. There is no necessity for such a designer to have to exist for eternity, just because that which he has designed does.

10. Darwin notes that it was random chance that organises life in the universe, according to the principles of evolution and natural selection.

11. The reason for species being so well suited to their environment was not due to a benevolent designer according to Darwin.

Issues for analysis and evaluation

The effectiveness of the challenges to the teleological argument for God's existence

Specification content
The effectiveness of the challenges to
the teleological argument for
God's existence.

Hume was adamant: The teleological argument for the existence of a designing
God was at best flawed and at worst entirely ineffective. The use of human
experience to conjure up analogies relating to a cosmic entity beyond human
experience was considered implausible by Hume – there was no empirical evidence
that could conclusively point towards the existence of such a being.

The contention that design is only apparent is an effective challenge. The order that
can be seen in the universe is not evidence of intention. Therefore there is no need
to conclude that this was the action of a designer God, thereby undermining claims
for His existence. To suggest otherwise would be illogical.

The modern mind, with access to the latest scientific evidence, proves time and
again an effective challenge to the teleological argument. Based on evidence
from 19th-century scientist Charles Darwin and his work on natural selection
and evolution, the teleological argument seems not to hold up under scrutiny.
The religious point of view that the world and everything in it was the result of
a divine design is undermined by Darwin's findings. These have been developed
over the last century with genetic research adding considerable weight to Darwin's
original theories.

In fact, the suggestion is that this argument is more of a God of 'gaps' argument
rather than based on empirical evidential claims. As such, it is outdated and
unnecessary in a rational scientific age.

However, it should be borne in mind that the teleological argument is based on
observation of apparent design, order and purpose in the universe (a posteriori),
i.e. a scientific method. In which case, the fundamentals of the argument are based
on the same assumptions as that of scientific theories. Surely this proves that not all
of the challenges to the argument are effective.

Equally, scientific theories are often in need of updating or proved to be false
– there have been plenty of examples over the centuries where what was once
accepted as effective scientific 'fact' has instead been overturned as new evidence
has come to light. In fact, many scientists recognise the precarious position their
theories are in, particularly in light of advancements in scientific understanding
of the universe that in themselves are not fully understood yet. Therefore,
scientific evidence against the teleological argument does not necessarily prove an
effective challenge. To develop this point further, contemporary scientists such as
Polkinghorne, Behe and Davies all support the design concept. Why would they risk
their reputations as scientific professionals, were there not something to it?

This shows that scientific evidence can be used to support as well as challenge the
teleological argument. In which case, the strength of the argument may come
down to a personal preference, negating the effectiveness of the challenges.

AO2 Activity *Possible lines of argument*

Listed below are some conclusions
that could be drawn from the AO2
reasoning in the accompanying text:

1. The challenges are effective as the
    argument has no sound empirical
    basis.

2. Scientifically evidenced arguments
    will always be more effective than
    philosophical religious arguments.

3. Any argument that is based on
    observation, experience and
    evidence should be considered
    effective.

4. Relying on scientific evidence
    to challenge the teleological
    argument is ineffective as it
    can also be used to support the
    argument.

Consider each of the conclusions
drawn above and collect evidence and
examples to support each argument
from the AO1 and AO2 material
studied in this section. Select one
conclusion that you think is most
convincing and explain why it is so.
Now contrast this with the weakest
conclusion in the list, justifying
your argument with clear reasoning
and evidence.

Specification content
Whether scientific explanations are
more persuasive than philosophical
explanations for the universe's
existence.

Whether scientific explanations are more persuasive than philosophical explanations for the universe's existence

The consideration of whether scientific explanations are more persuasive than philosophical explanations for the universe's existence can encompass a variety of explanations. Scientific discovery in the past century has occurred at a pace hitherto unknown in the history of the human race. Science is based on empiricism and rational knowledge acquired through the use of the five senses – it is easily and widely accepted.

The quantum explanations include the idea of 'random occurrences' to explain how the universe could have come into existence. The theory of quantum physics suggests that at the sub-atomic level our traditional understanding of a cause and effect universe is not necessarily relevant. This means that certain 'quantum' events can occur without an obvious 'cause'.

Interestingly, the widely accepted big bang theory indicates a starting point of the universe. The acceptance from the majority of the scientific community is that the universe definitely had a beginning, which the first parts of all cosmological arguments always attempt to prove. This is a point of agreement between science and philosophy. The contention then becomes 'what caused the starting point?' – with the scientific view being that it is unnecessary to posit a divine being, but to look instead for another, rational, scientific explanation.

Developing this point further, it is true to say that Science uses evidence-based rational thought to demonstrate how the universe began. Such thought underpins much of the workings of contemporary society. This is at odds with the suggestion of a divine being as the first cause of the universe. However, science works on assumptions that like causes produce like effects – deterministic existence of the universe lends itself to the model used to determine God as the first cause for the universe.

It should be taken into account that as there is no definitive answer as to how the universe began, then it is entirely rational to accept certain religious and philosophical arguments as having persuasive power. For instance, scientific observers have not proven beyond reasonable doubt that God is not the first cause of the universe.

Scientific evidence can only talk meaningfully about time after the Big Bang – not the moments before. This allows for the possibility of a divine being as the cause of the Big Bang, thus demonstrating that philosophical explanations for the universe's existence may be considered as persuasive.

Additionally, scientific explanations can often be extremely complex – and for many listening to contemporary scientific conversation about sub-quantum realities, multi-dimensional universes and other seemingly fantastical ideas, these explanations may in themselves seem so far-fetched that a common-sense philosophical explanation, taking an 'Ockham's razor' -type approach of not multiplying the difficulty for an explanation, seems to make more sense and could therefore be argued as being, ultimately, more persuasive – in that it can be more easily understood.

AO2 Activity *Possible lines of argument*

Listed below are some conclusions that could be drawn from the AO2 reasoning in the accompanying text:

1. Scientifically evidenced arguments will always be more effective than philosophical religious arguments.

2. The lack of clear evidence from science undermines how persuasive scientific explanations for the universe's existence are in the face of philosophical explanations from religion.

3. Religion relies too heavily on a God of the gaps approach to explaining the universe's existence – scientific explanations are far more persuasive.

4. Religious explanations should be accepted as valid because science cannot disprove them entirely.

Consider each of the conclusions drawn above and collect evidence and examples to support each argument from the AO1 and AO2 material studied in this section. Select one conclusion that you think is most convincing and explain why it is so. Now contrast this with the weakest conclusion in the list, justifying your argument with clear reasoning and evidence.

AO2 Developing skills

It is now time to reflect upon the information that has been covered so far. It is also important to consider how what you have learned can be focused and used for examination-style answers by practising the skills associated with AO2.

Assessment objective 2 (AO2) involves 'analysis' and 'evaluation'. The terms may be obvious but it is crucial to be familiar with how certain skills demonstrate these terms, and also, how the performance of these skills is measured (see generic band descriptors Band 5 for AS AO2).

Obviously an answer is placed within an appropriate band descriptor depending upon how well the answer performs, ranging from excellent, good, satisfactory, basic/limited to very limited.

▶ **Your next task is this:** develop each of the key points below by adding evidence and examples to fully evaluate the argument presented in the evaluation statement. The first one is done for you. This will help you in answering examination questions for AO2 by being able to ensure that 'sustained and clear views are given, supported by extensive, detailed reasoning and/or evidence' (Level 5 AO2 band descriptor).

A focus on evaluating how far scientific explanations for the universe's existence are more persuasive than philosophical explanations.

1. Science is based on empiricism and rational knowledge acquired through the use of the five senses – it is easily and widely accepted.

DEVELOPMENT: *This is because it is possible to fully justify in a physical sense and because rationality is the cornerstone of modern thinking in the West.*

2. Science is based on empiricism and rational knowledge acquired through the use of the five senses.

3. Quantum physics suggests that at the sub-atomic level our traditional understanding of a cause and effect universe is not necessarily relevant.

4. The big bang theory indicates a starting point of the universe.

5. Both scientific and philosophical arguments agree that the universe had a starting point.

6. Arguments based on empirical proofs are more likely to be persuasive.

7. Science uses evidence-based rational thought to demonstrate how the universe began.

8. Science works on assumptions that like causes produce like effects.

9. Religious philosophy is based as much on faith as it is on reason.

10. The philosophical arguments for God as the starting point of the universe are much older than the scientific ones.

11. Scientific evidence can only talk meaningfully about time after the Big Bang.

Key skills

Analysis involves identifying issues raised by the materials in the AO1, together with those identified in the AO2 section, and presents sustained and clear views, either of scholars or from a personal perspective ready for evaluation.

This means that it picks out key things to debate and the lines of argument presented by others or a personal point of view.

Evaluation involves considering the various implications of the issues raised based upon the evidence gleaned from analysis and provides an extensive detailed argument with a clear conclusion.

This means that the answer weighs up the various and different lines of argument analysed through individual commentary and response and arrives at a conclusion through a clear process of reasoning.

T2 Arguments for the existence of God – deductive

Specification content
Deductive proofs; the concept of a priori.

Key terms

A priori: without or prior to evidence or experience

Deductive proof: a proof in which, if the premises are true, then the conclusion must be true

Ontological argument: argument for the existence of God based on the concept of the nature of being

Premise: a statement or proposition used to construct an argument

Rodin's The Thinker

quickfire

2.1 What makes deductive proof different from inductive proof?

A: Deductive arguments – origins of the ontological argument

Deductive arguments

In Theme 1 we looked at the concept of inductive proofs, these are useful when basing an argument on evidence or experience. However, not all philosophical arguments have the luxury of drawing upon these two useful areas. Occasionally, it is necessary to argue based on no prior experience or evidence – and this is where the term **a priori** comes from. Philosophical arguments (and statements) can be made a priori and it is often useful to do so. This is the application of pure logical reasoning to come up with a conclusion and is known as deductive reasoning or **deductive proof**.

Deductive proofs are often composed of a series of **premises** or statements that, when stacked together, point towards a conclusion that is usually logically inescapable. For instance, look at the following:

[Premise 1] All oceans contain water.

[Premise 2] The Atlantic is an ocean.

[Conclusion] Therefore the Atlantic contains water.

Premise 1 is followed by premise 2 and these lead to a conclusion that is both logically sound and factually accurate.

However, this is all very well and good when the premises that point towards the conclusion are both accurate and true, but occasionally this is not the case. However, the conclusion that is drawn is still inescapable.

[Premise 1] All birds can fly.

[Premise 2] Penguins are birds.

[Conclusion] Therefore penguins can fly.

In this case the deductive proof leads to a conclusion that, whilst logically sound, is factually inaccurate. Why? Well the reason is that at least one of the premises is suspect (or wrong!) In this case, the premise 'All birds can fly' is not factually accurate and, because of this, the conclusion may not be accurate either.

Deductive proofs are incredibly powerful pieces of logical reasoning that, when well constructed, are virtually impossible to disagree with. Deductive proof is the basis for the **ontological argument** for the existence of God and, for its supporters, is the most persuasive form of philosophical argument that there is when positing the existence of a divine being.

AO1 Activity

Demonstrate your understanding of how deductive proofs are formed by writing five sets of deductive proofs – they can be about anything you like, as long as you follow the rules of *Premise + Premise = Conclusion*. Once you have completed this task, share your ideas with someone else in your class and get them to check that you have reasoned correctly.

Study tip

When answering questions on different types of proof, make certain that you
can clearly explain the differences between inductive and deductive proofs
by having a clear example for each. You should have an example prepared so
that you can use it as required. It is always worth checking with your teacher
that the example you have chosen is both accurate and relevant. This way you
can demonstrate at least 'good use of evidence and examples' (Level 4/5 AO1
response) to the examiner in response to explaining the different types of proof.

Anselm – God as the greatest possible being

In the eleventh century, monastic Anselm of Bec, later to be Archbishop of
Canterbury as part of the Norman invasion of England, composed the *Proslogion*
(sometimes referred to by its original title *Fides Quaerens Intellectum*, which when
translated means *'Faith seeking understanding')*. In this book he attempts to offer a
single rational proof for the existence of God. This single argument was expressed
in a deductive form.

Specification content

Anselm – God as the greatest possible
being (*Proslogion* 2).

Key term

Proslogion: a work written by
Anselm, used as a meditation, but
including within it the classical form of
the ontological argument

Anselm of Canterbury (1033–1109)

St Anselm

Key quote

I began to ask myself whether there might be found a single argument which would require no other for its proof than itself alone; and alone would suffice to demonstrate that God truly exists, and that there is a supreme good requiring nothing else, which all other things require for their existence and well-being; and whatever we believe regarding the divine Being. **(Anselm)**

Artist thinking of painting

quickfire

2.2 What was the use of reason for according to Anselm?

For Anselm, the relationship between **faith** and **reason** differed from some of the key thinkers that you may study elsewhere in the course. Faith for Anselm, came first. His faith was that God existed, that God was the source of all being and the ultimate good. Reason was employed to deepen his understanding of what his faith told him:

'For I do not seek to understand that I may believe, but I believe in order to understand. For this also I believe, that unless I believed, I should not understand.' (Anselm)

This leads the reader into the second chapter of his work, referred to as *Proslogion* 2. Opening with the reference to Psalm 14:1 he states, 'Truly there is a God, although the fool has said in his heart, "There is no God".'

Anselm presents the reader with the dichotomy of his investigation – that there are two positions in reference to the existence of God: acceptance or denial. To the modern mind this would translate as a theist versus atheist debate, but several biblical commentators do not believe that this is the case (and Anselm would have been well aware of this particular interpretation).

In modern terms, an atheist is a person who denies any possibility of the existence of a being such as a god. For Anselm's fool, it was more like a self-delusion in order to live a life of injustice and corruption – 'fooling' oneself that God's punishment could be avoided for such a course of action. This was a theme often repeated in the books of the Christian Old Testament. Hence the denial was not a rejection of a being called God but rather the rejection of having to face up to being accountable to the divine judge, called God, for one's actions in this life.

However we understand the fool, what is certain is that Anselm places him onto the losing side of the argument. *Proslogion* 2 invites the reader to consider God as 'a being than which nothing greater can be conceived'. Whilst we need to accept that Anselm's definition is a little on the vague side, it states the rational position that God is the greatest possible thing that can be thought of by the human mind.

This argument is then developed by Anselm who states that it is possible to exist in the mind and to exist in reality but that the two ideas are not mutually inclusive (i.e. they don't have to both be true at the same time – just because something exists in the mind does not mean it has to exist in reality). However, as God is considered to be the being than which nothing greater can be conceived, then in this case, he exists in both the mind and in reality – otherwise he is not the greatest possible being.

This is quite a confusing idea at first sight. It may be better to consider it as such:

(Premise 1) Beings exists in both the mind and in reality.

(Premise 2) God is the greatest possible being that can be thought of.

(Conclusion) In order to be the greatest thing that can be thought of, God must exist in both the mind and in reality.

The conclusion would be true if you accept the idea that it is 'greater' (or 'better') to exist in reality than in just the mind.

In essence this remains a difficult idea, and in fact, it initially seems logically weak in terms of its premises. It certainly attracted criticism, as we shall see later.

Anselm used the example of a painter and a painting – pointing out that, before it exists in reality, a painting needs to exist in the mind of the painter before it becomes a reality.

AO1 Activity

You are being asked to briefly explain Anselm's *Proslogion* 2 to a new student in the class. Write down what your answer would be in 200 words. If you are doing this a group, read out your answers. Take three examples and try to make one final version by extracting what is the best material from each one.

Anselm – God has necessary existence

Specification content

Anselm – God has necessary existence (*Proslogion* 3).

'God cannot be conceived not to exist.' Anselm starts Chapter 3 of his *Proslogion* by developing his theme of God as the greatest possible being from Chapter 2. He widens his definition to now include the idea that once you have understood what it means for God to be the greatest possible being, then, the next logical step is to conclude that God has necessary existence – i.e. that God cannot be thought not to exist.

Anselm's reasoning goes something like this: It is possible to think of a being who has the property of having to exist (i.e. that can be thought of as existing and not being able not to exist). It is also possible of thinking of something that does not have to exist. When thinking of the two, side by side, the one that cannot not exist is clearly greater than the one that does not have to exist.

Put another way – God, if he exists, is either a being which cannot be thought of as not existing (i.e. he is necessary) or he is a being which can be thought of as not existing (i.e. he is contingent). If the definition we use for God (as is the case from *Proslogion* 2) is that he is 'that than which nothing greater can be conceived' then God's existence must be necessary – as this is clearly greater than being contingent. In this Anselm presents us with the idea that God's existence is necessary and that this is an integral part of what it means to be God – a unique feature above that of all existent beings (i.e. necessary existence).

So, in summary, Anselm's idea of God as having necessary existence demonstrates that God is the greatest possible being that can be thought of, as anything which exists is greater than anything that does not.

Therefore if God is the greatest possible thing that there is, then he must, necessarily, exist in reality – not just as an idea. This is because otherwise anything that existed in reality would be greater than God (if he was only an idea) but because of our definition of God 'as the greatest possible being', then it follows that he must necessarily exist.

quickfire

2.3 What did Anselm mean by the term 'necessary existence'?

AO1 Activity

Pick out five to ten key words from each aspect studied here, for *Proslogion* 2 and *Proslogion* 3. Now come up with an acronym for each to help you remember. Test yourself with a partner. This will help you select and recall a core set of points to develop in an answer explaining each concept.

Key skills

Knowledge involves:

Selection of a range of (thorough) accurate and relevant information that is directly related to the specific demands of the question.

This means you choose the correct information relevant to the question set NOT the topic area. You will have to think and focus on selecting key information and NOT writing everything you know about the topic area.

Understanding involves:

Explanation that is extensive, demonstrating depth and/or breadth with excellent use of evidence and examples including (where appropriate) thorough and accurate supporting use of sacred texts, sources of wisdom and specialist language.

This means that you demonstrate that you understand something by being able to illustrate and expand your points through examples/supporting evidence in a personal way and NOT repeat chunks from a text book (known as rote learning).

Further application of skills:

Go through the topic areas in this section and create some bullet lists of key points from key areas. For each one, provide further elaboration and explanation through the use of evidence and examples.

AO1 Developing skills

It is now time to reflect upon the information that has been covered so far. It is also important to consider how what you have learned can be focused and used for examination-style answers by practising the skills associated with AO1.

Assessment objective 1 (AO1) involves demonstrating knowledge and understanding. The terms 'knowledge' and 'understanding' are obvious but it is crucial to be familiar with how certain skills demonstrate these terms, and also, how the performance of these skills is measured (see generic band descriptors Band 5 for AS AO1).

▶ **Your new task is this:** below is a weak answer that has been written in response to a question requiring an examination of Anselm's ontological argument. Using the band level descriptors you need to place this answer in a relevant band that corresponds to the description inside that band. It is obviously a weak answer and so would not be in bands 3–5. In order to do this it will be useful to consider what is missing from the answer and what is inaccurate. The accompanying analysis gives you observations to assist you. In analysing the answer's weaknesses, in a group, think of five ways in which you would improve the answer in order to make it stronger. You may have more than five suggestions but try to negotiate as a group and prioritise the five most important things lacking.

Answer

Anselm's ontological argument is used to prove God's existence [1]. It is based on the idea that God is the most amazing thing that exists in the universe [2]. Anselm states that the idea of God means he exists in the mind and in reality [3]. Anyone, even a fool, can think of God in their mind and that is important to Anselm's argument [4]. In his *Proslogion*, Anselm tells the reader that God must exist in the mind and in reality because reality is greater [5]. As God exists in reality and in the mind he is the greatest most amazing thing in the universe [6]. This is how Anselm proves God's existence using the ontological argument [7].

Analysis of the answer

[1] The statement gives no details beyond stating what the argument is for. Needs expanding and exploring.

[2] This paraphrases incorrectly the central theme of Anselm's argument.

[3] An opportunity is missed here to show accurate understanding. The stages of the argument are glossed over and summarised in such a way as to miss the point.

[4] This is poorly expressed – needs to state why it is important to the argument.

[5] Misses the point – this needs to be explained more clearly as it confuses the issue.

[6] The summary is accurate in general terms, although again, poor expression leads to a sense of confusion in the response.

[7] This is just a repeat of the first sentence. It does not properly show how Anselm proves God's existence.

Issues for analysis and evaluation

The extent to which 'a priori' arguments for God's existence are persuasive

Specification content

The extent to which 'a priori' arguments for God's existence are persuasive.

Arguments for God's existence can be categorised into 'a priori' and 'a posteriori' arguments. A priori arguments are arguments that are independent of our experience or any evidence that may present itself to us.

In general terms, the only thing needed for an a priori argument is an understanding of the language in which it is expressed! In this sense, it could be argued, that this very independence from experience means that they are intrinsically persuasive as they are not tainted by the experience of an individual or group, neither do they rely on evidence (which can often be found to be unreliable).

On the other hand, in general terms, a posteriori arguments, those based on evidence and experience, give us an empirical basis upon which we can prove, with scientific method, how reliable a particular claim or argument may be, that seems far more sensible to the 21st-century mind! We accept arguments about the reliability of medicines, technology and even educational systems based on empirical research, i.e. a posteriori research. We would not accept a priori that any of these things could be claimed as reliable thus proving that a posteriori arguments are more persuasive than a priori ones.

Countering this is the fact that a priori arguments tend to lead to inescapable conclusions – they state what is known and it is accepted as such. In this it could be considered that a priori arguments are more persuasive, particularly when dealing with subject matter such as the possible existence of God.

However, we should bear in mind the fact that a priori deductive proofs depend heavily on their premises in terms of providing sound arguments. If the premises are suspect, inaccurate or wrong then the conclusion that they lead to will inevitably also suffer from these defects. In this, the persuasiveness of an a priori argument for God's existence is considerably undermined.

The ontological argument, as an a priori form, depends on the understanding of what it means to be God. We accept certain facts about God, purely based on the definition of the word. In this, the assertion that God necessarily exists, because he is the greatest possible being that can be thought of and must possess all perfections, including that of existence, appears to be highly persuasive.

Countering this is the existence of the a posteriori arguments for God's existence, such as the cosmological and teleological forms. Both of these have enjoyed a lengthy existence as possible arguments for God's existence and are used by philosophers and theologians even today in the 21st century, accepting them as persuasive forms or proofs for the existence of God.

AO2 Activity *Possible lines of argument*

Listed below are some conclusions that could be drawn from the AO2 reasoning in the accompanying text:

1. A priori arguments for God's existence are entirely persuasive.

2. The persuasiveness of a priori arguments depends on our understanding of language

3. Arguments for the existence of God are not persuasive unless they are based on evidence and experience.

4. The persuasiveness of a priori arguments depends on your faith view.

5. A priori arguments are only persuasive when a posteriori arguments fail.

Consider each of the conclusions drawn above and collect evidence and examples to support each argument from the AO1 and AO2 material studied in this section. Select one conclusion that you think is most convincing and explain why it is so. Now contrast this with the weakest conclusion in the list, justifying your argument with clear reasoning and evidence.

Specification content

The extent to which different religious views on the nature of God impact on arguments for the existence of God.

The extent to which different religious views on the nature of God impact on arguments for the existence of God

According to the traditional concept of God in Classical Theism, God is omnipotent, omniscient and omnipresent. In other words, God can do all things, knows all things and is everywhere. This would be a view upheld by Christianity, Islam and Judaism – often collectively known as the western or Abrahamic religions.

When considering the theistic proofs considered so far (i.e. cosmological, teleological and ontological) it is worth reflecting on how much each of these is based on an understanding of God's nature as presented by these faiths.

For example, God's omnipotence is a key feature of both cosmological and teleological arguments which describe a being capable of creating a universe and designing a universe respectively. Were God not attributed with this power, then how could either of these feats be attributed to him? It must be considered vital to these arguments that God has these abilities (creator/designer) as an essential part of who he is considered to be.

Equally, the ontological argument describes God as possessing 'all perfections'. Indeed, this definition of God is the crux of the argument. Were it not so then the ontological argument would be a non-starter. The very idea of God is a God whose nature includes the idea of these perfections as a necessary part of who he is.

The question can then be asked 'what about other considerations about the nature of God? Would these arguments still work if God is described in any other form – e.g. impersonal, limited to a specific sphere of nature, entirely transcendent (i.e. beyond our physical world and incapable of interacting with it), etc. Certainly, this would seem to undermine the validity of all three arguments, as we traditionally understand them at least.

However, concepts of God beyond those recognised above do not necessarily entail such characteristics. In such cases, the nature of God – which might contain characteristics of limited power or malevolent intent – do not impede traditional questions regarding the existence of god in the face of the issues regarding evil and suffering for instance. (Polytheistic or dualist faith traditions could be included in this.) Whilst the traditional theistic arguments as outlined above, do not usually promote an understanding of the nature of God in this way, it certainly raises interesting questions about attempting to explain God's nature and asks why we assume the characteristics attributed to the God of Classical Theism.

In conclusion, traditional arguments for God's existence tend to arise out of specific faith traditions and, as a consequence, are intimately associated with the specific nature of God as described in that tradition. As such, it would seem that different religious views about the nature of God do indeed impact on arguments for the existence of God.

AO2 Activity *Possible lines of argument*

Listed below are some conclusions that could be drawn from the AO2 reasoning in the accompanying text:

1. God's nature informs arguments for his existence.

2. Arguments for God's existence that do not rely on specific faith claims about his nature are more persuasive than those that are dependent on such claims.

3. Without a clear understanding of the nature of God, it would be impossible to construct an argument for God's existence.

4. The validity of arguments for God's existence depends entirely on the religious views about the nature of God.

5. Arguments for God's existence work independently of any faith claims about his nature.

Consider each of the conclusions drawn above and collect evidence and examples to support each argument from the AO1 and AO2 material studied in this section. Select one conclusion that you think is most convincing and explain why it is so. Now contrast this with the weakest conclusion in the list, justifying your argument with clear reasoning and evidence.

AO2 Developing skills

It is now time to reflect upon the information that has been covered so far. It is also important to consider how what you have learned can be focused and used for examination-style answers by practising the skills associated with AO2.

Assessment objective 2 (AO2) involves 'analysis' and 'evaluation'. The terms may be obvious but it is crucial to be familiar with how certain skills demonstrate these terms, and also, how the performance of these skills is measured (see generic band descriptors Band 5 for AS AO2).

Obviously an answer is placed within an appropriate band descriptor depending upon how well the answer performs, ranging from excellent, good, satisfactory, basic/limited to very limited.

▶ **Your task is this:** below is a weak answer that has been written in response to a question requiring evaluation of the extent to which 'a priori' arguments for God's existence are persuasive. Using the band level descriptors you need to place this answer in a relevant band that corresponds to the description inside that band. It is obviously a weak answer and so would not be in bands 3–5. In order to do this it will be useful to consider what is missing from the answer and what is inaccurate. The accompanying analysis gives you observations to assist you. In analysing the answer's weaknesses, in a group, think of five ways in which you would improve the answer in order to make it stronger. You may have more than five suggestions but try to negotiate as a group and prioritise the five most important things lacking.

Key skills

Analysis involves identifying issues raised by the materials in the AO1, together with those identified in the AO2 section, and presents sustained and clear views, either of scholars or from a personal perspective ready for evaluation.

This means that it picks out key things to debate and the lines of argument presented by others or a personal point of view.

Evaluation involves considering the various implications of the issues raised based upon the evidence gleaned from analysis and provides an extensive detailed argument with a clear conclusion.

This means that the answer weighs up the various and different lines of argument analysed through individual commentary and response and arrives at a conclusion through a clear process of reasoning.

Answer

Proving God's existence is not an easy task. Philosophers have argued about this for thousands of years [1].

However, there are two main types of argument that can help prove God's existence: inductive, a posteriori and deductive, a priori [2].

The cosmological and teleological arguments are both inductive a posteriori arguments. The ontological argument is a priori and deductive. A posteriori arguments are arguments that are based on evidence so people can see what it is they are arguing about and it is very difficult to argue against when you have evidence to support your argument [3].

A priori arguments do not use evidence and so because of this they are very difficult to prove because people can always argue against you when there is no evidence to support your argument. However, some people think that some ideas are so obvious that no evidence is needed [4].

For instance it is a priori true that all bachelors are unmarried males and no evidence is needed to argue against that and so it is true with the idea of God, as Anselm defines him, there is no evidence needed because the word God means that he exists [5].

Therefore in my opinion a priori arguments can be very good at showing people how God's existence can be proved [6].

Analysis of the answer

[1] An introduction that does not properly address the question but instead focuses on the generic issue of God's existence being proven.

[2] Has a basic grasp of the concepts of a posteriori and a priori arguments.

[3] The explanation of a posteriori is limited, despite being accurately linked to the cosmological and teleological arguments, the candidate does not seems to have a proper grasp of what an a posteriori argument is.

[4] A clumsy and poorly expressed understanding of a priori arguments.

[5] A basic point that is not developed sufficiently and so is poorly expressed.

[6] A conclusion that is not linked to the question.

Specification content

Rene Descartes – concept of God as supremely perfect being; analogies of triangles and mountains/valleys.

Key quote

I clearly see that existence can no more be separated from the essence of God than can its having its three angles equal to two right angles be separated from the essence of a [rectilinear] triangle, or the idea of a mountain from the idea of a valley; and so there is not any less repugnance to our conceiving a God (that is, a Being supremely perfect) to whom existence is lacking (that is to say, to whom a certain perfection is lacking), than to conceive of a mountain which has no valley. (Descartes)

Key terms

Attribute: a descriptive characteristic that someone or something possesses

Perfection: the complete absence of flaws also the ultimate state of a positive trait

B: Deductive arguments – developments of the ontological argument

Rene Descartes – concept of God as supremely perfect being; analogies of triangles and mountains/valleys

For Descartes, the definition of God was that God was the most perfect being – or to put it another way – a being that possessed all **perfections**. Whilst Descartes is a little vague on precisely what is meant by the concept of 'perfection', the implication is that he means God possesses the very best form of all possible **attributes**.

When talking of the God of Classical Theism, the attributes of power, knowledge and love, are magnified so that he is all-powerful (omnipotent); all-knowing (omniscient) and all-loving (omnibenevolent). That is to say – God possesses each of those attributes in their perfect state. For Descartes, God as the supremely perfect being possesses all perfections and he includes within this the idea of existence that God possesses as an attribute. Were he not to possess the perfection of each and every positive attribute that it were possible to possess, then God would not be the supremely perfect being. Thus, the definition of God, for Descartes, is phrased in positive terms, unlike Anselm's negative 'God is that than which nothing greater can be conceived'.

Rene Descartes (1596–1650)

To help us understand this concept further Descartes uses two analogies:

The idea of a triangle:

Descartes points out that to think of a triangle is to necessarily think of a shape that has both three sides and interior angles that add up to 180°. It does not necessarily mean that this shape necessarily exists in any external reality but in order to think about the idea of a triangle there needs to be a set of criteria that can be understood by all and which forms part of the definition of what a triangle is.

Similarly with God: it is equally impossible to think of God unless one considers the attribute of existence as a necessary part of the definition of what God is. In summary – Descartes says the concept of God contains the idea of his existence as a necessary perfection that he possesses in the same way that the concept of a triangle refers to a shape with three sides and interior angles that add up to 180°. The attributes and the idea are inextricably linked in both cases.

Mountains and valleys:

The second analogy that Descartes makes use of is the idea that one cannot think of a mountain without thinking of the corresponding valley – for wherever there is one there is always, by definition, the other. This analogy is used by Descartes to reinforce the idea that it is impossible to divorce the ideas of God and the idea of his existence:

'....for from the fact that I cannot conceive a mountain without a valley, it does not follow that there is any mountain or any valley in existence, but only that the mountain and the valley, whether they exist or do not exist, cannot in any way be separated one from the other. While from the fact that I cannot conceive God without existence, it follows that existence is inseparable from Him, and hence that He really exists; not that my thought can bring this to pass, or impose any necessity on things, but, on the contrary, because the necessity which lies in the thing itself, i.e. the necessity of the existence of God determines me to think in this way. For it is not within my power to think of God without existence (that is of a supremely perfect Being devoid of a supreme perfection).'

Descartes is stating that God alone possesses this perfection (that is, of necessary existence) as the supremely perfect being, thereby proving that God, necessarily, exists.

Study tip

Make sure that you always answer the question set, paying particular attention to key words. This will ensure that you have the best chance of giving 'An extensive and relevant response which answers the specific demands of the question set' (L5 band descriptor AO1).

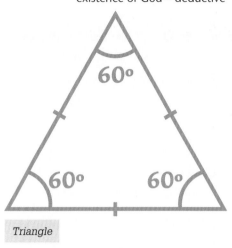

Triangle

Every mountain has a valley

quicKfire

2.4 What two analogies does Descartes make use of to help explain his ontological argument?

AO1 Activity

Descartes' arguments are relatively straightforward to follow, as long as you understand his analogies of the ideas of triangles and the link between mountains and valleys. Summarise these ideas in two separate diagrams that are drawn on one side of A4, this will help you to remember how they work to support Descartes' ontological argument.

Specification content

Norman Malcolm – God as unlimited being: God's existence as necessary rather than just possible.

Key quote 1

The doctrine that existence is a perfection is remarkably queer. It makes sense and is true to say that my future house will be a better one if it is insulated than if it is not insulated; but what could it mean to say that it will be a better house if it exists than if it does not? My future child will be a better man if he is honest than if he is not; but who would understand the saying that he will be a better man if he exists than if he does not? Or who understands the saying that if God exists He is more perfect than if He does not exist? One might say, with some intelligibility, that it would be better (for oneself or for mankind) if God exists than if He does not – but that is a different matter. (Malcolm)

Norman Malcolm – God as unlimited being: God's existence as necessary rather than just possible

In *The Philosophical Review* (1960) Norman Malcolm revisited the ontological argument and presented it in a form that responded to its previous critics and developed the argument further from that written by both Anselm and Descartes, centuries earlier.

Malcolm rejects both Anselm's argument stated in *Proslogion* 2 and that proposed by Descartes. Malcolm sides with both Gaunilo and Kant in their objections, namely that to state that something exists either because it is greater to exist in reality, or, because existence is a perfection and God possesses all perfections, are false arguments. You cannot merely add the concept of existence to a list of qualities that something has and then claim that it therefore exists! (see Key quote 1).

However, Malcolm does sympathise with the argument that Anselm puts forward in *Proslogion* 3, namely that he concludes (following his proof in *Proslogion* 2) that because God is the greatest possible being that can be thought of, then he must have necessary existence. This is, as seen earlier, a necessary consequence of being the greatest possible being that can be thought of – quite simply because a being that did not have necessary existence would be inferior to one that did have necessary existence. As both can be conceived then it is the being with necessary existence that is the greater – and as the greatest possible being must exist.

For Malcolm, the very fact that God is the greatest possible being that can be thought of, necessarily means that God should equally be described as an unlimited being (see Key quote 2)– that is to say, a being that has no limits – possesses all perfections to the greatest possible degree and, because God is considered as an unlimited being, then for the religious believer, he is worthy of worship. Were God not a being that was unlimited, then that would mean there were limits to some, if not all, aspects of his being, which in turn means he is not the greatest thing that can be thought of, would not fit our understanding of what it meant to be 'God' (as defined by Anselm) and therefore would not be worthy of worship. Thus, God must of necessity by definition be an unlimited being.

The big question about God

Malcolm summarises how the ontological argument shows God's existence to be necessary thus:

'If God, a being a greater than which cannot be conceived, does not exist then He cannot *come* into existence. For if He did He would either have been *caused* to come into existence or have *happened* to come into existence, and in either case He would be a limited being, which by our conception of Him He is not. Since He cannot come into existence, if He does not exist His existence is impossible. If He does exist He cannot have come into existence (for the reasons given), nor can He cease to exist, for nothing could cause Him to cease to exist nor could it just happen that He ceased to exist. So if God exists His existence is necessary. Thus God's existence is either impossible or necessary. It can be the former only if the concept of such a being is self-contradictory or in some way logically absurd. Assuming that this is not so, it follows that He necessarily exists.' (Malcolm)

AO1 Activity

On small revision cards create summaries of Malcolm's ontological argument. Support the explanations with relevant evidence from the passage, including quotations from Malcolm. This will help you select and recall a core set of points to develop in an answer to explaining Malcolm's version of the ontological argument and ensure that you are demonstrating 'Thorough, accurate and relevant knowledge and understanding of religion and belief.' (L5 band descriptor AO1)

Study tip

Make sure that you always answer the question set, paying particular attention to key terms. This will ensure that you have the best chance of giving 'An extensive and relevant response which answers the specific demands of the question set' (L5 band descriptor AO1).

Key quote 2

What Anselm did was to give a demonstration that the proposition 'God necessarily exists' is entailed by the proposition 'God is a being a greater than which cannot be conceived' (which is equivalent to 'God is an absolutely unlimited being'). (Malcolm)

quickfire

2.5 Under what conditions, according to Malcolm, would God's existence be impossible?

Key skills

Knowledge involves:

Selection of a range of (thorough) accurate and relevant information that is directly related to the specific demands of the question.

This means you choose the correct information relevant to the question set NOT the topic area. You will have to think and focus on selecting key information and NOT writing everything you know about the topic area.

Understanding involves:

Explanation that is extensive, demonstrating depth and/or breadth with excellent use of evidence and examples including (where appropriate) thorough and accurate supporting use of sacred texts, sources of wisdom and specialist language.

This means that you demonstrate that you understand something by being able to illustrate and expand your points through examples/supporting evidence in a personal way and NOT repeat chunks from a text book (known as rote learning).

Further application of skills:

Go through the topic areas in this section and create some bullet lists of key points from key areas. For each one, provide further elaboration and explanation through the use of evidence and examples.

AO1 Developing skills

It is now time to reflect upon the information that has been covered so far. It is also important to consider how what you have learned can be focused and used for examination-style answers by practising the skills associated with AO1.

Assessment objective 1 (AO1) involves demonstrating knowledge and understanding. The terms 'knowledge' and 'understanding' are obvious but it is crucial to be familiar with how certain skills demonstrate these terms, and also, how the performance of these skills is measured (see generic band descriptors Band 5 for AS AO1).

▶ **Your new task is this:** below is a strong answer that has been written in response to a question requiring an examination of the origins of the ontological argument. Using the band level descriptors you can compare this with the relevant higher bands and the descriptions inside those bands. It is obviously a strong answer and so would not be in bands 1–3. In order to do this, it will be useful to consider what is good about the answer and what is accurate. The accompanying analysis gives you clues and prompts to assist you. In analysing the answer's strengths, in a group, think of five things that make this answer a good one. You may have more than five observations and indeed suggestions to make it a perfect answer!

Answer

The ontological argument is an a priori, deductive argument for the existence of God. This means that it is not based on evidence or experience but rather on a prior understanding of what is already known – i.e. what the meaning of the word God entails. In this sense the definition of 'God' leads to the conclusion that God exists. [1]

The ontological argument, as it is recognised today, was first put forward by Anselm of Canterbury in his *Proslogion*. In this work Anselm considers two key points. Firstly, that God is the greatest possible being and secondly, that God has necessary existence. [2]

Anselm's first proof starts with reference to the verse in the Psalms that states 'The fool hath said in his heart there is no God'. Anselm uses this verse to demonstrate that to state that there is no God, when one is able to assert that such a concept exists, is indeed 'foolish'. For Anselm the word 'God' is defined thus: 'God is that than which nothing greater can be conceived'. From this he demonstrates that God must exist.

The argument runs thus – it is better to exist in reality than just in the mind, for things that only exist in the mind will always be inferior to things that have an external physical reality. As such, God – that than which nothing greater can be conceived – already exists as an idea in the mind. However, if God truly is the greatest possible being that can be thought of, then he must exist in reality as well. This is because if he did not, then anything that did exist in reality would automatically be considered to be greater than God. [3]

This in turn would mean that God would not be 'that than which nothing greater can be conceived' – which is a denial of the very definition of God – his essence, or 'ontos', means that he exists by definition. Only can a God that exists in reality can truly be the greatest possible thing that can be thought of. This is how Anselm develops his argument in *Proslogion* 3. That is, if God exists, he must be necessary. [4]

Anselm says that it is possible to think of a being who has the property of having to exist and that it is also possible of thinking of something that does not have to exist. When thinking of the two it is the one that cannot not exist that is greater than the one that does not have to exist. [5]

In other words, God, if he exists, he is either a being which cannot be thought of as not existing (i.e. he is necessary) or he is a being which can be thought of as not existing (i.e. he is contingent). If we use Anselm's definition for God, that he is 'that than which nothing greater can be conceived' then God's existence must be necessary. [6]

What Anselm is saying here is that if God is the greatest possible being that there is then he must, of necessity, exist in reality and not just as a concept in the mind. This is because otherwise anything that existed in reality would be greater than God (if he was only an idea) but because of our definition of God 'as the greatest possible being', then it follows that he must necessarily exist. [7]

Completed comments

1 Good introduction that provides an explanation of the philosophical framework upon which the ontological argument is formed.

2 Clearly outlines the two main aspects of Anselm's ontological argument.

3 Good identification of the beginnings of the argument that demonstrates accurate and relevant knowledge.

4 Very good use of both complex and technical language to show thorough understanding of the ontological argument.

5 Continues to develop the argument logically and accurately.

6 Accurately explains the argument by returning to the key definition.

7 Clearly rounds off Anselm's argument showing that they have made accurate reference to the *Proslogion* in formulating their response.

This section covers AO2 content and skills

Specification content

The effectiveness of the ontological argument for God's existence.

AO2 Activity *Possible lines of argument*

Listed below are some conclusions that could be drawn from the AO2 reasoning in the accompanying text:

1. The ontological argument effectively proves God's existence beyond any reasonable doubt.

2. Only later forms of the ontological argument are acceptable, the classical form from Anselm is entirely ineffective.

3. Using the ontological argument to prove God's existence is philosophically futile.

4. The ontological argument's effectiveness depends on your religious beliefs.

5. The effectiveness of the ontological argument is undermined by modern scientific thought.

Consider each of the conclusions drawn above and collect evidence and examples to support each argument from the AO1 and AO2 material studied in this section. Select one conclusion that you think is most convincing and explain why it is so. Now contrast this with the weakest conclusion in the list, justifying your argument with clear reasoning and evidence.

Issues for analysis and evaluation

The effectiveness of the ontological argument for God's existence

The ontological argument for God's existence has a thousand-year history in the annals of religious philosophy and deserves respect. As an a priori argument it is a rational proof whose logic is inescapable when the deductive form of its premises is accepted. For Anselm, this argument was entirely effective in confirming his own theistic beliefs – that God's existence was both obvious and necessary.

Theistic religions from the Abrahamic tradition, such as Christianity, Judaism and Islam, all accept the definition of God as proposed by Anselm and therefore they would also consider this to be an effective form of argument as it confirms their own faith views, that God is the greatest possible being, one which nothing greater can be thought of in the entire realm of reality.

What further demonstrates the effectiveness of the ontological argument is that it fits contemporary forms of philosophy and logic, such as the modal systems adopted by modern-day ontological argument philosophers, such as Malcolm.

The ontological argument, as an a priori form, depends on the understanding of what it means to be God. We accept certain facts about God, purely based on the definition of the word. In this, the assertion that God necessarily exists, because he is the greatest possible being that can be thought of and must possess all perfections, including that of existence, shows how effective the argument is.

We should also bear in mind the fact that the ontological argument, as an a priori argument, leads to an inescapable conclusion – i.e. that God exists. This makes it highly effective as long as one accepts the reasoning put forward in the argument!

However, not all philosophers or religious believers accept that the ontological argument is an effective proof for God's existence. Indeed, one of its earliest critics was Anselm's contemporary, Gaunilo, who rejected the idea that it was possible to define anything into existence.

Equally Immanuel Kant, centuries later, also rejected the argument, suggesting that Descartes was misusing the word 'exist'. It was not possible, in his view to simply add the word exist to a list of perfections that something did or didn't have – thereby showing the argument to be ineffective.

We should also appreciate, in line with these critiques, that whenever any of the premises of an a priori argument can be shown to be weak or inaccurate, then the conclusion that is produced by virtue of the reasoning will also be either weak or inaccurate – this links strongly to the views put forward by Kant.

In conclusion, the arguments against the ontological argument are sufficiently robust to undermine any reasonable claim that it is an effective argument in proving the existence of God.

Whether the ontological argument is more persuasive than the cosmological/teleological arguments for God's existence

Specification content
Whether the ontological argument
is more persuasive than the
cosmological/teleological arguments
for God's existence.

God's existence or non-existence has long been a debate for philosophers. Strong views are formed on both sides of the debate. In order to support this debate a number of different forms of 'proof' have been offered. These proofs exist in both a priori and a posteriori forms. The ontological argument is an a priori argument for the existence of God whilst both the cosmological and teleological arguments are a posteriori forms.

The persuasiveness of the ontological argument depends, as is so often the case, on the willingness of the individual to accept the deductive premises upon which it is based. If these premises are accepted – i.e. the idea that the definition of God is 'that than which nothing greater can be conceived' and the associated argument that this proves God has necessary existence (otherwise God cannot be the greatest possible thing that can be thought of) – then it is very difficult to deny the conclusion that God necessarily exists. This would make the ontological argument entirely persuasive.

However, if the premises are rejected – as Gaunilo, Kant and others did – then the ontological argument fails entirely. It is never accepted because the idea of existence following on from definition is seen as entirely fallacious and is not at all persuasive.

The cosmological argument is based on the empirical fact that there is a universe, and poses the question 'What started the universe?' from which the reasoning of philosophers such as Aquinas, Leibniz and Craig propose the answer as God.

The teleological argument starts from the philosophical observation that the universe contains evidence of design and that things within the universe appear to work towards an end or purpose, even when there is no obvious reason for this to happen. The conclusion inductively drawn by philosophers such as Aquinas, Paley and Tennant, is that the reason for this is God.

Both of the latter arguments use empirical evidence. In a scientific age, empirical evidence is always valued as a starting point for any persuasive argument and therefore, it could be argued, that these arguments are both more persuasive than the ontological argument, in proving the existence of God.

However, both of these inductive arguments are subject to a number of criticisms, not least of which is that even if all other ideas are accepted within the line of inductive reasoning, why does the ultimate conclusion for this inductive reasoning have to be God? To this, neither argument gives a definitive or persuasive answer.

It then becomes a matter of preference for the type of reasoning adopted in accepting a more persuasive form of argument for the existence of God. Those preferring an experience or evidence base will no doubt prefer the inductive arguments from cosmology or design – those who prefer the logical reasoning found in the deductive form of the ontological argument will prefer this. Some may therefore conclude that the relative persuasiveness of the arguments becomes a subjective matter, much like the acceptance or denial of belief in a divine being.

AO2 Activity *Possible lines of argument*

Listed below are some conclusions that could be drawn from the AO2 reasoning in the accompanying text:

1. The ontological argument is the most persuasive argument for the existence of God.

2. The cosmological/teleological arguments are the most persuasive arguments for the existence of God.

3. Neither of the arguments are persuasive.

4. All of the arguments are equally persuasive.

5. The arguments' relative persuasiveness will depend on the philosophical viewpoint of the individual.

Consider each of the conclusions drawn above and collect evidence and examples to support each argument from the AO1 and AO2 material studied in this section. Select one conclusion that you think is most convincing and explain why it is so. Now contrast this with the weakest conclusion in the list, justifying your argument with clear reasoning and evidence.

Key skills

Analysis involves identifying issues raised by the materials in the AO1, together with those identified in the AO2 section, and presents sustained and clear views, either of scholars or from a personal perspective ready for evaluation.

This means that it picks out key things to debate and the lines of argument presented by others or a personal point of view.

Evaluation involves considering the various implications of the issues raised based upon the evidence gleaned from analysis and provides an extensive detailed argument with a clear conclusion.

This means that the answer weighs up the various and different lines of argument analysed through individual commentary and response and arrives at a conclusion through a clear process of reasoning.

AO2 Developing skills

It is now time to reflect upon the information that has been covered so far. It is also important to consider how what you have learned can be focused and used for examination-style answers by practising the skills associated with AO2.

Assessment objective 2 (AO2) involves 'analysis' and 'evaluation'. The terms may be obvious but it is crucial to be familiar with how certain skills demonstrate these terms, and also, how the performance of these skills is measured (see generic band descriptors Band 5 for AS AO2).

Obviously an answer is placed within an appropriate band descriptor depending upon how well the answer performs, ranging from excellent, good, satisfactory, basic/limited to very limited.

▶ **Your task is this:** below is a strong answer that has been written in response to a question requiring evaluation of whether the ontological argument proves the existence of God. Using the band level descriptors you can compare this with the relevant higher bands and the descriptions inside those bands. It is obviously a strong answer and so would not be in bands 1–3. In order to do this it will be useful to consider what is good about the answer and what is accurate. The accompanying analysis gives you clues and prompts to assist you. In analysing the answer's strengths, in a group, think of five things that make this answer a good one. You may have more than five observations and indeed suggestions to make it a perfect answer!

Answer

In order to see whether the ontological argument proves the existence of God, it is important to consider, firstly, what we mean by proof. Three forms of proof are generally available to us: direct, deductive and inductive. Direct proof involves use of one or more of the five senses, and is sometimes also referred to as 'empirical proof'. In terms of proving the existence of God, this is one of the more contentious forms as claims of visions, miracles and other physical 'proofs' of God's existence are difficult to verify conclusively. **1**

Deductive proof uses premises to form a conclusion – thereby offering a form of 'logical' or rational proof. It is this form of proof that the ontological argument is based upon. The third type of proof is inductive and is the form utilised by the cosmological and teleological arguments. **2**

The relative success of the ontological argument, as a form of deductive proof, is heavily dependent – as all deductive proofs are – on the acceptance of the premises. For Anselm, these premises include the acceptance that the definition of the word God proves beyond reasonable doubt that he exists. God is that than which nothing greater can be conceived. It is also better to exist in reality than in the mind alone. Therefore if God is that than which nothing greater can be conceived, it necessarily follows that he exists not only in the mind but in reality as well. **3**

This argument, at first glance, appears convincing. However, it asks us to accept certain premises that some were unhappy to accept. For instance, the monk Gaunilo could not accept that you could simply move from a definition to an existent reality. He countered Anselm's argument by stating that were he to think of a perfect island then that must mean that that island also existed, otherwise it would not be a perfect island! This of course is an absurd idea. It would have seemed that Gaunilo had defeated Anselm's argument and that the ontological argument could not prove the existence of God. This was not the case though. **4**

In his response to Gaunilo, Anselm pointed out that the properties of an island and
the properties of God were entirely different. For instance, an island could always be
improved upon – this was not the case with God. God was unique, and because of
this the idea of his existence as necessary only applied to him – it did not, and could
not, apply to anything else in the physical world. Therefore Anselm believed that his
ontological argument had successfully proven God's existence. [5]

Descartes developed Anselm's ideas by explaining that the very idea of God meant
that he had to exist, in the same way that it was impossible to think about a triangle
without thinking of a three-sided shape, it was equally impossible to consider
the idea of God without equally thinking of a being that necessarily existed. This
therefore proved God's existence. [6]

Kant's objection to Descartes was that existence could not be treated like a
predicate and so it was philosophically unsound to move from a definition where
all perfections were claimed and then to include existence as a perfection. For
Kant, existence was not a property that a thing could lack – for if that were so, it
would not exist in the first place! Existence was an integral part of something in
the real world, but it was not a defining characteristic of that thing. Therefore whilst
he accepted that it was possible to hold the idea of God, it did not follow that God
actually existed – Kant seemed to have shown that the ontological argument had
not proven God's existence. [7]

By looking at the arguments as presented above, it would seem that the ontological
argument does not prove the existence of God. [8]

Completed hints

[1] Introduces the topic by looking at what is meant by the idea of proof.

[2] Continues outlining definitions of proof. The information is accurate.

[3] Introduces the ontological argument as presented by Anselm. Deals accurately
with the information.

[4] Introduces a counterpoint to the argument; makes good use of relevant
evidence.

[5] Introduces a counter-argument to the counterpoint. This demonstrates effective
evaluation of the subject material.

[6] Further evidence is added to support the argument by introducing a different
philosopher.

[7] The counter-argument is provided by reference to Kant's rejection of both
Anselm and Descartes' arguments.

[8] A brief conclusion that does not expand on a basic statement. Evidence is not
restated to support the conclusion being made.

C: Challenges to the ontological argument

Gaunilo, his reply to Anselm

Specification content

Gaunilo, his reply to Anselm; his rejection of idea of a greatest possible being that can be thought of as having separate existence outside of our minds; his analogy of the idea of the greatest island as a ridicule of Anselm's logic.

The ontological argument as presented by Anselm, was met with criticism by his contemporary, a monk by the name of Gaunilo of Marmoutier. In a work titled *On behalf of the fool*, Gaunilo replied to Anselm's proof by using an argument structure known as *reductio ad absurdum*. He makes a claim that in the same way that Anselm argues it is possible to argue the existence of God through the definition of God 'is that than which nothing greater can be conceived', then it must therefore be possible to have the idea of a perfect island and, because of this idea, then this island must exist:

The perfect island?

'Now if someone should tell me that there is such an island, I should easily understand his words, in which there is no difficulty. But suppose that he went on to say, as if by a logical inference: "You can no longer doubt that this island which is more excellent than all lands exists somewhere, since you have no doubt that it is in your understanding. And since it is more excellent not to be in the understanding alone, but to exist both in the understanding and in reality, for this reason it must exist. For if it does not exist, any land which really exists will be more excellent than it; and so the island already understood by you to be more excellent will not be more excellent.'

If a man should try to prove to me by such reasoning that this island truly exists, and that its existence should no longer be doubted, either I should believe that he was jesting, or I know not which I ought to regard as the greater fool: myself, supposing that I should allow this proof; or him, if he should suppose that he had established with any certainty the existence of this island.'

In other words, Gaunilo is stating that the idea of a something that can be thought of as existing separately outside of our minds, just because it is the greatest thing we can think of, is a logical nonsense. Just because you can define a greatest possible being does not automatically lead to the fact that one actually exists – and it here that he makes use of his island analogy to underline the absurdity of Anselm's argument.

Critics of Gaunilo suggest that he has misunderstood the ontological argument and is applying criticism incorrectly. The basic counter-argument to Gaunilo focuses on the idea that only God is necessary (non-contingent) and is the ground or source of his own being. If this is held to be true, then Anselm's definition is coherent. Gaunilo's island is a contingent object and, as such, possesses no **intrinsic maximum** (that is to say, you can always add something else to it to improve it or make it 'more perfect' than it already is – this is not true of the concept of a non-contingent God. God's perfection is a necessary part of him – the same cannot be said about islands (or any other contingent entity).

Key terms

Intrinsic maximum: a term often associated in the context of the ontological argument with English philosopher, Charles Dunbar Broad, to refer to the necessary properties of God – in that they must all possess this intrinsic maximum in order for the definition of God as the greatest possible being to be accurate

Reductio ad absurdum: an argument that shows a statement to be false or absurd if its logical conclusions were to be accepted

quickfire

2.6 Why did Gaunilo think Anselm's argument was flawed?

AO1 Activity

On small revision cards create a summary of the key points in Gaunilo's objections. Support the explanations with relevant quotes from Gaunilo. This will enable you to demonstrate 'Excellent use of evidence and examples' (L5 band descriptor AO1). This ensures that you are selecting the most important features for emphasis and clarity and supporting this with evidence, rather than just presenting a descriptive, or simple structure, for your answer.

Immanuel Kant's objection

In the 18th century, Prussian philosopher Immanuel Kant put forward a criticism towards Descartes' form of the ontological argument. Descartes had claimed that God possessed all perfections and that existence was one of those. However, Kant objected, it is inaccurate to describe existence as a perfection. The reasons for this were that the perfections that Descartes was referring to were attributes or '**predicates**'. Existence, said Kant, could not be a predicate simply because existence can be a thing that an object can possess or lack but it does not describe anything about the nature of an object.

For example, if we describe God as all-loving then we are describing a predicate that God has – it is a predicate (or attribute/characteristic) that tells us something about God's nature. The same is true when we describe God as omnipresent or omniscient. Were we to say 'God exists' what does that tell us about his nature? For Kant, it was for this reason that Descartes was mistaken in suggesting that God's existence was a determining predicate that he possessed.

To make this clearer, let us consider again what we mean be a predicate. If I say 'my car is silver' then I am describing something about my car that enables others to know something about it. I could go further and say that 'my car has four wheels', 'my car has five doors', my car has windscreen wipers, etc. All of these things are predicates of my car – they explain things about my car, things that it possesses and things that help others to understand something about the nature of my car. However, if I said 'my car exists' I am saying nothing about its nature – I am merely making the point that my car is in existence, as opposed to my car not being in existence.

Kant further elaborated on his denial of existence as a predicate by providing the example of 100 **thalers**. He asks the reader to consider what difference is held in the understanding of thalers by adding the phrase 'it exists' to the list of other predicates, (e.g. they are round, made of gold, etc.). He states that as nothing changes in our minds by adding this phrase, then it shows how existence is not a real predicate – despite the fact that 100 thalers in reality would have been preferable to 100 thalers in the mind alone! The word 'exists' adds nothing to our idea of God and therefore, suggests Kant's, Descartes' (and by association, Anselm's) ontological arguments fail a priori to prove the existence of God.

Study tip

When you use references to scholars and texts, try to make them manageable in size. Sometimes brief extracts are just as effective. In addition, do not just write down a quote to 'show off' without thinking about how it fits in with the point you are making.

Specification content

Immanuel Kant's objection – existence is not a determining predicate: it cannot be a property that an object can either possess or lack.

Immanuel Kant (1724–1804)

Key terms

Predicate: a defining characteristic or attribute

Thaler: currency used in 18th-century Prussia

quickfire

2.7 What was Kant's main objection to the ontological argument?

Key skills

Knowledge involves:

Selection of a range of (thorough) accurate and relevant information that is directly related to the specific demands of the question.

This means you choose the correct information relevant to the question set NOT the topic area. You will have to think and focus on selecting key information and NOT writing everything you know about the topic area.

Understanding involves:

Explanation that is extensive, demonstrating depth and/or breadth with excellent use of evidence and examples including (where appropriate) thorough and accurate supporting use of sacred texts, sources of wisdom and specialist language.

This means that you demonstrate that you understand something by being able to illustrate and expand your points through examples/supporting evidence in a personal way and NOT repeat chunks from a text book (known as rote learning).

Further application of skills:

Go through the topic areas in this section and create some bullet lists of key points from key areas. For each one, provide further elaboration and explanation through the use of evidence and examples.

AO1 Developing skills

It is now time to reflect upon the information that has been covered so far. It is also important to consider how what you have learned can be focused and used for examination-style answers by practising the skills associated with AO1.

Assessment objective 1 (AO1) involves demonstrating knowledge and understanding. The terms 'knowledge' and 'understanding' are obvious but it is crucial to be familiar with how certain skills demonstrate these terms, and also, how the performance of these skills is measured (see generic band descriptors Band 5 for AS AO1).

▶ **Your new task is this:** below is a fairly strong answer, although not perfect, that has been written in response to a question requiring an examination of the challenges to the ontological argument. Using the band level descriptors you can compare this with the relevant higher bands and the descriptions inside those bands. It is obviously a fairly strong answer and so would not be in bands 1, 2 or 5. In order to do this it will be useful to consider what is both strong and weak about the answer and therefore what needs developing.

In analysing the answer, in a group, identify three ways to make this answer a better one. You may have more than three observations and indeed suggestions to make it a perfect answer!

Answer

When Anselm formulated his ontological argument in the *Proslogion*, his statement that God was that than which nothing greater can be conceived, gave the idea of a God whose very existence could be proven through the simple definition of his name. The premises upon which this argument existed seemed effective and the inescapable conclusion of God's existence was thereby established.

However, the challenge that came from Gaunilo, a monk from Marmoutier, seemed to suggest that the ontological argument presented by Anselm was flawed and therefore failed to prove God's existence as the argument itself was seen, by Gaunilo, to be absurd. His response was that, to establish the existence of something merely by stating that it possessed all perfections was nonsense.

Gaunilo stated that were such a thing possible then it should be possible to define anything into existence – as long as that thing was held to possess qualities of perfection. His example was that of a perfect island – Gaunilo stated that this island must exist in reality because he could think of a perfect island in his mind. In doing this he was echoing Anselm's argument that God must exist in reality as well as in the mind as it was greater to exist in reality than in the mind alone.

Centuries later, Descartes developed Anselm's argument and stated that God was the supremely perfect being and that once that has been understood then it would be also understood that God necessarily existed; indeed, to think of God as not existing would be the same as trying to think of a triangle without three sides or a mountain existing without a valley.

Kant attacked this argument by saying that Descartes had misused the word existence. He said that existence was not a predicate – by which he meant, it was not a word that you could use to describe the nature of something. The concept of existence added nothing to our understanding of a thing – other then to state that that thing possessed an external reality. However, you could not just add existence to a list of predicates to cause them to come into reality. He gave the example of 100 thalers (money) which he said you could think of in the mind but when describing them, if you added, 'they exist' then you would not be adding anything different to the picture that you had of them in your mind and they certainly would not just magically appear. Therefore Kant challenged the ontological argument.

Issues for analysis and evaluation

The effectiveness of the challenges to the ontological argument for God's existence

Specification content

The effectiveness of the challenges to the ontological argument for God's existence.

Gaunilo's challenge to the ontological argument was in the fact that he felt that Anselm had used an absurd argument. Using the philosophical argument *reductio ad absurdum*, he showed that trying to define something into existence merely by definition was a ridiculous idea.

His presentation of the perfect island was in response to Anselm's definition of God as a being greater than which cannot be conceived. Gaunilo stated that he could think of an island of which none greater could be conceived but that did not mean that it actually existed – indeed, such a claim clearly made no sense. Gaunilo's challenge here appears particularly effective, attacking as it does the core of Anselm's argument.

However, Gaunilo did not appreciate that Anselm's claim was about God – and as God was that than which nothing greater can be conceived – then that definition applied to him alone. Gaunilo's concept of a perfect island could not work as an island can always be added to or improved – complete perfection (in the sense that nothing could ever be improved upon it) makes no sense when talking about a contingent reality such as an island. God was necessary – an island was not. This leads to Gaunilo's attack on Anselm's argument being considered ineffective as it did not make use of valid reasoning.

Kant's challenged Descartes' assertion that existence was a predicate of God. Descartes had stated that as the supremely perfect being, God possessed all perfections. Included within this was the 'perfection' of existence. However, Kant rejected this as he felt that Descartes's use of the word existence was incorrect. Predicates tells us something about the nature of the reality they are trying to describe. The concept of existence tells us nothing about the nature of a reality. Therefore, according to Kant, the ontological argument fails – and his challenge to the ontological argument is considered effective.

Some have questioned whether Kant's understanding of Anselm's original argument was fully accurate, though. It has been observed that Kant was talking about Anselm adding the concept of existence to the concept of God in order to make his argument work; however, other scholars have suggested that this misunderstands Anselm, who they say was instead asking his readers to compare something existing merely in the understanding with something existing in reality as well.

AO2 Activity *Possible lines of argument*

Listed below are some conclusions that could be drawn from the AO2 reasoning in the accompanying text:

1. Gaunilo's challenge was undermined by Anselm's use of deductive reasoning.

2. Kant's challenge was more effective than Gaunilo's.

3. The ontological argument is immune to challenge.

4. The effectiveness of the challenges to the ontological argument depend entirely on their definition of existence.

5. It is impossible to prove God's existence a priori and therefore the challenges are effective.

Consider each of the conclusions drawn above and collect evidence and examples to support each argument from the AO1 and AO2 material studied in this section. Select one conclusion that you think is most convincing and explain why it is so. Now contrast this with the weakest conclusion in the list, justifying your argument with clear reasoning and evidence.

Specification content

The extent to which objections to the ontological argument are persuasive.

The extent to which objections to the ontological argument are persuasive

The relative persuasiveness of the objections to the ontological argument depend on how far the individual considers these objections to be valid, as well as how far the original arguments were accepted as sound.

Gaunilo's objections centre on the claim that in the same way that Anselm argues it is possible to argue the existence of God through the definition of God as 'that than which nothing greater can be conceived', then it must therefore be possible to have the idea of a perfect island and, because of this idea, then this island must exist. Gaunilo says 'If a man should try to prove to me by such reasoning that this island truly exists …. I know not which I ought to regard as the greater fool myself, supposing that I should allow this proof, or him, if he should suppose that he had established with any certainty the existence of this island.' To demonstrate how persuasive an argument this could considered to be we should reflect on Gaunilo's stance that just because you can define a greatest possible being does not automatically lead to the fact that one actually exists.

However, there are critics of Gaunilo's position here. They state that he has misunderstood the ontological argument and is applying his criticism incorrectly. Gaunilo does not seem to understand that because of God's uniqueness the ontological argument only applies to him – no other being. This is because only God is necessary (non-contingent). All other beings are contingent and so cannot apply the same definition to themselves. This counter-argument, if accepted, considerably undermines any persuasiveness that Gaunilo may have had with his objection.

Contrary to the relative non-persuasiveness of Gaunilo's objections, the objections that are stated by Kant appear far more persuasive. This is because Kant does not attempt to directly undermine Anselm's argument by virtue of his definition but instead challenges Descartes' position. This, in turn, affects the position taken by Anselm on the nature of God. Kant shows Descartes reasoning in defining God's existence through a consideration of his perfections as invalid reasoning. Kant explains that existence, which was considered a perfection possessed by God is not a determining predicate – as existence cannot add anything to the idea of something. Only those qualities that add to the nature of God (e.g. omnipotence; omniscience; omnipresence, etc.) can be called predicates. Existence adds nothing new to our understanding of the nature of God and so cannot be called a predicate. This therefore undermines Descartes' position and strengthens the persuasiveness of Kant's objection.

However, if we accept that Kant had misunderstood Anselm and that the idea of adding the concept of existence to the concept of God was not what Anselm was suggesting, then the strength of Kant's objections are somewhat undermined. This would therefore demonstrate that Kant's objections are not as persuasive as at first thought.

AO2 Activity *Possible lines of argument*

Listed below are some conclusions that could be drawn from the AO2 reasoning in the accompanying text:

1. The persuasiveness of an argument depends on how valid its premises are.

2. Gaunilo's response is not persuasive.

3. Only ontological arguments based on valid premises can withstand objections to their reasoning.

4. Kant's understanding of predicates is the most persuasive objection to the ontological argument as presented by both Descartes and Anselm.

5. Kant's objections are persuasive because he is very effective at undermining a priori arguments.

Consider each of the conclusions drawn above and collect evidence and examples to support each argument from the AO1 and AO2 material studied in this section. Select one conclusion that you think is most convincing and explain why it is so. Now contrast this with the weakest conclusion in the list, justifying your argument with clear reasoning and evidence.

AO2 Developing skills

It is now time to reflect upon the information that has been covered so far. It is also important to consider how what you have learned can be focused and used for examination-style answers by practising the skills associated with AO2.

Assessment objective 2 (AO2) involves 'analysis' and 'evaluation'. The terms may be obvious but it is crucial to be familiar with how certain skills demonstrate these terms, and also, how the performance of these skills is measured (see generic band descriptors Band 5 for AS AO2).

Obviously an answer is placed within an appropriate band descriptor depending upon how well the answer performs, ranging from excellent, good, satisfactory, basic/limited to very limited.

▶ **Your task is this:** below is a reasonable answer, although not perfect, that has been written in response to a question requiring an examination of the strengths of the challenges to the ontological argument. Using the band level descriptors you can compare this with the relevant higher bands and the descriptions inside those bands. It is obviously a reasonable answer and so would not be in bands 5, 1 or 2. In order to do this it will be useful to consider what is both strong and weak about the answer and therefore what needs developing.

In analysing the answer, in a group, identify three ways to make this answer a better one. You may have more than three observations and indeed suggestions to make it a perfect answer!

Key skills

Analysis involves identifying issues raised by the materials in the AO1, together with those identified in the AO2 section, and presents sustained and clear views, either of scholars or from a personal perspective ready for evaluation.

This means that it picks out key things to debate and the lines of argument presented by others or a personal point of view.

Evaluation involves considering the various implications of the issues raised based upon the evidence gleaned from analysis and provides an extensive detailed argument with a clear conclusion.

This means that the answer weighs up the various and different lines of argument analysed through individual commentary and response and arrives at a conclusion through a clear process of reasoning.

Answer

The strengths of the challenges to the ontological argument are many. Gaunilo's challenge to the ontological argument clearly shows that Anselm's reasoning was absurd because he was trying to prove God's existence by giving a definition that included the idea that God had to exist.

This was not a good argument because, as Gaunilo said, if you could define things into existence then he could define a perfect island into existence and that didn't make any sense. It was impossible, from Gaunilo's point of view, to define anything into existence merely by saying that it had to exist, as part of the definition of what the thing was.

Some scholars think that Gaunilo was confused in his arguments, though, and therefore they weren't very strong. This is because Gaunilo did not make a distinction between contingent objects (which everything in the universe is) and non-contingent or necessary objects (which only God is). As God is the only non-contingent being in the universe then the ontological argument as presented by Anselm only applies to God and nothing else and because Gaunilo missed this point his criticism was not particularly strong.

However, a stronger form of challenge was made by Immanuel Kant who recognised that including existence as a describing word (or predicate) for God was inaccurate. This is because existence only tells you whether something is or not – it does not tell you what it is, or anything else about it, and therefore cannot be considered to be a proper predicate. Kant says that both Descartes and Anselm misunderstand this point in their arguments and because of this their ontological arguments should both be considered to be invalid.

Kant's challenged Descartes' assertion that existence was a predicate of God. Descartes had stated that as the supremely perfect being, God possessed all perfections. Included within this was the 'perfection' of existence. However, Kant rejected this as he felt that Descartes' use of the word existence was incorrect. Predicates tells us something about the nature of the reality they are trying to describe. The concept of existence tells us nothing about the nature of a reality. Therefore, according to Kant, the ontological argument fails – and his challenge to the ontological argument is considered effective.

This section covers AO1 content and skills

A: The problem of evil and suffering

Specification content

The types of evil: moral (caused by free-will agents) and natural (caused by nature).

The types of evil: moral (caused by free-will agents) and natural (caused by nature)

Evil is often considered to be anything that causes suffering. This suffering can occur in many different forms and can be the result of a moral action or an event that occurs in nature. As such, the nature of evil presents several philosophical issues. Consider the images in the diagrams – what sort of evil do they represent? What is the suffering that is caused by these types of evil? How do they differ?

Examples of Natural evil

Examples of evil

Examples of Moral evil

Key terms

Evil: anything that causes pain or suffering

Moral evil: evil caused as a result of the actions of a free-will agent

Natural evil: evil caused by the means of a force outside of the control of free-will agents – usually referred to as 'nature'

Broadly speaking evil can be categorised in two main ways: **moral evil** and **natural evil**.

Moral evil is understood as any suffering that is brought about through the actions of a free-will agent. Free-will agents have the ability to choose 'good' or 'evil'. As such, their actions can result in the suffering of others. It is important to realise that one of the main philosophical issues that is raised by this type of evil is that if evil is caused by an individual *that could have chosen to do good instead*, does that mean that God cannot be held accountable for evil's existence in the world? Examples of moral evil include murder, theft, violence, rape, slavery, child abuse, animal cruelty, terrorism, adultery, dishonesty, any form of negative discrimination and genocide.

Natural evil is understood as any suffering that is brought about as a consequence of the events outside of the control of free-will agents – most commonly those that occur as part of the natural order. Examples of natural evil include the suffering that results from earthquakes, tsunamis, flooding, drought, tornadoes, hurricanes, extremes in temperature – hot and cold, disease, ageing, crop failure, forest fires, pollution and global warming.

Occasionally free-will agents can set in motion a series of events that result in suffering that were not intended. It is therefore highly debatable as to whether this suffering constitutes moral evil or not.

Study tip

In order to demonstrate the higher-level skills, you should always explain fully any example of evil that you might use in an answer to illustrate moral or natural evil. This explanation must demonstrate how the example chosen causes suffering and is therefore considered as evil.

AO1 Activity

Compile a list of examples that show occurrences of the two main types of evil. You should then share these with a partner and take it in turns to write an explanation of how evil is shown through these examples and the effect it has on others.

The logical problem of evil: classical (Epicurus) – the problem of suffering

The problem of evil is an ancient philosophical and theological one. If a belief system suggests that the universe was created deliberately, out of nothing, by a God that is all-powerful, all-knowing and all-loving, then how is it possible that things within that universe can go wrong? Not only that, why is it that within that universe, the created beings which are again deliberately made by this God, suffer – often to appalling extremes.

Any response would seem to throw up some kind of philosophical contradiction to the characteristics of this God and this is why, despite numerous attempts by religious believers, theologians and philosophers, it remains a constant challenge to those that would believe in such a God (commonly referred to as the God of Classical Theism).

quickfire

3.1 Name the two main types of evil.

quickfire

3.2 Give an example of the two main types of evil.

Specification content

The logical problem of evil: classical (Epicurus) – the problem of suffering.

Key quote

Either God wants to abolish evil, and cannot; or he can, but does not want to. If he wants to, but cannot, he is impotent. If he can, but does not want to, he is wicked. If God can abolish evil, and God really wants to do it, why is there evil in the world? (Epicurus)

> ### Key terms
>
> Omnibenevolent: all-loving
>
> Omnipotent: all-powerful

John L. Mackie's (J. L. Mackie's) modern development – the nature of the problem of evil (inconsistent triad)

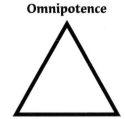

The Australian philosopher J. L. Mackie formulated the problem of evil into an 'inconsistent triad', which runs thus:

1. God is **Omnipotent**
2. God is **Omnibenevolent**
3. Evil Exists

Mackie points out that it is logically inconsistent for these three statements to exist simultaneously.

This is because if God were omnipotent he would have the power to remove evil as his omnipotence means that he is capable of any feat. The characteristic of omnipotence also includes the notion that God could have created a universe where there was no evil. For Mackie, omnipotence, as we will see later, incorporates omniscience and involves a clear definition of what he calls 'unqualified omnipotence', that is, omnipotence without any restrictions due to the constraints of the world.

If he were omnibenevolent then he, in his loving kindness towards his creation, would want to remove evil so that creation did not suffer. The idea that any omnibenevolent being would deliberately tolerate evil, and the horrendous suffering that it causes, is anathema to the very idea of omnibenevolence.

However, the existence of evil is so tangible in its effects and its scope that any denial of its existence would be nonsensical. Thus it is not possible for the three statements to co-exist.

An alternative solution to the problem is to try to resolve the inconsistent triad by removing one of the three points. Any such solution would read like so:

If we removed the characteristic of omnipotence from God, then we can understand why evil exists because, whilst God loves creation and wants to prevent evil, he does not have the power to do so. This solution echoes the philosophical stance taken by process theologians such as Whitehead, who claimed that God was part of the universe and was responsible for starting off the evolutionary process that led to humanity and, as such was responsible for what happened to his creation. However, such a God, as part of the universe, did not have sufficient power to remove evil. Process theologians regard this God as 'the fellow sufferer who understands' – being as much part of the universe as humanity. However attractive this solution appears, ultimately it does not satisfy those religious believers who believe that their God was responsible for creating the universe *ex nihilo* – and is therefore greater than all that exists within the universe.

So some suggest that we should remove the characteristic of omnibenevolence. In this case evil exists and God is omnipotent. Having the power to remove evil does not mean that God wants to. If he is not 'all-loving' then why should he care if his creation suffers? Such a God may even be considered as malicious, and may even enjoy seeing his creation suffer. However, such a God is so far from the imagination of all classical theistic religions as to be unrecognisable; the problem therefore remains.

> ### quickfire
>
> 3.3 What is meant by the term the 'God of Classical Theism'?

> ## Study tip
>
> Always make certain that you fully explain the inconsistent triad and how it could be solved by removing any one corner of the triangle. Candidates often lose marks because they do not explain this properly.

> ### quickfire
>
> 3.4 What is meant by the phrase 'the problem of evil'?

Finally then we can remove the fact that 'evil exists'. In doing so, God retains his characteristics of omnipotence and omnibenevolence and there is no contradiction for believers, in terms of God's characteristics. The assertion is that evil does not exist. After all, it may be our perception that is at fault. If we were able to see the universe, from a God's-eye view, then we may see that the suffering that creation faces is not the evil that we think it is, but rather has a purpose that we do not understand because we do not have God's perspective.

Imagine the situation of a toddler playing in the kitchen whilst the parent is using the oven. The oven piques the toddler's curiosity and he wanders over to it. Standing against the oven he reaches up to try and pull the pan off the top of the oven in order to see what is inside it. At this point the parent, alarmed at what is about to happen, may smack the toddler's hand away from the oven. In doing so, the toddler suffers from having a smacked hand. He cannot understand why the parent has just smacked the hand and is upset by the incident. He may even consider the parent to be cruel and unfair. However, what the toddler was unaware of was that the pan on top of the oven was full of boiling water and, had they succeeded in pulling it off the oven top, they would have been severely injured and suffered a far greater degree of pain than was caused by the smacking of the hand. The toddler did not have the parent's perspective, and, like the toddler, creation does not share God's (as the parent) perspective.

Danger ahead!

Attractive as this idea may at first appear, it has been largely rejected for the simple reason, as Hume points out, the effects of evil are felt too widely, and its presence attested too vividly for it to be dismissible.

Mackie, however, focused on the logical problem of evil in its purest sense. The logical problem arises because theists maintain that there are no limits to what an omnipotent being can do, but then, the so called 'solutions' or 'theodicies' that are proposed, actually limit God's power but misleadingly keep the term 'omnipotence'. Therefore, Mackie argues that the theodicies do not give a solution to the problem of evil since they have changed the premise (i.e. that God is omnipotent).

Mackie calls his theory the 'Paradox of Omnipotence'. He writes: 'This leads us to what I call the Paradox of Omnipotence: can an omnipotent being make things which he cannot subsequently control? Or, what is practically equivalent to this, can an omnipotent being make rules which then bind himself?'

From this he observes: 'It is clear that this is a paradox: the questions cannot be answered satisfactorily either in the affirmative or the negative. If we answer "Yes", it follows that if God actually makes things which he cannot control, or makes rules which bind himself, he is not omnipotent once he has made them: there are *then* things which he cannot do. But if we answer " No ", we are immediately asserting that there are things which he cannot do, that is to say that he is already not omnipotent.'

The only solution Mackie sees to this is to 'deny that God is a continuing being, that any time can be assigned to his actions at all', or, 'by putting God outside time'. In either case, this then is immediately compromised in considering any solution to the problem of evil that involves free will.

For many philosophers the problem of evil is simply insurmountable. The inconsistent triad presents a simple but devastating critique of the question of why an all-loving, all-powerful, God would allow his creation to suffer. However, this view has been challenged by a number of theists who maintain that the inconsistent triad and the problem of evil rest on assumptions that, if challenged, can open the debate.

quickpire

3.5 Explain what philosophers mean by the term 'inconsistent triad'.

Key quote

Quite apart from the problem of evil, the Paradox of Omnipotence has shown that God's omnipotence must in any case be restricted in one way or another, that unqualified omnipotence cannot be ascribed to any being that continues through time. And if God and his actions are not in time, can omnipotence, or power of any sort, be meaningfully ascribed to him? (Mackie)

For instance, one such assumption is the notion that just because God is all-powerful and all-loving, why would he necessarily want to remove evil immediately from the universe? Perhaps it does indeed serve some greater purpose of which we are currently unaware.

Aquinas, referencing his work on our understanding of God's nature, points out that what we understand as 'goodness' (or even evil for that matter) may not be the same as what God understands as goodness. After all, our understanding of goodness is often relative to the time and culture within which we live. We are limited by time as beings and the world and society that we live in are always changing. God, as a perfect being, is not subject to such change and therefore his understanding of concepts such as good and evil is likewise fixed and unchangeable, and may be very different to our own; in which case there is no logical contradiction within the 'inconsistent triad' and certainly no challenge to God's omnipotence.

William Rowe (intense human and animal suffering) and Gregory S. Paul (premature deaths)

Specification content

William Rowe (intense human and animal suffering) and Gregory S. Paul (premature deaths).

William Rowe in his work: *The problem of evil and some varieties of atheism* (1979) argued that, whilst it seemed reasonable for God to allow some limited suffering to enable humans to grow and develop, he could not accept God allowing what he called 'intense' suffering' Animal suffering also seemed pointless. Rowe used the example of a fawn caught in a forest fire as an example of pointless animal suffering. He argues:

- An omnipotent and omniscient being would know when intense suffering was about to take place.

- Such a being could prevent the suffering from happening.

- An all-loving being would probably prevent all evil and suffering that had no purpose and was pointless and avoidable.

- Such evil and suffering does happen.

- Therefore, probably God does not exist.

Rowe's approach is sometimes referred to as the evidential problem of evil, in that it involves a consideration of whether, and to what extent, the existence of evil can be used as evidence that can be used to argue the case against the existence of God. This should be recognised as being different from the problem of evil as presented by Epicurus and Mackie – that is more properly known as the logical problem of evil.

Gregory Paul argues that the death of so many innocent children challenges the existence of God. He estimates that since the time that God first spoke to man, as recorded in the sacred texts of the Abrahamic religions, that over 50 billion children have died naturally before reaching what Paul calls 'the age of mature consent' and some 300 billion human beings have died naturally but prenatally. Paul calls this 'the Holocaust of the children' and using this statistical information, he argues:

- Millions of innocent children suffer and die every year, from both natural and evil causes.

- These children are too young to be able to make choices about God – they have no free will.

- No all-loving, all-powerful being would permit such suffering.

- Therefore, God does not exist.

The problem of evil stated in this way is sometimes referred to as the statistical problem of evil.

Key quote

The modern Christian consensus followed by billions is so firmly overturned by human circumstances that it very probably is not possible to reconcile the Christian concept of a pacific creator with the state of the universe. (Paul)

AO1 Developing skills

It is now time to reflect upon the information that has been covered so far. It is also important to consider how what you have learned can be focused and used for examination-style answers by practising the skills associated with AO1.

Assessment objective 1 (AO1) involves demonstrating knowledge and understanding. The terms 'knowledge' and 'understanding' are obvious but it is crucial to be familiar with how certain skills demonstrate these terms, and also, how the performance of these skills is measured (see generic band descriptors Band 5 for AS AO1).

▶ **Your new task is this:** below is a below average answer that has been written in response to a question requiring an examination of how suffering is caused by the different types of evil and why this is a problem for religious believers. It is obviously a below average answer and so would be about band 2. It will be useful, initially, to consider what is missing from the answer and what is inaccurate. The accompanying list gives you some possible observations to assist you. Be aware, as not all points may be relevant! In analysing the answer's weaknesses, in a group, choose five points from the list that you would use to improve the answer in order to make it stronger. Then write out your additions, each one in a clear paragraph, remembering the principles of explaining with evidence and/or examples. You may add more of your own suggestions, but try to negotiate as a group and prioritise the most important things to add.

Key skills

Knowledge involves:

Selection of a range of (thorough) accurate and relevant information that is directly related to the specific demands of the question.

This means you choose the correct information relevant to the question set NOT the topic area. You will have to think and focus on selecting key information and NOT writing everything you know about the topic area.

Understanding involves:

Explanation that is extensive, demonstrating depth and/or breadth with excellent use of evidence and examples including (where appropriate) thorough and accurate supporting use of sacred texts, sources of wisdom and specialist language.

This means that you demonstrate that you understand something by being able to illustrate and expand your points through examples/supporting evidence in a personal way and NOT repeat chunks from a textbook (known as rote learning).

Further application of skills:

Go through the topic areas in this section and create some bullet lists of key points from key areas. For each one, provide further elaboration and explanation through the use of evidence and examples.

Answer

Suffering is a big problem not just for religious believers – it affects everybody at some point during their lives. Suffering is what happens as a result of evil, although some types of suffering are needed in order to improve a person's life – e.g. the type of suffering that is caused when a baby has an injection – it hurts but the result is that the baby is then protected from diseases.

However, suffering is linked to evil when the type of suffering produced does not seem to have any positive effect – such as when a person is murdered or when a house is destroyed by a bad storm.

Lots of people suffered during the Holocaust, which was a terrible event caused by Hitler and the Nazis during the 1930s and 1940s. As a result 6 million Jewish people lost their lives. Lots of other people lost their lives as well during this time because they disagreed with the Nazis. This type of suffering was caused by human beings and so is called moral evil.

Natural evil is when something other than humans causes evil. A famous example of this is the Boxing Day tsunami in 2004 when thousands of people suffered because of this terrible event.

Observations

- An introduction is needed to define the different types of evil.
- Needs to explain why evil causes suffering and how this is problematic for religious believers.
- Explain the concept of the God of Classical Theism.
- Include a reference from sacred writings to show why evil is a problem for religious believers.
- Needs to explain about the types of evil and how they produce suffering.
- Makes use of accurate terminology in relation to the classical and modern problems of evil.
- Needs to explain how each of the characteristics of the God of Classical Theism should cancel out the existence of evil.
- Explain how the specific types of evil produce suffering and how this occurs.
- Show how the existence of evil undermines the concept of the God of Classical Theism.
- Specific examples of evil should be fully explained to demonstrate how they produce suffering.
- Needs a summary at the end that relates to the question.

Specification content

The extent to which the classical form
of the problem of evil is a problem.

AO2 Activity *Possible lines of argument*

Listed below are some conclusions
that could be drawn from the AO2
reasoning in the accompanying text:

1. Evil is the result of God's creation.

2. The logical problem of evil cannot
   be overcome.

3. Only classical theists have an issue
   with the problem of evil.

4. The logical problem of evil is less
   important than the emotional and
   physical problem of evil.

5. Rejecting any one of God's key
   attributes helps to solve the
   classical logical problem of evil.

Consider each of the conclusions
drawn above and collect evidence and
examples to support each argument
from the AO1 and AO2 material
studied in this section. Select one
conclusion that you think is most
convincing and explain why it is so.
Now contrast this with the weakest
conclusion in the list, justifying
your argument with clear reasoning
and evidence.

Issues for analysis and evaluation

The extent to which the classical form of the problem of evil is a problem

In the 3rd century BCE, Epicurus is credited with posing the logical problem of
evil – in which is stated the formulation: 'Either God wants to abolish evil, and
cannot; or he can, but does not want to. If he wants to, but cannot, he is impotent.
If he can, but does not want to, he is wicked. If God can abolish evil, and God really
wants to do it, why is there evil in the world?'

Epicurus bases his assumption of an existent God who is attributed with divine
power and benevolence, favourably disposed towards the human race. However,
his formulation, sometime referred to as the 'Epicurean paradox', denies that it
is possible for such a God to exist alongside the existence of evil. This then, is the
classical logical problem of evil. The extent to which it can be considered a problem
rests, ultimately, on the predisposition of the individual.

For instance – any individual who discounts the existence of God is automatically
'rewarded' by the problem of evil not being a problem at all. For evil may well
exist but God does not. Alternatively, the believer may decide to attribute different
characteristics to God – causing him to be a god of malevolence or limited power –
or even a God who has no particular interest in the welfare of human beings –
a god apathetic to innocent human suffering. This, however, is sidestepping
the problem!

For the individual who concedes to a belief in God then it becomes quickly
apparent that the attributes of the said God are essential when considering to
what extent the classical problem of evil is a problem. Thus, if a belief in God is
held where God is considered to be an almighty power but to have no particular
fondness for humanity (or anything else in creation) then there is no contradiction
with the existence of evil – it may also be possible to dispute Epicurus' assertion
that such a God would be 'wicked' in that the fact of the matter may be that God
simply does not care about the existence of evil – therefore, he is not so much
wicked as apathetic where evil is concerned.

Equally, any believer that holds faith in a God who is loving towards his creation
but has no other particular attributes, must be willing to concede that, despite a
willingness to want to remove evil, He is unable to do so. This is the position held
by Process theologians, considering God as the 'fellow sufferer who understands'.
In such a case, whilst the fact that evil still exists is an emotional and physical
problem, it is no longer a logical one!

However, for the classical theist, holding to God's attributes of omnipotence and
omnibenevolence then there is no escaping the logical problem of evil as presented
to us by Epicurus – such a God – able to do anything and wanting to prevent our
suffering would surely not want us, as His creation, to suffer – would He?

The degree to which modern problem of evil arguments are effective in proving God's non existence

Ask almost any non-theist why they do not accept the existence of God as a believable proposition and, almost invariably, they will respond with reference to the amount of evil and suffering in the world. It seems entirely inconsistent that a God who is all-loving and all-powerful and has created the universe, could have put together His creation in such a way to allow the existence of evil and suffering – often to quite appalling extremes – thus undermining any counter claim regarding his supposed goodness and power.

Mackie's inconsistent triad – which shows the incompatibility of God's omnipotence and omnibenevolence with the existence of evil – is an effective 'argument' for undermining the existence of God – or so it seems. However, it must be noted that the inconsistency of the three statements is based on the assumption that God does indeed possess the stated characteristics and this may not actually be the case.

If God does indeed have both omnipotence and omnibenevolence then it seems virtually impossible to concede that evil exists, from a logical point of view. However, the overwhelming evidence of suffering within and among the entirety of creation – not just humanity – seems to make such a conclusion entirely nonsensical. Accepting this position would seem to therefore lead one to the inescapable alternative conclusion – i.e. that a God with the characteristics of omnipotence and omnibenevolence cannot exist.

However, if it is accepted, in line with Mackie's reasoning, that God is able to exist without one of those key attributes, then the modern problem of evil, much like the classical problem, no longer seems to be relevant. In other words – a God who is all-powerful but willing to let evil exist because he either doesn't care or consciously wants his creation to suffer – would still exist but would be significantly different from the God worshipped by the vast majority of theistic religions of the world today.

Perhaps, however, it is a God who is omnibenevolent and actively wants to stop the suffering experienced by creation but is unable to do so. The laws of the universe may bind this being, perhaps, and due to limitations to His power he is incapable of stopping the existence of evil. He may well still exist but would such a being be worthy of worship?

Evidential arguments, such as those proposed by William Rowe in which a whole range of suffering is brought as evidence against the existence of God, also mount a serious challenge to God's existence – how can an omnipotent and omnibenevolent God allow such horrors to occur and yet stand idly by whilst they continue to do so? Equally, the statistical problem of evil as presented by Gregory Paul, also shows a God who seems not to care about the destruction of literally billions of children since the time of the existence of the Abrahamic religions – the only sensible conclusion that can be drawn from this is that God simply does not exist.

Thus it would seem that modern problem of evil arguments – such as those outlined by Mackie, Rowe and Paul – do pose a significant challenge to believers in the God of Classical Theism and effectively seem to suggest his non-existence.

Specification content

The degree to which modern problem of evil arguments are effective in proving God's non-existence.

AO2 Activity *Possible lines of argument*

Listed below are some conclusions that could be drawn from the AO2 reasoning in the accompanying text:

1. Modern problem of evil arguments are more effective than classical arguments in proving God's non-existence.

2. Omnibenevolence is a less significant attribute than omnipotence when considering whether God is worthy of worship.

3. There are solutions to the modern problem of evil.

4. It is not God's non-existence that modern problem of evil arguments prove, rather it is God's traditional attributes that are challenged.

5. Modern problem of evil arguments are entirely ineffective in proving God's non-existence.

Consider each of the conclusions drawn above and collect evidence and examples to support each argument from the AO1 and AO2 material studied in this section. Select one conclusion that you think is most convincing and explain why it is so. Now contrast this with the weakest conclusion in the list, justifying your argument with clear reasoning and evidence.

Key skills

Analysis involves identifying issues raised by the materials in the AO1, together with those identified in the AO2 section, and presents sustained and clear views, either of scholars or from a personal perspective ready for evaluation.

This means that it picks out key things to debate and the lines of argument presented by others or a personal point of view.

Evaluation involves considering the various implications of the issues raised based upon the evidence gleaned from analysis and provides an extensive detailed argument with a clear conclusion.

This means that the answer weighs up the various and different lines of argument analysed through individual commentary and response and arrives at a conclusion through a clear process of reasoning.

AO2 Developing skills

It is now time to reflect upon the information that has been covered so far. It is also important to consider how what you have learned can be focused and used for examination-style answers by practising the skills associated with AO2.

Assessment objective 2 (AO2) involves 'analysis' and 'evaluation'. The terms may be obvious but it is crucial to be familiar with how certain skills demonstrate these terms, and also, how the performance of these skills is measured (see generic band descriptors Band 5 for AS AO2).

Obviously an answer is placed within an appropriate band descriptor depending upon how well the answer performs, ranging from excellent, good, satisfactory, basic/limited to very limited.

▶ **Your new task is this:** below is a below average answer that has been written in response to a question requiring an evaluation of the challenge to God's existence from the problem of evil. It is obviously a below average answer and so would be about lower band 2. It will be useful, initially, to consider what is missing from the answer and what is inaccurate. The accompanying list gives you some possible observations to assist you. Be aware, as not all points may be relevant! In analysing the answer's weaknesses, in a group, choose five points from the list that you would use to improve the answer in order to make it stronger. Then write out your additions, each one in a clear paragraph. Remember, it is how you use the points that is the most important factor. Apply the principles of evaluation by making sure that you: identify issues clearly; present accurate views of others making sure that you comment on the views presented; reach an overall personal judgement. You may add more of your own suggestions, but try to negotiate as a group and prioritise the most important things to add.

Answer

The problem of evil is a big problem. It tells us that it not possible for God to exist if evil also exists. The Australian philosopher Mackie tells us that it is inconsistent to think of God being all-powerful (omnipotent) all-loving (omnibenevolent) and for evil to exist at the same time.

God is responsible for causing things like the Boxing Day Tsunami of 2004 where lots of people lost their lives or their friends and family. If God loved us then this would not happen at all. God is also responsible for causing the terrible hurricanes that cause so much damage to property in America during August each year – how can a loving God do such things?

Some people say it is not God's fault because we have free will that means that we can cause evil and God is not allowed to stop us. This would mean that evil exists because we cause it, not God and therefore shows that the problem of evil does not successfully prove that God does not exist.

Overall, the problem of evil does challenge belief in the existence of God.

Observations

- An introduction that sets out what the problem of evil is and why it can be considered as challenging belief in the existence of God.

- Needs to clearly explain what is meant by each of the key attributes possessed by God and why these further support the idea that evil should not, logically, exist.

- Refer to Mackie and Epicurus to support the argument.

- Consider the types of evil and their relevance to the debate.

- Explore reasons for believing that the presence of evil would mean that it was impossible for God to exist.

- Use your understanding of deductive reasoning to demonstrate why the problem of evil could be considered to be a devastating challenge to the belief of classical theists.

- Needs a stronger counter-argument to defend the position of the classical theist.

- Should ensure that any examples included should clearly link to the evaluation of the contention in the question.

- Should avoid oversimplifications in expression and make effective use of specialist language

- A conclusion that is balanced, reflective of the argument presented and that clearly links to the question is needed.

B: Religious responses to the problem of evil: Augustinian type theodicy

Specification content
Augustinian type theodicy: Evil as a consequence of sin: evil as a privation; the fall of human beings and creation; the Cross overcomes evil, soul-deciding.

Religious responses to the problem of evil: Augustinian type theodicy

Despite several modern presentations to the contrary, Augustine's 'theodicy' is not a compact singular work but rather a strand that runs throughout much of his literary output. It has been observed by some of his commentators that Augustine was obsessed with the problem of evil and wrestled with it throughout his life – even before his conversion to Christianity. Therefore it must be remembered that any presentation of his theodicy that is demonstrated in a book such as this is a necessary simplification of Augustine's thoughts. The actual specifics can only be gained by reading through his vast writings – and taking on board the influences that he had from Manichaeism, Neo-Platonism and other competing thought systems that he found himself exposed to during his eventful life.

Adam and Eve being tempted in Eden

Evil as a consequence of sin

According to the Augustinian type theodicy, God's creation was originally free from evil. It did not exist before the sin of angels and humans. It first came into existence when angels, followed by humans, misused their wills and turned from God, their creator.

It is a fact of the created universe that God has called all things into existence *ex nihilo* and, through corruption and decay, they will all eventually lapse back into nothingness. Humans and angels are both part of the created order and therefore they are susceptible to change and therefore have the capability of turning away from God. It is precisely this turning – which involves an act of free will (namely, of choosing a lower rather than a higher good) – that brings about evil. However, the cause of humans and angels willing to do this remains a mystery beyond human understanding, according to Augustine.

As the gift of free will necessarily entails the concept of moral responsibility, it is humans that are ultimately responsible for sin and, consequently, evil – not God. This is because humans voluntarily choose sin.

Evil as a privation

It is important to realise, however, that evil is not in any way a 'substance' or part of the created order. The significance of this is that evil is then not something God creates. If it is a substance then God must have created it since he creates all things. God, being an omnibenevolent creator, cannot have created evil as a substance. Instead, evil indicates an absence or **privation** of part of God's created order. For example, when humans or angels 'turn away' from God it is this turning away that is a privation of God's original created order and purpose. The 'turning away' is then 'evil'.

God made every good thing but every good thing has the potential to be corrupted. Having that potential is not evil. Evil only occurs when the potential is realised and the good thing becomes corrupted. Everything that is created must be corruptible since it is subject to change. The very fact that things do corrupt shows they are in their nature, good. Evil is when they lose some of their goodness. Hence evil is a privation. Augustine referred to darkness as a metaphor for evil but darkness in the sense of the absence of light. Evil has no real being of its own. The reason that humans tend to be offended at the order of existing things is their finiteness, which does not allow seeing the whole picture as God does.

> **Key term**
> **Privation:** the absence or loss of something that is normally present (i.e. a privation of health means that a person is ill and not healthy)

Key term

Redemption: the act of saving something or someone. In the Christian context it refers to Jesus saving humanity from evil and sin

Study tip

Show awareness in your answers on this theodicy that Augustine's ideas were founded on a complex set of intellectual ideas that were combined with biblical teachings to produce his theodicy. Do not instantly dismiss his theodicy as 'simplistic' or 'naïve' because in doing so you are revealing your own understanding of Augustine to be flawed. He is regarded as being one of the greatest Christian thinkers that ever lived – so be cautious in your criticism and show respect to his views! (You don't have to agree with them but neither should you dismiss them as worthless either!)

The fall of human beings and creation

As all human beings are ultimately descended from Adam (in Augustine's words 'seminally present') then all human beings share Adam's guilt and sin. As we all share his guilt and sin we all deserve to face the same punishment. We suffer through 'moral evil' as that is humankind's fault through actions performed on the basis of free will.

The suffering that human beings face as part of the natural world (i.e. natural evil) is a direct result of the 'absence of good' caused in creation by the 'turning away' from God and therefore bringing corruption into the created order.

As an ultimate response to the question, 'Why did God choose to create this particular universe, even though he knew that human beings would abuse their freedom and sin?' Augustine replies, 'God judged it to be better to bring good out of evil, than to not permit any evil to exist.'

The Cross overcomes evil, soul-deciding

It is this point ('to bring good out of evil') that many Christians refer to as the 'happy mistake' (felix culpa). In this is the Christian belief that, were it not for the events of The fall of Adam and Eve (and therefore, all human beings), then God would never have needed to send Jesus into the world to save it from its sin.

Those who freely chose to accept Jesus as their saviour would be redeemed and, after this life, be reunited with God in Heaven. This is why the theodicy is sometimes regarded as a 'soul-deciding' theodicy.

An Augustinian type theodicy believes that this chance for humanity to seek redemption, through Christ, not only demonstrates that God is merciful but also that it underlines his justice.

AO1 Activity

Create an information poster that summarises the key points of an Augustinian type theodicy.

The felix culpa led to atonement through Jesus for Christians

Challenges to Augustinian type theodicies: validity of accounts in Genesis, chapters 2 and 3

Augustine's theodicy relies heavily on the accounts of the Creation and **The Fall** as depicted in the biblical book of Genesis, chapters 1–3. For the **literalist** Christian believer this means that the accounts are plausible and rooted in the revelation of divine scripture. Humankind's place in the created order, and the suffering that it faces, is clearly accounted for in the Genesis accounts. However, as soon as any other view of scripture is taken, Augustine's theodicy becomes problematic.

If the view of scripture is taken as non-literal and mythological, then any claim of historicity relating to the accounts of creation and fall become suspect. It is from this viewpoint that the most devastating attacks upon the theodicy arise. John Hick in his *Evil and the God of Love* (1966) considers many of these problems.

Scientific error – biological impossibility of human descent from a single pair (therefore invalidating the 'inheritance' of Adam's sin)

The idea that all human beings deserve to be punished because they are descended from Adam fails because it is a biological impossibility. With our advancements in scientific understanding of genetics and the human mind and body, the idea of one person's 'sin' being transferred to all of humanity is not possible. Neither is the idea that all humanity originated with one pair of human beings in the first place. If the Genesis account is not scientifically valid then Augustine's theory is not consistent or relevant to our experience of evil.

However, this is the genetic argument. What about evolution and Dawkins' idea that behavioural traits or 'memes' are 'inherited'? This could be argued to be compatible with the Hebrew concept of yetzer hara (tendency or inclination for evil inherent in a human being); however, the problem then arises that this is not a behavioural trait that is consistent, but is, according to the principles of evolution, subject to change and so cannot justify the 'inheritance' theory from a single pair of human beings. It appears that this single idea of inheritance is very problematic, and, according to science, an error.

quickfire

3.6 On what did St Augustine base his theodicy?

quickfire

3.7 What is meant by a privation?

quickfire

3.8 Why is the Fall of humanity a 'happy mistake?'

Key terms

Evolutionary theory: scientific theory, originally proposed in the 19th century that posited that life developed from simpler to more complex life forms via a process of natural selection and genetic mutation

Free will: the theological and philosophical concept that states that humans have the ability to choose freely between good and evil

Geological: the science relating to how the earth was formed

Contradiction of perfect order becoming chaotic – geological and biological evidence suggests the contrary

The perfect world becoming imperfect contradicts all **geological** scientific records and biological evidence. Geology sees the nature of the world as chaotic and unpredictable, even today, for example with earthquakes. Geologists would certainly deny a movement from initial perfection.

Evolutionary theory, according to biology, of the development of human beings as a result of a process of natural selection, mutation and evolution from earlier life forms is well evidenced. This reduces the plausibility of the creation account as an historical fact.

In addition, evolution does not always mean progress. It is a misapprehension to assume an intrinsic directionality that makes species more 'advanced'. This would be the stance taken against this understanding. Science cannot use 'value judgements' for evolution. For instance, if human beings, over time, 'regress', it is not seen as such but as simply another step in the evolutionary process. The matter of 'regression' is a point of view.

Moral contradictions of omnibenevolent God and existence of Hell; logical contradiction of perfect creation being susceptible to change

If a perfect world had been created then how is it possible that there was knowledge of good and evil necessary for the **free will** of humanity? This implies that evil already existed and therefore this can only be the responsibility of God.

Hell is part of the created order. This suggests that not only did God know that angels would rebel and human beings would fall but had also prepared a place of punishment for them. Why would an omnibenevolent (all-loving) God do this? The existence of Hell is not consistent with an all-loving God.

Perfection is immutable – it cannot change. So how can a perfect creation ever be less than perfect? Angels rebelled against God. This implies flaws in God's creation of the angels because why would rebellion occur in a perfect created order?

In addition, if human beings began by being perfect, then even though they are free to sin they need not do so. If they do, then they were not flawless to start with and so God must share the responsibility of their fall. It is hard to clear God from responsibility for evil since he chose to create a being whom he foresaw would do evil. (Note that Augustine argues that some angels were predestined to fall. If this view is not accepted then how did angels fall, given that they were perfect?) Surely in a perfect world they would have no reason to sin.

Finally, God is omniscient. Therefore he must have known in advance that angels would rebel and humans would fall – therefore he has to bear responsibility for the existence of evil as a result of the lack of good in creation.

The debate about the validity of Augustine's theodicy continues in modern religious philosophy, however. Modern supporters such as Plantinga and Miller suggest that much depends on how we interpret what Augustine meant by terms such as privation and free will. Others, such as Hick, consider that it is simply a product of its time and has no real relevance to the way in which we understand the world today.

quickfire

3.9 Describe one logical problem with Augustine's theodicy.

quickfire

3.10 Why does evolutionary theory undermine Augustine's theodicy?

AO1 Activity

Draw up a table that shows the scientific, moral and logical contradictions in Augustine's theodicy.

AO1 Developing skills

It is now time to reflect upon the information that has been covered so far. It is also important to consider how what you have learned can be focused and used for examination-style answers by practising the skills associated with AO1.

Assessment objective 1 (AO1) involves demonstrating knowledge and understanding. The terms 'knowledge' and 'understanding' are obvious but it is crucial to be familiar with how certain skills demonstrate these terms, and also, how the performance of these skills is measured (see generic band descriptors Band 5 for AS AO1).

▶ **Your new task is this:** below is a below average answer that has been written in response to a question requiring an examination of Augustinian type theodicies. It is obviously a below average answer and so would be about band 2. It will be useful, initially, to consider what is missing from the answer and what is inaccurate. This time there is no accompanying list to assist you. In analysing the answer's weaknesses, in a group, decide upon five points that you would use to improve the answer in order to make it stronger. Then write out your additions, each one in a clear paragraph, remembering the principles of explaining with evidence and/or examples.

Answer

Augustinian type theodicies are heavily based on the Bible and in particular the story from the Book of Genesis which explains how Adam and Eve disobeyed God by listening to the serpent and eating from the Tree of the Knowledge of Good and Evil which God had expressly told them they were not to eat from.

Using this story, known as 'The Fall' and combining it with the creation story in Genesis chapter 1 where God created everything perfectly ('and He saw that it was Good'), Augustine sets out, through several of his works, the fact that human beings fell short of what God intended for them. In doing so they disrupted the perfect world, brought evil into it in the form of natural evil and also, because they disobeyed God, moral evil.

Augustine shows how God did not create evil because evil is not a thing it is the lack of a thing – Augustine calls this a privation – and thus because it is not a thing God did not (could not) create it. Therefore showing that evil is not God's fault. It is human beings' fault because in turning away from God they caused the absence of Good – i.e. the privation of Good – so it is humans' fault not God's. Also because it was Lucifer in the form of a serpent that tempted Eve, that means that it is also the free will choice of an angel (fallen angel) that also disrupted God's perfect world.

However, showing that God is good and he doesn't want humans to suffer forever, he sent his son Jesus so that people that believe in him can be forgiven their original sin and end up in Heaven with God.

Key skills

Knowledge involves:

Selection of a range of (thorough) accurate and relevant information that is directly related to the specific demands of the question.

This means you choose the correct information relevant to the question set NOT the topic area. You will have to think and focus on selecting key information and NOT writing everything you know about the topic area.

Understanding involves:

Explanation that is extensive, demonstrating depth and/or breadth with excellent use of evidence and examples including (where appropriate) thorough and accurate supporting use of sacred texts, sources of wisdom and specialist language.

This means that you demonstrate that you understand something by being able to illustrate and expand your points through examples/supporting evidence in a personal way and NOT repeat chunks from a textbook (known as rote learning).

Further application of skills:

Go through the topic areas in this section and create some bullet lists of key points from key areas. For each one, provide further elaboration and explanation through the use of evidence and examples.

Specification content

Whether Augustinian type theodicies
are relevant in the 21st century.

AO2 Activity *Possible lines of argument*

Listed below are some conclusions that could be drawn from the AO2 reasoning in the accompanying text:

1. Science undermines the relevance of Augustinian type theodicies.

2. Augustinian type theodicies are only relevant for Christian believers.

3. Augustinian type theodicies are entirely irrelevant in the 21st century.

4. If the Book of Genesis is not reliable then neither are Augustinian type theodicies.

5. A belief in free will is essential for Augustinian type theodicies to be considered relevant.

Consider each of the conclusions drawn above and collect evidence and examples to support each argument from the AO1 and AO2 material studied in this section. Select one conclusion that you think is most convincing and explain why it is so. Now contrast this with the weakest conclusion in the list, justifying your argument with clear reasoning and evidence.

Issues for analysis and evaluation

Whether Augustinian type theodicies are relevant in the 21st century

The Augustinian type theodicies find their origin in the works of Augustine – the 4th/5th-century Christian Bishop of Hippo. Based largely on the account of The Fall in the Book of Genesis and the Christian understanding of the Atonement through the resurrection of Jesus, the theodicy demonstrates how evil was not part of God's plan for creation but rather was the unintended consequence of allowing free-will agents to exercise their moral choice. The question can then be asked – how historically accurate are these accounts? Did they actually occur? If not, then why should we believe anything that is based on them? In a 21st-century world of scientific enquiry and healthy scepticism, such ideas seem easy to dismiss and are therefore barely relevant.

The ability to have free will meant that a genuine choice between good or evil needed to be available – this meant that moral evil could theoretically thrive, if these free-will agents deliberately chose to turn away from good. Equally, the disobedience shown to God demanded a just punishment – which is where natural evil came from – a disruption of the perfect world created by God due to the evil choices of the free-will agents. Such a viewpoint also demands an assumption to believe that a divine being existed who 'programmed' His creation to act in a particular way. This idea seems difficult to comprehend in an age where evolutionary theory holds sway, where a consideration of how human beings were formed and developed is concerned.

The Augustinian account also presumes an acceptance of the belief in the existence of angels – indeed it is the fallen angel in the form of the serpent that is the catalyst for the events of the Fall – yet this is a strange notion for the 21st century where there is no empirical evidence for such creatures and certainly not in a way in which they are capable of taking the form of an animal and speaking directly with human beings – the whole account seems too fanciful to be taken seriously by the 21st-century mind – further depreciating the relevance of Augustinian type theodicies in the 21st century.

The view of evil as a privation depends on the acceptance of the concept of a perfect world where all things existed a state of goodness and perfection and that, only by a disruption of this, were absences of this goodness found and therefore 'evil' existed. However, in the 21st century, how believable is this? Evil is a very real presence in the world – as are its effects. As such, suggesting that evil is a 'lack of a thing' seems to belong purely to the realm of metaphysical speculation rather than cold harsh reality.

The salvation of human beings by acceptance of the sacrifice of Jesus is a comfort to those of the Christian faith, where a reconciled existence with God after death, offers hope of a future where pain and suffering will be nothing more than a distant memory. 'However, for those outside of this faith tradition no such comfort is offered and, as less than half of the planet's population are promised this salvation then what relevance does it have to the majority of people in the 21st century?

In conclusion, despite the appeal that they may have to believers from the Christian faith traditions, Augustinian type theodicies lack the scientific and historical credibility to be truly relevant in the 21st century.

The extent to which Augustine's theodicy succeeds as a defence of the God of Classical Theism

Specification content

The extent to which Augustine's theodicy succeeds as a defence of the God of Classical Theism.

The problem of evil is a long-standing challenge to believers in the God of Classical Theism. Throughout history there have been attempts to support this belief and to attack the problem of evil. One such example can be found in the theodicies (attempts to justify God in the face of the existence of evil) associated with the works of Augustine of Hippo.

Augustine's starting point is that God is not responsible for the creation of evil. Augustine refers to evil as a lack of goodness or a 'privation of good'. One way of trying to understand what is meant here is by considering the example of blindness. Blindness is the lack or privation of sight, and so this helps to explain the concept of evil being a lack or privation of good. Creating a 'lack of something' contradicts God's act of creation. If this point is taken as valid, then Augustine's theodicy is already a partially successful defence of the God of Classical Theism.

In further defence of the God of Classical Theism, Augustine points out that it is the free will of humans and angels that caused suffering. It was the deliberate turning away from divine commands, as explained in the Biblical account of the Fall, which resulted in the consequential destruction of the perfect order. It was not God's will for this to happen but rather the deliberate action of free-will agents. It should be recognised that evil is a direct result of the consequences of the Fall.

The Genesis account demonstrates the need for evil and suffering to exist as a consequence of the actions from free-will agents. It is necessary for a just God to punish wrongdoing. The introduction of natural evil (caused by the actions of fallen angels, who wreak havoc and human rebellion, which affected all of creation and subsequently distorting it) is therefore a deserved punishment. Again, if this view is accepted then Augustine's theodicy provides a successful defence of the God of Classical Theism, at least in part.

However, not all of Augustine's viewpoints are as easy to accept. The assertion that all humans are 'seminally present' in Adam and therefore, according to the inheritance of guilt doctrines, all descendants of Adam (i.e. all human beings) are deserving of punishment as they have inherited his sin, is a particularly difficult viewpoint to accept. This is because genetic and biological records show that it is biologically impossible (as well as genetically undesirable) for all humans to have descended from a single male. In this case Augustine's theodicy is not a successful defence of the God of Classical Theism.

Equally, the proposition that God demonstrates mercy through making provision for a way of redemption through Christ, leading to the Fall being referred to as the 'felix culpa' (happy mistake), is only of relevance to Christian believers. What about theists from other faith traditions? This part of the Augustine's theodicy simply does not work.

The moral and logical issues with the various contradictions within the Augustinian theodicy further undermine its validity as a defence of the God of Classical Theism in the face of the existence of evil.

Therefore, in conclusion, following the points made above, Augustine's theodicy fails as a successful defence of the God of Classical Theism.

AO2 Activity *Possible lines of argument*

Listed below are some conclusions that could be drawn from the AO2 reasoning in the accompanying text:

1. Augustine's theodicy is successful if the Book of Genesis is accepted as fact.

2. The contradictions within the Augustinian theodicy are what weaken it most.

3. It is impossible to defend the God of Classical Theism by using the Augustinian theodicy.

4. The Augustinian theodicy represents a partially successful defence of the God of Classical Theism.

5. Only Christians can make sense of the defence offered by the Augustinian theodicy.

Consider each of the conclusions drawn above and collect evidence and examples to support each argument from the AO1 and AO2 material studied in this section. Select one conclusion that you think is most convincing and explain why it is so. Now contrast this with the weakest conclusion in the list, justifying your argument with clear reasoning and evidence.

Key skills

Analysis involves identifying issues raised by the materials in the AO1, together with those identified in the AO2 section, and presents sustained and clear views, either of scholars or from a personal perspective ready for evaluation.

This means that it picks out key things to debate and the lines of argument presented by others or a personal point of view.

Evaluation involves considering the various implications of the issues raised based upon the evidence gleaned from analysis and provides an extensive detailed argument with a clear conclusion.

This means that the answer weighs up the various and different lines of argument analysed through individual commentary and response and arrives at a conclusion through a clear process of reasoning.

AO2 Developing skills

It is now time to reflect upon the information that has been covered so far. It is also important to consider how what you have learned can be focused and used for examination-style answers by practising the skills associated with AO2.

Assessment objective 2 (AO2) involves 'analysis' and 'evaluation'. The terms may be obvious but it is crucial to be familiar with how certain skills demonstrate these terms, and also, how the performance of these skills is measured (see generic band descriptors Band 5 for AS AO2).

Obviously, an answer is placed within an appropriate band descriptor depending upon how well the answer performs, ranging from excellent, good, satisfactory, basic/limited to very limited.

▶ **Your next task is this:** below is a below average answer that has been written in response to a question requiring an evaluation of Augustine's theodicy as a successful defence of the God of Classical Theism. It is obviously a below average answer and so would be about band 2. It will be useful, initially, to consider what is missing from the answer and what is inaccurate. This time there is no accompanying list to assist you. In analysing the answer's weaknesses, in a group, decide upon five points that you would use to improve the answer in order to make it stronger. Then write out your additions, each one in a clear paragraph. Remember, it is how you use the points that is the most important factor. Apply the principles of evaluation by making sure that you: identify issues clearly; present accurate views of others, making sure that you comment on the views presented; reach an overall personal judgement. You may add more of your own suggestions, but try to negotiate as a group and prioritise the most important things to add.

Answer

You could argue that Augustine was a very intelligent person and therefore was able to use this to help him put together an argument to prove that God existed, no matter what challenges were presented to him in terms of the problem of evil.

Augustine knew that human beings were sinful creatures and because of this, we were far more likely to make bad moral choices rather than good ones. This is because we had free will. It is not God's fault that we made these choices – he gave us freedom to choose and we chose the wrong thing. In this case it is clear that the theodicy is successful.

However, Augustine's arguments are limited because of the time at which he lived. We know a lot more about science and how the world works than he did and we can see that many of his ideas make no scientific sense.

In conclusion, Augustine's theodicy is not a successful defence of the God of Classical Theism.

C: Religious responses to the problem of evil: Irenaean type theodicy

Religious responses to the problem of evil: Irenaean type theodicy

Unlike Augustine, who held that the responsibility for the existence of evil was due to the actions of free-will agents deliberately turning away from God, Irenaeus maintained that the presence of evil in the created order was a deliberate action of an omnibenevolent God who wanted his creation to develop the qualities that would make them spiritually perfect. His ideas are a result of his interpretation of Genesis 1:26. However, like Augustine, his theodicy was never presented as a complete work but rather arose from his ideas about the place of humankind in the universe and the relationship that they have with God.

Vale of soul-making: human beings created imperfect; epistemic distance; second-order goods; eschatological justification

Irenaeus regards this life as a place where human beings develop their potential and grow from the 'image' (possessing the potential qualities of God's spiritual perfection) to the 'likeness' (actualising those qualities) of God, through the trials and tribulations that they face and the decisions that they make. For every moral decision faced where a good choice is freely made, then the individual develops more fully towards spiritual maturity. Certain moral qualities were intrinsic to human beings but Irenaeus theodicy shows how second-order goods such as courage, forgiveness and compassion can only develop as a response to the suffering of ourselves and others. This was the essence of moving from 'image' to 'likeness'.

Irenaeus of Lyons (130CE–202CE)

Evil is a necessary facet of life that enables humans to develop. Without it, decisions in life would have no real value. For instance, a person would never really appreciate being in good health unless they had experienced being ill. As previously stated, second-order goods or virtues such as courage, patience and perseverance could never be developed if there were not the challenges in life that tested such virtues. Suffering not only enables humans to become stronger, it also allows them to appreciate goodness more. For Irenaeus, the ability for human beings to be able to freely choose to do good was therefore instrumental in achieving God's purpose for his creation.

Irenaeus makes use of an analogy of God as a craftsman working with human beings as his material and suggests that humans should allow God to mould them into perfection by acting in faith towards God and allowing the experiences of life, both good and bad, to make us into a perfectly crafted item. He also makes the point that those who resist God will be punished in the next life. Unlike Augustine, Irenaean type theodicy allows for God's mercy to continue into the next life where individuals who have rejected God in this life will have the opportunity to earn his forgiveness and develop into spiritual perfection in the next. This eschatological justification for evil allowed God to remain both just and good in the face of the temporary suffering experienced by creation. This is what the philosopher and theologian John Hick was to argue.

Specification content

Religious responses to the problem of evil: Irenaean type theodicy: Vale of soul-making: human beings created imperfect; epistemic distance; second-order goods; eschatological justification.

Key person

Irenaeus of Lyons: second–third-century Early Christian Bishop who is chiefly remembered for his writings against the heresy of Gnosticism – a major threat to Christian orthodoxy in the first few centuries of the Church's history. He also influentially stated that human beings had been made imperfect and needed to grow towards perfection, which he believed could only be done by making the proper response to God through Christ.

Key quotes

Then God said, 'Let us make humankind in our image, according to our likeness.' (Genesis 1:26)

God made man a free [agent] from the beginning, possessing his own power, even as he does his own soul, to obey the behests of God voluntarily, and not by compulsion of God. For there is no coercion with God, but a good will [towards us] is present with Him continually. (Irenaeus)

And the harder we strive, so much is it the more valuable; while so much the more valuable it is, so much the more should we esteem it. (Irenaeus)

Key terms

Epistemic distance: a distance measured in terms of knowledge rather than space or time

Soul-making: a process where the soul is developing towards spiritual perfection by gaining the wisdom to always make the correct moral choices when faced with the ambiguities of life as a human being

John Hick developed Irenaeus' theodicy in his book *Evil and the God of Love* (1966). Hick describes Irenaeus' theodicy as a 'soul-making' theodicy (a reference to John Keats idea that the world was a proving ground for human beings who earned their salvation, not simply by belief in a saviour figure, but rather by working through the trials and tribulations of everyday existence). Hick also makes the point that in order to be truly free, human beings had to be created at an 'epistemic distance' from God.

In this, humans were placed in a situation where the existence and non-existence of God were equally likely. This therefore allowed true human freedom to exist in terms of how they then responded to God. God could not create humans who were spiritually perfect or who were immediately aware of his existence for the simple reason that, in the first instance, goodness developed through free choice is more valuable than goodness that is 'ready-made' and, in the second instance, this would restrict choices made as humanity would be constantly aware of being 'watched' and would therefore make all decisions in the light of this knowledge. Hick also accepted the idea that God's mercy would allow for all human beings to complete the process of developing spiritual perfection – if not in this life, then in the next.

Key quotes

He shall overcome the substance of created nature. For it was necessary, at first, that nature should be exhibited; then, after that, what was mortal should be conquered and swallowed up by immortality, and the corruptible by incorruptibility, and that man should be made after the image and likeness of God, having received the knowledge of good and evil. (Irenaeus)

The common cognomen of this world among the misguided and superstitious is 'a vale of tears' from which we are to be redeemed by a certain arbitrary interposition of God and taken to Heaven – What a little circumscribed straightened notion! Call the world if you please 'The vale of Soul-making'. (Keats)

Key person

John Hick: 1922–2012. Hick was one of the most influential religious philosophers of the 20th and early 21st centuries. His most famous works include *Faith and Knowledge* (1957); *Evil and the God of Love* (1966); *Death and the Eternal Life* (1976); *Philosophy of Religion* (various editions – most recently 4th edition, published 1990) and *The New Frontier of Religion and Science: Religious Experience, Neuroscience and the Transcendent* (2006). He died in February 2012.

AO1 Activity

Create two mind maps – one for Irenaeus and one for John Hick. Detail their ideas on each mind map so that you are clear who said what with regards to the theodicy. This will mean that you will be able to demonstrate 'thorough, relevant and accurate knowledge' with regards to key philosophers (AO1 Level 5 response) in your answers to questions regarding Irenaean type theodicies.

Specification content

Challenges to Irenaean type theodicies: concept of universal salvation unjust; evil and suffering should not be used as a tool by an omnibenevolent God; immensity of suffering and unequal distribution of evil and suffering.

Challenges to Irenaean type theodicies

The modern re-workings of this theodicy, with its sympathies towards scientific appreciations of the development of life on earth, have given it a lease of life and plausibility that the Augustinian theodicy has not been able to enjoy to the same extent. Developing into spiritual maturity has a resonance with faiths outside of the Christian framework – and possibly echoes Hick's own views on religious pluralism. However, despite many of its attractions, the Irenaean theodicy has also attracted fierce criticism.

The concept of universal salvation is unjust

If all humans will eventually achieve perfection, no matter what they have done in the past, how does this encourage good moral behaviour in the here and now? If the end result is guaranteed by God, what is the point of the pilgrimage? Indeed, if there is universal salvation then do we have free will to refuse to mature?

quickfire

3.11 Which biblical verse is the foundation of the Irenaean type theodicy?

The concept of universal salvation seems to undermine the efforts of human beings to develop their own spiritual maturity. If God will eventually realise everyone to this state, does that suggest free will is limited? I.e. do human beings have the free will to refuse this development to spiritual perfection?

Evil and suffering should not be used as a tool by an omnibenevolent God

Suffering should never be an instrument of a loving God. Hurting someone is more akin to abuse than it is to love.

In addition, a number of criticisms involve suggestions of better ways to achieve this process. For example, why did the natural environment have to be created through a long, slow, pain-filled evolutionary process? Why could an omnipotent God not do it in 'the twinkling of an eye'? Equally, if we go on to another life to reach maturity, then why did God not simply make our earthly spans much longer, so that we could reach the Celestial City on earth, or at least get closer? Indeed, is there any evidence for other lives?

Could not the greater goods be gained without such evil and suffering? As a Christian theodicy, it seems to make the role of Jesus as saviour and atoning (making amends) for all sins, superfluous and unnecessary.

Immensity of suffering and unequal distribution of evil and suffering

The immense suffering endured by some does not make up for any possible reward of spiritual perfection. Suffering is not evenly spread – this implies inconsistency with God's mechanism of perfection.

Does the end justify the means? The suffering experienced, for example, in Auschwitz during the Holocaust or random acts of terror killing innocents, cannot justify the ultimate joy. Indeed, in the Holocaust, people were ruined and destroyed more than made or perfected. It is hard to see how this fits God's design and human progress.

It would appear, then, that the intensity of the suffering felt by many makes this a 'soul-breaking' rather than a 'soul-making' theodicy.

Study tip

Remember that criticisms of any argument can weaken or strengthen depending on the viewpoint that a person holds. For example, one of the criticisms of soul-making is only a strong criticism if a person holds to a Christian view of the atonement. If they don't then it holds no value as a criticism.

AO1 Activity

Produce an information poster that details the key challenges to Irenaean type theodicies – linking in the key part of the theodicy that they challenge – this will help strengthen both your AO1 understanding and your AO2 evaluation skills.

Many Jews suffered at the hands of the Nazis

Key quote

Who has inflicted this upon us? …. Who has allowed us to suffer so terribly up till now? It is God that has made us as we are, but it will be God, too, who will raise us up again. If we bear all this suffering and if there are still Jews left, when it is over, then Jews, instead of being doomed, will be held up as an example. (Anne Frank)

Key skills

Knowledge involves:

Selection of a range of (thorough) accurate and relevant information that is directly related to the specific demands of the question.

This means you choose the correct information relevant to the question set NOT the topic area. You will have to think and focus on selecting key information and NOT writing everything you know about the topic area.

Understanding involves:

Explanation that is extensive, demonstrating depth and/or breadth with excellent use of evidence and examples including (where appropriate) thorough and accurate supporting use of sacred texts, sources of wisdom and specialist language.

This means that you demonstrate that you understand something by being able to illustrate and expand your points through examples/supporting evidence in a personal way and NOT repeat chunks from a textbook (known as rote learning).

Further application of skills:

Go through the topic areas in this section and create some bullet lists of key points from key areas. For each one, provide further elaboration and explanation through the use of evidence and examples.

AO1 Developing skills

It is now time to reflect upon the information that has been covered so far. It is also important to consider how what you have learned can be focused and used for examination-style answers by practising the skills associated with AO1.

Assessment objective 1 (AO1) involves demonstrating knowledge and understanding. The terms 'knowledge' and 'understanding' are obvious but it is crucial to be familiar with how certain skills demonstrate these terms, and also, how the performance of these skills is measured (see generic band descriptors Band 5 for AS AO1).

▶ **Your new task is this:** below is a list of several key points bulleted in response to a question that has been written requiring an examination of Irenaean-type theodicies. It is obviously a very full list. It will be useful, initially, to consider what you think are the most important points to use in planning an answer. This exercise, in essence, is like writing your own set of possible answers that are listed in a typical mark scheme as indicative content. In a group, select the most important points you feel should be included in a list of indicative content for this question. You will need to decide upon two things: which points to select; and then, in which order to put them in an answer.

List of indicative content:

- Evil is a deliberate part of God's plan.
- Augustinian type theodicies are very different from Irenaean type theodicies.
- Irenaeus was an Early Christian bishop who lived in Lyons, Gaul.
- Humans are created Imago Dei.
- All humans will eventually be united with God in spiritual perfection in Heaven – this provides an eschatological justification for the suffering faced in life.
- God is able to mould people into perfection if they act in faith towards him.
- Evil is a necessary part of human existence.
- 'Let us make man in our image, after our likeness' (Genesis 1:26).
- Human beings were created at an epistemic distance from God (distance in knowledge) as that allows for free will to exist.
- Second-order goods such as courage and compassion can only develop when humans beings are faced with the problems caused by evil and suffering.
- Genuine choice means good and evil need to be genuine possibilities and have genuine consequences.
- When humans freely choose to do good rather than evil, they fulfil God's purpose for his creation.
- 'Image' means having the potential to be like God whereas 'likeness' means demonstrating God-like qualities.
- The process of developing into spiritual perfection may take longer than just one mortal lifespan.
- Those who resist God by choosing evil will be punished in the next life.
- God is both omnipotent and omnibenevolent.
- It is impossible to appreciate being healthy unless you have been ill, this shows why suffering is needed to help us understand how to choose to do good.

Issues for analysis and evaluation

Whether Irenaean type theodicies are credible in the 21st century

Specification content

Whether Irenaean type theodicies are credible in the 21st century.

Irenaean type theodicies find their origins in the mid-3rd century CE. Irenaeus of Lyons, in reflecting on the relationship that human beings had with God and the place that they occupied in the created order, realised that humans were unique. As such, humans were the only created being that had been made Imago Dei (in the image of God) and as such possess the potential to develop the sort of characteristics of God himself and become 'like God'. This idea was based on the verse in Genesis 1:26 'Let us make man in our image, after our likeness'. As far as the 21st century is concerned, this idea fits in with the scientific understanding that life on earth develops qualities that help it survive more effectively within the natural environment (as per Natural Selection and the Theory of Evolution). In this sense, the Irenaean type theodicies appear to have some credibility in the 21st century.

However, others may state that basing a theodicy on a document that is nearly 3000 years old makes any claim for credibility suspect at least. The idea that the existence of evil and suffering can be explained away as some kind of 'spiritual workout' may even sound obscene to some – particularly those whose suffering is so acute that seeing any positives come from it is virtually impossible.

In fact the very immensity of suffering that has occurred throughout human history from genocides, such as those faced by the Bosnian Serbs, the victims of Stalin, the peoples of Rwanda and European Jewry (and those are just events from the past 80 years of recorded human history), completely undermine the idea that suffering is there to help individuals become spiritually mature – such an idea becomes abhorrent if that is the price that needs to be paid – what sort of God would exact such a terrible cost from His creation?

Where the theodicies may have credibility in the 21st century is in the promise of hope given to all. The suggestion that this process of developing from image to likeness will one day be realised by all human beings, no matter how long it takes for each individual gives something for everyone to aspire to in the sense that suffering and pain will be removed for ever and all will be able to partake in spiritual perfection in an eternity with God. Such is the hope for those that follow Liberation Theology – in that, one day suffering will be overcome and God will restore us to him in the original relationship envisioned in Eden.

Objections to this view are many though. Critics would claim that the idea of a universal salvation appears abhorrent. Does this mean that some of the most wicked, evil and cruel humans ever to have lived will be given precisely the same eventual reward as those humans who dedicated their lives to good works, selfless acts and the improvement of others? Do we really mean that Gandhi and Stalin will be treated the same? How does this demonstrate God's justice? Why should anyone even bother to try in this life now, if eventually we will all end up in Heaven? The idea seems preposterous and seriously undermines any credibility this theodicy may have in the 21st century.

In conclusion, despite the initial attractiveness of human development and a universal hope of eternal reward, the contradictions contained with Irenaean type theodicies are too severe for this theodicy to be able to maintain any credibility in the 21st century.

AO2 Activity *Possible lines of argument*

Listed below are some conclusions that could be drawn from the AO2 reasoning in the accompanying text:

1. Irenaean type theodicies are not credible because they do not take the issue of evil seriously enough.

2. It is the unfairness of the theodicies that causes the lack of credibility in the 21st century.

3. If the Bible is accepted as a reliable source then the Irenaean theodicy makes perfect sense.

4. Developing spiritual perfection is a credible idea because it relates closely to the theory of evolution.

5. The Irenaean type theodicies lack credibility in the 21st century because they are not equipped to deal adequately with the intensity, immensity and utter unfairness caused by evil and suffering.

Consider each of the conclusions drawn above and collect evidence and examples to support each argument from the AO1 and AO2 material studied in this section. Select one conclusion that you think is most convincing and explain why it is so. Now contrast this with the weakest conclusion in the list, justifying your argument with clear reasoning and evidence.

Specification content
The extent to which Irenaeus'
theodicy succeeds as a defence of the
God of Classical Theism.

The extent to which Irenaeus' theodicy succeeds as a defence of the God of Classical Theism

The problem of evil is a long-standing challenge to believers in the God of Classical Theism. Throughout history there have been attempts to support this belief and to attack the problem of evil. One such example can be found in the theodicies (attempts to justify God in the face of the existence of evil) associated with the works of Irenaeus of Lyons.

Irenaeus bases his main ideas on Genesis 1:26 that states: 'Let us make man in our image, after our likeness'. The basic thread that runs throughout Irenaeus' works (the theodicy was never written as a composite – it is a theme that runs throughout many of his writings) is that human beings were made in God's image – in other words had the potential to be like God, but only through undergoing the trials of suffering that life presents and responding to these appropriately (freely choosing to do good rather than evil) would we develop into God's likeness – i.e. would fully actualise God's qualities within ourselves. In this Irenaeus faces the problem of evil head on and admits that evil exists. Not only does it exist, but it was also part of God's plan for humanity. God, in Irenaeus' view, has deliberately created evil so that we could develop our spiritual qualities and become better people. In this sense, the Irenaean theodicy is a successful defence of the God of Classical Theism because he admits the 'third corner' of the inconsistent triad but overcomes this by stating that there is a very clear reason for the existence of evil – to help human beings achieve spiritual and moral perfection.

Irenaeus speaks of God being like a craftsman, and evil is one of his tools that allows him to mould humans into perfection when they act in faith towards him (i.e. they freely choose to do good in the face of evil and suffering). The theodicy is also successful if we consider John Hick's development of Irenaeus' theodicy when he makes the point that God's mercy extends beyond this life and that, by virtue of his divine mercy, all human beings will eventually develop into spiritually perfect beings and be united with him in Heaven. This would, at first glance, seem another successful defence of the God of Classical Theism in the face of the existence of evil – in that the promise is that, one day, it will not only be overcome, but that all individuals will one day achieve the end that God has set out for them and all of creation will be one in harmony together.

Unfortunately for supporters of the Irenaean theodicy there are too many issues that are unresolved. The extent of suffering is not evenly spread. Not all humans experience the same amount of suffering in their lives and some manage to become moral and spiritually good people even without undergoing trials of suffering and evil. In fact, some of those that undergo suffering have so much to deal with that they do not develop but actually regress – some into cycles of violence and cruelty themselves, some in taking their own lives because they cannot stand to suffer another moment. Neither of these is taken account of in the theodicy and both pose a serious challenge to its effectiveness as a defence of the God of Classical Theism. Furthermore, the concept of universal salvation seems to entirely undermine any reason for choosing to do the right thing in the here and now – what's the point if all humanity will eventually up with God anyway?

Therefore, in conclusion, following the points made above, the Irenaean theodicy fails as a successful defence of the God of Classical Theism.

AO2 Activity Possible lines of argument

Listed below are some conclusions that could be drawn from the AO2 reasoning in the accompanying text:

1. Irenaean type theodicies weaken the concept of God's omnipotence.

2. Irenaean type theodicies are incompatible with a loving God.

3. Irenaean type theodicies suggest that God is arbitrary in distributing evil and suffering, incompatible with the God of Classical Theism.

4. Irenaean type theodicies do not explain why an all-knowing God would allow such a complex plan.

5. Irenaean type theodicies are successful because they are the only way of explaining free will.

Consider each of the conclusions drawn above and collect evidence and examples to support each argument from the AO1 and AO2 material studied in this section. Select one conclusion that you think is most convincing and explain why it is so. Now contrast this with the weakest conclusion in the list, justifying your argument with clear reasoning and evidence.

AO2 Developing skills

It is now time to reflect upon the information that has been covered so far. It is also important to consider how what you have learned can be focused and used for examination-style answers by practising the skills associated with AO2.

Assessment objective 2 (AO2) involves 'analysis' and 'evaluation'. The terms may be obvious but it is crucial to be familiar with how certain skills demonstrate these terms, and also, how the performance of these skills is measured (see generic band descriptors Band 5 for AS AO2).

Obviously an answer is placed within an appropriate band descriptor depending upon how well the answer performs, ranging from excellent, good, satisfactory, basic/limited to very limited.

▶ **Your new task is this:** below is a list of several key points bulleted in response to a question that has been written requiring an evaluation of the Irenaean theodicy as a successful defence of the God of Classical Theism. It is obviously a very full list. It will be useful, initially, to consider what you think are the most important points to use in planning an answer. This exercise, in essence, is like writing your own set of possible answers that are listed in a typical mark scheme as indicative content. In a group, select the most important points you feel should be included in a list of indicative content for this question. You will need to decide upon two things: which points to select; and then, in which order to put them in an answer.

List of indicative content:

- Acceptance of the Irenaean type theodicy could call into question the omnibenevolence of God if the purpose of life is to grow through suffering.
- Surely such a God would find a more compassionate mechanism to allow Creation to grow and develop towards God?
- This theodicy is incompatible with the biblical accounts of Creation, the Fall and Atonement.
- There is no room for the redemptive power of salvation through Christ.
- Idea of suffering leading to moral/spiritual development is not a universal experience.
- It is possible for some individuals to develop and others not to.
- Some suffering causes death rather than development.
- Others develop moral virtues and spiritual maturity without excessive suffering.
- The theodicy fails to account for the excessive extent of evil/suffering that some experience.
- It also fails to explain the uneven distribution of suffering.
- The concept of universal salvation is morally inconsistent – if all eventually go to Heaven, there is no incentive to do good rather than evil.
- However, some observers may consider that the Irenaean type theodicy provides a purpose for suffering.
- Unlike Augustine, Irenaeus's concept of development is compatible with a scientific view of evolution.
- The theodicy also involves genuine human responsibility, which is therefore respecting of the doctrine of genuine human free will.
- The theodicy promotes human growth/development in achieving moral virtue as a key aim in life and encourages positive behaviour of individuals within society.
- The theodicy also maintains a belief in and purpose for life after death.

Key skills

Analysis involves identifying issues raised by the materials in the AO1, together with those identified in the AO2 section, and presents sustained and clear views, either of scholars or from a personal perspective ready for evaluation.

This means that it picks out key things to debate and the lines of argument presented by others or a personal point of view.

Evaluation involves considering the various implications of the issues raised based upon the evidence gleaned from analysis and provides an extensive detailed argument with a clear conclusion.

This means that the answer weighs up the various and different lines of argument analysed through individual commentary and response and arrives at a conclusion through a clear process of reasoning.

T4 Religious experience (part 1)

Specification content

The nature of religious experience with particular reference to Visions – sensory; intellectual; dreams.

Key terms

Corporeal: of a material nature, physical

Dreams: in terms of visions, the unconscious state where knowledge or understanding is gained through a series of images or a dream-narrative, that would not normally be available to the individual in the conscious state

Intellectual: in terms of visions, that which brings the recipient(s) knowledge and understanding

Sensory: a vision where external objects/sounds or figures convey knowledge and understanding to the recipient

Visions: the ability to 'see' something beyond normal experiences – e.g. the vision of an angel; such visions usually convey information or insight concerning a specific religious tradition

A: The nature of religious experience

The nature of religious experience with particular reference to Visions – sensory; intellectual; dreams

A vision can be defined as something seen other than by ordinary sight, i.e. a supernatural or prophetic sight experienced whilst awake or during sleep, and especially one that conveys a revelation or message of some form.

There are different types of vision. Like other types of religious experiences, they have been classified and grouped differently by different scholars. In the main, in terms of their nature, they have either **sensory** or **dream based** qualities and can often contain an **intellectual** aspect.

A vision has a sensory characteristic if it is to do with sense experience. In other words it is where external objects, sounds or figures appear before the recipient. A vision can also have an intellectual quality if the vision brings the recipient(s) a message of inspiration, insight or instruction. It can also contain warnings! Some dreams can involve visions wherein the unconscious state experiences a series of images or a dream-narrative, which would not normally be available to the individual in the conscious state.

Obviously, these classifications are fluid and a particular vision may have more than one quality, for example sensory visions often can convey some kind of knowledge and understanding to the person or people who experience the vision.

Sensory visions can be summarised in three ways. Group visions are seen by more than one person, for example Angels of Mons, where during the First World War a vision of St George and a phantom bowman halted the Kaiser's troops. Others claimed that angels had thrown a protective curtain around the British troops saving them from disaster. Sensory visions can also be individual, seen by only one person, for example Bernadette of Lourdes who claimed to have been instructed by an apparition of the Virgin Mary to dig a hole and a healing spring would appear. The place was Lourdes. A slight variation is that a sensory vision can be **corporeal** in nature and have an object that is external and appears to be physical in nature, but only visible to certain people, for example the appearances of angels.

Individual visions, however, are often imaginative or dream based, internal visions wherein the image is produced in the person's imagination and has no existence external to that person, for example John's visions of strange creatures in the Book of Revelation. This also brought a message to understand. Therefore, as above, as well as having a specific quality of being dream based, it can also be intellectual. Another example of a dream-based religious experience would be when the wise men were warned in a dream not to return to Herod (Matthew 2:12).

The actual content of visions can be very varied. For example, there could be an image or event in which there is a message, for example Peter's vision of the large sheet descending (Acts 10:9-16). The sheet contained all kinds of animals and reptiles and birds. A voice told Peter to kill and eat. When he refused, the voice told him that he should not call anything impure that God has made clean. Peter then realised that he could eat with a Gentile.

Key quote

When I saw the vision of his bleeding head, our Lord also showed my soul the unpretentious manner of his loving. I saw that for us he is everything that is good, comforting, and helpful. He is our clothing who wraps us up and holds us close for love … and with this insight he also showed me a little thing, the size of a hazelnut, lying in the palm of my hand. It seemed to me as round as a ball. I gazed at it and thought, 'What can this be?' The answer came thus, 'It is everything that is made.' I marveled how this could be, for it was so small it seemed it might fall suddenly into nothingness. Then I heard the answer, 'It lasts, and ever shall last, because God loves it. All things have their being in this way by the grace of God.' (**Julian of Norwich**)

A vision could also contain religious figures, for example St Teresa of Avila's most famous was of an angel holding a long spear and at the end of the spear was something like a fire. This seemed to pierce her heart several times and when it was withdrawn it left her 'completely afire with a great love for God'.

The vision experience could also be of a place of significance, for example Guru Nanak's vision of God's court in which he was escorted into God's presence and commanded to drink a cup of nectar.

Visions can also contain fantastic creatures or figures, for example Ezekiel's vision of four living creatures (Ezekiel 1:6-14). Each had a face of a man, and on the right side had the face of a lion, and on the left the face of an ox; each also had the face of an eagle.

As we have seen, a vision could deliver a specific message, for example the final judgement and images of the end of the world in the Book of Revelation (Revelation 20:12–15). This describes the dead being judged according to what they had done. Anyone's name that was not found in the book of life was thrown into the lake of fire.

Key quote

… it penetrated into my entrails. When he drew out the spear he seemed to be drawing them out with it, leaving me all on fire with a wondrous love for God. (**Teresa of Avila**)

Study tip

Do not narrate but use the examples to identify and discuss the features of type and form of vision. Be aware that visions can be part of a conversion, or a mystical experience, but that visions are also a separate type of religious experience.

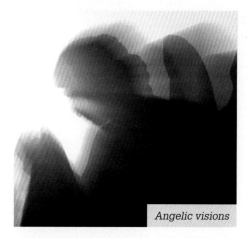
Angelic visions

Key quote

In the year that King Uzziah died, I saw the Lord sitting on a throne, high and lofty; and the hem of his robe filled the temple. Seraphs were in attendance above him; each had six wings: with two they covered their faces, and with two they covered their feet, and with two they flew. And one called to another and said: 'Holy, holy, holy is the Lord of hosts; the whole earth is full of his glory.' The pivots on the thresholds shook at the voices of those who called, and the house filled with smoke. And I said: 'Woe is me! I am lost, for I am a man of unclean lips, and I live among a people of unclean lips; yet my eyes have seen the King, the Lord of hosts!' Then one of the seraphs flew to me, holding a live coal that had been taken from the altar with a pair of tongs. The seraph touched my mouth with it and said: 'Now that this has touched your lips, your guilt has departed and your sin is blotted out.' Then I heard the voice of the Lord saying, 'Whom shall I send, and who will go for us?' And I said, 'Here am I; send me!' (**Isaiah 6:1–8**)

Specification content

The nature of religious experience
with particular reference to
Conversion –individual/communal;
sudden/gradual.

Key term

Conversion: in the religious context
the change of state from one form of
life to another

quickfire

4.1 State three ways in which a vision
can be experienced.

Key quote

We only have to glance at religious
history to see the enormous vitality
and significance of experience in
the formation and development of
religious traditions. Consider the
visions of the Prophet Muhammad,
the conversion of Paul, the
enlightenment of the Buddha. These
were seminal events in human
history. And it is obvious that the
emotions and experiences of men
and women are the food on which
the other dimensions of religion
feed: ritual without feeling is cold,
doctrines without awe or compassion
are dry, and myths which do not
move hearers are feeble. (Smart)

The nature of religious experience with particular reference to Conversion –individual/ communal; sudden/gradual

The word 'conversion' means 'to change direction' or 'to turn around'. It is a process of change that alters one's view of the world and one's personal place in it.

Conversions are usually a personal experience but not always. There are many examples of communal conversions. The classic example of communal or collective conversion is in Acts of the Apostles chapter 2. The disciples were gathered in a room and received the Holy Spirit:

'When the day of Pentecost came, they were all together in one place. Suddenly a sound like the blowing of a violent wind came from Heaven and filled the whole house where they were sitting. They saw what seemed to be tongues of fire that separated and came to rest on each of them. All of them were filled with the Holy Spirit and began to speak in other tongues as the Spirit enabled them.' (Acts 2: 1–4)

Although this in itself is a dramatic collective religious experience, it is what happened next that is relevant here. Peter then took courage and addressed the crowds, preaching to them and encouraging them to repent. The crowd responded and many were converted:

'When the people heard this, they were cut to the heart and said to Peter and the other apostles, "Brothers, what shall we do?" Peter replied, "Repent and be baptised, every one of you, in the name of Jesus Christ for the forgiveness of your sins. And you will receive the gift of the Holy Spirit. The promise is for you and your children and for all who are far off – for all whom the Lord our God will call." With many other words he warned them; and he pleaded with them, "Save yourselves from this corrupt generation." Those who accepted his message were baptised, and about three thousand were added to their number that day.' (Acts 2:37–41)

Characteristic features of a conversion

The psychologist and philosopher William James understood conversion only in psychological terms; however, he discussed a number of key features of conversion that have remained important to scholars today.

A conversion can be either gradual or sudden. However, even sudden conversions may have had prior sub-conscious development. Billy Graham agreed that conversion did not have to be an instant dateable experience.

A conversion is often volitional or self-surrendering, meaning that the conversion might involve the giving up of the personal will, either freely (volitional) or with resistance and an internal battle (self-surrendering).

A conversion can be passive or active, which means either the experience comes upon them somewhat unexpectedly without them deliberately seeking it, or someone might specifically seek a spiritual experience by going to an evangelistic meeting.

Conversions are often transforming in that the conversion might involve a thorough-going transformation creating a 'new person' or as Paul writes 'a new creation' (2 Corinthians 5:17).

Different descriptions of, and explanations for, conversions

There are various ways in which a conversion experience can be explained, some of which may overlap.

A conversion that involves the unifying of the inner self. This is how the American psychologist and philosopher, William James (*The Varieties of Religious Experience*, 1902), understood conversion. He saw it in psychological terms rather than a miraculous occurrence. The divided self was an awareness of incompleteness.

Sometimes a conversion can be a matter of intellectual persuasion; this involves conflict between two systems of thought where the new one is seen as 'true'. It can also be one of moral transformation; this is where someone changes how they live their life as a result of where it is the change in lifestyle that is the key factor.

A conversion can be from no religion to a faith. For example, Augustine, who became Bishop of Hippo in 395CE, a key thinker in the development of the Christian Church writes of his conversion, 'As I came to the end of the sentence, it was as though the light of confidence flooded into my heart and all the darkness of doubt was dispelled'. It can also be from one faith to another faith. For example, Sundar Singh, who was raised a devout Sikh, was dissatisfied with Sikhism and he sought ultimate meaning in Hinduism and Christianity. Disenchanted with both he made to kill himself unless God revealed himself. Then he had a vision of Jesus and became an active Christian for the rest of his life.

A conversion can even be from faith (believing) to faith (trusting), or as some may put it, 'from mind to heart'. For example, John Wesley was aware that he did not have a faith in Christ as a personal saviour but he saw that others had. Then, in 1738 he records how he felt his heart strangely warmed. 'I did trust Christ, Christ alone, for salvation; and an assurance was given me, that he had taken away my sins, even mine ...'.

Saul of Tarsus – Road to Damascus conversion experience

Sometimes conversions are categorised under the headings 'intellectual' and 'moral'. An example of an intellectual conversion would be C.S. Lewis, the author of the Narnia Chronicles and professor at Oxford. He recounts how in 1931 he walked and talked for hours with the author J.R.R. Tolkein about myth and Christianity and became convinced that Jesus was the Son of God. Augustine is an example of a moral conversion, in that his wayward life was challenged when he read the words from Romans which exhorts the reader to abandon the works of the flesh and to be clothed with Christ.

Study tip

Clearly, not all the features that appear in the various lists occur in every example of a religious experience. Therefore, a number of examples may be required if the features are to be illustrated and discussed.

AO1 Activity

Write a series of revision cards that detail specific examples of religious visions or religious conversion accounts. This will provide useful reference materials in preparation for examination questions focussing on this area of the specification.

Key quote

And when I received the book, a guidance that would explain everything to me – who I was; what was the purpose of life; what was the reality and what would be the reality; and where I came from – I realised that this was the true religion. (Yusuf Islam, formerly Cat Stevens)

Key quote

In the evening I went very unwillingly to a society in Aldersgate Street, where one was reading Luther's Preface to the Epistle to the Romans. About a quarter before nine, while he was describing the change which God works in the heart through faith in Christ, I felt my heart strangely warmed. I felt I did trust in Christ, Christ alone for salvation, and an assurance was given me that he had taken away my sins, even mine, and saved me from the law of sin and death. (Wesley)

quickfire

4.2 What can be considered to be the defining characteristic of a religious conversion?

Specification content

The nature of religious experience with particular reference to Mysticism – transcendent; ecstatic and unitive.

The nature of religious experience with particular reference to Mysticism – transcendent; ecstatic and unitive

A departure from a logical, rational view of religion is the experience cited by religious believers of mysticism. The term has become somewhat loosely translated in recent times to refer to a range of experiences, often erroneously attributed to a vague kind of 'new-age' approach to religious practices and experiences. Whilst there may well be veins of mystical experiences to be found within such areas, the history of such things is older by far. Mystical experiences are described in the most ancient religious traditions that we know of. From ancient texts such as the Bhagavad Gita in Hinduism to accounts of medieval mystics such as Julian of Norwich and Meister Eckhart, mysticism has a rich and diverse history.

What then is the *nature* of mystical experience? To this question there are numerous responses but certain themes run throughout all of them. Ed Miller regards it as *'the pursuit of a transcendent, unitive experience with the absolute reality'* (*Questions that Matter*, Miller, 1995) and offers the following helpful summary:

1. **Transcendent:** not localisable in space or time
2. **Ineffable:** not expressible in language
3. **Noetic:** conveying illumination, truth
4. **Ecstatic:** filling the soul with bliss, peace
5. **Unitive:** uniting the soul with reality.

Miller is not alone in making use of these particular terms to define mystical experiences. Commentators such as William James (who makes use of several of the above categories) and Walter Stace define mystical experiences in different ways but admit to a series of common features that all such experiences are said to have.

Religious mystics also often speak of a mystical ascent. In some ways similar to the Platonic view of reality, where there is, effectively, a ladder or staircase. These steps begin in the earthly, mundane world but, with regular practice and divine assistance, the individual can transcend their own reality and make an ascent of this ladder, to gain unity with the ultimate reality. It is often described metaphorically as a journey from darkness to light.

Transcendent mysticism is associated with the mystical experiences that take the practitioner 'beyond' the realm of the normal everyday experience. Transcendental realities are often described in language that refers to 'other worldly' or 'different dimensions', both of which are vague descriptions of a feeling of moving beyond this physical realm to the realm of the 'other', the realm of the spirit. Such experiences encompass other types of mystical experience such as ecstasy and unitive experience as the believer feel that they have become one with the transcendent reality whilst effectively disengaging for a while, from the temporal and physical world of the empirical senses. Most religious traditions have aspects of transcendental mysticism within them. One of most notable of these is Sufism, the mystical group within Islam focused on divine union with Allah through meditation, dance, and other mystic practices, and the tradition that Rumi, a 13th-century Persian poet and arguably the most famous mystic from the Islamic tradition, was associated with.

Rumi believed that all individuals have a yearning within them that is due to the feeling of separation that all beings instinctively feel. He recognised that whilst Allah was both high in the heavens and closer to man than his own jugular vein, humankind was still separated from Allah and only by spiritual purification through love could union with God (tawhid) be truly achieved. Rumi believed that the human spirit was designed for the singular underlying purpose to draw into a deeper relationship with God. He developed the practice known as Sema, a sacred dance, where Sufis constantly turn on the left foot; (the turning, according to

Key terms

Ecstatic: an overwhelming feeling of bliss or peace

Ineffable: that being of which a person cannot speak as no words can describe the experience

Mysticism: a religious experience where union with God or the absolute reality is sought or experienced

Noetic: knowledge gained through mystical experience that would otherwise not be available to the recipient through ordinary means

Transcendent: that which lies beyond the everyday realm of the physical senses

Unitive: the feeling of complete oneness with the divine

Ladder to Heaven

Rumi, is a metaphor for 'a blessed state of every fibre of an individual's being turning on the axis of the merciful and compassionate creator and sustainer of all things.') this turning is meant to generate a spiritual ascent to Allah. This message of yearning to be united with Allah forms the central message in his poem *The Song of the Reed Flute*. Here Rumi invites the listener to understand the secret of human existence by hearkening to the message hidden in the plaintive tones of the reed flute. If, reasoned Rumi, the most basic purpose of the human spirit was to put a person in relationship with the divine then all other relationships within the created order, especially those with other human beings, are mystical gateways into a closer relationship with the creator. This highly significant part of Rumi's mystical experience was played out in his own relationship with his mentor, Shams. He noted how through this close relationship he felt that he became closer in his relationship with Allah. Rumi believed poetry, music, and dance were all direct doorways to the divine and, due to these convictions, he founded the Mevlevi order of Sufis, famous for their Whirling Dervishes.

Whirling Dervishes

The mystical **ecstatic** experience is well documented and discussed in the work of a wide range of mystics, philosophers and scholars from other traditions. Teresa of Avila regards ecstasy as the suspension of the exterior senses: 'One perceives that the natural heat of the body is perceptibly lessened; the coldness increases, though accompanied with exceeding joy and sweetness.' (Autobiography, Teresa). Others in the Christian tradition describe it as the closest a mortal being can get to the feeling of what it must be like for departed souls to be in the presence of God. Followers of Eastern religious traditions also describe feelings of mystical ecstasy – often centred around intense meditative practices such as those in the later stages of Vipissana meditation in Buddhism and Yogic practices in Hinduism. Broadly speaking, ecstasy can be described to have two effective states then – one which relates to an interior sensation where the mind becomes utterly focussed on a subject (usually religious in nature) and the other element is the physical suspension of the normal activity of the sense, such that the individual appears to be in a trancelike state in 'which they are not easily disturbed. However, upon wakening, most are able to describe, in some measure, the intensity of their experiences albeit in highly symbolic language.

The **unitive** type of mystical experience tends to cover a range of similar types of experiences, rather than describing a single identifiable experience. The concept of union involves a removal of the separation between the individual and God. Many Christian mystics have claimed such experiences, including St Bernard of Clairvaux, the French Cistercian Abbott, who described the experience as a 'mutuality of love'; the German mystic (and student of Meister Eckhart), Henry Suso, stated that the experience was like a man who : '... is entirely lost in God, has passed into him, and has become one spirit with him in all respects, like a drop of water which is poured into a large portion of wine. Just as this is lost to itself, and draws to itself and into itself the taste and colour of the wine, so it likewise happens to those who are in complete possession of blessedness.'

Key quote

Now listen to this reed-flute's deep lament – About the heartache being apart has meant:

Since from the reed-bed they uprooted me – My song's expressed each human's agony,

A breast which separation's split in two – Is what I seek, to share this pain with you:

When kept from their true origin, all yearn – For union on the day they can return.

(Rumi)

Key quote

The most important, the central characteristic in which all fully developed mystical experiences agree, and which in the last analysis is definitive of them and serves to mark them off from other kinds of experiences, is that they involve the apprehension of an ultimate nonsensuous unity in all things, a oneness or a One to which neither the senses nor the reason can penetrate. In other words, it entirely transcends our sensory-intellectual consciousness. **(Stace)**

Key quote

The mystical experience is a transient, extraordinary experience marked by feelings of being in unity, harmonious relationship to the divine and everything in existence, as well as euphoric feelings, noesis, loss of ego functioning, alterations in time and space perception, and the sense of lacking control over the event. **(Lukoff)**

Specification content

The nature of religious experience
with particular reference to Prayer –
types and stages of prayer according
to Teresa of Avila.

The nature of religious experience with particular reference to Prayer – types and stages of prayer according to Teresa of Avila

She was born on 15 March 1515 in Spain. Her family inspired the young Teresa to take her religious life seriously and in 1535 she joined an order of Carmelite nuns. After a severe illness which left Teresa partially paralysed for three years, she became somewhat disillusioned with her religious practices, especially prayer. However, a vision of the 'sorely wounded Christ' was to re-energise Teresa's spiritual journey and inspire her to write her great works on prayer.

Teresa's approach to mystical experience was through her four stages of prayer. She believed that true union with God could only be achieved by intense concentration and disciplining oneself through a life of prayer that would, by a series of stages, allow a person to reach that union:

'To say something, then, of the early experiences of those who are determined to pursue this blessing and to succeed in this enterprise ... it is in these early stages that their labour is hardest, for it is they themselves who labour and the Lord Who gives the increase. In the other degrees of prayer the chief thing is fruition, although, whether at the beginning, in the middle or at the end of the road, all have their crosses, different as these may be. For those who follow Christ must take the way which He took, unless they want to be lost.' (*Autobiography*)

Teresa firmly believed that it was not possible for an individual to achieve that union by themselves but that, only through God's grace, could a person move through the various stages:

'The beginner must think of himself as of one setting out to make a garden in which the Lord is to take His delight, yet in soil most unfruitful and full of weeds. His Majesty uproots the weeds and will set good plants in their stead. Let us suppose that this is already done -- that a soul has resolved to practise prayer and has already begun to do so. We have now, by God's help, like good gardeners, to make these plants grow, and to water them carefully, so that they may not perish, but may produce flowers which shall send forth great fragrance to give refreshment to this Lord of ours, so that He may often come into the garden to take His pleasure and have His delight among these virtues.' (*Autobiography*)

Teresa is often associated with teaching on the various stages of prayer. She compares these stages to the ways in which a garden (the metaphor that she has already established to represent the state of a person's spiritual self) is looked after:

'The garden can be watered in four ways: by taking the water from a well, which costs us great labour; or by a water-wheel and buckets, when the water is drawn by a windlass...; or by a stream or a brook, which waters the ground much better, for it saturates it more thoroughly and there is less need to water it often, so that the gardener's labour is much less; or by heavy rain, when the Lord waters it with no labour of ours, a way incomparably better than any of those which have been described.' (*Autobiography*)

Whilst her definitions of prayer from her autobiography are highly significant, many observers believe that the real insight into mystical experience is found in Teresa's final work: *The Interior Castle*. Moving on from her analogy of a watered garden, Teresa now considers the soul to be like a castle that contains seven suites or mansions (the original Spanish term, which is often used in English considerations of Teresa's teachings is *las moradas*). The first three mansions refer to the type of prayer that Teresa speaks about in detail in earlier works such as her *Autobiography*. These prayers, whilst allowing the individual to come closer to God, do not give the same level of union that can eventually be gained. This union is to be found within the fourth to the seventh mansions, where Teresa represents the various degrees of mystical prayer.

quickpire

4.3   How did Teresa of Avila describe religious ecstasy?

The water wheel as a metaphor for prayer

The first of these, found in the fourth mansion, is the prayer of consolations from God, better known as the Prayer of Quiet. Teresa describes this as a state where the human will is completely captivated by God's Love. This now has the individual operating on the mystical level and, as such, they experience, peace and spiritual delight. Sometimes the experience is so intense that the individual can faint or appear semi-comatose – this state is referred to by St Teresa as a 'sleep of the faculties'.

Within the fifth mansion Teresa describes the next stage as the prayer of simple union: 'God implants himself in the interior of the soul is such a way that, when it returns to itself, it cannot possibly doubt that God has been in it and it has been in God'.

The sixth mansion contains the longest of Teresa's mystical descriptions and is occasionally disputed as to precisely what was being described. It is commonly known as the stage of spiritual marriage. The main experiences associated with this stage can include rapture, feelings of painful longing, spiritual ecstasy and visions. The over-riding characteristic is the sense of wanting to be able to spend every possible moment alone with the divine 'spouse' and the complete rejection of all things that can get in the way of such moments.

The seventh and final mansion is regarded as the highest possible state of prayer that is achievable on earth. The soul is regarded as having reached a state of transforming union or, as it is more commonly known, the stage of 'mystical marriage'. It is the stage where complete unity with the divine is felt, to the extent where an intimate and perceptive awareness, knowledge and understanding of the person of the divine is intuitively felt.

AO1 Activity

Draw a poster with seven concentric circles – in each circle label the description of prayer given by Teresa for the Interior Mansion. This will enable you to have a visual reminder of the seven mansions and will help promote your ability to show 'Thorough, accurate and relevant knowledge and understanding of religion and belief.' (AO1 Level 5 descriptor).

Teresa of Avila (1515–1582)

Key quotes

Teresa says beginners should use determination to overcome distractions while praying and devoutly contemplate Christ. At the second stage, the soul has quieted and gains greater clarity. The will is lost in God but other human faculties, such as imagination, remain distracted. In the third stage, Christ becomes the gardener; the soul is given over to God blissfully but the union with God remains incomplete. The fourth stage is a trance. Union with God is complete; the senses stop and consciousness of the body fades. (Lapointe)

We should desire and engage in prayer, not for our enjoyment, but for the sake of acquiring the strength which fits us for service. … Believe me, Martha and Mary must work together. … I will end by saying that we must not build towers without foundations, and that the Lord does not look so much at the magnitude of anything we do as at the love with which we do it. If we accomplish what we can, His Majesty will see to it that we become able to do more each day. (Teresa of Avila)

Key term

Prayer: in simple terms, communication with the divine

quickfire

4.4 What metaphor does Teresa of Avila employ to describe the various stages of prayer?

Key skills

Knowledge involves:

Selection of a range of (thorough) accurate and relevant information that is directly related to the specific demands of the question.

This means you choose the correct information relevant to the question set NOT the topic area. You will have to think and focus on selecting key information and NOT writing everything you know about the topic area.

Understanding involves:

Explanation that is extensive, demonstrating depth and/or breadth with excellent use of evidence and examples including (where appropriate) thorough and accurate supporting use of sacred texts, sources of wisdom and specialist language.

This means that you demonstrate that you understand something by being able to illustrate and expand your points through examples/supporting evidence in a personal way and NOT repeat chunks from a text book (known as rote learning).

Further application of skills:

Go through the topic areas in this section and create some bullet lists of key points from key areas. For each one, provide further elaboration and explanation through the use of evidence and examples.

AO1 Developing skills

It is now time to reflect upon the information that has been covered so far. It is also important to consider how what you have learned can be focused and used for examination-style answers by practising the skills associated with AO1.

Assessment objective 1 (AO1) involves demonstrating knowledge and understanding. The terms 'knowledge' and 'understanding' are obvious but it is crucial to be familiar with how certain skills demonstrate these terms, and also, how the performance of these skills is measured (see generic band descriptors Band 5 for AS AO1).

▶ **Your new task is this:** below is a list of indicative content that could be used in response to a question requiring an examination of the descriptions of prayer from Teresa of Avila. The problem is that it is not a very full list and needs completing! It will be useful, as a group, to consider what is missing from the list. You will need to add at least five points that you would use to improve the list and/or give more detail to each point that is already in the list. Then, as a group, agree on your final list and write out your new list of indicative content, remembering the principles of explaining with evidence and/or examples.

If you then put this list in order of how you would present the information in an essay you will have your own plan for an ideal answer.

List of indicative content:

- God's grace is necessary for fruitful prayer.
- Prayer develops in stages.
- Prayer is like watering a garden.
- Teresa's mystical teaching on prayer is described in the Interior Castle.
- The human will is captured by God.
- A semi-comatose state can seem to occur.
- Spiritual ecstasy.
- Mystical marriage.
- *Your added content*
- *Your added content*
- Etc.

Issues for analysis and evaluation

The impact of religious experiences upon religious belief and practice

Some may argue that religious experiences are not the same as sense experiences. God is not material. God does not have a definite location. How would you recognise it was God that you were experiencing? However, just as people are known to each other by a kind of awareness and understanding of the mind rather than through our physical body, so in the same way people claim to experience God, who is non-physical, and this has great impact upon both religious belief and practice.

A way of assessing the impact of religious experiences upon religious belief and practice is with the experience of conversion. A conversion essentially initiates two things: firstly, the belief in God's existence or the truth of another religion; and secondly, a change of behaviour in the new convert. For example, Augustine, who became Bishop of Hippo in 395CE a key thinker in the development of the Christian Church, converted from atheism to believer and had a major impact on the belief and practice of others. In the same way, Sundar Singh, who was raised a devout Sikh, had a vision of Jesus and became an active Christian for the rest of his life.

The extent of change varies but the impact still remains on the individual. In addition, this impact can influence others.

Swinburne proposed the principles of credulity and testimony. This stated that it is reasonable to believe that the world is probably as we experience it to be. He argues that other people's testimony of religious experiences provide good reason to believe that God exists. Many people, on the basis of apparent direct experiences of God, take it that God exists. This has also had impact upon others, who may also base their belief in God upon the acceptance of another's religious experience. All founders of world faith had this impact upon others. Religion, based on the experience of its founders has been a powerful force in history, and modern researchers such as David Hay suggest it is widespread.

William James was particularly interested in the effects of religious experience on people's lives and believed that the validity of the experience rests upon the effects it produces. In his book, 'The Varieties of Religious Experience' where he documented many examples of religious experience, he saw that the effects of these experiences were powerful and positive. They changed the lives of communities and individuals so much so that he saw this as powerful evidence for both a belief in God and the validity of such belief. However, some argue that James is too subjective as he focuses more on the truth of the experience for the individual, rather than whether or not this relates to the idea of a God who exists in the 'real world'.

Overall, belief and practice are impacted upon inevitably by religious experience but it is the range of this impact that differs, from just the individual, to world-wide communities as in the case of religious founders.

Although the powerful force of religious experience is often used by many to suggest that a belief in God is a viable option and a possibility, or in some cases, sound evidence for God's existence, it should be remembered that not all accept this extent of the impact of religious experience. Others, such as Bertrand Russell, would argue 'the fact that a belief has a good moral effect upon a man is no evidence whatsoever in favour of its truth'. For example, one can be influenced by a character from a good story but that does not mean the character is real.

In conclusion, it is probably best to admit that whilst religious experience does inevitably have a powerful impact upon religious belief and practice, its impact is limited to those that believe and cannot extend to sound and firm philosophical proof that the object of that religious experience is objectively real.

This section covers AO2 content and skills

Specification content

The impact of religious experiences upon religious belief and practice.

AO2 Activity *Possible lines of argument*

Listed below are some conclusions that could be drawn from the AO2 reasoning in the accompanying text:

1. Religious experience has a major impact on both belief and practice.

2. Religious experience has a major impact on an individual's belief but not always that of others.

3. Religious experience has most impact on the practice of individuals in that it changes their lives.

4. Religious experience has a major impact on both belief and practice but is still not evidence that it is true or that God exists.

5. Religious experience has a major impact on both belief and practice and could be argued to be strong evidence, or proof, that God exists.

Consider each of the conclusions drawn above and collect evidence and examples to support each argument from the AO1 and AO2 material studied in this section. Select one conclusion that you think is most convincing and explain why it is so. Now contrast this with the weakest conclusion in the list, justifying your argument with clear reasoning and evidence.

Specification content

Whether different types of religious experience can be accepted as equally valid in communicating religious teachings and beliefs.

AO2 Activity *Possible lines of argument*

Listed below are some conclusions that could be drawn from the AO2 reasoning in the accompanying text:

1. All religious experiences have the same value for communicating or evidencing religious belief and specific teachings.

2. All religious experiences have the some value for communicating or evidencing religious belief and specific teachings but it depends upon the type of experience.

3. Some religious experiences are better at communicating or evidencing religious belief and specific teachings.

4. Not all religious experiences can communicate or evidence religious belief and specific teachings.

5. Religious experiences are not intended to have the same value for communicating or evidencing religious belief and specific teachings.

Consider each of the conclusions drawn above and collect evidence and examples to support each argument from the AO1 and AO2 material studied in this section. Select one conclusion that you think is most convincing and explain why it is so. Now contrast this with the weakest conclusion in the list, justifying your argument with clear reasoning and evidence.

Whether different types of religious experience can be accepted as equally valid in communicating religious teachings and beliefs

The main issue here is whether or not all religious experiences have the same value for communicating or evidencing religious belief and specific teachings.

There is certainly a widespread lack of uniformity of religious experiences. There are so many different types, all of which have varying impact. In addition, as regards the religious teachings, it could be argued that the messages, visions, information and beliefs apparently transmitted in religious experiences are so diverse and contradictory that it is impossible for the majority of religious experiences to be real and accurate, and therefore a valid tool for communicating religious truths.

For example, in Zen Buddhism, religious experiences do not lead to Buddhists claims of a creator God, but rather that meditation makes you fully in touch with the true nature of reality. Opposed to this is the claim of some Christians that they meet with God or Jesus in their religious experiences. It appears, then, that religious experiences could suggest that God, or the impersonal spiritual experience, is relative to, and dependent upon, cultural beliefs that we will understand and interpret.

However, different experiences recounted do not mean they are all in error. Maybe only one religion is correct so the other religious experiences are false, but those of that one religion are true. This is a more internal debate between religions. Some may say that their religious experience allows them to have a pluralistic outlook, for example Hick and Gandhi. Others may have a more exclusivist approach and claim that their religious experience is the single truth.

Aside from this problem there is another issue. This is the key problem of ineffability. Many religious experiences are beyond verbal description. There are no words that can describe the experience, so it is not possible for others to understand. The experience is subjective and private, it is not open to anyone else. The experience is personal, it is not possible to fully understand unless we have the experience. If all this is true then how can ineffable religious experiences be as valid in communicating or evidencing religious belief and specific teachings as other forms of religious experiences?

Equally we should consider what the primary purpose of a religious experience is – is it for the individual alone? Is it only meant to deepen faith or is it there to be used as an exemplar for teaching others and sharing the experience? What if others misunderstand the experience? Does it demean its original value for the recipient? One may also consider that certain types of religious experience may be considered 'superior' to others within a faith tradition for the alleged value that they may have in communicating or consolidating a particular belief or faith tradition, thereby potentially making those who do not experience this feel inferior or unworthy.

Despite this, it may be safe to conclude that religious experiences are a valid way of communicating or evidencing religious belief and specific teachings for religious believers. However, the real question of whether or not they all have an equal impact for this purpose is quite clearly dependent upon the type of religious experience it is.

AO2 Developing skills

It is now time to reflect upon the information that has been covered so far. It is also important to consider how what you have learned can be focused and used for examination-style answers by practising the skills associated with AO2.

Assessment objective 2 (AO2) involves 'analysis' and 'evaluation'. The terms may be obvious but it is crucial to be familiar with how certain skills demonstrate these terms, and also, how the performance of these skills is measured (see generic band descriptors Band 5 for AS AO2).

Obviously an answer is placed within an appropriate band descriptor depending upon how well the answer performs, ranging from excellent, good, satisfactory, basic/limited to very limited.

▶ **Your new task is this:** below is a list of indicative content that could be used in response to a question requiring an evaluation of the impact of religious experience upon belief and practice. The problem is that it is not a very full list and needs completing! It will be useful, as a group, to consider what is missing from the list. You will need to add at least six points (three in support and three against) that you would use to improve the list and/or give more detail to each point that is already in the list. Remember, it is how you use the points that is the most important factor. Apply the principles of evaluation by making sure that you: identify issues clearly; present accurate views of others, making sure that you comment on the views presented; reach an overall personal judgement. You may add more of your own suggestions, but try to negotiate as a group and prioritise the most important things to add.

Then, as a group, agree on your final list and write out your new list of indicative content, remembering the principles of explaining with evidence and/or examples.

If you then put this list in order of how you would present the information in an essay you will have your own plan for an ideal answer.

List of indicative content:

In support
- Greater impact than cerebral factors
- Begins and/or deepens commitment to religious belief and practice in a unique way
- *Your added content*
- *Your added content*
- Etc.

Against
- Religious upbringing has a greater impact
- Sacred writings are more important than religious experiences fro belief and practice
- *Your added content*
- *Your added content*
- Etc.

Key skills

Analysis involves identifying issues raised by the materials in the AO1, together with those identified in the AO2 section, and presents sustained and clear views, either of scholars or from a personal perspective ready for evaluation.

This means that it picks out key things to debate and the lines of argument presented by others or a personal point of view.

Evaluation involves considering the various implications of the issues raised based upon the evidence gleaned from analysis and provides an extensive detailed argument with a clear conclusion.

This means that the answer weighs up the various and different lines of argument analysed through individual commentary and response and arrives at a conclusion through a clear process of reasoning.

This section covers AO1
content and skills

Specification content

William James' four characteristics of
mystical experience: ineffable, noetic,
transient and passive.

B: Mystical experience

William James' four characteristics of mystical experience

William James' *Varieties of Religious Experience* (1902) is still regarded as one of the most significant and influential studies of religion of the 20th century. Amongst other subjects, James details a classification of mysticism within lectures 16 and 17 of the work. These are instrumental observations of mystical experience and no serious study of the subject can be undertaken without reflecting on James's contributions.

Here follow the explanations of the classifications in James' own words (All quotes from James' *Varieties of Religious Experience*):

1. 'Ineffability – The handiest of the marks by which I classify a state of mind as mystical is negative. The subject of it immediately says that it defies expression, that no adequate report of its contents can be given in words. It follows from this that its quality must be directly experienced; it cannot be imparted or transferred to others. In this peculiarity mystical states are more like states of feeling than like states of intellect. No one can make clear to another who has never had a certain feeling, in what the quality or worth of it consists. One must have musical ears to know the value of a symphony; one must have been in love one's self to understand a lover's state of mind. Lacking the heart or ear, we cannot interpret the musician or the lover justly, and are even likely to consider him weak-minded or absurd. The mystic finds that most of us accord to his experiences an equally incompetent treatment.'

James first class of mystical experience is the one most commonly cited by mystics such as Teresa of Avila, Eckhart, Rumi and others. It is atypical of a mystical experience that it is so profound, that mundane language cannot express it. It also represents, as James acknowledges, the greatest challenges to the authenticity of the experience. However, James continues, just because it cannot be 'proved' should not detract from its value; indeed, he implies, it is more to do with the deficiency of the empiricist than it is with any such deficiency of the mystic, that the experience cannot be described.

2. 'Noetic quality – Although so similar to states of feeling, mystical states seem to those who experience them to be also states of knowledge. They are states of insight into depths of truth unplumbed by the discursive intellect. They are illuminations, revelations, full of significance and importance, all inarticulate though they remain; and as a rule they carry with them a curious sense of authority for after-time.'

The gaining of a special kind of knowledge, or insight, is another hallmark of the work of mystics down the ages and this is what James refers to when he considers the noesis (gaining of knowledge) of the mystics' experiences.

3. 'Transiency – Mystical states cannot be sustained for long. Except in rare instances, half an hour, or at most an hour or two, seems to be the limit beyond which they fade into the light of common day. Often, when faded, their quality can but imperfectly be reproduced in memory; but when they recur it is recognised; and from one recurrence to another it is susceptible of continuous development in what is felt as inner richness and importance.'

In the third classification, James relates the fleeting nature of the mystical experience and demonstrates, through the evidence that he collects, that such experiences may be very intense and have lasting consequences for the recipient, yet in terms of the time in which they take, they are relatively short-lived.

Key quote

One may say truly, I think, that personal religious experience has its root and centre in mystical states of consciousness. Mystical states indeed wield no authority due simply to their being mystical states. But the higher ones among them point in directions to which the religious sentiments even of non-mystical men incline. They tell of the supremacy of the ideal, of vastness, of union, of safety, and of rest. They offer us hypotheses, hypotheses which we may voluntarily ignore, but which as thinkers we cannot possibly upset. The supernaturalism and optimism to which they would persuade us may, interpreted in one way or another, be after all the truest of insights into the meaning of this life. (James)

4. 'Passivity – Although the oncoming of mystical states may be facilitated by preliminary voluntary operations, as by fixing the attention, or going through certain bodily performances, or in other ways which manuals of mysticism prescribe; yet when the characteristic sort of consciousness once has set in, the mystic feels as if his own will were in abeyance, and indeed sometimes as if he were grasped and held by a superior power. This latter peculiarity connects mystical states with certain definite phenomena of secondary or alternative personality, such as prophetic speech, automatic writing, or the mediumistic trance. When these latter conditions are well pronounced, however, there may be no recollection whatever of the phenomenon and it may have no significance for the subject's usual inner life, to which, as it were, it makes a mere interruption. Mystical states, strictly so called, are never merely interruptive. Some memory of their content always remains, and a profound sense of their importance. They modify the inner life of the subject between the times of their recurrence. Sharp divisions in this region are, however, difficult to make, and we find all sorts of gradations and mixtures.'

The fourth and final classification notes the important feature that the experience tends to be 'done to' the recipient and that, even when the recipient goes searching for the experience, the actual moment itself is governed by a being or force external to the will of the mystic. The suggestion is also that these events have a transformative effect on the individual, whose life will very often be changed after the experience.

AO1 Activity

In pairs, take turns in testing each other with the definitions of each of William James' four characteristics for mysticism. In an examination situation it can be easy to mix ideas, terms and definitions – so regular memory testing with a partner can help avoid this. It is also likely to help you ensure your material in the exam response is a '... relevant response which answers the specific demands of the question set'.

Key person

William James: born to a wealthy family in North America in 1842, and brother to the notable American novelist Henry James, William explored several academic disciplines during the first part of his life before settling on the relatively new discipline of psychology. His work inspired many of the 20th century's greatest thinkers, including Ludwig Wittgenstein (allegedly the only book written by a modern philosopher that Wittgenstein would have on his own bookshelf was James' *Varieties of Religious Experience*!). A philosophical pragmatist, James nonetheless stated his belief that religious experience was ultimately beyond the realm of empirical science to ever prove as 'true'. Of such experience he observed: the further limits of our being plunge, it seems to me, into an altogether other dimension of existence from the sensible and merely 'understandable' world.

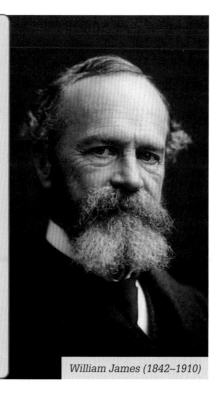

William James (1842–1910)

Key terms

Passive: in this context, where the mystical experience is 'done to' the recipient – it is not instigated by the individual or group but is instead due to some kind of external force or influence

Transient: an experience that is short lived yet has far-reaching and/or long-lasting consequences

quickfire

4.5 What are the four identifying features of mystical experiences, according to William James?

Specification content

Rudolf Otto – the concept of the numinous; mysterium tremendum; the human predisposition for religious experience.

Key terms

Anthropology: the study of human beings, their culture and social development

Naturalism: that which arises from real life or the world of nature

A numinous experience?

Key quote

'Holiness' – 'the holy' – is a category of interpretation and valuation peculiar to the sphere of religion … while it is complex, it contains a quite specific element or 'moment', which sets it apart from 'The Rational' … and which remains inexpressible.' (Otto)

quickfire

4.6 What, in simple terms, does Otto mean by the phrase 'mysterium tremendum'?

Rudolf Otto – the concept of the numinous; mysterium tremendum; the human predisposition for religious experience

Otto's approach, in his *The Idea of the Holy*, was to look at the aspects of religious experience that were beyond the scope of rational and empirical reasoning. Instead there is a focus on the 'feelings' of the recipient that, in many ways, was the first time such an approach to the study of religious experience had been attempted. Otto drew on the history of religion, as he was familiar with it, and combining it with his interest in **anthropology** and **naturalism**, produced an investigation into the subjective field of religious and mystical experiences.

For Otto, the word 'holy' had several wide-ranging connotations, not all of which he found helpful when trying to describe the feelings in the religious or mystical experience. He therefore made use of the term **numinous.** This words derives from the Latin word 'numen', which refers to a supernatural divine power. This sets it apart from the ethical and moral connotations that holy may also have. Thus the individual who experiences the numinous, is one who feels the presence of a supernatural divine power as part of their religious or mystical experience.

For Otto, the idea that human beings can be in receipt of the numinous is part of the natural inclination of humanity towards the spiritual realm. Whilst human experience is often described in term of the rational – particularly when dealing with the mundane aspects of human existence, Otto believed that there was also a significant dimension of human existence that yearned for that which he termed as the 'non-rational' – i.e. that which could not easily be explained by reference to standard empirical means. In this Otto is not stating that experiences of the numinous were irrational – which implies a lack of sanity or sensibility, a lack of stability in the interaction and experience – but rather the non-rational being that which was entirely stable as an experience just not definable in rational terms.

In Chapter 4 of the *The Idea of the Holy*, Otto addresses the numinous experience as being 'the deepest and most fundamental element in all strong and sincerely felt religious emotion'. He describes this as having a particularly profound effect on the individual in receipt of the numinous experience and states that the only way to sum up the intensity of this experience is by using the Latin expression 'mysterium tremendum'. As Otto states, 'the feeling of it may at times come sweeping like a gentle tide, pervading the mind with a tranquil mood of deepest worship. It may pass over into a more set and lasting attitude of the soul, continuing, as it were, thrillingly vibrant and resonant, until at last it dies away and the soul resumes its profane, non-religious mood of everyday experience.'

As he continues to describe the intensity of the mysterium tremendum, Otto is trying to describe the profound intensity that is associated with a deeply felt religious experience. In doing so he further illuminates our understanding of his concept of the numinous as an expression of religious awe and wonder in the presence of the supernatural divine power.

AO1 Activity

Using an example from the world religion in your course of study, record how a religious experience in that tradition might be considered as 'numinous'. You should then use this recorded example in any answer that addresses Otto's concept of the numinous – this will help promote 'Excellent use of evidence and examples' (Level 5 AO1 response) in your answer.

AO1 Developing skills

It is now time to reflect upon the information that has been covered so far. It is also important to consider how what you have learned can be focused and used for examination-style answers by practising the skills associated with AO1.

Assessment objective 1 (AO1) involves demonstrating knowledge and understanding. The terms 'knowledge' and 'understanding' are obvious but it is crucial to be familiar with how certain skills demonstrate these terms, and also, how the performance of these skills is measured (see generic band descriptors Band 5 for AS AO1).

You are now nearing the end of this section of the course. From now on the task will have only instructions with no examples; however, using the skills you have developed in completing the earlier tasks, you should be able to apply what you have learned to do and complete this successfully.

▶ **Your new task is this:** you will have to write a response under timed conditions to a question requiring an examination of the characteristics of mystical experience. You will need to focus for this and apply the skills that you have developed so far:

> **1. Begin with a list of indicative content. Perhaps discuss this as a group. It does not need to be in any order.**

> **2. Develop the list using examples.**

> **3. Now consider in which order you would like to explain the information.**

> **4. Then write out your plan, under timed conditions, remembering the principles of explaining with evidence and/ or examples.**

Use this technique as revision for each of the topic areas that you have studied. The basic technique of planning answers helps even when time is short and you cannot complete every essay.

Key skills

Knowledge involves:

Selection of a range of (thorough) accurate and relevant information that is directly related to the specific demands of the question.

This means you choose the correct information relevant to the question set NOT the topic area. You will have to think and focus on selecting key information and NOT writing everything you know about the topic area.

Understanding involves:

Explanation that is extensive, demonstrating depth and/or breadth with excellent use of evidence and examples including (where appropriate) thorough and accurate supporting use of sacred texts, sources of wisdom and specialist language.

This means that you demonstrate that you understand something by being able to illustrate and expand your points through examples/supporting evidence in a personal way and NOT repeat chunks from a text book (known as rote learning).

Further application of skills:

Go through the topic areas in this section and create some bullet lists of key points from key areas. For each one, provide further elaboration and explanation through the use of evidence and examples.

Specification content

The adequacy of *James'* four
characteristics in defining
mystical experience.

AO2 Activity *Possible lines of argument*

Listed below are some conclusions
that could be drawn from the AO2
reasoning in the accompanying text:

1. James' four characteristics are
   adequate for defining mystical
   experience.

2. James' four characteristics in
   defining mystical experience are
   just one of many different ways of
   studying mystical experience.

3. James' four characteristics are
   more than adequate in defining
   mystical experience because they
   are the standard set in the study of
   mystical experiences.

4. James' four characteristics in
   defining mystical experience
   have been better developed and
   expressed by others.

5. James' four characteristics in
   defining mystical experience are
   adequate but not definitive.

Consider each of the conclusions
drawn above and collect evidence and
examples to support each argument
from the AO1 and AO2 material
studied in this section. Select one
conclusion that you think is most
convincing and explain why it is so.
Now contrast this with the weakest
conclusion in the list, justifying
your argument with clear reasoning
and evidence.

Issues for analysis and evaluation

The adequacy of *James'* four characteristics in defining mystical experience

William James' characteristics of mystical experiences have been the standard for
classification of the features of a mystical experience now for many years. Many
scholars have used, debated, accepted, challenged or developed them. The issue
really is can James' identified features be seen to be adequate in the light of the
work of other scholars?

James, as we know, identified four features of mysticism. The first feature is
ineffability. This means that no adequate account of the experience can be given in
words. It defies expression. Phrases such as 'the dissolution of the personal ego' are
empty to those who have not experienced such things. A second feature is its noetic
quality, that is, apparent insight into the depths of truths unobtainable by the
intellect alone. They have a force of certainty and reality. Mystical experiences are
also transient, which means that the states cannot be maintained for long periods
of time. Though the states are remembered, they are imperfectly recalled. Usually
they leave the recipient with a profound sense of the importance of the experience.
Finally, mystical experiences have the feature of passivity whereby there is a sense
of feeling that one is taken over by a superior power.

These all appear to be perfectly sound but whether or not they are adequate
depends upon whether any other scholarly observations have added, superseded
or challenged them. If we compare Otto's numinous classification of religious
experience as the mystical element we can see there is nothing new really added
to James' characteristics of a mystical experience. Otto identified a number of
elements such as awefulness (a sort of profound unease), overpoweringness
(inspires a feeling of humility), energy or urgency (compelling), wholly other
(totally outside normal experience) and fascination (causes the subject of the
experience to be caught up in it). Most of these are really elaborations upon, or
alternative definitions for, James' four features.

In a way the same can be said of the philosopher F.C Happold who identified
another three characteristics of the mystical experience: consciousness of the
oneness of everything; a sense of timelessness; and, the idea that the ego is
not the real 'I' but that there is something that lies behind the usual experience
of self. These appear to have similarities with both numinous and James' four
characteristics.

However, if we look at the work of the Italian medieval theologian and philosopher
St Bonaventure, we can see a different perspective on mystical experiences which
really focuses on the process of mysticism rather than an analysis of its common
features. Bonaventure identified three stages of a mystic experience: the purgative
stage when the mystic is purified and prepared for the experience through
meditation; the illuminative stage when the mystic is affected both in his intellect
and his feelings – illuminated both cognitively and emotionally; and, the unitive
stage when the mystic gains a continuing union with God.

In conclusion, it appears that James' four characteristics in defining mystical
experience are adequate enough as they have stood the test of time. Nonetheless,
this does not means that they are definitive and, as we have seen, there are other
more elaborate articulations of a mystical experience. In addition, it is evident
from the work of Bonaventure that just identifying features is only one aspect of
studying mystical experiences and there are other perspectives, such as the process
of a mystical experience, that are equally worthy of analysis and evaluation.

The adequacy of *Otto's* definition of 'numinous'

Rudolph Otto, a Protestant theologian, in his book *The Idea of the Holy*, tried to identify and describe what made a religious experience uniquely religious, as opposed to just an ordinary experience. The main issue here is not just Otto's definition but really the basis of that definition and the implications that it brings. Rudolph Otto said of the numinous experience 'there is no religion in which it does not live as the innermost core and without it no religion would be worthy of the name'. In other words, the claim of the numinous is that it is the one *essential* and valid religious experience as opposed to just an experience.

Central to this investigation, however, was the underlying assumption and conviction that a personal encounter with God is for every religious believer. Again, Otto was convinced that everyone could have a personal encounter with the spiritual or the divine and that it does not necessarily have to involve overt dramatic sensory or dream experiences Otto's numinous was a very individual and personal experience.

Despite this, Otto also held that its dramatic nature lay in what the religious experience invoked within the individual, namely, that the mysterium tremendum also prompted the fascinans, that is, an intense fascination with the experience itself. This then provided a platform from which a religious believer interprets the world around them.

The problems with this account of the numinous is that it has very little to say about the nature of God or the specific details about a specific religious belief. It provides no instruction or edification other than a sense of awareness of the 'other'. Indeed, Otto himself held that God cannot be known through the senses nor through the process of rational thought; God was 'wholly other'.

Other objections include the fact that it is too vague as to wonder how any theological ideas could follow after the experience due to the fascinans as Otto held. In this sense it appears limiting, especially as there are well-documented types of experience that are entirely different to the numinous.

Another criticism has been to suggest Otto reduces the concept of religious experience to a simple 'feeling' when there is clearly much more to religious experiences than that.

But the most powerful critique of Otto's numinous really involves that which he set out to demonstrate – that every individual can experience the divine. The real question is, however, due to such a general and diluted description of the religious experience as the numinous, how do we then know that it is God that is the object of this experience?

In conclusion, it would seem that Otto's numinous is adequate in describing what some, if not all, religious experiences may 'feel like', but beyond that it has clear limitations as the criticisms above would attest. It really tells us nothing more. However, it may be possible to use the definition of numinous in conjunction with other religious experiences as a basis for study and this, it is evident, is as far as its adequacy may extend.

Specification content

The adequacy of *Otto's* definition of 'numinous'.

AO2 Activity *Possible lines of argument*

Listed below are some conclusions that could be drawn from the AO2 reasoning in the accompanying text:

1. Otto's numinous definition is adequate in describing all religious experiences.

2. Otto's numinous definition is adequate in describing some religious experiences.

3. Otto's numinous definition is inadequate because it is far too vague.

4. Otto's numinous definition is inadequate because it imparts nothing of significance regarding the truths behind such an experience.

5. The adequacy of Otto's numinous definition is confined to the individual and nothing more.

Consider each of the conclusions drawn above and collect evidence and examples to support each argument from the AO1 and AO2 material studied in this section. Select one conclusion that you think is most convincing and explain why it is so. Now contrast this with the weakest conclusion in the list, justifying your argument with clear reasoning and evidence.

Key skills

Analysis involves identifying issues raised by the materials in the AO1, together with those identified in the AO2 section, and presents sustained and clear views, either of scholars or from a personal perspective ready for evaluation.

This means that it picks out key things to debate and the lines of argument presented by others or a personal point of view.

Evaluation involves considering the various implications of the issues raised based upon the evidence gleaned from analysis and provides an extensive detailed argument with a clear conclusion.

This means that the answer weighs up the various and different lines of argument analysed through individual commentary and response and arrives at a conclusion through a clear process of reasoning.

AO2 Developing skills

It is now time to reflect upon the information that has been covered so far. It is also important to consider how what you have learned can be focused and used for examination-style answers by practising the skills associated with AO2.

Assessment objective 2 (AO2) involves 'analysis' and 'evaluation'. The terms may be obvious but it is crucial to be familiar with how certain skills demonstrate these terms, and also, how the performance of these skills are measured (see generic band descriptors Band 5 for AS AO2).

Obviously an answer is placed within an appropriate band descriptor depending upon how well the answer performs, ranging from excellent, good, satisfactory, basic/limited to very limited.

You are now nearing the end of this section of the course. From now on the task will have only instructions with no examples; however, using the skills you have developed in completing the earlier tasks, you should be able to apply what you have learned to do and complete this successfully.

▶ **Your new task is this:** you will have to write a response under timed conditions to a question requiring an evaluation of whether Otto's definition of the numinous is an adequate description of religious experience. You will need to focus for this and apply the skills that you have developed so far:

> 1. **Begin with a list of indicative content. Perhaps discuss this as a group. It does not need to be in any order. Remember, this is evaluation, so you need different lines of argument. The easiest way is to use the 'support' and 'against' headings.**

> 2. **Develop the list using examples.**

> 3. **Now consider in which order you would like to explain the information.**

> 4. **Then write out your plan, under timed conditions, remembering to apply the principles of evaluation by making sure that you: identify issues clearly; present accurate views of others making sure that you comment on the views presented; reach an overall personal judgement.**

Use this technique as revision for each of the topic areas that you have studied. The basic technique of planning answers helps even when time is short and you cannot complete every essay.

C: Challenges to the objectivity and authenticity of religious experience

This section covers AO1 content and skills

Challenges to the objectivity and authenticity of religious experience: with reference to Caroline Franks Davis

Caroline Franks Davis in her 1989 work *The Evidential Force of Religious Experience*, listed three distinct forms of challenge to the validity of claims of religious (mystical) experiences.

Description-related challenges

When any event is described that claims itself to be an experience of 'God' or 'The Divine' then a claim is being made for which there is no proof. This description is therefore not valid. Furthermore the claim is inconsistent or contradictory with normal everyday experience and, for this reason, should be rejected. It is not a claim that is in any sense valid, merely a misunderstanding of the experience on the part of the recipient.

Subject-related challenges

In this challenge, the recipient (subject) of the religious experience is put under suspicion. It may be claimed that they are unreliable as a source, they may be considered to be suffering from a mental illness or to have been suffering delusions brought about by some sort of substance misuse. In such cases they are not in a position to properly understand what they have experienced and, as such, must have their claims dismissed.

Object-related challenges

The final type of challenge focuses on the alleged object of the experience. The challenge is that the likelihood of having experienced something such as the recipient claims is so unlikely as to be entirely untrue. The suggestion of God (the object) having been experienced is no more likely than a claim of having seen an 8ft green alien or a flying antelope. As we are unlikely to believe anyone that claimed experience of the latter two examples, why then should we believe the claim of someone who was said to have experienced God?

AO1 Activity

With a group of three, learn a specific category of challenge from Franks Davis. Once this has been done, you should research further information on your challenge and then share your findings with the others in the group. In this way you will develop your understanding of the material and be able to demonstrate 'thorough, accurate and relevant knowledge and understanding of religion and belief' (Level 5 AO1 response) in your written answers.

The very nature of mystical experiences (whatever their type and whoever undergoes them), seems to belong to a bygone era. Reading accounts of mystical experiences in ancient religious texts seems perfectly natural as does considering the experiences of the famous mystics from the traditions of the various world religions. However, when faced with such claims in an age seemingly dominated by empiricism, science, rationality and evidential proofs, scepticism tends to come into play and doubt as to their occurrences, or at least, to the authenticity of such experiences, seems to be the automatic response.

Specification content

Challenges to the objectivity and authenticity of religious experience: with reference to Caroline Franks Davis (description-related; subject-related and object-related challenges). Claims of religious experience rejected on grounds of misunderstanding; claims delusional – possibly related to substance misuse, fantastical claims contrary to everyday experiences.

Key quote

With arguments against the plausibility of religious doctrines and reductionist accounts of religious experiences now widely accepted, and with many people leading atheistic lives ... religious individuals can no longer assume that experiences judged to be 'genuine' by fellow believers are immune from further attack. They are challenged on all sides, by philosophers, psychologists, sociologists, anthropologists, members of other religious traditions and even by members of their own tradition with widely differing views. (Franks Davis)

quickfire

4.7 What are Caroline Franks Davis three categories of challenge?

Specification content

Challenges: individual experiences valid even if non-verifiable; claims could be genuine – integrity of individual; one-off experiences can still be valid even if never repeated.

The two explorers

Further debates about the challenges

In trying to establish the reliability of any mystical experience, some criteria for establishing truth must first be agreed upon. However, due to the very nature of mystical experiences, most philosophers agree that such criteria are virtually impossible to verify. This is due to the fact that, by their very nature, mystical experiences are subjective and not objective.

If something is objective and verifiable, it is something that relates to external facts that can be agreed upon by the observers – it is possible to prove by one or more of the five senses, it is something that can be described and multiple observers will come to the same conclusion about the same thing, e.g. the colour of the car is red.

If something is subjective then it tends to be based upon opinion, personal judgement, belief or assumption and is more difficult to verify. It is likely to be interpreted in different ways by multiple observers and these views may change according to time and context, e.g. this is the best car in the world to drive.

Due to the very fact that communicating mystical experiences depends entirely on the perception of the experience by the recipient – or in some cases the witnesses of the recipient – it is considered as a subjective experience. As scientific empiricism tends to reject subjective accounts out of hand, then this presents a serious challenge to the 'truth' of any mystical experience. However, equally, the experience remains valid for the individual, or group of individuals, even if by its very subjectivity, it is non-verifiable. This would also extend to the idea that the claim for the one-off experience can still be valid – a repetition of the event is not required for it to retain its validity.

The work of the Vienna Circle and the logical positivists did much to help clarify our understanding of how language is used to convey knowledge and ideas, as well as the conditions where that language could be considered either meaningful or meaningless. Any claim made by a religious believer about a mystical experience may seem to be an ordinary claim about their perception of the state of reality (whichever reality they may be referring to) but as their claim lacks any empirical evidence to support it, and as such experiences are neither analytic a priori nor synthetic a posteriori, they are considered by the logical positivists to be meaningless.

A further difficulty is posed by Anthony Flew's falsification principle, which stated that propositions could be made meaningful if there was some evidence that could count against them. However, Flew stated that as religious believers allow nothing to count against their beliefs, then all religious statements, including those of the mystic, were ultimately meaningless. He used John Wisdom's parable of the Gardener to support his point:

'Once upon a time two explorers came upon a clearing in the jungle. In the clearing were growing many flowers and many weeds. One explorer says, "Some gardener must tend this plot." The other disagrees, "There is no gardener." So they pitch their tents and set a watch. No gardener is ever seen. "But perhaps he is an invisible gardener." So they set up a barbed-wire fence. They electrify it. They patrol with bloodhounds. (For they remember how H. G. Well's The Invisible Man could be both smelt and touched though he could not be seen.) But no shrieks ever suggest that some intruder has received a shock. No movements of the wire ever betray an invisible climber. The bloodhounds never give cry. Yet still the Believer is not convinced. "But there is a gardener, invisible, intangible, insensible, to electric shocks, a gardener who has no scent and makes no sound, a gardener who comes secretly to look after the garden which he loves." At last the Sceptic despairs, "But what remains of your original assertion? Just how does what you call an invisible, intangible, eternally elusive gardener differ from an imaginary gardener or even from no gardener at all?"'

Flew's point was that for a religious believer, they would always offer a qualification as to why no evidence could be found to count against their own beliefs and, as religious experiences are essentially ones where there are no clear and agreed upon criteria which can be used to count against them, they too must, according to Flew's criteria, be considered meaningless.

Using alternative explanations, based on the objective worlds of science and nature, is nothing new in terms of critiquing events that fall into the religious and mystical sphere. When considering the possibility of miracles occurring, David Hume in *An Enquiry Concerning Human Understanding* (1748) stated that it was not impossible that miracles could occur, it was merely impossible to ever prove that one had in fact occurred. Transferring this naturalistic view to religious experiences, a similar problem is faced. Due to their highly individualistic nature (for the most part) religious experiences are not open to rational enquiry, and, thus, are treated with suspicion at best and derision at worst.

The scientific fields of sociology, psychology and anthropology have all made huge advances in understanding the human condition within the past century and, in doing so, have all examined the religious dimension of humankind's existence and sought to offer alternative theories as to what is actually being experienced.

For instance, studies by the anthropologist Ioan Lewis have shown a close and intelligible connection in pre-industrial societies between the incidence of religious ecstasy and the need of individuals and groups to legitimatise claims made upon the larger society. Sigmund Freud held the view that all religious experiences were nothing more than the result of the repression of sexual urges. Re-interpreting Teresa's vision of the angel piercing her soul in the light of Freudian imagery is very easy to do but has come under criticism itself for being too reductionist. Others have commented that the characteristics of religious experiences bear remarkable resemblances to the effects felt by those who use alcohol and drugs such as LSD, which can stimulate the brain into hallucinating and experiencing so-called alternative realities.

Despite these challenges, the British philosopher Richard Swinburne proposed the principle of credulity. Swinburne argues that what someone claims to perceive is probably the case unless there are special reasons for thinking the experience is false. He then listed four special reasons that might cast doubt on the validity of the event. The special reasons (principle of credulity) are:

- If the person was unreliable (e.g. drugged).
- If similar perceptions are shown to be false (e.g. drug induced by taking LSD).
- If there is strong evidence that the object of the experience was not present, did not exist (e.g. a mirage).
- If the event experienced can be accounted for in other ways as a reality and not just in your imagination.

If all lines of investigation above are exhausted then how do we explain a religious experience? Again, the heart of the argument is that religious experience concerns the reliability of our sense experiences. However, when someone tells us about their experience, rather than us having the experience ourselves, should we believe them?

Swinburne uses the principle of credulity to develop his principle of testimony. He argues that other people's testimony of religious experiences provides good reason to believe that their religious experience is valid and is part of his overall argument that God exists.

In other words, in the absence of special considerations, it is reasonable to believe that the experiences of others are probably as they report them to be. This is Swinburne's principle of testimony. Therefore, religious experiences are validated and serve as strong evidence for the existence of God, according to Swinburne. The integrity of the individual is maintained and according to this argument one-off experiences can still be valid even if never repeated.

Freud (1856–1939) dismissed religious belief as a form of neurosis

AO1 Activity

Produce a list of the key challenges to the objectivity and authenticity of religious experiences and provide an example for each challenge on your list, e.g. the challenge from Falsification – Wisdom's parable of the Gardener. This will help you develop a deeper understanding of the subject material and support your ability to develop skills in producing 'extensive depth and/or breadth' (Level 5 AO1 response) in your answers.

Key skills

Knowledge involves:

Selection of a range of (thorough) accurate and relevant information that is directly related to the specific demands of the question.

This means you choose the correct information relevant to the question set NOT the topic area. You will have to think and focus on selecting key information and NOT writing everything you know about the topic area.

Understanding involves:

Explanation that is extensive, demonstrating depth and/or breadth with excellent use of evidence and examples including (where appropriate) thorough and accurate supporting use of sacred texts, sources of wisdom and specialist language.

This means that you demonstrate that you understand something by being able to illustrate and expand your points through examples/supporting evidence in a personal way and NOT repeat chunks from a text book (known as rote learning).

Further application of skills:

Go through the topic areas in this section and create some bullet lists of key points from key areas. For each one, provide further elaboration and explanation through the use of evidence and examples.

AO1 Developing skills

It is now time to reflect upon the information that has been covered so far. It is also important to consider how what you have learned can be focused and used for examination-style answers by practising the skills associated with AO1.

Assessment objective 1 (AO1) involves demonstrating knowledge and understanding. The terms 'knowledge' and 'understanding' are obvious but it is crucial to be familiar with how certain skills demonstrate these terms, and also, how the performance of these skills is measured (see generic band descriptors Band 5 for AS AO1).

You are now nearing the end of this section of the course. From now on the task will have only instructions with no examples; however, using the skills you have developed in completing the earlier tasks, you should be able to apply what you have learned to do and complete this successfully.

▶ **Your new task is this:** you will have to write another response under timed conditions to a question requiring an examination of the challenges to the objectivity and authenticity of religious experience. You will need to do the same as your last AO1 Developing skills task but with some further development. This time there is a fifth point to help you improve the quality of your answers.

> 1. **Begin with a list of indicative content. Perhaps discuss this as a group. It does not need to be in any order.**

> 2. **Develop the list using examples.**

> 3. **Now consider in which order you would like to explain the information.**

> 4. **Then write out your plan, under timed conditions, remembering the principles of explaining with evidence and/ or examples.**

> 5. **Use the band descriptors to mark your own answer, considering carefully the descriptors. Then ask someone else to read your answer and see if they can help you improve it in any way.**

Use this technique as revision for each of the topic areas that you have studied. Swap and compare answers to improve your own.

Issues for analysis and evaluation

The extent to which the challenges to religious experience are valid

This section covers AO2
content and skills

Specification content

The extent to which the challenges to religious experience are valid.

The first challenge to religious experiences is that they are not really the same as sense experiences, even if they have sensory elements to them. However, it could be contended that just as we are known to each other by a kind of direct apprehension rather than through our physical body, so in the same way we may be able to experience God who is non–physical and so the challenge has its obvious limitations.

Another challenge is that a direct experience of God is impossible as suggested by the empiricist philosopher David Hume. How can that which is 'wholly other' be partly revealed? If there is something 'wholly other' we could not possibly have knowledge or experience of it. This claim of a direct experience of God does not really make sense for many people. The response of religious believers, however, could be that it may be possible for God to enter into time and space and it is also a reasonable argument to believe that God would seek to interact with creation.

It has been argued by the logical positivists that a religious experience cannot be verified. The nature of religious experiences are such that they have their own level or 'reality' or 'fantasy' that is quite separate to meaningful logical analysis. Pitted against this are that some religious experiences appear to be shared by many people and so cannot be fabricated or 'fantasy'. Indeed, there may be criteria external to the experience that would add weight to its validity, for example if the experience makes a noticeable difference to religious life of the person. Swinburne adds to this that the onus is on the sceptic to show the experience is delusive.

Although some experiences may be experienced by more than one person, there is still the issue of the lack of overall uniformity of religious experiences. They are so different and sometimes contradictory. Which one is valid and which one is true? However, God may reveal himself in terms of cultural beliefs that we will understand and interpret and the fact that there are different experiences recounted do not mean they are all in error. Maybe only one religion is correct so the other religious experiences are false, but those of that one religion are true?

Science has provided challenges to religious experiences; for example, in the field of physiology and neurology and the experiments by Persinger. Such challenges conclude that religious experiences once again have clear materialistic explanations. However, it could be argued that the neurological changes associated with religious experiences may mean such activity does in fact perceive a spiritual reality, rather than the explanation being that it is solely the brain that is causing those experiences. Stimulating the temporal lobes, such as in Persinger's Helmet, may not induce, that is, be the cause of, the religious experience but rather be the process that can facilitate it. It is clearly difficult to isolate what is the cause and what is the effect.

Finally, there are psychological explanations such as collective neurosis, the primal horde and the Oedipus Complex suggested by Freud and the arguments of Jung that provide a positive, but materialistic account of religious experiences. However, it should be indicated that such theories, especially on the part of Jung, were never intended to debate issues of authenticity or validity with regard to the truth claims of religious experiences. Instead they simply provide a suitable explanation for the process by which human beings encounter such experiences. Indeed, Jung's theory of archetypes can be more simply explained by the fact that all human beings share similar experiences.

In conclusion, key questions still remain despite the challenges. For example, if

Richard Dawkins, born 1941

Richard Dawkins believed that those who claimed to have undergone religious experiences were at best misguided. Taking part in the Persinger's Helmet experiment, Dawkins claimed to have felt nothing other than a mild tingling sensation.

there is a God, why doesn't he reveal himself to everyone, especially if he wants us to believe in him? Then again, although some have claimed religious experiences might be explained by natural causes, is it reasonable to think that all claimed religious experiences are wrong? Richard Dawkins himself tried out Persinger's Helmet and he claimed it did not produce any sensation of a religious experience. So what conclusion can be drawn? Does it weaken or strengthen the challenge to religious experience? Although challenges are clearly valid, the solutions are far from being confirmed.

AO2 Activity *Possible lines of argument*

Listed below are some conclusions that could be drawn from the AO2 reasoning in the accompanying text:

1. Challenges to religious experience are valid and can accurately account for them.
2. Challenges to religious experience are valid but have their limitations.
3. Challenges to religious experience are not valid because they have been adequately responded to.
4. Challenges to religious experience are valid but so too are possible counter-arguments.
5. Challenges to religious experience are valid but the answers and explanations of the phenomenon of religious experience are still uncertain.

Consider each of the conclusions drawn above and collect evidence and examples to support each argument from the AO1 and AO2 material studied in this section. Select one conclusion that you think is most convincing and explain why it is so. Now contrast this with the weakest conclusion in the list, justifying your argument with clear reasoning and evidence.

The persuasiveness of Franks Davis' different challenges

Franks Davis has put forward three distinct challenges to the authenticity of religious experiences. In order to assess their persuasiveness, we need to consider each challenge in turn.

The first challenge is the description-related challenge, which argues that when any event is described that claims itself to be an experience of 'God' or 'The Divine', then a claim is being made for which there is no proof. This invalidates the description because the claim is inconsistent or contradictory with normal everyday experience. A religious experience, therefore, is merely a misunderstanding of the experience on the part of the recipient.

Whilst this challenge seems reasonable, there is a major flaw in the reasoning. Aside from the issue of 'proof', which has its own problems in philosophy, the real problem with this challenge is with the limited understanding of 'experience'. It is clear that this is a very materialist-based assumption akin to the empiricism of Hume. Experience may not just be a matter of normal everyday experience. Indeed, what makes religious experience different is that it could be argued to be an experience of the 'abnormality' of a possible spiritual realm that filters into the normal.

The second challenge is to do with subject-related challenges. This challenge, suspects that the recipient (subject) of the religious experience is unreliable as a source, and that they may be considered to be suffering from a mental illness or to have been suffering delusions brought about by some sort of substance misuse. Impaired perceptions and understanding thus mean that the recipient must have their claims dismissed.

Again, this challenge seems quite logical. However, aside from the objections raised to scientific and psychological explanations, the work of Richard Swinburne in using his principles of credulity and testimony are a strong defence of those who claim to have had a religious experience. Swinburne proposed the principle of credulity, stating that it is reasonable to believe that the world is probably as we experience it to be unless there are special reasons for thinking the experience is false. In the light of some challenges to the objections raised, he argues that religious experiences can therefore be verified. If this is the case, then, Swinburne uses the principle of credulity as part of his argument to derive his principle of testimony, which then argues that other people's testimony of religious experiences provides good reason to believe that God exists because one seems to perceive is probably the case (principle of credulity). This is because many people, on the basis of apparent (perceptual rather than inferred) direct experiences of God, take it that God exists and in the the absence of special considerations, it is reasonable to believe that the experiences of others are probably as they report them (principle of testimony). Although Swinburne uses this as part of his overall argument for the existence of God, the points he make do challenge the persuasiveness of Franks Davis' subject-related challenges.

Finally, the object-related challenges centre on the likelihood of having experienced something such as the recipient claims being so unlikely as to be entirely untrue. However, it could be argued that the nature of the experience is very different from a hypothetical experience of a flying antelope and some would also suggest that it merely points to the possibility for something else 'existing' in a different way than we normally perceive, that is, in a spiritual sense.

In conclusion, although the challenges put forward by Franks Davis do appear persuasive, it is clear that if these challenges are themselves challenged, their persuasiveness is also questioned.

Richard Swinburne, born 1934

Richard Swinburne refuted the idea that religious experiences could be easily dismissed and with his principles of testimony and credulity, stated that people should be believed when they claimed to have had an experience that might be described as religious, unless there were strong grounds to doubt what they had said.

AO2 Activity *Possible lines of argument*

Listed below are some conclusions that could be drawn from the AO2 reasoning in the accompanying text:

1. Franks Davis' different challenges are persuasive in that they recount and highlight some of the central problems with religious experiences.

2. Franks Davis' different challenges are not persuasive at all as there are many responses that have been given to them.

3. Franks Davis' different challenges are really an amalgamation of general challenges to religious experiences that have already been well debated.

4. Franks Davis' different challenges are persuasive for those who already assume that there is nothing beyond the material real, that is, they are materialists.

5. Franks Davis' different challenges are not persuasive because they have a clear materialistic basis and allow no possibility of a religious experience in the first place.

Consider each of the conclusions drawn above and collect evidence and examples to support each argument from the AO1 and AO2 material studied in this section. Select one conclusion that you think is most convincing and explain why it is so. Now contrast this with the weakest conclusion in the list, justifying your argument with clear reasoning and evidence.

AO2 Developing skills

It is now time to reflect upon the information that has been covered so far. It is also important to consider how what you have learned can be focused and used for examination-style answers by practising the skills associated with AO2.

Assessment objective 2 (AO2) involves 'analysis' and 'evaluation'. The terms may be obvious but it is crucial to be familiar with how certain skills demonstrate these terms, and also, how the performance of these skills is measured (see generic band descriptors Band 5 for AS AO2).

Obviously an answer is placed within an appropriate band descriptor depending upon how well the answer performs, ranging from excellent, good, satisfactory, basic/limited to very limited.

Key skills

Analysis involves identifying issues raised by the materials in the AO1, together with those identified in the AO2 section, and presents sustained and clear views, either of scholars or from a personal perspective ready for evaluation.

This means that it picks out key things to debate and the lines of argument presented by others or a personal point of view.

Evaluation involves considering the various implications of the issues raised based upon the evidence gleaned from analysis and provides an extensive detailed argument with a clear conclusion.

This means that the answer weighs up the various and different lines of argument analysed through individual commentary and response and arrives at a conclusion through a clear process of reasoning.

You are now nearing the end of this section of the course. From now on the task will have only instructions with no examples; however, using the skills you have developed in completing the earlier tasks, you should be able to apply what you have learned to do and complete this successfully.

▶ **Your new task is this:** you will have to write another response under timed conditions to a question requiring an evaluation of the extent to which the challenges to religious experience are valid. You will need to do the same as your last AO2 Developing skills task but with some further development. This time there is a fifth point to help you improve the quality of your answers.

1. **Begin with a list of indicative content. Perhaps discuss this as a group. It does not need to be in any order. Remember, this is evaluation, so you need different lines of argument. The easiest way is to use the 'support' and 'against' headings.**

2. **Develop the list using examples.**

3. **Now consider in which order you would like to explain the information.**

4. **Then write out your plan, under timed conditions, remembering to apply the principles of evaluation by making sure that you: identify issues clearly; present accurate views of others making sure that you comment on the views presented; reach an overall personal judgement.**

5. **Use the band descriptors to mark your own answer, considering carefully the descriptors. Then ask someone else to read your answer and see if they can help you improve it in any way.**

Use this technique as revision for each of the topic areas that you have studied. Swap and compare answers to improve your own.

T1 Ethical thought

Specification content
Meta-ethical theory.

Key terms

Applied ethics: the debates that arise when ethical *issues* are considered

Ethics: from the Greek 'ethike' meaning habit or behaviour and closely related to the word ethos, it is a study of the framework of guiding principles that direct an action

Meta-ethics: the debates that arise when the *nature* of ethics is considered

Moral: a term used to describe ethical behaviour

Normative ethics: the debates that arise when ethical *theories* are considered

Key quotes

The unexamined life is not worth living. (Socrates)

Two things fill me with wonder: the starry sky above and the moral law within. (Kant)

Our duty can be defined as that action which will cause more good to exist in the universe than any possible alternative. (Moore)

A man without ethics is a wild beast loosed upon this world. (Camus)

quickfire

1.1 What does meta-ethics study? Give an example.

A: Divine Command theory

An introduction to ethics

The study of **ethics** examines the guiding principles that direct an action. Ethics as a discipline is a study of the various systems of **moral** values that exist today. Ethics analyses not only how these values direct a person's actions if they wish to be morally good, but it also identifies the obligations behind the purpose of doing right rather than wrong.

The framework of guiding principles that is identified through a study of ethics is called an ethical theory. For those involved, acting consistently within this framework is acting morally, or sometimes referred to as right behaviour. Sometimes a person, sometimes referred to as a 'moral agent' in ethics, may choose to act contrary to a given framework and so be said to be acting immorally or wrongly. In ethics, right and wrong generally have stronger meanings than just error or misjudgement. There is often an implied 'going against character' or failing to be the sort of person required in relation to set expectations – a standard of which the moral agent has fallen short. There is an indication that the moral agent has done something he or she is obliged *not* to do.

Meta-ethical theory

In the study of ethics there is a distinction made between meta-ethics and normative ethics. **Meta-ethics** is the study of the nature of ethical thinking, for example a consideration of why we act as we do, or, whether or not 'right' and 'wrong' are dependent upon self-interest, subjective view or objective standards. **Normative ethics** is the study of the content of, or the principles that underlie, a specific ethical theory. **Applied ethics** is the term used to describe the debates that arise when normative ethical theories are applied to issues that arise in practice in the real world.

Ethics, then, considers meaning behind terms such as 'moral' and 'right', studies proposed theories that outline what is considered as 'moral' and 'right' behaviour, and, considers how such theories work in practice.

This first Theme of your course will consider three meta-ethical questions:

Section A: Whether or not ethical behaviour is independent of a divine being?

Section B: Whether or not ethical behaviour is to do with virtues more than rules?

Section C: Whether or not ethical behaviour originates with self-interest?

Key terms used in categorising ethical theories

Philosophers have identified common links between the various ethical theories and have categorised them into groups. It is important to have an understanding of these terms as they will arise throughout the A Level course.

Absolutists believe that there exists a standard of right and wrong that is fully and totally binding on all human beings. Those who are religious may feel that this absolute standard proceeds from the mind and will of a supreme being. Those who are not religious may believe that the standard simply exists.

Relativists believe that there is no absolute right or wrong. They do not see morality as imposing a binding obligation on human beings to behave in a particular way. They see morality as the response of human communities to issues of how to behave in relation to each other. There are no absolute rules, but there are norms of behaviour that promote goodwill and happiness or some other desirable objective.

A relativist can say that she finds a certain course of action unjust or morally wrong, but it is difficult for her to conclude that someone else should feel that this action was wrong. To the absolutist, a wrong course of action is something that they are under a binding and absolute obligation *not* to do.

Whereas the absolutist would have to say: 'This is wrong for me and for you and for everyone', the relativist could say: 'This is wrong for me but may be right for you,' which is something the absolutist could never say.

There is some ambiguity in the terms absolutist and relativist in that they are not always mutually exclusive but can overlap; for example, relativist systems may have an absolutist element. Hence, moral relativists might agree on very basic human values, such as respect for property, even though they may interpret this very differently.

In ethics, a theory is described as **subjective** if its truth is dependent on the person's view. Mackie observes: 'What is often called moral subjectivism is the doctrine that, for example, "This action is right" means "I approve of this action", or more generally that moral judgements are equivalent to reports of the speaker's own feelings or attitudes.'

A theory is described as **objective** if its truth is independent of a person's view. This is sometimes referred to as moral realism and the idea is that moral values are like mathematical numbers. Julia Driver comments: 'Moral truth can have a basis similar to mathematical truth. I can't see $2 + 2 = 4$; I know it to be true nevertheless. When I see four apples grouped out there in the world, I know "There are four apples" is true, even though I don't see a big fat "4" flashing over them. Am I justified in believing in moral facts? If I am justified believing in numbers, this line of reasoning goes, then yes.'

It seems natural to link subjective with relativist, since both terms imply freedom of choice of the individual: nothing is fixed and immovable. However, there is also a sense in which subjective can be linked to absolutist. For example, you might conclude that no ethical theory can be absolutist since our values stem from our own feelings and choices. However, you may also think that some of those feelings and choices are universal to human beings, and so apply to everyone. This implies that it is not a contradiction to have an ethical theory that is subjectively grounded but holds to absolute values.

quickfire

1.2 What is a moral agent?

Key terms

Absolutist: an ethical system that believes there exists a standard of right and wrong that is fully and totally binding on all human beings

Objective: a theory that is independent of personal view

Relativist: an ethical system that believes there is no absolute right or wrong

Subjective: a theory that is dependent on a personal view

Key quote

At the descriptive level, certainly, you would expect different cultures to develop different sorts of ethics and obviously they have; that doesn't mean that you can't think of overarching ethical principles you would want people to follow in all kinds of places. (Singer)

Key terms

Consequentialism: an ethical theory based on considering consequences

Deontological: a theory that explores obligation or duty

Teleological: a theory concerned with the end purpose or goal of an action

Key quote

An ethical dilemma arises when two or more causes of conduct may be justifiable in any given set of circumstances, possibly resulting in diametrically opposed outcomes. **(Mason and Laurie)**

An ethical dilemma often raises questions about the consequences of various actions that could be taken. Indeed, it is often the case that thinking about the goal of a particular action persuades us whether or not to take that action. Such an approach that focuses on the consequences is called a **teleological** ethical theory.

Teleological comes from the Greek, meaning end or purpose. In such theories, the rightness or wrongness of an action is identified by the consequences it produces. If the theory held that the action that best resulted in 'the good of the majority' was the criterion for judging right action, then the right action would be the one that produces the most good for the majority. It is the result and not the action, which directs the right course of behaviour. This approach is also called **consequentialism**, since it claims that the value of the consequences of our actions is decisive for their moral status as right or wrong.

Deontological comes from the Greek, meaning obligation or duty. In such theories there is a relationship between duty and the morality of human actions. Therefore, deontological ethical theories are concerned with the acts themselves, irrespective of any consequences of those acts. For instance, a deontologist might argue that murder was wrong whatever the situation or consequence, and therefore euthanasia was morally wrong.

The study of applied ethics is complex and difficult because it is the point at which principles are tested in the real world. Applied ethics often involves an ethical dilemma, that is, the potential conflicting nature of set principles. This sometimes challenges a person to re-examine and re-interpret these principles.

AO1 Activity

Create some study cards with some key terms you have learned about in this section.

Study tip

It is important when writing an answer in ethics to use the correct terminology with reference to ethical theories.

Specification content

God as the origin and regulator of morality; right or wrong as objective truths based on God's will/command, moral goodness is achieved by complying with Divine Command; Divine Command a requirement of God's omnipotence; Divine Command as an objective meta-physical foundation for morality.

Divine Command theory: God as the origin and regulator of morality

Plato wrote a dialogue entitled *Euthyphro*, in which a character named Euthyphro takes his father to court, charging him with murder. His father failed in care and attention and allowed a worker to die. Socrates, a philosopher, is at the court awaiting his own trial, and so he engages Euthyphro in dialogue about moral goodness. In the dialogue Socrates poses the question that has become known as the Euthyphro dilemma:

Socrates 469–399 BCE

Euthyphro: 'Well, I should certainly say that what's holy is whatever all the Gods approve of, and that its opposite, what all the Gods disapprove of, is unholy...'

Socrates: 'We'll soon be in a better position to judge, my good chap. Consider the following point: is the holy approved by the Gods because it's holy, or is it holy because it's approved?' (Plato)

In other words, Socrates is asking whether God

110

commands things because they are good in themselves, or are things good because God commands and approves them? Put simply, does good exist independently, and separate from approval, or does good exist as a consequence of it being approved?

This is the first meta-ethical question for consideration.

Divine Command theory, also known as theological voluntarism, proposes that God has established eternal, objective principles of morality. As Frankena puts it, 'the standard of right and wrong is the will or law of God'.

Followers of the Divine Command accept that there is an objective standard for ethics but that the standard is not external to God, but rather originates with God. In simple terms, that which God says is good becomes good. Right or wrong as objective truths are based on God's will and command. This raises a problem.

If God were to command things because they are good, then this implies that there is a standard of goodness independent of God. This would mean, then, that God is no longer the creator of everything. There would be a standard of values outside of his control and creativity. However, Divine Command proposes that the ethical template for what is good originates with God and cannot be external from God. The idea of a Divine Command theory is a requirement of God's omnipotence.

JAT Robinson summarises this position well in his book *Honest to God*: 'They are the commandments which God gives, the laws which he lays down ... They come down direct from Heaven, and are eternally valid for human conduct ... Certain things are always "wrong" and "nothing can make them right", and certain things are always "sins", whether or not they are judged by differing human societies to be "crimes".'

Robert Adams' 'Modified Divine Command theory'

The problems that this view raises are numerous, but there is another problem that relates to the Euthyphro dilemma, namely, that if something is good because God wills it is good, then can God will to be good that which we may consider evil? As Frankena puts it: 'If God were to order the exact opposite of what we generally take him to have ordered or of what we take to be right, then, by the hypothesis in question, this would be what we ought to do.' This is often referred to as the arbitrariness problem.

Certainly, some have argued that this is exactly in keeping with depictions of God and his followers in the Bible, as Baggini points out: 'Christian texts seem to provide evidence that this is precisely what their God has done'. This is justified further in the writings of William of Ockham who argues that God can perform acts that according to common law are evil, but without involving any evil. This even extends to those who are on earth and subject to 'Divine Command'.

Key quotes

I reply that hatred, theft, adultery, and the like may involve evil according to the common law, in so far as they are done by someone who is obligated by a Divine Command to perform the opposite act. As far as everything absolute in these actions is concerned, however, God can perform them without involving any evil. And they can even be performed meritoriously by someone on earth if they should fall under a Divine Command, just as now the opposite of these, in fact, fall under a Divine Command. (**William of Ockham**)

There are, however, certain exceptions to the law against killing, made by the authority of God himself. There are some whose killing God orders, either by law, or by an express command to a particular person at a particular time. (**Augustine**)

Robert Adams born 1937

quickpire

1.3 What is an absolutist ethical theory?

Key quote

Any action is ethically wrong
if and only if it is contrary to
the commands of a loving God.
(Adams)

Key term

Omnibenevolence: God's all-loving
nature

quickpire

1.4 What is another term for
consequentialism?

quickpire

1.5 Which characteristic of God is most
important in Divine Command theory?

Specification content

Challenges: the Euthyphro dilemma
(inspired by Plato); arbitrariness
problem (Divine Command
theory renders morality as purely
arbitrary); pluralism objection
(different religions claim different
Divine Commands).

Key quote

The idea that God could just decree
that all that we thought evil was in
fact good and vice versa seems to
make a mockery of the seriousness
of ethics. It makes right and wrong
ultimately arbitrary. (Baggini)

The major issue of Divine Command theory – leading to any ethical system it proposes being arbitrary, that is, dependent on the whim of a creator God – has led to a development and refinement in Divine Command theory, proposed by Robert Adams.

Adams argued that because morality is grounded in the character of God, who is perfectly good, then God's commands are rooted in God's character. Since a characteristic of God is his **omnibenevolence**, then whatever God commands will inevitably reflect this, God's character. That is not the same thing as saying that God and good are identical. God is not the very same thing as goodness. Goodness is an essential characteristic of God, it is grounded in the character of God. Morality, therefore, reflects at all times the omnibenevolent character of God.

This means, then, that morality cannot be arbitrary because it is grounded in the unchanging omnibenevolent nature of God. In the same way God cannot therefore be subject to a moral law that exists external to him either.

Key quote

On the Modified Divine Command theory, the moral law is a feature of God's nature. Given that the moral law exists internal to God, in this sense, God is not subject to an external moral law, but rather *is* that moral law. God therefore retains his supreme moral and metaphysical status. Morality, for the modified Divine Command theorist, is ultimately grounded in the perfect nature of God. (Austin)

Challenges to Divine Command theory

The obvious challenge from the Euthyphro dilemma is traditionally seen to have two aspects to it. Firstly, is morality arbitrary if it is down to the command of a divine being? Secondly, if God decides upon what is good then does this suggest God does this because they are right and good independent of God? In other words, traditional Divine Command theory may be suggesting that morality is indeed a matter external to God.

Robert Adams, in his Modified Divine Command theory, has addressed this matter in pointing out that both the arbitrariness and external objectivity issues are redundant when one considers Divine Command as an expression of God's omnibenevolence. However, not all are convinced. For some philosophers this just extends the problem and does not solve it. For example, Julian Baggini perceptively observes, 'This doesn't seem to work, however, because the dilemma can just be restated: is God's nature good because it is good or good because it is God's'! The debate about Robert Adams' Modified Divine Command theory continues.

Key quote

For regressive avoidance, morality must not have ultimate grounds in obedience to independent commanders: God must possess moral characteristics in want of no further authority ... why is morality seen as needing an external lawgiver when, finally, a moral rabbit is pulled from a divine hat, a rabbit in no need of an external anything? (Cave)

There are also clear problems with Divine Command theory when it comes to consider the relationship between religion and morality as there are very different ethical systems and principles that can be found within the religions of the world. The questions this raises include: 'which system is right?' and, 'are these systems compatible?'. It is very clear that although there may be some common moral ideas identified between religions, there are also differences.

In addition, not only do we have different systems but we also have the problem of identifying a specific religious ethic within a religion and then the variety of interpretations this may be given. For example, consider the conflicting interpretations of Shari'a found in the different law schools within Islam, or, the variety of understandings and applications of the precepts within Buddhism, or, the different views on Old Testament law within Christianity. Many conflicts arise between some very respected and virtuous principles: for example, 'Thou shalt not kill' is directly challenged by the principle of agape when it comes to issues of abortion and euthanasia. Can Gandhi's understanding and use of ahimsa as an absolute principle work in a time of war?

In addition, there are the more controversial aspects of conflict when a small minority group within a religion may propose specific interpretations of ethical principles based upon a particular reading of religious texts as Divine Command that other groups within that same religion may disagree with. There are a number of examples ranging from women's' rights to matters of punishment for homosexuality.

For example, some Christians still condemn homosexuality, whether in terms of sexuality or the acts involved. They often refer to Biblical texts from both the Old and New Testaments. However, there is a problem when it comes to Leviticus 20:13, which states 'If a man has sexual relations with a man as one does with a woman, both of them have done what is detestable. They are to be put to death; their blood will be on their own heads.' This raises several problems for Divine Command theorists.

If God commands this then the full letter of the law is to be applied and homosexual men should receive the death penalty. But this is contrary to 21st-century law. Also, how does the Bible then address homosexual women? Although Romans 1:26–28 recognises female homosexuality, it does not prescribe the death penalty for them as it does for men in Leviticus 20:13. In addition, what about wider teachings of tolerance and forgiveness taught by Jesus? Do such wider teachings supersede this text? If so, does that mean the Divine Command can be relative to a particular historical and social context? If not, then Divine Command must advocate slavery as acceptable as it is not condemned in the Bible along with many other views that are seen as unacceptable today. The main challenge, then, to Divine Command is that it has no flexibility to adapt to the changing views about morality that are accepted by most people today.

AO1 Activity

Write down a conversation that Socrates would have with Robert Adams about the nature of morality. Included reference to the Euthyphro dilemma, the nature of good, the origins of good, and God's nature.

Key quote

If there are reasons why God deems an action to be 'right' or 'wrong', then it is really those reasons that provide the account of 'right' and 'wrong' and not God's will. (Driver)

quickfire

1.6 Explain one problem associated with Divine Command theory.

Study tip

When writing an answer on ethics always try to back up the point you are making with clear examples or reference to evidence, or quotes, drawn from the works of scholars.

Key skills

Knowledge involves:

Selection of a range of (thorough) accurate and relevant information that is directly related to the specific demands of the question.

This means you choose the correct information relevant to the question set NOT the topic area. You will have to think and focus on selecting key information and NOT writing everything you know about the topic area.

Understanding involves:

Explanation that is extensive, demonstrating depth and/or breadth with excellent use of evidence and examples including (where appropriate) thorough and accurate supporting use of sacred texts, sources of wisdom and specialist language.

This means that you demonstrate that you understand something by being able to illustrate and expand your points through examples/supporting evidence in a personal way and NOT repeat chunks from a text book (known as rote learning).

Further application of skills:

Go through the topic areas in this section and create some bullet lists of key points from key areas. For each one, provide further elaboration and explanation through the use of evidence and examples.

AO1 Developing skills

It is now time to reflect upon the information that has been covered so far. It is also important to consider how what you have learned can be focused and used for examination-style answers by practising the skills associated with AO1.

Assessment objective 1 (AO1) involves demonstrating knowledge and understanding. The terms 'knowledge' and 'understanding' are obvious but it is crucial to be familiar with how certain skills demonstrate these terms, and also, how the performance of these skills is measured (see generic band descriptors Band 5 for AS AO1).

Obviously, an answer is placed within an appropriate band descriptor depending upon how well the answer performs, ranging from excellent, good, satisfactory, basic/limited to very limited.

For starters, try using the framework / writing frame provided to help you in practising these skills to answer the question below.

As the units in each section of the book develop, the amount of support will be reduced gradually in order to encourage your independence and the perfecting of your AO1 skills.

EXAM PRACTICE: A WRITING FRAME

A focus on examining the different versions of Divine Command theory.

Divine Command theory proposes that …

This means that it is objective because …

The theory suggest that morality is not external to God because …

The problems with the first form of Divine Command theory …

Robert Adams developed …

Adams' theory has the advantage of …

Not all philosophers are convinced by Adams because …

In conclusion, Divine Command theory …

Issues for analysis and evaluation

Whether morality is what God commands

This section covers AO2 content and skills

Specification content

Whether morality is what God commands.

The issue here is whether or not we can accept the views put forward by Divine Command theory that morality originates with God. Divine Command theory holds that morality originates with the will of God but, as we have seen, there has been an ancient challenge from Socrates who asks Euthyphro whether God commands things because they are good in themselves, or are things good because God commands and approves them? This brings with it two problems: firstly, the objection that morality is arbitrary; and, secondly, even if God commands what is good, it could be because they are already good and independent of God.

On the one hand, we have seen how Robert Adams defends the Divine Command theory in his modified version by pointing out that because morality is grounded in God it cannot be arbitrary because it depends upon God's omnibenevolent character and so whatever God commands is a reflection of this. In addition, if morality is grounded in the character of God then it cannot be external.

As we have seen, Julian Baggini rejects Adam's response because it just extends the problem and he states, 'This doesn't seem to work, however, because the dilemma can just be restated: is God's nature good because it is good or good because it is God's?'

There are clear strengths to Divine Command theory. It is consistent with religious belief and takes all responsibility away from human beings to make crucial decisions. Its template becomes a secure and consistent guide for life.

However, there are clear weaknesses. First of all, there are inconsistencies. Indeed, some philosophers have argued that Divine Command theory does confirm morality as arbitrary if one looks at the Old Testament and God's interventions. Both Augustine and William of Ockham have confirmed that God can will anything in relation to morality. But this then raises the question as to God's omnibenevolence.

Again, another line of criticism in accepting that Divine Command theory is a suitable explanation for the origins of morality is that there are too many inconsistencies both between, and within, religions to accept that morality originates with God. For instance, take the issues of abortion and euthanasia and the many different responses.

Finally, there are other explanations that some philosophers see as more suitable as an explanation for the origin of morality that have more naturalistic or rational justifications, for example virtue theory.

In conclusion, it appears to be clear that it is religious belief that dictates the answer for many; however, there still remains the issue of how, with God as the originator of morality, do religious thinkers justify the challenges brought against God's omnibenevolent nature?

This is particularly problematic when we consider such matters as homosexuality and slavery, and the questions and inconsistencies that are raised. How is a verse like Leviticus 20:13 which states 'If a man has sexual relations with a man as one does with a woman, both of them have done what is detestable. They are to be put to death; their blood will be on their own heads.' compatible with an omnibenevolent God?

AO2 Activity *Possible lines of argument*

Listed below are some conclusions that could be drawn from the AO2 reasoning in the accompanying text:

1. Divine Command theory is acceptable as an explanation for the origin of morality.

2. Modified Divine Command theory solves any problems associated with the idea that morality is what God commands.

3. The Euthyphro dilemma is too problematic for any theory suggesting morality originates with God.

4. There are too many inconsistencies both between, and within, religions to accept that morality originates with God.

5. There are better meta-ethical explanations for the origins of morality other than with God.

Consider each of the conclusions drawn above and collect evidence and examples to support each argument from the AO1 and AO2 material studied in this section. Select one conclusion that you think is most convincing and explain why it is so. Now contrast this with the weakest conclusion in the list, justifying your argument with clear reasoning and evidence.

Whether Divine Command theory is superior to virtue theory or ethical egoism

There are clearly several good reasons why Divine Command theory may be argued as superior to other explanations for the origins of morality.

First of all it is consistent in that it is absolutist and universal. The main principles of morality are clearly set out in religious texts. It is also helpful for many because it takes away responsibility from human beings and guides them throughout their lives in moral concerns. Divine Command theory, in its essence, has also stood the test of time and whilst there are some minor concerns and inconsistencies, there is an overall core belief about the will of God in relation to morality within and between religious traditions.

There are, however, problems that one could suggest make it inferior to other theories about the origins of ethics. Firstly, it is very inflexible in nature compared to the other two theories when it is applied as a theory to ethics. There is also the consideration that it is less virtuous overall, and even Christianity through the teachings of Jesus appears to promote the development of virtue over the idea that there is a fixed set standard of moral codes to adhere to. Virtue theory has this strength over Divine Command theory.

Divine Command theory does not account for differences that arise, nor does it cope well with modern-day problems that are not specifically referenced in religious texts. Here emerge possible accusations of potential intolerance towards alternative ways of dealing with problems, for example, with a fixed and unalterable view of 'you shall not kill' when faced with issues such as embryology, abortion and euthanasia. Both virtue theory and ethical egoism allow for differences, and, in the case of ethical egoism, would encourage differences and promote tolerance for the actions of individuals in private matters.

Finally, Divine Command theory does not allow individual growth of a person, unlike the other two theories of ethics. This is because Divine Command theory does not address the issues of intentions and virtues when it comes to ethical decisions. It does not allow a person to reflect upon the reasoning behind the actions, nor does it allow a person to take responsibility for their decision making. There appears to be a simplistic and blind following of rules with Divine Command theory without any insight into their nature and purpose, and ultimately, the validity of such rules.

In conclusion, it could be argued that superiority is clearly a matter of perspective in relation to the purpose of morality. For example, as we have seen from the above, for the religious believer that yearns for consistency, simplicity and certainty, Divine Command theory may be a more superior theory to adopt. For a more individualistic, flexible and personal approach to morality in the modern world there are those people, both religious and non-religious, that may prefer the focus of developing virtuous behaviour as an alternative. On a more individual level there are those who may feel that morality is a matter of personal preference and engagement with moral issues in the pursuit of the self-interest advocated by ethical egoism may be the superior option.

AO2 Activity Possible lines of argument

Listed below are some conclusions that could be drawn from the AO2 reasoning in the accompanying text:

1. Divine Command theory is superior to other theories.

2. Virtue theory is more superior because it promotes responsibility.

3. Ethical egoism is more suitable and flexible an explanation for today and therefore more superior to either virtue theory or Divine Command theory.

4. It is not important which theory is a superior theory, but rather which is more practical for society today.

5. There is no single theory that is superior to another as they all have problems.

Consider each of the conclusions drawn above and collect evidence and examples to support each argument from the AO1 and AO2 material studied in this section. Select one conclusion that you think is most convincing and explain why it is so. Now contrast this with the weakest conclusion in the list, justifying your argument with clear reasoning and evidence.

AO2 Developing skills

It is now time to reflect upon the information that has been covered so far. It is also important to consider how what you have learned can be focused and used for examination-style answers by practising the skills associated with AO2.

Assessment objective 2 (AO2) involves 'analysis' and 'evaluation'. The terms may be obvious but it is crucial to be familiar with how certain skills demonstrate these terms, and also, how the performance of these skills is measured (see generic band descriptors Band 5 for AS AO2).

Obviously, an answer is placed within an appropriate band descriptor depending upon how well the answer performs, ranging from excellent, good, satisfactory, basic/limited to very limited.

For starters, try using the framework / writing frame provided to help you in practising these skills to answer the question below.

As the units in each section of the book develop, the amount of support will be reduced gradually in order to encourage your independence and the perfecting of your AO2 skills.

Have a go at answering this question by using the writing frame below.

Key skills

Analysis involves identifying issues raised by the materials in the AO1, together with those identified in the AO2 section, and presents sustained and clear views, either of scholars or from a personal perspective ready for evaluation.

This means that it picks out key things to debate and the lines of argument presented by others or a personal point of view.

Evaluation involves considering the various implications of the issues raised based upon the evidence gleaned from analysis and provides an extensive detailed argument with a clear conclusion.

This means that the answer weighs up the various and different lines of argument analysed through individual commentary and response and arrives at a conclusion through a clear process of reasoning.

EXAM PRACTICE: A WRITING FRAME

A focus on evaluating whether morality originates with what God commands.

The issues to discuss here relate to …

On the one hand it could be argued that morality originates with God because …

The advantage of the Divine Command theory is …

On the other hand, there are problems with Divine Command theory as outlined by Euthyphro …

Although Robert Adams has addressed some of the initial problems associated with the Euthyphro dilemma …

There are also other problems associated with Divine Command theory such as …

In addition …

In conclusion, based upon this discussion, it can be seen that …

B: Virtue theory

An ethical system based on personal qualities

With virtue theory, or as it is often called, the theory of virtue ethics, we see a clear shift away from identifying ethical theory as being found in 'rules' or 'principles', to the quality, correct manner or disposition (**hexis**) of a human being. Right or wrong are therefore not a matter of rules but of personal character and qualities that an individual exhibits in his or her behaviour. Virtue theory is all about how an individual can develop the correct 'character' (**ethos**) so as to behave virtuously, and, accordingly, that way which is morally correct.

Specification content

Ethical system based on defining the personal qualities that make a person moral; the focus on a person's character rather than their specific actions.

Key quotes

People have recognisable reasons for doing what is right because doing what is right, it is argued, is likely to lead to their happiness. Morality and personal happiness are entwined. (**Cave**)

Aristotle tells us that the well-being or eudaimonia which is the good for man is an activity in accordance with virtue … one can do or show too little or too much of something, one can go too far or not far enough; what constitutes the right amount, the virtuous choice, is determined as the man of practical wisdom would determine it; and he is the man who is good at choosing the means to the end of eudaimonia. (**Mackie**)

Key terms

Arete: a Greek word meaning virtue

Ethos: a Greek word used by Aristotle for character of a person

Eudaimonia: a Greek word used by Aristotle to define the end purpose of human life to be happiness, flourishing or fulfilment

Hexis: a Greek word used by Aristotle for a person's manner of behaviour

Aristotle's moral virtues

The Greek word **eudaimonia** is key to understanding virtue theory. For Aristotle, the word meant happiness or 'well-being' in the sense of being successful or fulfilled. However, it is not a disposition like a virtue but rather an activity of the virtuous person. Eudaimonia is the end product generated, the outcome of being virtuous.

Specification content

Aristotle's moral virtues (based on the deficiency; the excess and the mean).

The goal of virtue theory, then, is to create the good life, to be happy and fulfilled through cultivating virtues (**arete**). It is sometimes known as aretaic ethics. Eudaimonia is integral to every virtuous thing that we do in life. Rather than it being some sort of abstract substance to tap into, 'happiness is an activity of the soul in accordance with virtue' according to the philosopher Roger Scruton; that is, it is more about 'doing' than 'being'. This is very significant as the optimum disposition for eudaimonia is in accordance with virtuous behaviour. The goal of virtue theory is to cultivate a virtuous disposition that brings about eudaimonia through virtuous actions.

Key quote

Every art and every inquiry, and similarly every action and pursuit, is thought to aim at some good; and for this reason the good has rightly been declared to be that at which all things aim. (**Aristotle**)

Virtue theory is grounded in Aristotle's book *The Nicomachean Ethics*, however, the origins of virtue theory tie in with Aristotle's whole view about the universe, the four causes and idea of teleology (an ultimate goal).

Key quote

Happiness means the general condition of fulfilment or 'success'. It is absurd to ask why we should pursue it, since success or fulfilment is what every activity intends. (**Scruton**)

Eudaimonia, then, incorporates the idea of well-being, 'peace', and goodwill to all but it also incorporates the physical good life. Aristotle's virtue theory is a holistic philosophy that must have a social context and the end result of enabling people to live together.

Key quote

Happiness, then, is something final and self-sufficient, and is the end of action. (**Aristotle**)

Overall, there are three aspects to happiness according to Aristotle: (1) a life of enjoyment, (2) a life with freedom and, (3) being a philosopher (a life of reflection and contemplation). The most important virtue of all, wisdom, is the overall characteristic of a person that can maintain all three. Such wisdom is not easily gained and the good life is not so easily and quickly achieved. As Aristotle says, 'But we must add "in a complete life". For one swallow does not make a summer, nor does one day; and so too one day, or a short time, does not make a man blessed and happy.'

> ## AO1 Activity
>
> Try and write a brief description of a fictional town that is called Eudaimonia. In your description write down the ideal features that ensure it is Eudaimonia!

Study tip

Any answer in an examination should always select the key relevant points, that is, the appropriate information relevant to the focus of the question. Try to explain the points in your own words. This demonstrates more personal understanding or 'ownership' of the knowledge.

Moral and intellectual virtues

Aristotle wrote, 'Since happiness is an activity of soul in accordance with perfect virtue, we must consider the nature of virtue; for perhaps we shall thus see better the nature of happiness.' The Greek term arete means 'virtue' but it also conveys the meaning of moral excellence, intellectual excellence and also physical excellence. Virtue is the idea of being how we are meant to be or being 'fit for purpose'.

Aristotle 384–322 BCE

According to Aristotle, there are two kinds of virtue: moral and intellectual. The moral virtues are acquired through habit and developed through practice. In contrast, the intellectual virtues are developed by education.

The moral virtues as discussed by Aristotle are:

1. Courage
2. Temperance
3. Liberality
4. Generosity (munificence or magnificence)
5. Pride (high-mindedness, concerned with honour)
6. Right or proper ambition
7. Patience
8. Truthfulness
9. Wittiness
10. Friendliness
11. Modesty
12. Righteous indignation.

The intellectual virtues as discussed by Aristotle include:

1. Intelligence or insight
2. Scientific knowledge by demonstration and conclusion
3. Wisdom
4. Artistic endeavour through the guidance of reason
5. Prudence, i.e. Understanding of good, or common sense to make the right choice.

quickfire

1.7 What does virtue theory concern itself with?

quickfire

1.8 Why is virtue theory not about rules?

quickfire

1.9 Why is the word eudaimonia significant?

quickfire

1.10 Where can we find Aristotle's ideas about virtue theory?

Key quote

Virtue too is distinguished into kinds in accordance with this difference; for we say that some of the virtues are intellectual and others moral, philosophic wisdom and understanding and practical wisdom being intellectual, liberality and temperance moral. (Aristotle)

Key quote

Virtue, then, being of two kinds, intellectual and moral, intellectual virtue in the main owes both its birth and its growth to teaching (for which reason it requires experience and time), while moral virtue comes about as a result of habit, whence also its name (ethike) is one that is formed by a slight variation from the word ethos (habit). (Aristotle)

The scales of justice

quicKpire

1.11 Explain how a moral virtue is different from an intellectual virtue.

quicKpire

1.12 Why is justice an important virtue for Aristotle?

Key quote

Virtue, then, is a state of character concerned with choice, lying in a mean … Now it is a mean between two vices, that which depends on excess and that which depends on defect; and again it is a mean because the vices respectively fall short of or exceed what is right in both passions and actions, while virtue both finds and chooses that which is intermediate. Hence in respect of its substance and the definition which states its essence virtue is a mean, with regard to what is best and right an extreme. (Aristotle)

Key terms

Akrasia: incontinent, that is, lacking self-restraint and uncontrolled

Akrates: one who is weak-willed and overcome by vices

Enkrates: one who is tempted, but strong, and lives in the mean

Sophron: one who effortlessly lives according to the mean

Once again, it is important to note that such virtues are not easily learned but rather cultivated carefully. Aristotle compares the development of such virtues with at first a 'sketch' that gradually develops into a picture.

Aristotle also devotes a chapter of his book to the virtue of 'justice', although it is clear that whilst being a virtuous state, it is more a collective outcome of virtuous behaviour per se. He writes: 'Justice in this sense, then, is not part of virtue but virtue entire, nor is the contrary injustice a part of vice but vice entire. What the difference is between virtue and justice in this sense is plain from what we have said; they are the same but their essence is not the same; what, as a relation to one's neighbour, is justice is, as a certain kind of state without qualification, virtue.'

Study tip

This section is full of new concepts. In revising, instead of just drawing up a glossary of key words try changing this into a flow chart that links each aspect of the topic together. Sometimes candidates start to explain one thing and then get carried away and move from the focus of the question. Stay focused

Aristotle's doctrine of the mean

For Aristotle cultivating virtues was to balance the two extremes of excess and deficiency. Each extreme brought with it an associated vice. Balancing the virtues and achieving the mean is no easy feat: 'Hence also it is no easy task to be good. For in everything it is no easy task to find the middle' (Aristotle).

Aristotle's doctrine of the mean produces three types of person:

1. The **sophron** who naturally lives in the mean without effort.

2. The **enkrates** who is tempted but has strong enough will power to live in the mean.

3. The **akrates** ('person without will or weak-willed person') who is weak and cannot live in the mean by overcoming temptation of the vices. Such a character according to Aristotle is said to be incontinent (**akrasia**).

Aristotle's account of the mean can be summarised in the following table:

Excess associated vice	Mean (virtue)	Deficiency associated vice
Rashness	Courage	Cowardice
Licentiousness	Temperance	Insensibility
Prodigality	Liberality	Illiberality
Vulgarity	Generosity	Pettiness
Vanity	Pride/High-mindedness	Humility
Over ambition	Proper ambition	Lack of ambition
Boastfulness	Truthfulness	Understatement
Irascibility	Patience	Lack of spirit
Buffoonery	Wittiness	Boorishness
Obsequiousness	Friendliness	Cantankerousness
Shyness/bashfulness	Modesty	Shamelessness
Envy/spitefulness	Righteous indignation	Malicious enjoyment/callousness

Pythagoras c.570–c.495 BCE

There are, according to many commentators on Aristotle, four key virtues that are of most importance to Aristotle: temperance (moderation); courage; together with justice; and wisdom. These virtues were seen to be the most important for a character to develop, with wisdom being the virtue that manages and drives them all and, naturally, producing a morally virtuous, or 'just' outcome.

It is no surprise, then, that the greatest advocate of virtue, according to Aristotle is the philosopher, that is, the one who pursues the 'loving' (philos) and 'wise' (sophos). This phrase was first used by Pythagoras, the ancient Greek philosopher and mathematician, to describe himself.

> **Key quote**
>
> Wisdom, thoroughly learned, will never be forgotten. (Pythagoras)

> **Key quote**
>
> It is better to be silent than to dispute with the Ignorant. (Pythagoras)

> **Key quote**
>
> Do not say a little in many words but a great deal in a few. (Pythagoras)

AO1 Activity

The virtues table above includes some very technical words to describe specific qualities. See if you can find out alternative, simpler words to describe each one. This will help you become familiar with them. Although you will not have to know them all, it is good to be familiar with a few to use as examples in an answer.

Study tip

When discussing virtue theory, do not simply list the virtues but be selective using Aristotle's three characters to exemplify them. Some candidates confuse the virtues and the vices, especially since Aquinas lists pride as one of the seven sins.

Jesus' teachings on virtues

There is a long history of encouraging virtues in the Christian tradition, much of which can be traced back to the Old Testament and such works as Ecclesiastes in particular. Although traditionally many people may associate Christianity and its teachings with rules and commandments, in the Sermon on the Mount, found in Matthew's Gospel chapters 5–7, the first section begins with Jesus promoting specific inward qualities or virtues.

> **Specification content**
>
> Jesus' teachings on virtues (the Beatitudes).

Key quote

Even more striking, when seen against the background of Greek ethics, is the positive value which Christianity attaches to qualities such as meekness and humility, in contrast to self-assertion and world success. This is a central theme of Jesus' Sermon on the Mount, which begins with the Beatitudes. (Norman)

Key quote

The Spirit of the Sovereign Lord is on me, because the Lord has anointed me to proclaim good news to the poor. He has sent me to bind up the broken-hearted, to proclaim freedom for the captive and release from darkness for the prisoners, to proclaim the year of the Lord's favour and the day of vengeance of our God, to comfort all who mourn, and provide for those who grieve in Zion – to bestow on them a crown of beauty instead of ashes, the oil of joy instead of mourning and a garment of praise instead of a spirit of despair. They will be called oaks of righteousness, a planting of the Lord for the display of his splendour. (Isaiah 61:1–3)

Key quote

There are six things the Lord hates, seven that are detestable to him: haughty eyes, a lying tongue, hands that shed innocent blood, a heart that devises wicked schemes, feet that are quick to rush into evil, a false witness who pours out lies and a person who stirs up conflict in the community. (Proverbs 6:16–19)

Each virtue is considered 'blessed' and has a corresponding spiritual reward. Jesus' blessing is praise and affirmation in recognition of the virtuous quality demonstrated. The text reads:

'Blessed are the poor in spirit, for theirs is the kingdom of Heaven.
Blessed are those who mourn, for they will be comforted.
Blessed are the meek, for they will inherit the earth.
Blessed are those who hunger and thirst for righteousness, for they will be filled.
Blessed are the merciful, for they will be shown mercy.
Blessed are the pure in heart, for they will see God.
Blessed are the peacemakers, for they will be called children of God.
Blessed are those who are persecuted because of righteousness, for theirs is the kingdom of Heaven.'

(Matthew 5:3–12)

So the virtues identified by Jesus are: poor in spirit; mourning; meek; a hunger and thirst for righteousness; mercy; purity of heart; peacemakers; and, the persecuted for the sake of righteousness.

The virtues have been the subject of much theological debate over the centuries. Some scholars see them as echoes of Isaiah 61:1–3 that refers to freedom from poverty, heartbreak, imprisonment and mourning, declaring hope for the righteous who are in despair, and comfort for those who mourn. Alternatively, it can be viewed as the antithesis of Proverbs 6:16–19 which describes the unrighteous character. There are many different ways of understanding these but below is a general summary of views about what each one means.

Virtue	Meaning
Poor in spirit	The term poor in spirit is often interpreted as an understanding of poverty in relation to the whole person; that is, physical, mental and spiritual. For example, those who are oppressed, enslaved, have their rights taken from them. Such people are humble before God. This also incorporates those who are 'poor in spirit' through an awareness of their own insignificance, hopelessness and helplessness before God.
Mourning	The idea of 'mourning' extends beyond the immediate concern for loss of a loved one to the loss of possessions, status, or even health. It is the state of recognising concern and regret for the current situation of being separated from God. It is also 'mourning' for the state of the whole world in general.
Meek	Psalm 37:11 reads that 'The meek will possess the land'. Meekness is not weakness but more a description of discipline and self-control exhibiting a gentle disposition towards others.
Hungry and thirsty for righteousness	This is often understood as a desire for the virtuous outcome of justice in life in relation to the kingdom of God. It is often understood as depicting the virtue of seeking righteousness or justice in a personal, spiritual, social and global sense.
Mercy	Through humility and an awareness of God's mercy, Christians are encouraged to display mercy towards others, not because it brings the reward of God's mercy, but because it is a virtuous disposition in itself.

Virtue	Meaning
Pure in heart	Often understood as sincerity of character that wills and determines the correct choices and decisions in life without the contamination of selfish drives.
Peacemakers	Traditionally ascribed to the role of the Messiah, those who follow suit and work for peace in a world of conflict truly appreciate the nature of God's kingdom.
Persecuted for the sake of righteousness	Such character displays a willingness to suffer for religious and moral principles but simultaneously display an underlying determination to survive and stand up for what is right despite the obstacles.

quicKfire

1.13 Where in the Old Testament can we find examples of virtues encouraged?

AO1 Activity

Look at Aristotle's virtues and those given by Jesus. Are there any similarities? Are there differences? Write some down.

Study tip

It is always good to be able to quote from religious texts in an answer to support your explanation or argument. The beatitudes are quite lengthy but try to shorten them so that they are more useful as quotes.

Jesus preaching the Sermon on the Mount (painting by Carl Heinrich Bloch)

Specification content

Challenges: virtues are not a practical guide to moral behaviour; issue of cultural relativism (ideas on the good virtues are not universal); virtues can be used for immoral acts.

Key quote

He has all the virtues I dislike and none of the vices I admire.
(Churchill)

Key quote

We value virtue but do not discuss it. The honest bookkeeper, the faithful wife, the earnest scholar get little of our attention compared to the embezzler, the tramp, the cheat.
(Steinbeck)

A war hero wearing medals

Challenges to virtue theory

Virtue theory can be seen to be an alternative and attractive way to pursue ethical standards. Although the virtues are self-focused, they are in fact 'other regarding'. Despite beginning with the self, virtue theory then moves on to develop a character that responds best to others and hence builds an ideal community. There is therefore a strong social context for virtue theory and in this way it can be viewed as a very practical system. It focuses on the way we behave and not simply what we believe should be the case!

In addition, the virtuous person is an exemplar of good character, and virtue theory therefore has clear guiding principles. It also acknowledges the fact that such exemplars (philosophers) can serve as good role models. Indeed, Aristotle argued that the wisdom in application and the delivery of justice for society ensure that it works and is not subjective.

Virtue theory could also appeal to feminist thinkers as an alternative to the rules and duties that, some argue, are stereotypically a male way of approaching life. Most of the systems in place have been devised by men, for men.

Despite various attractive aspects of virtue theory, there are challenges that have been raised.

The main issue with virtue theory as a system is that it does not conveniently fall within the 'deontological' or 'teleological' category due to its focus on characteristics of a person. Nonetheless, its links with Aristotle and Aquinas have caused some to question whether or not it is really a form of Natural Law. Others see it as more 'teleological' due to its focus on achieving eudaimonia.

There have been more specific challenges.

Virtues are not a practical guide to moral behaviour

As a system, virtue theory can be argued to be arbitrary, imprecise and vague because it lacks a focus on real behaviour in relation to real-life situations. More guidance is required if it is to be effective as a moral system.

In virtue theory there is also too much dependence on the potential goodness of others. It is naive in this respect and has an unconditional trust that allows for no overall control or individual quality control. It is, essentially, too individualistic because it deals primarily with the individual and so is not practical for society as a whole.

Overall, it seems too complex for many human beings to apply; even Aristotle recognised that not everyone has the same ability when resisting vice.

Cultural relativism and the use of virtues for immoral acts

Do virtues really exist? For example, there are various degrees of behaviour and there have been clear instances in the history of the world when one society's virtue is considered another society's vice.

For example, take the virtue of courage. Courage could be seen as putting up with injustice and persecution in one society or system of belief, whereas it could be seen as an active participation in the challenge to tyranny in defence of one's own rights in another society. Warriors have often been praised for their courage. There are many more examples associated with other virtues.

As a system virtue theory can be contradictory – if there are differences in expressing a virtue then which is the right one to choose? It is very subjective.

Indeed, virtue theory has been argued to be self-centred; for example, the idea of well-being can be understood as self-interest, or, at the very least have the potential for this. In the light of this there is no guarantee that the action one agent performs has a moral outcome as it does not really consider the consequences for others.

AO1 Developing skills

It is now time to reflect upon the information that has been covered so far. It is also important to consider how what you have learned can be focused and used for examination-style answers by practising the skills associated with AO1.

Assessment objective 1 (AO1) involves demonstrating knowledge and understanding. The terms 'knowledge' and 'understanding' are obvious but it is crucial to be familiar with how certain skills demonstrate these terms, and also, how the performance of these skills is measured (see generic band descriptors Band 5 for AS AO1).

▶ **Your new task is this:** from the list of ten key points below, choose six that you feel are the most important in answering the question above the list. Put your points in order of priority explaining why they are the six most important aspects to mention from that topic. This skill of prioritising and selecting appropriate material will help you in answering examination questions for AO1.

A focus on outlining the challenges to virtue theory.

1. The main issue with virtue theory as a system is that it does not conveniently fall within the 'deontological' or 'teleological' category due to its focus on characteristics of a person.

2. Its links with Aristotle and Aquinas have also caused some to question whether or not it is really a form of Natural Law and therefore in essence a deontological system.

3. Virtue theory is 'teleological' due to its focus on achieving eudaimonia but this makes it potentially subjective.

4. Virtue theory can be accused of being arbitrary, imprecise and vague because it lacks a focus on real behaviour in relation to real life situations.

5. Virtue theory has very little practical guidance.

6. Virtue theory has very little overall quality control in determining what is correct, and therefore good, behaviour.

7. Virtue theory is too dependent on the goodness of others.

8. Virtue theory places too much focus on the individual and could be accused of being self-centred.

9. It is too complex and intelligent a system for all and only relevant for the philosopher.

10. Are there really such things as virtues?

Key skills

Knowledge involves:

Selection of a range of (thorough) accurate and relevant information that is directly related to the specific demands of the question.

This means you choose the correct information relevant to the question set NOT the topic area. You will have to think and focus on selecting key information and NOT writing everything you know about the topic area.

Understanding involves:

Explanation that is extensive, demonstrating depth and/or breadth with excellent use of evidence and examples including (where appropriate) thorough and accurate supporting use of sacred texts, sources of wisdom and specialist language.

This means that you demonstrate that you understand something by being able to illustrate and expand your points through examples/supporting evidence in a personal way and NOT repeat chunks from a text book (known as rote learning).

Further application of skills:

Once you have made your choices and selected your information, compare them with another student. See if together you can decide on six and their correct order, this time, in sequence for answering a question.

Specification content

Whether being a good person is
better than just doing good deeds.

AO2 Activity *Possible lines
of argument*

Listed below are some conclusions
that could be drawn from the AO2
reasoning in the accompanying text:

1. Anyone can do good deeds but not
   everyone is sincere.

2. Developing good character is more
   important than doing good deeds.

3. Good deeds and good character
   are inseparable.

4. Doing good deeds is the priority
   and developing good character is
   only secondary to this.

5. Developing virtues is the only way
   to consistently do good deeds.

Consider each of the conclusions
drawn above and collect evidence and
examples to support each argument
from the AO1 and AO2 material
studied in this section. Select one
conclusion that you think is most
convincing and explain why it is so.
Now contrast this with the weakest
conclusion in the list, justifying
your argument with clear reasoning
and evidence.

Issues for analysis and evaluation

Whether being a good person is better than just doing good deeds

The main issue for debate here is the challenge that this assertion makes to traditional views of morality as following set instructions and codes of behaviour to become moral and be a good person. Virtue theory holds that this is far too simplistic and that being a good person involves more than this.

The central problem with the idea that doing good deeds makes one a good person is that just following rules is not really edifying for 'character'. In other words, such a simplistic understanding of goodness is just superficial because it is grounded in the action and not in the person. For instance, a good deed may be done with impure motives, without good intention. Someone who is angry and wants to be violent towards others may not act accordingly because of rules, but does that make them 'good' in character when they are full of hate and bad intentions? In the same way, a person may give to charity but if they are only doing this from a reluctant duty or to appear good to others does that mean they are good?

Nevertheless, an alternative line of argument could be that a person still chooses right over wrong, good over bad, and so really, even with insincere intentions, does that make them less good than another that performs acts graciously? After all, the end product is the same.

Virtue theory would counter this by arguing that developing virtues enables people to learn to become moral beings and promotes a change and development in character that will last; just following rules does not make one good intrinsically but simply indicates that a person has done the right thing. For virtue theory, the idea of developing virtue is actually a process of self-development whereby a person grows in moral character, in goodness or arete (virtue) and recognises 'good' beyond the action itself and integral to the person.

Virtue theory would argue that being a good person involves developing independence and responsibility in order to do good deeds naturally and without the necessities of external, dependent structures.

In addition, the virtuous person is an exemplar and therefore the clear guiding principles arise from within rather than being imposed on from without. It also acknowledges the fact that such exemplars (philosophers) can serve as good role models and therefore assist others in their pursuit of good character. Therefore, virtue theory does indeed agree with the sentiment that being a good person is better than just doing good deeds.

Nevertheless, there are problems with the view that being a good person is better than just doing good deeds. The main problem is that if no good deeds are done then how can a person be good? Good deeds underline good character and define it.

In conclusion, there is much to say about the argument that goodness is more than just good acts; however, it is also important to consider that good deeds are a strong indicator for goodness of character.

Whether virtue theory is useful when faced with a moral dilemma

A moral dilemma is defined, according to scholars, as a situation when two or more courses of conduct may be justifiable in any given set of circumstances, possibly resulting in diametrically opposed outcomes. The issue, then, for virtue theory, is whether or not it can be applied meaningfully when faced with, say for example, a case of injustice like persecution.

In terms of a Christian response, some could argue that the beatitudes appear to avoid fighting for justice but just accept injustice as it states, 'blessed are those who are persecuted because of righteousness, for theirs is the kingdom of Heaven'. In terms of Aristotle's virtues, courage has different understandings. It could, on the one hand, support the beatitude above, or, alternatively, courage could mean to stand up and fight against persecution.

In virtue theory there is, one could argue, some idea of 'duty' and 'doing the right thing'; however, this is not really explicitly stated in relation to how the virtues need to be applied. Indeed, the question could be asked, 'are the virtues really moral absolutes?'. This problem, then, makes virtue theory uncertain for some. Due to the fact that virtue theory sees every moral dilemma as contextual it is therefore open to interpretation and debate, and therefore potentially confusing.

The problem with having no rules to follow is that it could encourage an 'anything goes' society, which is certainly not consistent with religion nor with the philosophy or Aristotle. Indeed, the liberal and relative aspect to virtue theory means that it will not appeal to the more conservative, traditional religious followers or those who wish for a more structured approach to ethics. This point may also indicate that there are other ethical systems that are more attractive to follow when facing a moral dilemma, systems that are more structured and absolute.

However, some thinkers see virtue theory as merely an extension of Natural Law or of the teachings of Jesus and therefore the underlying principles for each can be referred to for guidance in specific cases in partnership with considerations of virtuous character and behaviour.

One could argue that one of the great strengths of virtue theory is that it stresses altruism, that is, a concern for the well-being of others. This is a teaching consistent with all forms of religion and philosophy and a useful principle when facing moral dilemmas. The virtues are self-focused but are in fact 'other regarding'. Although it begins with the self it then moves on to develop a character that responds best to others and hence build an ideal community that can face moral dilemmas.

Indeed, it could be argued that if virtue theory were not useful then people such as Aquinas would not have developed the theory later in conjunction with Natural Law. Moreover, there is a clear social context for virtue theory in the writings of Aristotle and in this way it is a very practical system. It focuses on the way we behave and not simply what we believe should be the case!

Since the virtuous person is an exemplar for others, he or she can serve as a good role model for others in facing moral dilemmas. One could argue that the wisdom in application and the delivery of justice for society ensure that it works and is not subjective.

In conclusion, it can be seen that virtue theory can certainly be of use when facing moral dilemmas, although it should be recognised that there are limitations. If one is looking for a more absolutist solution to moral dilemmas, then virtue theory may not be suitable.

Specification content

Whether virtue theory is useful when faced with a moral dilemma.

AO2 Activity *Possible lines of argument*

Listed below are some conclusions that could be drawn from the AO2 reasoning in the accompanying text:

1. Virtue theory is a good way of solving moral dilemmas.

2. Virtue theory, based much on moral character of the individual, has the danger of being subjective and therefore not always reliable in solving moral dilemmas.

3. There are better theories and systems of morality to use than virtue theory when facing moral dilemmas.

4. Virtue theory needs to be used in conjunction with other methods of moral decision making in order for it to be effective.

5. Virtue theory is really based in more concrete, absolutist theories and so in itself is not useful in addressing moral dilemmas.

Consider each of the conclusions drawn above and collect evidence and examples to support each argument from the AO1 and AO2 material studied in this section. Select one conclusion that you think is most convincing and explain why it is so. Now contrast this with the weakest conclusion in the list, justifying your argument with clear reasoning and evidence.

Key skills

Analysis involves identifying issues raised by the materials in the AO1, together with those identified in the AO2 section, and presents sustained and clear views, either of scholars or from a personal perspective ready for evaluation.

This means that it picks out key things to debate and the lines of argument presented by others or a personal point of view.

Evaluation involves considering the various implications of the issues raised based upon the evidence gleaned from analysis and provides an extensive detailed argument with a clear conclusion.

This means that the answer weighs up the various and different lines of argument analysed through individual commentary and response and arrives at a conclusion through a clear process of reasoning.

AO2 Developing skills

It is now time to reflect upon the information that has been covered so far. It is also important to consider how what you have learned can be focused and used for examination-style answers by practising the skills associated with AO2.

Assessment objective 2 (AO2) involves 'analysis' and 'evaluation'. The terms may be obvious but it is crucial to be familiar with how certain skills demonstrate these terms, and also, how the performance of these skills is measured (see generic band descriptors Band 5 for AS AO2).

Obviously an answer is placed within an appropriate band descriptor depending upon how well the answer performs, ranging from excellent, good, satisfactory, basic/limited to very limited.

▶ **Your task is this:** from the list of the 12 key points below, select six that are relevant to the evaluation task below. Put your selection into an order that you would use to address the task set. In explaining why you have chosen these six to answer the task, you will find that you are developing a process of reasoning. This will help you to develop an argument from this to decide how far morality is just a matter of good deeds.

A focus on evaluating whether there is more to morality than just doing good things.

1. Following rules is too simplistic.

2. Rules do not make a person good, only obedient and subject to a law.

3. Doing good things is a feature of morality but not the only one.

4. Being a good person involves developing virtues.

5. Being a good person means knowing what is right and wrong.

6. Just doing good deeds tell us nothing about the person other than they have done a good act.

7. Morality should involve an appreciation of motives and intentions behind good acts.

8. Developing virtues is more important than performing good deeds.

9. Good deeds are a key feature of morality and the gauge by which morality is measured.

10. Morality incorporates much more than mere actions.

11. Without good deeds there can be no morality.

12. Good actions are the essence of morality.

C: Ethical egoism

Ethical egoism is a meta-ethical investigation that is focused on the agent, that is, individual character, to give an understanding of 'norm' or behaviour. In looking at the individual character, and the motives behind an individual's actions, there is a very important question that emerges.

Do we behave in a manner that is purely driven by our self-interest?

Ethical egoism: a normative agent focused ethic based upon self-interest as opposed to altruism

In 1928, H. A. Pritchard delivered a lecture entitled 'Duty and Interest' in which he questioned the true motive behind a dutiful action. Richard Norman writes: 'Pritchard's central argument is this: if justice is advocated on the grounds that it is advantageous to the just person, it is thereby reduced to a form of self-interest'. In other words, 'duty is not really duty unless it is done for duty's sake'.

If we act because the end product is advantageous to us, whether we are consciously aware of the fact or not, we are, in essence, acting from self-interest. This is the key meta-ethical point of focus for what is called **ethical egoism**.

The distinction between ethical egoism and psychological egoism

For those who advocate any form of ethical egoism as a moral theory, this idea of 'self-interest' is the chief concern of their philosophical enquiry. As we have seen above, ethical egoism is the study of self-interest as one possible explanation for some moral actions. Ethical egoism as a theory suggests that this is the best way to act.

Key quote

Psychological egoism is a theory of of human nature that purports to describe what motivates people to act. Ethical egoism, on the other hand, is normative. It purports to tell us how people ought to act. (**Driver**)

There is, however, a difference between ethical egoism and **psychological egoism**. Peter Cave writes: 'Some scorn morality. They argue that we always act for our own sake, in our own self-interest or, more accurately, in what we perceive to be self-interest.' This is psychological egoism. Cave continues, 'A different egoism, ethical egoism, is that we 'ought always to act self-interestedly'. Julia Driver notes that 'Ethical egoism is not committed to the truth of psychological egoism'.

In other words, to say that we always act out of self-interest (psychological egoism) is not the same thing as arguing that we should always act out of self-interest (ethical egoism). In essence, they are very different claims.

Ethical egoism is, therefore, a normative agent focused ethic based upon self-interest, as opposed to **altruism**, and is a directive by which one should be guided to behave.

Julia Driver writes, 'Altruistic actions are those that are performed for the sake of others – purely for the sake of others. The psychological egoist denies that there are such acts.' The response of the psychological egoist is interesting in response to donating money to charity. They would suggest that the motive could be to look good in front of others, to support a moral system to which they are duty-bound, or, to avoid shame and personal anguish if they decide not to give. All such explanations reveal the root intention of self-interest.

This section covers AO1 content and skills

Specification content
Normative agent focused ethic based on self-interest as opposed to altruism; ethical theory that matches the moral agent's psychological state (psychological egoism); concentration on long-term self-interests rather than short-term interests.

Key terms
Altruism: selfless concern for the well-being of others

Ethical egoism: the normative view that holds that all action ought to be motivated by self-interest

Psychological egoism: the descriptive view that all human action is motivated by self-interest

Key quote

Within our own moral culture, largely as a product of the Christian tradition, an altruistic concern for others is widely held to be a, or even the, supreme value. If, however, in caring for other people, I do so because I think that it will make my own life happier, then it would seem that it is not really a concern for others which motivates me, but a concern for myself. (**Norman**)

Key quote

Psychological egoism offers an account of human nature and is non-normative. It concerns how people actually behave, not how they ought to behave. If we hold that all human action is motivated by self-interest, we're making a strong universal claim. We're denying that altruistic actions are ever performed. (**Driver**)

quickfire

1.14 What is the difference between ethical egoism and psychological egoism?

Long-term and short-term self-interests

Ethical egoism does not necessarily mean, however, that we always act selfishly in the narrow understanding of the word. Acting out of self-interest can be amalgamated with an action that demonstrates concern for others, as we have seen above in Pritchard's observation of 'duty'.

For some, this is what distinguishes ethical egoism from psychological egoism in that it could be argued that acting in one's own self-interest is more than just being selfish but that it involves a much more complex consideration of both short-term and long term-benefits. After all, an action that overtly benefits another in the short term may have the covert purpose of self-benefit in the long term.

Frankena writes, 'It should be noted that an ethical egoist need not be an egotist or even an egotistic and selfish man in the everyday sense of these terms. Ethical egoism is an ethical theory, not a pattern of action or trait of character, and is compatible with being self-effacing and unselfish in practice.'

The outworking of self-interest could be short term, for example in giving to charity or in sacrificing time by visiting an elderly relative. Interests are served immediately by making one feel good about doing the right thing, or, alternatively interests could be considered as part of a long-term plan such as developing character or earning merit for a greater cause such as the afterlife in terms of religions.

In the same way, acting out of self-interest can be seen as serving long-term interests. Peter Cave cites the 18th-century economist Adam Smith who recognised that 'It is not from the benevolence of the butcher, the brewer, or the baker, that we expect our dinner, but from their regard to their own interest.' One only thinks of the slogans, 'serving the customer' and the 'customer is always right' to realise that supermarkets care about the customer simply because it is in their own long-term self-interest to do so.

Giving to the poor

Max Stirner

Max Stirner was born in Germany in 1806. His real name was Johann Caspar Schmidt but he used Max Stirner as a literary pseudonym. He studied at three universities in Germany and is known to have attended lectures by Hegel on the philosophy of religion. In short, a man of no real notable academic repute in his day, he worked as a humble teacher but in later life did work as an academic translator and a journalist, none of which were well paid. Max Stirner's key work was the book entitled *The Ego and his Own* published in 1844 in German (*Der Einzige und sein Eigentum*); however, the circulation was minimal and although it received some brief critical acclaim and provoked a response from the philosopher, Feuerbach, it was not an overall success financially or academically. Stirner lived most of his later life in poorer circumstances, often pursued by creditors and he died of fever in 1856.

Despite this, Stirner's ideas have influenced many people. Stirner's ideas have also been interpreted in different ways. For some, he was the forerunner of Friedrich Nietzsche in terms of the style and substance of his writing. For others, he was a pioneer of the sort of existentialism found in Sartre. He also had a great influence on the early thoughts of Karl Marx. Today, he is often held as the rational advocator of the anarchist movement in his recognition of the illegitimate claims of the state.

In short, there are things written about Max Stirner and then there are the things that Max Stirner actually wrote. In a sense, the work of Stirner is oddly anachronistic in that in his day he was not really understood, and it is only a recent emergence of scholarly interest in his work that has drawn out a true appreciation of the complexity of his thought.

In essence, Stirner accepted the stance of psychological egoism only in so far as he recognised the role of what others identified as self-interest in making moral decisions. However, the irony is, he argued that the notion of self-interest was deluded because it incorrectly identified the true nature of the 'self'. Once the true self is realised, the assertions of psychological egoism are weakened and a clearer picture emerges of what pure self-interest really involves. Yes, Stirner agreed that actions should be driven by self-interest, but, it is only when we understand what the self actually is, that we can be truly free to act accordingly.

Stirner's work is not really methodical. It appears random at times, almost chaotic, repetitive and according to the *Stanford Encyclopedia*, 'his unusual style reflects a conviction that both language and rationality are human products which have come to constrain and oppress their creators'. However, with patience and careful reading, some main themes can be identified. In short, Stirner argues his case progressively throughout several stages of argument as follows:

- That self-interest as is commonly understood is always a slave to something other than the 'self' or ego and so is not true 'self-interest'.

- That it is misguided to think that we actually are free to make moral choices in relation to religious or philosophical systems of moral behaviour because such systems control us.

- That true egoism is a matter of realising what is 'own' and 'ownness' by not being driven by religious, philosophical or materialistic frameworks that enslave us, but to gain mastery over one's self.

- That the true self needs to be free from the constraints of any external ideologies and not controlled from within by the senses, so that it is truly 'self', and therefore, unique.

- The only way to engage one's uniqueness in the world is to cooperate with other unique individuals by being part of a union of egoists.

Specification content

Max Stirner, self-interest as the root cause of every human action even if it appears altruistic; rejection of egoism for material gain; union of egoists.

quicKpire

1.15 What is an altruistic action?

Key quote

There looks to be a stark contrast between the often melodramatic tone of Stirner's best-known work, on the one hand, and the rather less sensational events of his own life, on the other. (*Stanford Encyclopedia*)

Max Stirner 1806–1856

Key quote

It would also be a mistake to think of Stirner as advocating a normative proposition about the value of self-interested action as ordinarily understood. Stirnerian egoism needs to be distinguished from the individual pursuit of conventional self-interest. (*Stanford Encyclopedia*)

Key term

Einzige: ego

quickfire

1.16 Why did Stirner argue we were not really free in our moral choices?

Key quote

Totally different from this *free* thinking is *own* thinking, *my* thinking, a thinking which does not guide me, but is guided, continued, or broken off, by me at my pleasure. The distinction of this own thinking from free thinking is similar to that of own sensuality, which I satisfy at pleasure, from free, unruly sensuality to which I succumb. **(Stirner)**

Key quote

There is no sinner and no sinful egoism! **(Stirner)**

Key quote

I decide whether it is the *right thing* in me; there is no right *outside* me. **(Stirner)**

The delusion of the past and the true nature of self-interest: the ego (Einzige)

Psychological egoism sees self-interest as the root cause of every human action, even if it appears altruistic. Stirner acknowledges this explanation but questions its truth. Stirner argued that we have had a false notion of liberty in our approach to thinking; he denies there is such a thing in a sense because a conventional understanding of self-interest is always slave to something, whether it be an obvious religious moral duty or obligation, or one that is more subtle and non-religious, yet still brings with it a moral duty or obligation. He writes, 'When one looks to the *bottom* of anything, *i.e.* searches out its *essence*, one often discovers something quite other than what it *seems* to be'. These revelations of 'essence' Stirner refers to as 'spooks' or 'ghosts'.

The *Stanford Encyclopedia* supports this understanding of Stirner: 'Stirner is occasionally portrayed as a psychological egoist, that is, as a proponent of the descriptive claim that all (intentional) actions are motivated by a concern for the self-interest of the agent. However, this characterisation of Stirner's position can be questioned ... Moreover, at one point, Stirner explicitly considers adopting the explanatory stance of psychological egoism only to reject it.'

Instead, Stirner calls for human beings to recognise their enslavement to the duty and obligation imposed by such moral frameworks and re-focus on what the self or ego desires and wills. He writes, 'Why will you not take courage now to really make *yourselves* the central point and the main thing altogether?' Therefore, any person that thinks they are acting independently in making moral choices is misguided as it is not the agent that directs the moral behaviour but rather the ideal that controls them. Stirner adds, 'The habit of the religious way of thinking has biased our mind so grievously that we are terrified at ourselves in our nakedness and naturalness; it has degraded us so that we deem ourselves depraved by nature, born devils.'

In a critical attack on both religion and philosophy, Stirner scorns the idea that adopting belief systems and moral frameworks will lead to self-development and moral improvement. For Stirner, adopting such normative ethical frameworks only enslaved the self or ego. He refers to an example of a philosopher or free thinker who 'thinks he is through with God and throws off Christianity as a bygone thing'. That thinker would still, according to Stirner, reject incest and adultery with a 'moral shudder' because the philosopher or free thinker is still subject to a belief in a moral framework.

If we consider the following scenario, we can see how Max Stirner's thought works. Some poor people ask for money. These are some possible responses:

'I choose to give them money; however, every reason for which I could do this is related to my own self-interest.'

In other words, it appears that I am free and have chosen a course of action because it is in my own interest. Psychological egoism proposes this. However, Stirner questions this conclusion that the underlying motive is self-interest. For example, Stirner would see an underlying obligation:

'I give them money because it makes me feel happy BUT it is also my duty.'

Stirner would argue that I am not free because, despite my self-interest in pursuing happiness, I am still a slave as this feeling of happiness is only in relation to what my conscience tells me is my duty. Stirner rejects psychological egoism because it seems the self is obliged by the duty 'one should help those in need'. Again:

'I do not give them money (I justify my decision in any of several ways to make me feel better).'

Stirner would argue that I am not free because I feel guilty as I am still a slave to what my conscience tells me I should do. I have justified my actions and have good reasons for going against the general rule of conscience, for example, in arguing there are charities and welfare to support them. Again Stirner rejects psychological egoism because the self is still slave to some obligation: one should, unless there is good reason not to, help those in need.

'I give them money reluctantly.'

The Stirnerian response would be that I am not free because I just do what my conscience tells me is my obligation, despite me not wanting to. Psychological egoism is once again rejected because the self is still slave to the obligation of conscience: to not help those in need would mean I am bad and not fulfilling my duty of helping those in need.

Stirner has sometimes been referred to as advocating amoralism, that is, to reject morality outright. This is not entirely true and we have to be careful here not to draw the incorrect conclusion. Stirner appears to reject fixed moral obligations and not values. As the *Stanford Encyclopedia* states: 'Morality, on Stirner's account, involves the positing of obligations to behave in certain fixed ways. As a result, he rejects morality as incompatible with egoism properly understood. However, this rejection of morality is not grounded in the rejection of values as such, but in the affirmation of what might be called non-moral goods ... his rejection of the legitimacy of moral claims is not to be confused with a denial of the propriety of all normative judgement.'

The future of self is to realise ownness (Eigenheit)

Stirner made an important distinction between what is perceived as the self and ownness. The philosopher who thinks (s)he is free and independent needs to recognise that to be truly such they must be freed from all obligation to any conscious or sub-conscious ideal. They must realise their 'ownness' (Eigenheit): 'I am my *own* only when I am master of myself, instead of being mastered either by sensuality or by anything else (God, man, authority, law, State, Church, etc.); what is of use to me, this self-owned or self-appertaining one, my selfishness pursues.'

Therefore, in relation to the example of giving to the poor (above) Stirner would argue:

'I do as I will/please.'

In other words, I am free because it is nothing to do with whether it is a good or bad thing to give money to a poor person, but rather because I am my own person (ownness) and not a slave to any obligation. Max Stirner argued that this is true freedom and true self interest.

Key quote

Away, then, with every concern that is not altogether my concern! You think at least the 'good cause' must be my concern? What's good, what's bad? Why, I myself am my concern, and I am neither good nor bad. Neither has meaning for me. (Stirner)

The future of the self is to activate uniqueness (Einzig)

An awareness of ownness is one thing, but the implications of what ownness truly means can only be realised through the appreciation of oneself as unique (Einzig). This is Stirner's evaluation of the true self, of the true egoist. In short, being unique means individual freedom from all external conceptual theories that could be imposed. Stirner writes, 'I am *owner* of my might, and I am so when I know myself as *unique.*'

Key quote

Thousands of years of civilisation have obscured to you what you are, have made you believe you are not egoists but are called to be idealists ('good men'). Shake that off! Do not seek for freedom, which does precisely deprive you of yourselves, in 'self-denial'; but seek for yourselves, become egoists, become each of you an almighty ego. Or, more clearly: just recognise yourselves again, just recognise what you really are, and let go your hypocritical endeavours, your foolish mania to be something else than you are. (Stirner)

Key quote

The man who is set free is nothing but a freed man, a *libertinus*, a dog dragging a piece of chain with him: he is an unfree man in the garment of freedom, like the ass in the lion's skin. (Stirner)

Key term

Eigenheit: ownness, the idea of mastering oneself

quickfire

1.17 According to Stirner, what makes us truly free to make choices?

Key quote

Ownness includes in itself everything own, and brings to honor again what Christian language dishonored. But ownness has not any alien standard either, as it is not in any sense an *idea* like freedom, morality, humanity, etc.: it is only a description of the *owner*. (Stirner)

Key quote

Egoism does not think of sacrificing anything, giving away anything that it wants; it simply decides, what I want I must have and will procure. (Stirner)

Key quote

I am *owner* of my might, and I am so when I know myself as *unique*. In the *unique one* the owner himself returns into his creative nothing, of which he is born. Every higher essence above me, be it God, be it man, weakens the feeling of my uniqueness, and pales only before the sun of this consciousness. **(Stirner)**

This does not, however, mean that being a unique individual, and everyone becoming unique, is the same thing as everyone being equal; equality is just another conceptual and idealistic framework for all humanity to kneel to. Stirner writes, 'But I am not an ego along with other egos, but the sole ego: I am unique. Hence my wants too are unique, and my deeds; in short, everything about me is unique.' The true unique egoist has a true appreciation of their self, which inevitably, being unique, cannot be equated with another.

In addition, this activation of uniqueness needs also to be free from excessive sensual appetites, or, to be more accurate, that the self is not controlled by these appetites or under any obligation to them. The *Stanford Encyclopedia* states, 'Stirner not only rejects the legitimacy of any subordination to the will of another but also recommends that individuals cultivate an ideal of emotional detachment towards their own appetites and ideas.'

In relation to the example of giving money to a poor person, we can develop Stirner's egoism further:

'Once I recognise that I am my own self and not accountable to any obligation I then become aware of my own true unique self and can judge accurately what course of action I will to do that serves my own true unique nature and so I will give, or not, according to this.'

I am truly free and act according to my self-interest which is not determined by any sense of duty or obligation nor is it driven by a greed or hunger for materialistic gain. This is the best way to behave for me, not because I should do it (nor should it become a rule that binds me), but because it is what I will. This also links to the idea that Stirner rejects egoism as a means for material gain and leads to the idea that it is not, in essence, anti-social.

Union of egoists

Stirner's argument suggests, then, that relationships towards others and how one behaves as the true egoist all hinge upon one's own unique nature. Whilst this does not lead to an obligation of equality for all as individuals, it certainly does not advocate greed for material gain. In the same way, Stirner's egoism is not anti-social and he is keen to advocate co-operation between egos.

Much of Stirner's work in *The Ego and his Own* is directed towards the notion of the secular state and political ideologies. Ownership was a big issue for Stirner and was one that, for him, should not be dictated by any outside agent or government. But at the same time he was practical and recognised that the only way forward was to develop a special community that was unprincipled other than having in common the recognition of the uniqueness of the egoist. He called this the union of egoists and promoted the idea that society should be composed in such a way in which the idea of cooperation prevailed in recognition of one's uniqueness so that one's true identity is asserted. Although an ideal in itself, Stirner was well aware of the deconstructing force of the concept of a union and the condition of uniqueness and also the practical difficulties this may have involved.

The *Stanford Encyclopedia* states: 'The egoistic future is said to consist not of wholly isolated individuals but rather in relationships of "uniting", that is, in impermanent connections between individuals who themselves remain independent and self-determining.' The union of egoists would respect the uniqueness of each member, support them in their unique pursuit of their individual goals whilst still having no shared final ends. It is a true cooperation of egos.

Key quote

Why will you not take courage now to really make yourselves the central point and the main thing altogether? **(Stirner)**

Challenges to ethical egoism

In short, there are many challenges to ethical egoism. In terms of Stirner, the most obvious one is the difficulty in understanding his work. As the *Stanford Encyclopedia* attest: 'The plurality of interpretations of his own work might well have amused Stirner and encouraged him in his view that there could be no legitimate constraints on the meaning of a text.'

Destruction of a community ethos

One criticism is that ethical egoism can destroy a **community ethos** in promoting the will of the individual over the will of the people. The state and laws are there for the benefit of the majority and as a guard against exploitation of any individual against another.

In response, Stirner would argue that it is this very aim to free people that is the formula that enslaves them. This claim has often been interpreted as advocating anarchy and official opposition towards, and fight to eliminate, the state.

It is true that any state or system is illegitimate for Stirner's ethical egoism, since this essentially causes conflict between the individual's uniqueness and an obligation to serve the law. For Stirner, the demands of the state are not binding on the individual but in no way does this mean an active affront to oppose or eliminate the state system. It is up to each individual to decide whether or not to agree with the state's demands. It is Stirner's views, according to the *Stanford Encyclopedia*, that 'whilst individuals have no duty to overthrow the state, Stirner does think that the state will eventually collapse as a result of the spread of egoism'.

Social injustices and bigotry could occur as individuals put their own interests first

The next criticism of ethical egoism is the most obvious, that, in pursuing one's own interests there will, inevitably, be a conflict of interests with others. This could inevitably lead to social injustices and **bigotry**.

One can see how this could arise by just considering Stirner's words: 'Now am I, who am competent for much, perchance to have no advantage over the less competent? We are all in the midst of abundance; now shall I not help myself as well as I can, but only wait and see how much is left me in an equal division?'

This immediately provokes accusations of inequality in all aspects of social life, ethical actions and political administration. Indeed, how can one society live according to the demands and needs specific to countless individuals without injustice and bigotry?

Specification content

Challenges: destruction of a community ethos; social injustices could occur as individuals put their own interests first; a form of bigotry (why is one moral agent more important than any other?).

Key terms

Bigotry: intolerance and narrow-mindedness

Community ethos: the character or spirit of a community

AO1 Activity

You have read the reasons above for the challenges to ethical egoism. For each of the two main challenges, think of some practical examples of 'destruction of a community ethos' and 'bigotry' that would support the explanations above.

Key skills

Knowledge involves:

Selection of a range of (thorough) accurate and relevant information that is directly related to the specific demands of the question.

This means you choose the correct information relevant to the question set NOT the topic area. You will have to think and focus on selecting key information and NOT writing everything you know about the topic area.

Understanding involves:

Explanation that is extensive, demonstrating depth and/or breadth with excellent use of evidence and examples including (where appropriate) thorough and accurate supporting use of sacred texts, sources of wisdom and specialist language.

This means that you demonstrate that you understand something by being able to illustrate and expand your points through examples/supporting evidence in a personal way and NOT repeat chunks from a text book (known as rote learning).

Further application of skills:

Go through the topic areas in this section and create some bullet lists of key points from key areas. For each one, provide further elaboration and explanation through the use of evidence and examples.

AO1 Developing skills

It is now time to reflect upon the information that has been covered so far. It is also important to consider how what you have learned can be focused and used for examination-style answers by practising the skills associated with AO1.

Assessment objective 1 (AO1) involves demonstrating knowledge and understanding. The terms 'knowledge' and 'understanding' are obvious but it is crucial to be familiar with how certain skills demonstrate these terms, and also, how the performance of these skills is measured (see generic band descriptors Band 5 for AS AO1).

▶ **Your new task is this:** you need to develop each of the key points below by adding evidence and examples to fully explain each point. The first one is done for you. This will help you in answering examination questions for AO1 by being able to 'demonstrate extensive depth and/or breadth' with 'excellent use of evidence and examples' (Level 5 AO1 band descriptor).

Question focus on ethical and psychological egoism

1. Psychological egoism concerns itself with the explanation of all moral decision making as originating from self-interest.

DEVELOPMENT: *It argues that morality is not imposed upon us by external systems but that we choose which systems to use in relation to what is best for us.*

2. Both ethical egoism and psychological egoism explain that even altruistic actions have selfish motives.

3. Ethical egoism is concerned with the idea that we ought to base our ethical decisions in self-interest.

4. Max Stirner argued that ethical egoism was the way we should make ethical decisions.

5. One of the key criticisms of ethical egoism is that it is arbitrary.

6. Another criticism of ethical egoism is that it has the potential to produce evil acts.

7. Ethical egoism, if adopted by all, would mean an anarchist society.

8. Psychological egoism challenges altruism.

9. Ethical egoism does not necessarily mean that it is purely selfish in its outcomes.

10. The outworking of ethical egoism can be either short term or long term.

Issues for analysis and evaluation

The extent to which ethical egoism inevitably leads to moral evil

This section covers AO2 content and skills

Specification content

The extent to which ethical egoism inevitably leads to moral evil.

The main potential problem with ethical egoism is that there is no absolute, as Max Stirner writes, 'I decide whether it is the *right thing* in me; there is no right *outside* me'. This has led to the criticism that ethical egoism will inevitably lead to a person perfoming immoral actions at the expense of others. But is this a valid criticism?

Certainly there is no control other than the individual will and the theory of ethical egoism, if accepted, would need to trust a person to be truly disciplined. But it could be argued that individuals are not responsible enough to do this. Indeed, individuals are not true to themselves, as Stirner observes that many think they are free and individual but in fact they are enslaved and directed by some form of framework they have subscribed to. Stirner writes, 'The man who is set free is nothing but a freed man ... he is an unfree man in the garment of freedom, like the ass in the lion's skin' and again, 'The freer the people, the more bound the individual'.

Ethical egoism has also been accused of encouraging bigotry through promoting self-interest over others and seeing oneself as more important. This would inevitably lead to conflict in interests and disagreement. In addition, it has the potential for anarchy in society, the consequences of which could be very unsavoury.

Despite this, it could be argued that Stirner's vision of the self leads to a virtuous self-interest and so this does not necessarily lead to moral evil. He writes, 'I love men too – not merely individuals, but every one. But I love them with the consciousness of egoism; I love them because love makes *me* happy, I love because loving is natural to me, because it pleases me. I know no "commandment of love".'

Indeed, psychological egoism and ethical egoism both support the idea that a focus on self-interest can lead, and often does lead, to moral good. In fact, all current systems, according to both psychological egoism and Max Stirner, do depend on a form of self-interest in decision making, despite deferring to an agreed framework.

In conclusion, it appears that although there are potential problems anticipated by many who are critical of ethical egoism, and the charge that it inevitably leads to moral evil is a possibility, it is not necessarily the case if one truly understands the complexity behind Stirner's ethical egoism. But despite Stirner's development of the theory, the main problems do remain and it is the potential to lead to moral evil that is of most concern. The key to the answer is really how far people can operate individually and yet simultaneously with each other. In the end, the system advocated by ethical egoism and its coherent outworking depends upon co-operation with, and the involvement of others, as a union of egoists.

Nonetheless, it has been seen already that the idea of a union of egoists brings its own problems in trying to maintain a delicate balance between the will of the individual that is accurately calculated, and that of the needs of other individuals. Some would go as far to say that this is impossible in, and certainly not a practical solution for, society as a whole.

AO2 Activity Possible lines of argument

Listed below are some conclusions that could be drawn from the AO2 reasoning in the accompanying text:

1. Any moral system dependent on self-interest inevitably leads to moral evil.

2. Self-interest does not have to lead to moral evil but it can do.

3. True self-interest underpins all moral systems and so the evidence suggests self-interest does not lead to moral evil.

4. Self-interest makes one more co-operative.

5. Ethical egoism is good in theory, but is not workable in practice and will inevitably lead to moral evil.

Consider each of the conclusions drawn above and collect evidence and examples to support each argument from the AO1 and AO2 material studied in this section. Select one conclusion that you think is most convincing and explain why it is so. Now contrast this with the weakest conclusion in the list, justifying your argument with clear reasoning and evidence.

Specification content

The extent to which all moral actions
are motivated by self-interest.

The extent to which all moral actions are motivated by self-interest

This issue really concerns the debate between psychological egoism, ethical egoism and the different interpretations given to the term self-interest.

The position of psychological egoism is that whether we like it or not, we are all driven by self-interest. The classic example is, in the words of Richard Norman, 'in caring for other people, I do so because I think that it will make my own life happier, then it would seem that it is not really a concern for others which motivates me, but a concern for myself'. In which case, all our actions can be traced back to motives of self-interest.

Some philosophers challenge this view. Peter Cave argues, 'Sometimes people act simply for the sake of others. Parents help children for the children's sake. Environmentalists save the beached whale for the sake of that whale beached.' In addition, there needs to be a clarification of what self-interest means. Max Stirner has questioned the reliability of ascribing everything to self-interest.

On the other hand, if all moral actions are not motivated by self-interest, ethical egoism suggests that the best way forward is that they ought to be. Ethical egoism is the normative version of self-interest based ethics. Julia Driver confirms this when she writes, 'Psychological egoism is a theory of human nature that purports to describe what motivates people to act. Ethical egoism, on the other hand, is normative. It purports to tell us how people ought to act.'

Indeed, such an approach questions a possible assumption one could make in reading the claim, that self-interest is a bad thing. As Frankena writes, 'It should be noted that an ethical egoist need not be an egotist or even an egotistic and selfish man in the everyday sense of these terms. Ethical egoism is an ethical theory, not a pattern of action or trait of character, and is compatible with being self-effacing and unselfish in practice.'

Max Stirner stripped away the delusions associated with conventional ideas of self-interest to re-define the self as the 'unique' when he wrote, 'I am *owner* of my might, and I am so when I know myself as *unique*. In the *unique one* the owner himself returns into his creative nothing, of which he is born.' This means that all moral actions can only be motivated by self-interest when we have a true vision of what the self consists of.

In conclusion, it is clear that there is a case for all moral actions to be motivated by self-interest, if, by 'self-interest' one means a choice, whether conscious or unconscious, in the conventional sense. However, this is not the case if, by self-interest, the statement means we are all enlightened to the extent of the egoist Max Stirner portrays. Overall, it seems, then, that whilst we are motivated by individual choice and preference, whether or not self-interest is the true description of this depends upon the interpretation and understanding one ascribes to the term 'self-interest'.

As Max Stirner himself argued, once the true nature of the self is discovered, it is only then that we are in a position to debate the issue of whether self-interest is the determining factor behind ethical actions, or indeed, whether it should be.

AO2 Developing skills

It is now time to reflect upon the information that has been covered so far. It is also important to consider how what you have learned can be focused and used for examination-style answers by practising the skills associated with AO2.

Assessment objective 2 (AO2) involves 'analysis' and 'evaluation'. The terms may be obvious but it is crucial to be familiar with how certain skills demonstrate these terms, and also, how the performance of these skills is measured (see generic band descriptors Band 5 for AS AO2).

Obviously an answer is placed within an appropriate band descriptor depending upon how well the answer performs, ranging from excellent, good, satisfactory, basic/limited to very limited.

▶ **Your next task is this:** develop each of the key points below by adding evidence and examples to fully evaluate the argument presented in the evaluation statement. The first one is done for you. This will help you in answering examination questions for AO2 by being able to ensure that 'sustained and clear views are given, supported by extensive, detailed reasoning and/or evidence' (Level 5 AO2 band descriptor).

Question focus on an evaluation of ethical egoism as causing moral confusion

1. It has been argued that ethical egoism is arbitrary because it is based upon individual interests.

DEVELOPMENT: *This means there is no overall structure to this form of ethical system other than the general guide to do as it pleases you. In other words, there is no absolute and so no real guidance for the individual.*

2. Ethical egoism cannot control society and promotes social injustice through inequality.

3. Individuals are not responsible enough to make moral decisions independently.

4. Individuals are not true to themselves, as Stirner argues people are really slaves to what they think are their own views but are really principles they choose from systems already in place.

5. Ethical egoism encourages bigotry.

6. Ethical egoism encourages anarchy.

7. Ethical egoism is misunderstood as it promotes virtuous, mature, and disciplined behaviour on the part of the individual.

8. The union of egoists shows that ethical egoism encourages co-operation not chaos.

Key skills

Analysis involves identifying issues raised by the materials in the AO1, together with those identified in the AO2 section, and presents sustained and clear views, either of scholars or from a personal perspective ready for evaluation.

This means that it picks out key things to debate and the lines of argument presented by others or a personal point of view.

Evaluation involves considering the various implications of the issues raised based upon the evidence gleaned from analysis and provides an extensive detailed argument with a clear conclusion.

This means that the answer weighs up the various and different lines of argument analysed through individual commentary and response and arrives at a conclusion through a clear process of reasoning.

Aquinas' Natural Law – a religious approach to ethics

Specification content

Natural Law derived from rational thought; based on a belief in a divine creator (the highest good as being the rational understanding of God's final purpose).

Key quote

The idea of Natural Law is sometimes described as the view that there is an unchanging, normative order that is part of the natural world. (**Buckle**)

quickfire

2.1 What was the goal of Natural Law for Aristotle?

Key quote

From the beginning Natural Law theories drew on disparate elements, which, waxing and waning at different times, shaped and reshaped the doctrine accordingly. (**Buckle**)

A: Thomas Aquinas' Natural Law: laws and precepts as the basis of morality

Aquinas' four levels of law (eternal, divine, natural and human)

Natural Law is based on a particular view about nature and the universe. That view is that the universe has a natural order that works to achieve an 'end' or 'purpose' (telos). This order, direction and purpose is determined by a supernatural power. Human beings are part of the natural world and so they too have a 'purpose' or 'nature'. It is a nature that is in all human beings. Natural Law is therefore about acting in such ways that we consistently move towards this 'purpose'. Despite its teleological focus, Natural Law is often classed as a normative, deontological theory that identifies principles of duty, that is, how we ought to behave.

Some argue that the ideals behind Natural Law can be traced back to ancient philosophers such as Aristotle. Aristotle thought the teleological goal for man was to live a life of a certain kind, that is, to be reasoning creatures and to use reason to recognise how to behave (i.e. morally). It is when human beings act morally that their purpose of telos is fulfilled. Hence the combination of reason and moral action are in accordance with the natural order of things.

Overall, Aristotle saw the goal (purpose) of human life as 'eudaimonia' (happiness). He argued that we pursue other goals in order ultimately to achieve happiness. Confusion can arise because of modern usage of the word 'happiness'. For Aristotle, 'happiness' was very different from 'pleasure', since he regarded the pursuit of pleasure for its own sake as mere gratification. In contrast, happiness was living well and being fulfilled, since it involved behaving rationally (i.e. consistent with human nature and order of the natural world). Therefore, he thought that making reasoned choices would lead to happiness. In this thinking we can see the germination of classical Natural Law.

It is with the Roman lawyer, Cicero, where the account of a Natural Law made its first systematic appearance: 'True law is right

Aristotle 384–322 BCE

reason in agreement with nature; it is of universal application. Unchanging and everlasting; it summons to duty by its commands, and averts from wrongdoings by its prohibitions.' For Cicero, the 'author' of this law was God. This connection between Natural Law and an eternal or divine law was developed by the medieval theologian and philosopher Thomas Aquinas.

Aquinas was born (1125CE) into a Europe that was emerging from the 'Dark Ages' (a period of intellectual 'darkness' cause by the decline of the Roman Empire). At this time, the Church was coming under increasing threat as more and more people began to question the authority claims of the Church. It was at around this time that the crusaders were bringing back new religious and intellectual ideas from the Holy Land (which included the work of Aristotle translated into Arabic). Aquinas studied Aristotle's works at the University of Naples at the age of 14 and he was greatly influenced by what he read.

In particular Aquinas agreed with Aristotle that rationality (the ability to reason) was a key element of human existence. He also realised that if the truths of teachings of the Bible and Christianity could be shown to be based on reason, and not just faith, then Aquinas could help defend the faith against rising challenges. Aquinas also used many of Aristotle's terms in his Natural Law theory; for example, he supported Aristotle's idea of there being 'efficient' and 'final' causes.

Aquinas agreed with Aristotle that everything in the world had a purpose, but unlike Aristotle he argued that this purpose was given to it by God. Aquinas also incorporated into his Natural Law theory Aristotle's ideas of the importance of cultivating the cardinal virtues; but for Aquinas this was in order to develop as a human being and fulfil one's true nature in relation to God.

For Aquinas, the Natural Law was located in the activity of human reasoning. By applying reason to moral problems, we will find that we act consistently with the Natural Law. Such acts are deemed good acts, or natural good, since they are in line with our true human nature and purpose. For Aquinas, the Natural Law was created by God and designed to achieve the ultimate purpose – to enjoy fellowship with God and to be perfect in the image of God. For Aquinas, obeying Natural Law meant doing actions that develop our image to reflect as closely as possible the image of God; however, true perfection of this was not possible in our lives on earth.

For Aquinas, reason still played a key role in his development of Natural Law, despite its divine origin. God was seen as the source of the Natural Law, which was rooted in the human mind. When reasoning about moral questions takes place, then good reasoning will coincide with the Natural Law. Aquinas saw God as having designed us for the end of perfection. He believed that we were made in God's image and our purpose was to eventually reflect this image perfectly. Unlike earlier philosophers such as Aristotle and the Stoics, Aquinas believed in a personal creator God. He also saw the final purpose of human beings in terms of the eternal rather than the temporal.

Key quote

Natural Law is the same for all men … there is a single standard of truth and right for everyone … which is known by everyone. (Aquinas)

Key quote

True law is right reason in agreement with Nature; it is of universal application. Unchanging and everlasting; it summons to duty by its commands and averts from wrongdoing by its prohibitions. (Cicero)

Thomas Aquinas 1225–1274

The Bible is part of divine law

Specification content

Natural Law as a form of moral absolutism and a theory which has both deontological and teleological aspects.

Key term

Casuistry: the art of applying key principles to an ethical case

Key quote

Casuistry is the science of judging cases of conscience, or moral problems. (Holmes)

Aquinas did not think that this perfection could be discovered by Natural Law alone. He also appealed to 'eternal law' and 'divine law':

- Eternal law we only know in part since it refers to the principles by which God governs the universe.
- Divine law refers to the Bible which guides us in reaching our goal of perfection. However, although such revelation is aimed at correcting that which was impaired by the Fall of human beings, Aquinas believed that such perfection was not achievable in this life, but only after death.
- Natural Law is the part of the eternal law that applies to human choices in identifying the primary precepts and can be known by our natural reason.
- Human law involves a recognition of a need to seek the common good by establishing custom and tradition of rules based in experienced judgements. Aquinas did, however, recognise that this level of law could sometimes involve wrong reasoning and lead to injustice, arguing, 'if in any point it deflects from the law of nature, it is no longer a law but a perversion of law'.

This idea that there is a universal natural standard of good needed to be worked out. Natural Law is within all of us but it is not like a physical law that has to be followed. It derives from reason and reason needs to be applied carefully and coherently in order to avoid an erroneous outcome.

AO1 Activity

Compare Aquinas' Natural Law with that of Aristotle and highlight the ways in which it is different. Then create some flash cards to write down key terms and the different levels of Natural Law.

Natural Law as a form of moral absolutism and a theory which has both deontological and teleological aspects

Natural Law ethics involve using reason to work out the morally correct behaviour that is in accordance with the goal of being human. They are usually regarded as being deontological and absolutist:

1. Deontological because what should be done is seen as being determined by fundamental principles that are not based on consequences.
2. Absolutist because they identify the right action by means of the primary precepts.

The word 'casuistry' originates from the Latin word casus meaning case. Casuistry is when core principles of pre-determined moral behaviour are applied to a 'case', context or situation. Reason is used to apply the rule and determine judgement on the morality of the situation.

For some, this is not, strictly speaking, a teleological approach due to the predetermined absolute principles that are brought to the case. However, others have seen it as teleological because in applying the predetermined absolute principles, the end result is considered. The fact that the term casuistry comes from the word 'case' suggests that a given context and 'end' results are considered and so the teleological aspect of Natural Law is often accepted.

The five primary precepts

The primary precepts apply to all human beings without exception. They are good acts because they lead us towards the main human purpose or goal. The most fundamental one that underpins them all is 'act in such a way as to achieve good and avoid evil'.

This summary identifies the most basic natural inclination. From this Aquinas then identified more general inclinations or tendencies. In one sense they can be seen as fundamental principles that must be followed in order to achieve the required ends. Although there is debate about how many precepts Aquinas identified, it is usually agreed that there are five. These five principles are:

1. Preserve innocent life ('the preservation of its own being … whatever is a means of preserving human life')

2. Orderly living in society

3. Worship God

4. Educate children

5. Reproduce to continue the species.

Whether or not acts lead us towards God depends upon whether the action fits the purpose that humans were made for. If the action helps us to fulfil that purpose then it is good. The primary precepts help us to identify what are our God-given purposes in life and therefore they identify which acts are 'good'. If we fulfil these purposes they will bring us closer to God and our ultimate goal of re-establishing a 'right' relationship with God and by doing so, gain eternal life with God in Heaven.

The secondary precepts and the importance of keeping the precepts

From these primary precepts, secondary ones can be deduced. The difference between the primary and secondary is that the primary precepts are always true and held universally, without exception. They are also self-evident. In contrast, the secondary precepts are not strictly universal since they may not hold in certain circumstances. They are also derived from reasoning from the primary precepts.

An example of a secondary precept would be 'do not steal'. This reflects the primary precept of 'orderly living in society.' However it is accepted that sometimes situations occur whereby not following secondary precepts may be supported by another primary precept. For example, if the act of stealing was for the purpose of feeding a hungry child then the primary precept of preserving innocent life takes precedence. In such a case the act is justified. Natural Law always demands that a primary precept is adhered to. It is this sort of 'working out' that is casuistry. Again, its teleological influence can be seen here.

The theologian Ronald Preston thought that the flaw with casuistry was with those who made use of casuistry, that is those that applied it, and not with the discipline of casuistry itself. Indeed, he maintains that casuistry is essential: it involves the careful use of thought in applying general principles to particular circumstances: 'Christian ethics would be an exercise in ignorance without it'.

AO1 Activity

Using the terms that have been used to describe Aquinas' Natural Law, create a mind map which summarises each concept. Make sure that you use examples, where appropriate, from the scriptures or key quotes. This helps with the ability to select and present the key, relevant features of the material you have read.

Specification content

The five primary precepts (preservation of life, ordered society, worship of God, education and reproduction of the human species) as derived from rational thought and based on the premise of 'doing good and avoiding evil'.

Specification content

The secondary precepts which derive from the primary precepts; the importance of keeping the precepts in order to establish a right relationship with God and gain eternal life with God in Heaven.

quickfire

2.5 How does casuistry help Natural Law?

Study tip

There are many examples of specialist language and vocabulary in this topic. Make sure that you don't get confused by the different words which are used to describe the main terms associated with Natural Law. Your ability to use the terms accurately in an examination answer would distinguish a high level answer from one that is simply a general response.

Key skills

Knowledge involves:

Selection of a range of (thorough) accurate and relevant information that is directly related to the specific demands of the question.

This means you choose the correct information relevant to the question set NOT the topic area. You will have to think and focus on selecting key information and NOT writing everything you know about the topic area.

Understanding involves:

Explanation that is extensive, demonstrating depth and/or breadth with excellent use of evidence and examples including (where appropriate) thorough and accurate supporting use of sacred texts, sources of wisdom and specialist language.

This means that you demonstrate that you understand something by being able to illustrate and expand your points through examples/supporting evidence in a personal way and NOT repeat chunks from a text book (known as rote learning).

Further application of skills:

Go through the topic areas in this section and create some bullet lists of key points from key areas. For each one, provide further elaboration and explanation through the use of evidence and examples.

AO1 Developing skills

It is now time to reflect upon the information that has been covered so far. It is also important to consider how what you have learned can be focused and used for examination-style answers by practising the skills associated with AO1.

Assessment objective 1 (AO1) involves demonstrating knowledge and understanding. The terms 'knowledge' and 'understanding' are obvious but it is crucial to be familiar with how certain skills demonstrate these terms, and also, how the performance of these skills is measured (see generic band descriptors Band 5 for AS AO1).

▶ **Your new task is this:** below is a weak answer that has been written in response to a question requiring an explanation of Aquinas' Natural Law. Using the band level descriptors you need to place this answer in a relevant band that corresponds to the description inside that band. It is obviously a weak answer and so would not be in bands 3–5. In order to do this it will be useful to consider what is missing from the answer and what is inaccurate. The accompanying analysis gives you observations to assist you. In analysing the answer's weaknesses, in a group, think of five ways in which you would improve the answer in order to make it stronger. You may have more than five suggestions but try to negotiate as a group and prioritise the five most important things lacking.

Answer

Aquinas thought that the primary precepts of Natural Law apply to all human beings without exception. They are good acts because they lead us towards the main human purpose or goal which is to worship God. **1**

Aquinas argued that we had to think carefully about what is right and wrong and by reasoning we can work it out. **2**

The most fundamental precept is 'act in such a way as to achieve good and avoid evil'. The Roman Catholic Church has used Natural Law as a means of making moral decisions for over seven hundred years and this shows that the theory is still popular. For example, the primary precepts include worship God which is referred to in the 10 commandments. Another precept is 'to reproduce' which is one of God's first commands to humans. **3**

Natural Law is an absolutist theory and it is too strict. Some Christians would allow abortion (which breaks the primary precept of reproduction) if it was the most 'loving thing to do' but if a woman had been raped Natural Law would not allow abortion as this would break the primary precept 'to reproduce'. **4**

Overall, Aquinas' Natural Law has other secondary precepts but they are not as important as the primary ones. **5**

Analysis of the answer

1 The answer goes straight into the precepts without explaining how they originate. The answer then states an important point but does not expand on it.

2 This point on reasoning is relevant but it is not explained at all well and suggests that the writer has no idea of why reason is the basis of Natural Law.

3 The first sentence is relevant but does not explain how it is not the primary precepts as such. The second sentence goes off at a tangent and does not stay focused. The third sentence comes back to the specific precepts and states two without development.

4 The point about absolutist is relevant but does not relate to anything else and does not explain why it may be considered an absolutist theory.

5 The last sentence shows no real evidence of understanding the secondary precepts at all. Overall there is no explanation of how the precepts are derived nor why they are important for Natural Law theory.

Issues for analysis and evaluation

The degree to which human law should be influenced by Natural Law

Specification content

The degree to which human law should be influenced by Natural Law.

It could be argued that Natural Law could influence human law in positive ways and that it has much to offer. It gives clear cut, objective and universal guidance, for example the primary precepts tell us what are right and wrong. The purpose of human law is to keep order and indeed one of the primary precepts of Natural Law reflects this.

It also supports specific human laws such as the prohibition of murder. In fact, it could be argued that human law is based in the traditions of Natural Law, such as society has been centred around the principles of the 10 commandments. Experience tells us that 'do not steal' leads to an ordered society, again this reflecting the fact that one key primary precept is 'an ordered society'.

Like human law, Natural Law can be deduced by referring to the natural order of things and does not rely on unpredictable consequences. It also gives due place to reason in making laws and ethical decision making. This could be argued to be a major help to establishing and applying human laws. Indeed, our society's legal system is based upon the principles of casuistry and working out how to apply general principles of law to specific cases, sometimes working our secondary levels of application just like the secondary precepts. Furthermore, Natural Law encourages virtuous behaviour and can create an image of the ideal citizen.

However, an alternative line of argument is that is does have its problems, which would not be acceptable in working out and applying human law. For example, it is based on the assumption that what Aquinas considered to be 'natural' is always right. This is too intolerant today and if it did influence human law then we would not allow homosexuality or same sex marriage on account of the primary precept to reproduce. Indeed, there is no debate allowed within the Natural Law framework to consider the fact that people in same sex relationships might disagree with Aquinas's view and argue that their sexuality is natural to them.

In addition, many people do not believe in a divine creator and therefore would not see a theory which is based on belief in God as an adequate basis for human law as it would not apply to all humans. In this respect some would argue that it is also outdated and that society has changed, even progressed beyond Natural Law ideas. For example, many would argue that allowing abortion is the most loving thing to do now, yet not only does it break the primary precept 'to protect life' it also would deny abortion. Abortion is part of human law and permissible.

In conclusion, while there is much of value that Natural Law may bring to society, it tends to be too absolutist in its application and therefore too intolerant for it to be a basis of human law. This does not, however, mean that it is of no use at all in helping guide some aspects of human law, for example, virtuous behaviour and the creation of an ordered society.

It must be remembered that the theory of Natural Law is based in centuries of philosophical debate and discussion and is very comprehensive in nature. It would therefore be a mistake to reject the whole of Natural Law without serious consideration.

AO2 Activity *Possible lines of argument*

Listed below are some conclusions that could be drawn from the AO2 reasoning in the accompanying text:

1. Natural law is not an adequate basis for human law as it would not be fair to everyone.

2. Natural law is an adequate basis for human law as they both have much in common.

3. Natural law is not an adequate basis for human law because it is far too dated for the modern world.

4. Natural law should influence human law but it has its limitations.

5. Natural law is not an adequate basis for human law because it tends to be adopted mostly by religious traditions.

Consider each of the conclusions drawn above and collect evidence and examples to support each argument from the AO1 and AO2 material studied in this section. Select one conclusion that you think is most convincing and explain why it is so. Now contrast this with the weakest conclusion in the list, justifying your argument with clear reasoning and evidence.

Specification content

The extent to which the
absolutist and/or deontological
nature of Natural Law works in
contemporary society.

The extent to which the absolutist and/or deontological nature of Natural Law works in contemporary society

One line of argument in response to this is that Natural Law is too restrictive and does not allow people to act following their conscience. It sets absolute standards that must be adhered to and there is clearly no flexibility. Any absolutist system does not allow for individual expression or individual reasoning that challenges set precepts.

In addition, many people prefer to make decisions based on love or happiness rather than strict rules, and there are more flexible teleological or agent-based systems such as Situation Ethics, Utilitarianism or virtue theory that are perhaps more applicable in our world today. One could even go as far as to say it is too simplistic and does not reflect the complexities of ethics in today's contemporary world.

Indeed, many people have rejected the 'deontological' approach in favour of approaches which allow them more autonomy (freedom of choice). These rules are seen as universal and applicable to all at all times, yet they themselves are hundreds of years old and whilst they may not have changed, society has changed. An obvious example is that divorce is now accepted by law but according to Natural Law this breaks the primary precept of an 'ordered society'. Another example would be to not accept homosexuality as legal and to outlaw abortion. For many this would be a regression and not progress.

Atheists or humanists would not want to follow a deontological religious ethical theory as they do not believe God is the source of morality. They do not believe that a divine being decides what is 'right' or 'wrong' for humans. Whilst not all Natural Law is religious, the principles behind it are still based in ancient thought and culture.

Nonetheless, those who favour a deontological approach to an ethical or legal system would argue that Natural Law's rules are eternal and unchanging so they can apply to all people at all times.

They would argue that Natural Law provides clear rules for people to live by and that there are no 'grey' areas or complicated issues. For example it is quite clear that any sexual act which is not open to the possibility of reproduction is wrong as it challenges one of the primary precepts.

In addition, it has been the basis of some religious moral thinking such as the Roman Catholic Church and has stood the test of time. Millions of people adhere to it today. The fact that sacred texts support such an approach for many religious believers would approve of its use as a guide in today's society.

In conclusion, there is an extent to which Natural Law works in contemporary society but this is only partial. Some would say it is the important things that Natural Law is useful for such as virtuous behaviour and a strict moral code that disapproves of anti-social behaviour such as violence, stealing and murder. In this way it is still valuable. However, in the eyes of the law, there can be no disagreement with the conclusion that its extent of value stops when certain issues of family law, medical ethics and sexuality are considered. Here the proposals put forward by Natural Law would clearly not work today.

AO2 Activity *Possible lines of argument*

Listed below are some conclusions that could be drawn from the AO2 reasoning in the accompanying text:

1. Deontological systems such as Natural Law can work in contemporary society because they give clear rules.
2. Deontological systems such as Natural Law cannot work in contemporary society because they are too inflexible.
3. Deontological systems such as Natural Law cannot work in contemporary society because they are too dated and can be accused of being intolerant.
4. Deontological systems such as Natural Law can work in contemporary society as it is clear much of our legal tradition and moral behaviour has its roots in Natural Law.
5. Deontological systems such as Natural Law cannot work in contemporary society as we have progressed beyond such simplistic systems.

Consider each of the conclusions drawn above and collect evidence and examples to support each argument from the AO1 and AO2 material studied in this section. Select one conclusion that you think is most convincing and explain why it is so. Now contrast this with the weakest conclusion in the list, justifying your argument with clear reasoning and evidence.

AO2 Developing skills

It is now time to reflect upon the information that has been covered so far. It is also important to consider how what you have learned can be focused and used for examination-style answers by practising the skills associated with AO2.

Assessment objective 2 (AO2) involves 'analysis' and 'evaluation'. The terms may be obvious but it is crucial to be familiar with how certain skills demonstrate these terms, and also, how the performance of these skills is measured (see generic band descriptors Band 5 for AS AO2).

Obviously an answer is placed within an appropriate band descriptor depending upon how well the answer performs, ranging from excellent, good, satisfactory, basic/limited to very limited.

▶ **Your task is this:** below is a weak answer that has been written in response to a question requiring evaluation of whether Natural Law is an excellent system for making moral decisions today. Using the band level descriptors you need to place this answer in a relevant band that corresponds to the description inside that band. It is obviously a weak answer and so would not be in bands 3–5. In order to do this it will be useful to consider what is missing from the answer and what is inaccurate. The accompanying analysis gives you observations to assist you. In analysing the answer's weaknesses, in a group, think of five ways in which you would improve the answer in order to make it stronger. You may have more than five suggestions but try to negotiate as a group and prioritise the five most important things lacking.

Key skills

Analysis involves identifying issues raised by the materials in the AO1, together with those identified in the AO2 section, and presents sustained and clear views, either of scholars or from a personal perspective ready for evaluation.

This means that it picks out key things to debate and the lines of argument presented by others or a personal point of view.

Evaluation involves considering the various implications of the issues raised based upon the evidence gleaned from analysis and provides an extensive detailed argument with a clear conclusion.

This means that the answer weighs up the various and different lines of argument analysed through individual commentary and response and arrives at a conclusion through a clear process of reasoning.

Answer

Some disagree with this statement because they say how can we be sure that the 'telos' or purpose of a particular object or action as defined by Natural Law is correct? For example, Natural Law says the main purpose of sex is reproduction, but what if its main purpose is pleasure? **1**

Also, Natural Law is based on the belief that God created a world and everything within it for a purpose, but many people would challenge this idea. **2** An atheist would have no reason to follow this theory as they don't believe in God. **3**

Aquinas believed that all of mankind has the same universal nature, but is there such a thing as a universal human nature? **4** For example, Eskimos think it is acceptable to allow elderly relatives to die in the cold to stop them becoming a burden on their family. This would not be acceptable to people in British society today. **5**

Therefore it is not that excellent. **6**

Analysis of the answer

1 Whilst the point raised here is valid it could have been explained more clearly. For example, why is the concept of the 'telos' so important within Natural Law? God designed everything with a purpose and therefore fulfilling its intended design is good. This could then be challenged.

2 A valid point that is partially supported by reasoning.

3 However, the reasoning is simplistic. The challenge is not about whether or not God exists but about whether or not I have a purpose.

4 The candidate needs to explain why Aquinas believed there was a 'universal human nature', i.e. we were all created this way by God. Also they could introduce scholars who reject this idea because from the study of the various cultures around the world that there doesn't appear to be a universal human nature.

5 The example of the Eskimos is good to use.

6 A poor conclusion with no real justification nor link to the above reasoning.

This section covers AO1
content and skills

Specification content

The need for humans to be more God-like by developing the three revealed virtues (faith, hope and charity).

The Apostle Paul c.4 BCE–c. 62–64 CE

quickfire

2.6 Why is it important to clarify agape as the Greek word for love?

Key terms

Agape: Greek word for pure, unconditional love

Beatific vison: the state of perfect happiness through supernatural union with God

Key quote

Faith has to do with things that are not seen and hope with things that are not at hand. (Aquinas)

B: Aquinas' Natural Law: the role of virtues and goods in supporting moral behaviour

The three revealed virtues

One way that correct reasoning can be developed is through the cultivation of certain virtues. Aquinas identified three theological virtues (revealed in the Bible) that are known as the three revealed virtues; he actually referred to them as 'articles of faith'. These are:

1. Faith   2. Hope   3. Love (charity).

Although charity is the word often used in translation, it is derived from the Greek word for 'love' used by Paul in 1 Corinthians chapter 13, 'ἀγάπη' (**agape**), which is often understood as pure, unconditional love as opposed to sexual, empathetic (usually associated with family love), and, affection (usually associated with friendship) which are different Greek words but also translated as 'love'.

1 Corinthians reads:

'If I speak in the tongues of men or of angels, but do not have love, I am only a resounding gong or a clanging cymbal. If I have the gift of prophecy and can fathom all mysteries and all knowledge, and if I have a faith that can move mountains, but do not have love, I am nothing. If I give all I possess to the poor and give over my body to hardship that I may boast, but do not have love, I gain nothing.

Love is patient, love is kind. It does not envy, it does not boast, it is not proud. It does not dishonour others, it is not self-seeking, it is not easily angered, it keeps no record of wrongs. Love does not delight in evil but rejoices with the truth. It always protects, always trusts, always hopes, always perseveres.

Love never fails. But where there are prophecies, they will cease; where there are tongues, they will be stilled; where there is knowledge, it will pass away. For we know in part and we prophesy in part, but when completeness comes, what is in part disappears. When I was a child, I talked like a child, I thought like a child, I reasoned like a child. When I became a man, I put the ways of childhood behind me. For now we see only a reflection as in a mirror; then we shall see face to face. Now I know in part; then I shall know fully, even as I am fully known.

And now these three remain: faith, hope and love. But the greatest of these is love.'

For Aquinas these are the superlative virtues that define and direct all other virtues. As they are the absolute and superlative they are perfect. However, they are aspirational in that they cannot be fully achieved in this world, being far above the capacity of a human being, but should be a standard that is aimed at. It is with God's grace through these virtues that enables a human being to strive towards perfection. Of course, the final and absolute end is supernatural union with God. This state of perfect happiness, towards which the superlative virtues guide human beings, is known as the **beatific vision**. As Aquinas writes, human beings 'attain their last end by knowing and loving God'.

In order, faith is more than just an intellectual acknowledgement of assent to the divine. Faith is an act of will for Aquinas: it is 'an act of intellect which assents to the divine truth at the command of the will, moved by God's grace'. Faith involves the whole person and reflects a total outpouring and deference to the divine as an active assertion.

Secondly, hope is the constant and consistent trust in achieving the beatific vision. This is like an inspired positive state of being, a spiritual energy that drives a person in pursuit of final end. It is a pure form of desire focused on the highest aim alone. It is an underlying virtue that supports the active participation in other non-theological, moral virtues.

Finally, the greatest of them all is love (charity). Love for God is reflected in the love for one's neighbour and is the real key to Aquinas' view of morality. Love is the one virtue that actively directs all other virtues towards God. As reflected in 1 Corinthians 13, without love, all other virtues are 'nothing', meaningless and empty. Love also has the healing property that restores our 'fallen' nature.

Key quotes

You shall love the Lord your God with all your heart and with all your soul and with all your mind. This is the great and first commandment. And a second is like it: You shall love your neighbour as yourself. On these two commandments depend all the Law and the Prophets. (Matthew 22:38–40)

God is love. Whoever lives in love lives in God, and God in them …. There is no fear in love. But perfect love drives out fear, because fear has to do with punishment. The one who fears is not made perfect in love. (1 John 4:16–18)

One vital aspect of love as a virtue for Aquinas is that it incorporates the 'gift' of wisdom, a virtue in itself and so significant in the thought of Aristotle also. But for Aquinas, wisdom was the insight into the supernatural truths of creation, the goodness of God and the beatific vision; the 'sovereign good, which is the last end …' This is crucial to moral philosophy as it is those who are wise and have a comprehensive understanding of the goodness of God that can then direct others towards the virtuous life. In this sense the superlative virtue of love is the essence of all other virtues in that it directs them towards the correct end.

> ## AO1 Activity
>
> Design a diagram that will help to summarise the three revealed virtues and that also links to the idea of the beatific vision.

Four cardinal virtues

As well as the superlative revealed virtues, Aquinas identified some natural virtues. He argued that one way correct reasoning can be developed is through the cultivation of specific natural virtues and he identified four virtues as the most important of these. These are known as the 'cardinal virtues':

1. **Prudence**　　2. **Temperance**　　3. **Fortitude**　　4. **Justice.**

For Aquinas these were the main framework for moral behaviour that helped human beings become more God-like in their application.

Prudence involves being able to make sound judgements in reasoning. It is the application of 'wisdom concerning human affairs', that is, 'right reason with respect to action'. Prudence involves being aware of both the moral principles established through Natural Law but also the specific situation wherein such principles need to be applied. In effect, prudence is the basis of casuistic endeavour.

In other words, prudence is the capability and competency of rational evaluation of circumstances in order to establish direct true and good courses of action. It does this in three steps: counsel, which is a consideration of possible courses of action; judgement, which decides upon the correct course of action; and, command, which is the application of that judgement. This is the art of casuistry.

Aquinas relates prudence to other virtues that depend upon it such as memory, intelligence, docility, shrewdness, reason, foresight, circumspection, and caution.

Temperance is all about moderation and we can see here the idea of Aristotle's doctrine of the mean. It involves sobriety and restraint. Temperance has the ability

Key quote

A new command I give you: Love one another. As I have loved you, so you must love one another. By this everyone will know that you are my disciples, if you love one another. (John 13:34–35)

Key quote

The things that we love tell us what we are. (Aquinas)

Specification content

The need for humans to be more God-like by developing the four cardinal virtues (fortitude, temperance, prudence and justice).

Key terms

Courage: a cardinal virtue involving physical, moral or spiritual endurance and strength of character

Justice: a cardinal virtue involving guidance in how we act towards others

Prudence: a cardinal virtue involving sound judgement

Temperance: a cardinal virtue involving balance and restraint

quickfire

2.7　Give an alternative word to explain each of the four cardinal virtues.

Key quote

Actions are about singular matters: and so it is necessary for the prudent man to know both the universal principles of reason, and the singulars about which actions are concerned. (Aquinas)

to purify and refine physical pleasures. He writes, 'sensible and bodily goods ... are not in opposition to reason, but are subject to it as instruments which reason employs in order to attain its proper end'.

Part of temperance is also the virtue of humility, of knowing how to present oneself in the correct and balanced manner. Meekness, generosity and studiousness and also part of temperance as they restrain such vices as anger and vanity.

The virtue of courage, sometimes also referred to as fortitude, incorporates discipline, patience, endurance and perseverance in the face of difficult circumstances, whether physical, moral or spiritual. A courageous person will not be beaten or broken by stress and sorrow. Courage also encourages nobility of character and one that is not controlled by fear on the one hand, yet on the other hand not subject to reckless, irresponsible or rash behaviour.

The final cardinal virtue is justice. It is interesting to note that whilst the first three are to do with individual qualities, the last cardinal virtue has a specific focus on others, that is, our actions towards them. It is less to do with our own character but more to do with how our actions are governed. Justice covers the law, both general as regards community welfare and also individual cases. It also involves the specific way in which matters are administrated, both in terms of goods and responsibilities which, according to Aquinas, 'are [fairly] apportioned among people who stand in a social community' and in 'due proportion'.

It is interesting to note that Aquinas' idea of justice does not mean equality for all, but recognises individual needs, relative to circumstances and needs. For example, someone in poverty requires more assistance from justice than a wealthy person.

AO1 Activity

Use your knowledge and understanding of both the revealed virtues and the cardinal virtues to complete the following task: A person has been caught stealing from the funds of a local charity. They feel very guilty and sorry for what they have done and turn to you for help. How would you encourage them to act and what advice would you give in applying the virtues? This practises the AO1 skill of being able to show an accurate understanding of ethical concepts.

Study tip

Remember to use examples when explaining the four cardinal virtues so that you can fully explain your answer.

Aquinas' definition of different types of acts and goods

Specification content

Aquinas' definition of different types of acts and goods: internal acts (the intention of the moral agent when carrying out an action) and external acts (the actions of a moral agent); real goods (correctly reasoned goods that help the moral agent achieve their telos) and apparent goods (wrongly reasoned goods that don't help the moral agent achieve their God-given purpose).

Internal acts and external acts: intention and action

Aquinas made a distinction between the intention of an act and the act itself. For those looking on, it may well be judged that an action was good. However, if the onlooker knew the real motive or intention, then it may well be seen rather differently. Likewise it is not acceptable to do a bad act intentionally even if the aim is to bring about good outcomes.

This approach to understanding intentions is important when applying Natural Law to moral dilemmas. It is at the heart of what is known as the 'doctrine of double effect'. This states that even if a good act results in bad consequences, then it is still right to do that act. It is still right to do that act, even if it was known that bad consequences would result. The important issue is the intention. If the intention was not to bring about these bad consequences, then the unfortunate side effects do not make the act morally wrong.

Classical formulations of the principle of double effect require that four conditions be met if the action is to be morally permissible:

1. That we do not wish the evil effects, and make all reasonable efforts to avoid them;
2. That the immediate effect be good in itself;
3. That the evil is not made a means to obtain the good effect;
4. That the good effect be as important (proportionate) at least as the evil effect.

An example of this would be treating a pregnant woman for cancer in order to save her life but at the same time destroying the unborn child. Since the death of the unborn child was not the intention of the act that produced it but rather an unfortunate side effect, then the act that brought it about is deemed good and morally right, according to Natural Law ethics.

Real goods and apparent goods: right and wrong reasoning

As we have seen, Natural Law is within all of us but it is not like a physical law that has to be followed. It derives from reason but sometimes the reasoning can be incorrectly directed or applied.

Reason should tell us what we should desire, since we have a natural inclination. This should lead us to our goal of perfection (image of God). This is what is known as a real good, for example being generous and giving to charity, with correct intention of course!

However, Aquinas recognised that sometimes we do not do the things that we should. We can reason wrongly.

One example of reasoning wrongly would be if a good was pursued that actually was not a good as understood by Natural Law (i.e. it did not develop perfection). It is what is referred to as an apparent good. It was the philosopher Socrates who first made this distinction and pointed out that we never desire anything that we do not, at the moment of desiring it, judge to be good; this personal judgement, however, does not make the action good. Aquinas argued that it is our fallen nature that can lead us astray to choose things that we desire, but which may not be contributing to our development into the image of God. An example of an apparent good would be following our desires for something that seems good at the time but not in line with our good overall in relation to Natural Law such as eating as much as possible because the food tastes good. This shows a lack of the cardinal virtue of temperance and cultivates a greedy character. Therefore, Aquinas did not believe that people choose to be 'evil' but rather they performed evil acts because they used their ability to reason incorrectly.

AO1 Activity

Prepare a 30-second YouTube blog explaining how Natural Law distinguishes between actions and intentions, and real and apparent goods. Give examples and this task will allow you to show that you understand the reason why certain decisions may be made as part of ethical theory.

Study tip

Do not confuse real and apparent goods. Make sure you know them accurately. Using examples for each will help you remember.

Key terms

Apparent good: apparent good is a vice or sin that takes us further away from the ideal human nature that God had planned for us

External act: an action that is seen to be good or bad but one that does not correlate with, nor is consistent with, the intention behind it

Internal act: an action that is consistent with intention whether good or bad

Real good: real good is a characteristic that will help people to become closer to the ideal human nature that God had planned for us

Food is good but this does not justify greed

quickfire

2.8 Why is intention important in Natural Law?

quickfire

2.9 What is the difference between real and apparent goods?

Key skills

Knowledge involves:

Selection of a range of (thorough) accurate and relevant information that is directly related to the specific demands of the question.

This means you choose the correct information relevant to the question set NOT the topic area. You will have to think and focus on selecting key information and NOT writing everything you know about the topic area.

Understanding involves:

Explanation that is extensive, demonstrating depth and/or breadth with excellent use of evidence and examples including (where appropriate) thorough and accurate supporting use of sacred texts, sources of wisdom and specialist language.

This means that you demonstrate that you understand something by being able to illustrate and expand your points through examples/supporting evidence in a personal way and NOT repeat chunks from a text book (known as rote learning).

Further application of skills:

Go through the topic areas in this section and create some bullet lists of key points from key areas. For each one, provide further elaboration and explanation through the use of evidence and examples.

AO1 Developing skills

It is now time to reflect upon the information that has been covered so far. It is also important to consider how what you have learned can be focused and used for examination-style answers by practising the skills associated with AO1.

Assessment objective 1 (AO1) involves demonstrating knowledge and understanding. The terms 'knowledge' and 'understanding' are obvious but it is crucial to be familiar with how certain skills demonstrate these terms, and also, how the performance of these skills is measured (see generic band descriptors Band 5 for AS AO1).

▶ **Your new task is this:** below is a strong answer that has been written in response to a question requiring an examination of the religious basis of Aquinas' Natural Law. Using the band level descriptors you can compare this with the relevant higher bands and the descriptions inside those bands. It is obviously a strong answer and so would not be in bands 1–3. In order to do this it will be useful to consider what is good about the answer and what is accurate. The accompanying analysis gives you clues and prompts to assist you. In analysing the answer's strengths, in a group, think of five things that make this answer a good one. You may have more than five observations and indeed suggestions to make it a perfect answer!

Answer

The Christian denomination that has been most influenced by Aquinas' Natural Law is the Roman Catholic Church. Their theology follows the strict rules and guidelines set out by Aquinas. Catholics believe in Natural Law when it states that all moral decisions can be made using our God-given reason. Aquinas developed Aristotelian ideas that everything has a purpose described as our 'telos'. Aquinas, unlike Aristotle, believed this purpose was given by God. Our 'telos' is to reach fellowship with God through the decisions we make using our ability to reason. Any action that does not bring about causality or fulfil its final purpose is wrong. This is the fundamental religious basis of Natural Law. **1**

Aquinas determined that Natural Law has five primary precepts: to worship God; self-preservation and preservation of the innocent; to live in an ordered society; to learn; and, continuation of the species through reproduction. He then explained the secondary precepts which demonstrate the primary precepts in action. For example, in order to live in an ordered society, we need the secondary precept 'do not kill'. Many Catholics still accept the use of Natural Law because it gives them a clear set of rules by which to lead their lives. The Roman Catholic Church upholds the precept of 'an ordered society' by maintaining an absolutist approach to issues such as abortion and euthanasia which would break this precept. The primary precepts are also supported by the Bible; for example, in Genesis it states the one of our main purposes is reproduction. **2**

As a deontological theory Natural Law focuses on the action that is performed and Aquinas described both 'exterior' and 'interior' acts. The exterior act is the act itself and the interior act is its motive. For an act to be good both the exterior and interior acts must be good. Many Roman Catholics still accept his ideas and believe that doing the right action for the right reasons will improve oneself and enable humans to get closer to God. This is consistent with the teachings of the New Testament for example, 'God is love. Whoever lives in love lives in God, and God in them' according to 1 John 4:16–18. **3**

Aquinas also encourages the development of cardinal virtues such as inner strength-fortitude or temperance (everything in moderation). Jesus taught that virtues were very important for Christians, such as in the Beatitudes. Scholars such as Peter Vardy agree that the idea of improving the self and soul is very appealing to religious believers who aim to get closer to God. [4]

Aquinas believed that the main purpose of sex was reproduction – as outlined in the primary precepts. Any sexual activity that frustrates this final cause such as homosexual sex is therefore wrong. This is the reason why many Roman Catholics hold the view that homosexual sex is not permissible because it does not lead to the fulfilment of the 'telos' of sex –reproduction. For many Christians this has a biblical basis on Old Testament teaching and the idea of procreation fits in with the creation stories and Adam and Eve in Genesis. [5]

Overall, it can be clearly seen how Aquinas' Natural Law has a clear religious basis, from being grounded in God as 'telos', the nature of the precepts, the nature of actions and the development of virtuous character, all supported by Christian religious texts. [6]

Hints

1. Basis in God.
2. Evidence.
3. Explanation and link.
4. Virtues.
5. Example of application.
6. Clarity.

Completed hints

1. The answer has carefully selected accurate and relevant information. Specialist vocabulary is also used accurately. A clear religious basis for Aquinas' Natural Law is established.

2. The answer has clearly linked the primary and secondary precepts here, not only to each other, but also to Roman Catholic teachings and to biblical evidence.

3. The answer has clearly defined interior and exterior acts here and explained why these concepts are important to religious believers.

4. In addition to this he has identified the cardinal virtues and their link to human personal development. He has supported the point he has made with a scholarly opinion.

5. Here the answer has clearly identified why Roman Catholics would support Natural Law's view on homosexual acts.

6. A concise but accurate summary.

Issues for analysis and evaluation

The strengths and weaknesses of Natural Law

Natural Law clearly has many strengths otherwise it would have not been as influential as it has been throughout history.

The first attraction and strength is that it is based on what it means to be human. To be human means acting in line with your true nature and following our natural inclinations. When the theory is applied, it assumes the special status of human beings.

Natural Law also reveals a universal law, and is therefore not relative to culture or a religion. This means that the primary precepts are common to all. Because it is about following natural inclinations, then the application to a moral issue is always the same, wherever you are and whoever you are.

Natural Law appeals to common sense and some versions, for example that posed by Aristotle, do not need God for its authority. It also gives a clear basis for morality, there is an authority and a clear justification for actions allowed and it is clear how Natural Law is applied. For instance, the primary precepts are clearly identified and justified. It is clear for all to see why abortion is wrong.

Natural Law also judges the intrinsic value of actions regardless of outcomes – it is the action itself, not the outcomes, that decides whether an act is moral. This avoids the problem of seemingly doing an action that appears good but in fact has evil motives. In such cases the theory does not identify those acts as good. This seems a correct judgement.

It could also be argued that its application seems clear even when there appears a conflict within the system itself. Whilst the application of the primary precepts is straightforward, the doctrine of double effect allows for possible conflicts of primary precepts.

Finally, it does encourage virtuous behavior such as love, wisdom, justice and temperance. These are valuable in any society.

However, there are some strong challenges to Natural Law. Perhaps the most significant one is often referred to as the naturalistic fallacy. It is unreasonable to expect someone who does not believe in the existence of a moral God, to accept that what simply exists as human nature has moral authority. It is argued that describing the facts of any situation never leads to making a value judgement. What 'is' (fact) does not imply what 'ought to be' (value). In other words there seems to be a mistake in reasoning (fallacy) in identifying morality with another concept (i.e. nature).

Indeed, what does it mean to say an action is 'natural'? Does it just mean that it refers to the action that is common to a particular group?

There is also a question over whether or not there really is a common human nature? Surely the fact that cultures have different values challenges the idea of a common nature; for example, the Spartan nature was to kill weak or defective children whereas this is certainly not universal. Some would deny there was any such thing as a human nature. Indeed, human nature seems to change. For instance, the debate about homosexuality has raised questions about what is natural.

There is also the challenge that if there is a constant unchanging human nature and a Natural Law that stems from it, how is it that so many through the centuries have got human nature so wrong, for example slavery and apartheid were considered as natural.

As Natural Law is a major component of Roman Catholic doctrine, its legalism might seem to some to be in conflict with a Christian stance. It is action centred rather than people and consequence centred. This is particularly evidenced in Natural Law approaches to abortion and euthanasia.

The doctrine of double effect assumes that a sharp distinction can be drawn between directly intending a result and merely foreseeing it. If a result can be foreseen, then in performing the action the person must be intending the consequence. For instance, the acceptance of collateral damage from a bombing raid. If it is known that many innocent lives will be lost, then is the act moral? It also raises the issue that Natural Law itself raises about intentions and real and apparent goods.

In conclusion, just as with any system there are key strengths and weaknesses. Rather than judging the overall quality of Natural Law, it may be better to point out that, for many, there are consequentialist systems that are preferable to Natural Law simply because they are more flexible and suitable for today's world.

AO2 Activity *Possible lines of argument*

Listed below are some conclusions that could be drawn from the AO2 reasoning in the accompanying text:

1. The strengths of Natural Law can withstand criticisms as they have done throughout time.
2. The weaknesses with Natural Law are far too strong for it to remain a valuable ethical system today.
3. Since most of our laws are a reflection of Natural Law is it still valid today.
4. Natural Law will remain valid if it will focus more in application on virtues and goods in casuistry rather than on precepts.
5. Other ethical theories that are either more flexible or consequentialist are preferable to Natural Law.

Consider each of the conclusions drawn above and collect evidence and examples to support each argument from the AO1 and AO2 material studied in this section. Select one conclusion that you think is most convincing and explain why it is so. Now contrast this with the weakest conclusion in the list, justifying your argument with clear reasoning and evidence.

A consideration of whether Natural Law promotes injustice

We can see how this issue may be raised because on the one hand Natural Law fails to recognise that some acts, for example sex, can have more than one purpose. As a result this clearly discriminates against those who perform an act without fulfilling its purpose, for example pre-marital relationships and homosexuality.

As it is inflexible at times, Natural Law fails to move with the times and promotes what some would see as 'old-fashioned' and out of date ideals. For example, this can clearly be seen in the fact that divorce is viewed as wrong and yet is legal; likewise, abortion is legal but viewed as wrong by Natural Law.

Unlike relativistic theories such as Situation Ethics, Natural Law fails to consider the personal situation in which a person finds themselves. Some people argue it could be more loving to allow non-married couples to express their love for each other through sex. Moreover, it does not, in considering the context, reflect the true application of law, which always considers 'mitigating circumstances' for any crime committed. Natural Law simply applies universal principles almost like a 'one size fits all' theory. This is certainly inconsistent with modern justice. However, some would argue that there are clear ways in which Natural Law promotes justice by providing humans with a set of rules which they can live by and it promotes a sense of community. This is very important for social justice.

Specification content

A consideration of whether Natural Law promotes injustice.

Natural Law also promotes universal and eternal laws: so human beings know, regardless of the century they live in or where they live, what is acceptable and what is not. People have the primary precepts as guidance. In this sense it both promotes and supersedes human justice, as it recognises that God punishes those who do wrong and sin as they move further away from reaching the goal of eternal life with God. This is a very significant aspect for those religious believers that follow Natural Law.

Finally, it promotes justice by advocating basic human rights such as the right to life, the right to education and the right live in an ordered society. No-one would disagree with these today.

In conclusion, it appears that although Natural Law does have its flaws when applied rigidly and has the potential to cause injustice, the fact that its very basis is to promote virtue, love and protection of the innocent through an ordered society means that it would be very harsh to agree and make a general statement that Natural Law promotes injustice.

AO2 Activity *Possible lines of argument*

Listed below are some conclusions that could be drawn from the AO2 reasoning in the accompanying text:

1. The statement cannot be true because one of the virtues, and indeed a purpose of Natural Law, is to see that justice is served.

2. The inflexible nature of Natural Law leads to injustice in practice.

3. Overall, Natural Law does not promote injustice but there are potential problems with it in application.

4. If Natural Law were followed, it would clearly promote injustices and there are several examples of this.

5. If applied carefully, sensitively and with good reasoning in a Christian manner, Natural Law could never promote injustice.

Consider each of the conclusions drawn above and collect evidence and examples to support each argument from the AO1 and AO2 material studied in this section. Select one conclusion that you think is most convincing and explain why it is so. Now contrast this with the weakest conclusion in the list, justifying your argument with clear reasoning and evidence.

AO2 Developing skills

It is now time to reflect upon the information that has been covered so far. It is also important to consider how what you have learned can be focused and used for examination-style answers by practising the skills associated with AO2.

Assessment objective 2 (AO2) involves 'analysis' and 'evaluation'. The terms may be obvious but it is crucial to be familiar with how certain skills demonstrate these terms, and also, how the performance of these skills is measured (see generic band descriptors Band 5 for AS AO2).

Obviously an answer is placed within an appropriate band descriptor depending upon how well the answer performs, ranging from excellent, good, satisfactory, basic/limited to very limited.

▶ **Your task is this:** below is a strong answer that has been written in response to a question requiring evaluation of Natural Law as a good basis for making moral decisions. Using the band level descriptors you can compare this with the relevant higher bands and the descriptions inside those bands. It is obviously a strong answer and so would not be in bands 1–3. In order to do this it will be useful to consider what is good about the answer and what is accurate. The accompanying analysis gives you clues and prompts to assist you. In analysing the answer's strengths, in a group, think of five things that make this answer a good one. You may have more than five observations and indeed suggestions to make it a perfect answer!

Key skills

Analysis involves identifying issues raised by the materials in the AO1, together with those identified in the AO2 section, and presents sustained and clear views, either of scholars or from a personal perspective ready for evaluation.

This means that it picks out key things to debate and the lines of argument presented by others or a personal point of view.

Evaluation involves considering the various implications of the issues raised based upon the evidence gleaned from analysis and provides an extensive detailed argument with a clear conclusion.

This means that the answer weighs up the various and different lines of argument analysed through individual commentary and response and arrives at a conclusion through a clear process of reasoning.

Answer

For many believers across the world Natural Law does provide an excellent basis for making moral decisions. Its absolutist approach determines that some actions are always right or always wrong. This provides people with clear cut consistent rules. Natural Law echoes the Ten Commandments in the Bible such as 'do not kill'. [1]' Natural Law is still used by the Roman Catholic Church, the largest Christian denomination in the world. It must therefore provide an excellent basis for making moral decisions as it is still used by many as part of their faith. The Pope criticised relativist theories as 'moving towards a dictatorship of relativism' where the individual only looks out for themselves. In contrast, Natural Law is based on goodness for all humanity. It promotes precepts such as 'an ordered society'. It also promotes the Golden Rule of Christianity – 'Do unto others as you would have them do unto you' through cardinal virtues such as justice. [2]

However, many have criticised Natural Law's absolutist approach. For example, some philosophers have observed that what is 'good' or acceptable varies within different cultures and believed that there is no such thing as a universal human nature. [3] The idea that all of humanity is given the gift of reason also seems unrealistic as not everyone has the ability to reason. Reformist Protestants such as Martin Luther have also criticised Natural Law and Roman Catholic theology for the emphasis they place on human reason, as he believed that the Bible was the highest form of authority. [4]

Many also believe that Natural Law is outdated in its views on abortion and euthanasia and the strict rules it applies prevent people from doing what they believe to be right. It was a firm belief in Natural Law that led to the Pope condemning the widespread use of contraception in poverty-stricken African countries when surely allowing this would be the most loving answer to providing a better quality of life? [5]

Whilst many favour the rules-based approach given by Natural Law and the way it allows them to have a clear moral stance on many issues, I think it is fundamentally flawed as people's perception of what is a rational decision will vary according to their cultural background – what is considered rational and right in one culture may not be in another. **6**

Hints

1 Focus.

2 Understanding.

3 Examples.

4 Role of authority.

5 Develop.

6 Link.

Completed hints

1 The answer has clearly focused on the question and has made a valid point on the benefits of Natural Law's absolutist approach.

2 The second half of the paragraph displays clear understanding of one of the core principles of Natural Law and of one of the virtues.

3 Some good examples of evaluation are given here pointing out two of the major weaknesses of Natural Law. The fact that not everyone has the ability to reason could be developed further with an example.

4 The reference to Martin Luther shows a mature understanding of the issue of the importance of scriptural authority over Natural Law.

5 Whilst the points raised here are perfectly valid, they could be developed – what are Natural Law's views on abortion and euthanasia and why are these views held? Why according to Natural Law would contraception not be allowed?

6 An appropriate conclusion has been drawn that clearly links to the arguments presented above. Perhaps an example could have been used to illustrate the point made? But still, overall very good.

Natural Law is still used by the Roman Catholic Church

C: Aquinas' Natural Law: application of the theory

The issues arising from abortion

An abortion can be defined as the termination of a pregnancy before 24 weeks. Abortions are available on the National Health Service (NHS) but women seeking them must be referred by a doctor. According to the Brook Advisory Service '… although the normal legal limit for abortion is 24 weeks, it is usually easiest to get an abortion on the NHS if a woman is under 12 weeks pregnant'.

There are two classifications of abortion: medical and surgical. The first, achieved by means of an abortion pill (mifepristone) and a tablet (prostaglandin) inserted into the vagina 36 to 48 hours later, is a **medical abortion**. It involves no surgery and, in effect, is like heavy menstruation; however, it is not available in all areas.

The second type involves surgery and is called a **surgical abortion**. Most commonly, it is achieved through vacuum aspiration or suction and is available up to the week 13 of pregnancy. Women usually recover within a few hours and can go home the same day. In later stages of pregnancy, a process of dilation and evacuation is used, which involves opening the cervix and entering the womb, then removing the contents by means of surgical instruments as well as suction.

One of the important issues surrounds the question of exactly the moment of the beginning of 'humanness'. The beginning of 'humanness' is debated in philosophical, ethical and legal circles but, biologically speaking, the beginning is at conception. In its broadest terms, the development, that is, the actualisation of the potentiality to become fully human, takes the following course:

1. conception
2. **zygote** (pre-embryo, 0–5 days)
3. **blastocyst** (a group of multiplying cells, pre-embryo, 5–14 days)
4. **embryo** (14 days to 8 weeks)
5. **foetus** (8 weeks onwards)
6. new born (birth, usually between 38 and 42 weeks).

It is interesting that the stage of pregnancy is calculated from the first day of the woman's last period. Despite such accuracy of science and technology, even the stage of conception is arguably vague and the timings given above assume normal growth rates.

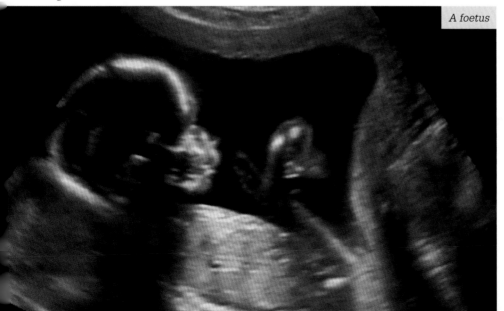

A foetus

This section covers AO1
content and skills

Specification content

Aquinas' Natural Law: application of the theory. The application of Aquinas' Natural Law to the issue of: abortion.

Key terms

Blastocyst: a group of multiplying cells

Embryo: an animal in the early stage of development before birth; in humans, the embryo stage is the first three months after conception

Foetus: the unborn baby from the end of the eighth week after conception (when the major structures have formed) until birth

Medical abortion: abortion by means of the abortion pill

Surgical abortion: abortion by means of the suction method

Zygote: a cell formed by the union of a male sex cell (a sperm) and a female sex cell (an ovum), which develops into the embryo according to information encoded in its genetic material

quickfire

2.10 What is the legal timeframe for an abortion?

Key quote

Personhood may be one thing and human life another; hence it is possible to argue that, while the zygote may not be a person, there is no logical alternative to regarding it as the first stage in human life. (Mason and Laurie)

Key quote

The basic argument against abortion, on which all others build, is that the unborn child is already a human being, a person, a bearer of rights, and that abortion is therefore murder. (Mackie)

Key quote

Whether or not abortion should be legal turns on the answer to the question of whether and at what point a foetus is a person. This is a question that cannot be answered logically or empirically. The concept of personhood is neither logical nor empirical: it is essentially a religious, or quasi-religious idea, based on one's fundamental (and therefore unverifiable) assumptions about the nature of the world. (Campos)

David Steel born 1938

quickfire

2.11 When was the Abortion Act introduced?

quickfire

2.12 What are the two conditions of the act in considering an abortion necessary?

Key quote

What is to be done with a live foetus? The 1990 Act absolves the gynaecologist of destruction only and not the killing of a 'creature in being'. (Mason and Laurie)

The changes in the law against abortion reflect changes in attitude and begin with the Offences Against the Person Act (1861), which depicts procuring a miscarriage as a criminal act. The problem was that there was no option for therapeutic activity. In 1929 the Infant Preservation Act allowed the preservation of the mother's life as reason for a termination.

David Steel introduced the Abortion Act 1967 that stated: 'two doctors must agree that an abortion is necessary. It is deemed necessary if:

1. The woman's physical health is threatened by having the baby or any existing children would be harmed mentally or physically by the woman proceeding to have the baby.

2. There is a high risk the baby would be handicapped.

This was clarified by the Embryology Act 1990 (Section 37). According to Mason and Laurie '... it now states that a person is not guilty of an offence under the law of abortion when termination is performed by a registered practitioner and two registered medical practitioners have formed the opinion in good faith that the continuance of the pregnancy would involve risk, greater than if the pregnancy were terminated, of injury to the physical or mental health of the pregnant woman or any existing children of her family.' The legal limit was also reduced from 28 weeks to 24 weeks; however, the Act also removed time restrictions for a foetus aborted due to abnormality.

AO1 Activity

An **acrostic** is a form of writing in which the first letter of each line spells out a word. Using the word 'Abortion', aim to write out **eight** facts or key words which you feel sum up the important aspects of the issue.

Study tip

There are many examples of specialist language and vocabulary in this topic. Make sure that you don't get confused by the different terms that are used to describe issues related to abortion. Your ability to use the terms accurately in an examination answer would distinguish a high level answer from one that is simply a general response.

This raises a key legal issue in that an abortion for reason of abnormality does absolve the gynaecologist of destruction of the foetus but not of unlawful killing of a 'creature in being'. For instance, if such an abortion entitles the foetus to a birth and death certificate, then surely such a 'person' is protected by the full extent of the law?

Peter Singer raises the issue of personhood when he writes: 'To kill a human adult is murder, and is unhesitatingly and universally condemned. Yet there is no obvious sharp line which marks the zygote from the adult. Hence the problem.'

Key quote

The dilemma of the gynaecologist who is there to relieve a woman of her foetus, however, is that 'there is now an infant who, on any interpretation, is entitled to a birth certificate, and, if necessary, a certificate as to the cause of death'. (Mason and Laurie)

Another related issue involves the **sanctity of life**, which is the belief that life is in some way sacred or holy, traditionally understood as being given by God. Kant actually gives the idea of the sanctity of life a non-religious perspective based on purely ethical grounds, and philosophers such as Peter Singer have long called for a shift from talking about the sanctity of life towards a more universal discussion about the value of life.

The key debates, then, consider when an act can be classed as killing, or even murder, and at which point potential human life acquires such value as to make abortion an ethical injustice.

This leads into more specific questions concerning the nature and status of the foetus.

One of the major problems with the abortion debate is that there are blurred and inaccurate definitions for the terminology. For example, those campaigning against abortion (**pro-life**) and those campaigning for the rights of women to have abortions (**pro-choice**), interpret the terms *life* and *unborn* differently. For one group, the idea of a human person includes the stage of an embryo, while the other considers only that stage beyond birth.

It is important, therefore, to establish what such interested parties actually mean when they refer to a baby, a person and a life. This is intrinsic to this aspect of the debate and therefore it is important to consider some different views. There are several arguments concerning the application of the status of personhood to the embryo, foetus or child. These tend to be based on either biological stages or related to philosophical and religious principles or concepts.

Biological debates depend upon physical evidence to define the status of the foetus. Some argue that the status of personhood is only applied at actual physical **birth**. This is the first true point of independence and individuality. Others argue for the point of **viability**, that is, the status of personhood is awarded at that time when the unborn can exist beyond any dependence on the mother. A more traditional approach has been defining the start of human life by what is known as the **quickening** when the 'child' is first felt to move, although this does vary from individual to individual and therefore has no standardised point. Finally, some would suggest life begins at the point when **potential** for life begins (at conception).

Philosophical or religious arguments are based on concepts or principles beyond the physical evidence. Some would argue that life begins at the point of **consciousness** when the ability to think and reason is clearly evidenced. Others argue for **ensoulment** when it is believed that the soul enters the body. This point is debated as proposals between 40 and 90 days have been offered, but the argument defies accuracy.

Peter Vardy makes an important point when he observes that arguments are based upon the meaning of words, or what he calls '**relational factors**'. What he means by this is that there are different interpretations or understandings of the same words. Until accurate definitions of key terms are agreed, the stage at which personhood status is awarded can never be universal.

Key quote

We may take the doctrine of the sanctity of human life to be no more than a way of saying that human life has some very special value …. The view that human life has unique value is deeply rooted in our society and is enshrined in our law. (**Singer**)

Key terms

Birth: the point at which the child is separated from the mother and becomes a separate entity

Consciousness: awareness of self

Ensoulment: the point when the soul enters the body

Potential: the possibility, at conception, of becoming a human person

Pro-choice: supporting women's rights to have abortions

Pro-life: against abortion

Quickening: traditionally, when the child is first felt to move inside the mother

Relational factors: different interpretations of the same words or terms, depending on the viewpoint of the observer

Sanctity of life: the belief that life is sacred or holy, given by God

Viability: the ability to grow and develop into an adult, especially the ability of the child to exist without dependence on the mother

Key quote

The only absolute in the saga is that 'life' as it is generally understood begins with the formation of the zygote; on this view, the conservative Roman Catholic view represents the only tenable option – the difficulty is that it is also the least practical solution to the question. (Mason and Laurie)

Key quote

Definitions intended for statistical use are not, however, necessarily the same as those to be applied in practice. (Mason and Laurie)

Key quote

… I will neither give a deadly drug to anybody who asked for it, nor will I make a suggestion to this effect. Similarly I will not give to a woman an abortive remedy. In purity and holiness I will guard my life and my art …. What I may see or hear in the course of the treatment or even outside of the treatment in regard to the life of men, which on no account one must spread abroad, I will keep to myself, holding such things shameful to be spoken about. If I fulfil this oath and do not violate it, may it be granted to me to enjoy life and art, being honoured with fame among all men for all time to come; if I transgress it and swear falsely, may the opposite of all this be my lot. (Hippocratic Oath – Classical version)

quickfire

2.13 Identify two key areas of discussion from the biological debates concerning the beginning of human life.

One final consideration is that there is a clear disparity in the development of individuals. During life, although there are broad timescales at which people mature, develop and grow, there is, by the very nature of individuality, a blurring of the exact moment one moves from adolescence to adulthood, from childhood through puberty and so forth. Why are the early stages of development any different?

AO1 Activity

Find out how the Hippocratic Oath has been modified for doctors today and explain why.

Hippocrates 460–370 BCE

HIPPOCRATES HIRACLIDÆ F. COVS.
Ex marmore antiquo.

The application of Natural Law to the issue of abortion

For those who accept Aquinas' doctrine of Natural Law and seek to apply this to the issue of abortion, believe that the key primary precept involved here is that of preserving innocent life. Hence the act of abortion is seen as inherently evil because of the intentional and direct killing of an innocent human being. This would apply to all situations including the cases of rape or incest.

The debate, however, will then focus on when a foetus can be considered as a person. Opinions vary between regarding it as the moment of conception or choosing the time of the appearance of a certain feature, such as neural activity. This is where there could be some debate.

Study tip

Being able to make accurate reference to sacred texts, and/or sources of wisdom where appropriate is vital if you wish to gain a high level in your answer. However, make sure that the quotations that you use are relevant to the point that you are making in your answer.

There is another approach that could, however, be taken. Professor of Ethics, Howard Kainz has argued that in the case of abortion, two other precepts are perhaps even more relevant to the issue of abortion than the 'preservation of life principle', that of the right to procreation and the right to nurture offspring. He argues that in the case of abortion there are those who defend the right of the woman if her life is in danger: 'Those who apply the first precept often make an exception for situations threatening the life of the mother, since there is a conflict between two rights to life.' However, for Kainz, this opens up another area of debate regarding rape in that 'if every woman has a right to conceive and procreate, and if this right implies that she has a right to make that choice *voluntarily*, no more obvious infractions of that right than rape and incest can be contemplated'. In other words, if one uses a principle of exception for the first precept, then one has to admit the possibility that there could be exceptions in applying the two precepts of right to procreation and nurturing offspring. Just as one has a right to preserve one's life, one also has an equal right to preserve one's choice to procreate. Rape clearly violates this choice. Indeed, it is then a question of conflicting principles that exist within the primary precepts as they stand. This would then obviously open up the debate or real and apparent goods but still raise more questions.

Kainz, however, argues that despite all this confusion, a more virtuous approach to rape may be more Christian in terms of the dilemma of abortion. He argues that 'Christian principles may supersede considerations of conflicts of right related to Natural Law' and that a woman who decides to nurture a child after rape or who sacrifices her own life due to a problem pregnancy in order for the child to survive are classic examples of virtuous behaviour that demonstrate 'going the extra mile'. He writes, 'from the standpoint of Natural Law, such decisions would belong in the category of heroic virtue — sacrifices of personal rights that go beyond any normal call to maternal responsibility'.

Specification content

Aquinas' Natural Law: application of the theory. The application of Aquinas' Natural Law to the issue of: abortion.

Pope Pius XI 1857–1939

Key quote

Whether inflicted upon the mother or upon the child, [abortion] is against the precept of God and the law of nature: 'Thou shalt not kill'. (Pope Pius XI)

Key quote

On the other hand, it should be recognised that application of the second precept may change our perspective on some of the common exceptions many are willing to allow regarding the prohibition of abortion … in light of the second precept, a conflict of rights obtains also in the cases of rape and incest. For, if every woman has a right to conceive and procreate, and if this right implies that she has a right to make that choice *voluntarily*, no more obvious infractions of that right than rape and incest can be contemplated. (Kainz)

Key quotes

When suffering is the result of following an ethical principle then we need to look very carefully at our ethical principle and ask whether we are applying it too inflexibly. (Hope)

The doctor's dilemma is self-evident – is he or she practising truly 'good' medicine in keeping alive a neonate who will be unable to take a place in society or who will be subject to pain and suffering throughout life? (Mason and Laurie)

It is perverse to seek a sense of ethical purity when this is gained at the expense of the suffering of others. (Hope)

Specification content

Aquinas' Natural Law: application of the theory. The application of Aquinas' Natural Law to the issue of: voluntary euthanasia.

Key term

Euthanasia: literally meaning a gentle or easy death, it is the controversial and, in some cases, illegal action of allowing a terminally ill person to die with dignity, avoiding pain and suffering

Kainz does raise an important issue but also indicates that Natural Law has an obligation to reason, through the art of casuistry, and clearly take into account Christian virtues. However, some would be reluctant to accept that even the virtue of agape (love), the greatest of divine virtues, can be stretched beyond what the primary precepts identify as its key application. Critics may suggest that this is not a true understanding of the application of such virtue.

Key quote

It goes without saying, however, that Christian principles may supersede considerations of conflicts of right related to Natural Law. Deciding to bring a child into the world after a rape, for example, would be in the same category as gospel admonitions to 'go the other mile', 'lend to others without hoping for repayment', 'turn the other cheek,' etc. In situations of problem pregnancies like ectopic gestation, a woman deciding to forfeit her own right to life and her right to nurture and raise her children to bring her child to term would be going even further in 'other miles'. From the standpoint of Natural Law, such decisions would belong in the category of heroic virtue — sacrifices of personal rights that go beyond any normal call to maternal responsibility. (Kainz)

Interestingly enough, the doctrine of double effect, however, does permit the death of the foetus, but only as a by-product of another act. This means that the intention was not to kill the foetus. For instance, in the case of the use of chemotherapy or the performance of a hysterectomy to remove a cancerous uterus, when it would lead to the death of the foetus. However, as that is not the intention of the act, but rather a by-product, the removal of the cancerous uterus is acceptable.

It is quite clear that in its application, Natural Law itself is not as clear as some would suggest and, arguably, how it first appears to present itself.

AO1 Activity

Write a newspaper column response as a Roman Catholic follower of Natural Law to a woman who has been considering an abortion giving clear reasons for your advice.

The issues arising from euthanasia

The issue of euthanasia is equally as complex as abortion and for similar reasons. The context is the end, as opposed to the beginning, of life, yet some of the principles are the same. Certainly, the ethical issues identified progress under similar headings.

The first problem involves the technical difficulties surrounding the different definitions and types of euthanasia. There is a clear disparity in law both between countries and the ways in which legislation is applied.

The meaning of the word derives from the Greek eu thanatos, interpretations of which include good, easy, gentle (eu) and death (thanatos). The key idea goes beyond the mere descriptive term and encompasses an idea of a death that is beneficial for the party involved. Tony Hope, Professor for Medical Ethics at the University of Oxford and author of a key text for student doctors, *Medical Ethics and Law: The Core Curriculum*, offers the distinctions between different types of euthanasia. Here we are interested in voluntary euthanasia, sometimes referred to in its more narrow application as physician-assisted suicide. Hope identifies the following:

- Euthanasia: one person kills another with intention or allows another's death for the other's benefit.
- Active euthanasia: one person actions another's death for the other's benefit
- Voluntary: the request to die by the person who competently wishes it so.

Voluntary euthanasia is therefore also known as active euthanasia.

The history of the legal status of voluntary euthanasia reflects many of the issues that arise when considering whether any proposed change in law may actually 'work'.

In 1961 suicide was decriminalised. Despite this, the Suicide Act 1961 was very explicit that to aid or assist suicide in any way was still a crime.

As with the debate surrounding abortion, there are two central principles at stake. The first is whether or not killing should be allowed in any circumstances. The second relates to the value that is given to life in respect of issues such as sanctity or quality, whether for religious, ethical or philosophical reasons.

In the consideration of abortion, the second area for debate was the point at which it could be said that life actually begins. The problems associated with establishing the start of a life could be deemed similar to those related to the end of life.

Generally, a physical end of life can be determined medically. However, for a person in a coma, for example, who is kept alive artificially and yet still demonstrates signs of consciousness, the issue is problematic. Such a situation again calls into question the definition of life and even whether a physical definition suffices. This is a key question in the euthanasia debate.

Related to this issue are also the philosophical questions about quality of life. Is there a point at which one can conclude that life has lost its value? If so, exactly when should this be and who is going to decide?

There is also the issue of the patient refusing to accept treatment, which is allowed by law, even where refusal may result in harm to themselves. The only exception would be if they were determined not to have the mental capacity or competency to make such a decision.

This mainly refers to those who are dying. They have the right not to prolong their life, by refusing treatment. They do not have the right, however, to hasten an end to their life by administering a different course of medication. Does this pose a contradiction? If a person refuses treatment to prolong life then have they shortened their life? How, in principle, is this different from shortening life in another way? Thus, humans have the legal right to the opportunity to extend life but not to shorten it. Where death is inevitable, humans can only stave it off and are not allowed to welcome it.

There appears to be an uncomfortable inconsistency here. Consciously refusing treatment, knowing that the consequence is death, is seen as acceptable. Consciously willing medication of which the consequence is also death, only sooner and with less pain, is unacceptable. It is this delicate dilemma – if, indeed, it is one – that is at the very heart of the euthanasia debate: namely, just how far should a person's individual rights extend over their own body, fate and destiny?

Ethically, perhaps people should have a duty to prevent the prolonged and meaningless suffering of others. In addition, consideration should be given to the impact that a prolonged and painful death may have on others, such as close family and friends.

quickfire

2.14 What is voluntary euthanasia?

quickfire

2.15 When was suicide decriminalised?

Key quote

Patients have the right to decide how much weight to attach to the benefits, burdens, risks and the overall acceptability of any treatment. They have the right to refuse treatment even where refusal may result in harm to themselves or in their own death, and doctors are legally bound to respect their decision. **(General Medical Council)**

Arguments against the introduction of a law that allows euthanasia point to the very real risk of abuse:

- How could such a law be effectively monitored?
- Would it be in the best interests of society as a whole?
- Would it be a workable law?
- Further, does euthanasia go against the Hippocratic Oath?
- Is it interfering with the natural or divinely ordained course of events?

For medical practitioners there is no clear legal guideline other than advice given by such bodies as the British Medical Association in 2001 or the Royal College of Paediatrics and Child Health. However, such guidelines are very vague with respect to active intervention and the withholding of curative medical treatment. Even doctors are unsure and clearly vulnerable, both legally and ethically.

Medical practitioners have no clear legal guidelines

Key quote

A patient's condition may improve unexpectedly, or may not progress as anticipated, or their views about the benefits, burdens and risks of treatment may change over time. You should make sure that there are clear arrangements in place to review decisions. (General Medical Council)

AO1 Activity

As a doctor write down the concerns that you may have if you were to be involved with someone that was terminally ill and was considering euthanasia.

Specification content

Aquinas' Natural Law: application of the theory. The application of Aquinas' Natural Law to the issue of: voluntary euthanasia.

The application of Aquinas' Natural Law to the issue of: voluntary euthanasia

The primary precept of preserving innocent life is also the key principle when faced with the issue of euthanasia. It is often expressed in terms of 'the sanctity of life' argument. Sanctity means 'the quality of being sacred or holy'. Natural Law teaches that there is something special about a human being that is above and beyond that of animals. Therefore it should be protected. The taking of another's life, even if they request it, is not therefore morally acceptable. By the same argument, the taking of one's own life (suicide) is equally an immoral act.

The Catechism of the Catholic Church defines euthanasia as 'an act or omission which, of itself or by intention, causes the death of handicapped, sick, or dying persons – sometimes with an attempt to justify the act as a means of eliminating suffering.'

This would be the objection of Natural Law to an approach that suggests casuistry and a consideration of virtues or of ends is subordinate to the application of primary precepts. It also suggests that there are dangers in what may be considered virtuous and entitled 'mercy' killing, is really an apparent good only.

However, there are some instances of uncertainty in the application of even the first precept. As Professor Ian Harriss has argued, in a paper on euthanasia and applied ethics in 2005, there are still some questionable applications of the first precept that exist today in the name of Natural Law. He writes, 'In Spain, where the Catholic faith and Natural Law have exerted a strong influence on policy, an intervention with the direct intention of either accelerating death or killing the patient is considered morally wrong, but the heavy use of sedation implies that unconsciousness, either disease-induced, or drug-induced, is generally perceived as the best way out.'

Although administering drugs to end a life is unacceptable, it could be argued that it is morally acceptable, under Natural Law, to give a large dose of morphine to control the pain of a terminally ill patient, even if it was foreseen that the morphine would shorten the patient's life. Whatever the consequences, the intention was not to kill the person, but to bring relief to their pain. This is the application of the principle of double effect.

However, again, in response to this application of Natural Law, Harriss writes, 'Natural Law theory is inherently hostile to utilitarian arguments, and this is seen to full effect in the assertion that there is a 'slippery slope' that must be avoided at all costs. In its concession to the doctrine of double effect, however, Natural Law theory is compromised by a latent concession to Utilitarianism.' Is the application of double effect therefore a true absolutist application of Natural Law?

Obviously there are other applications of Natural Law to consider such as whether legalising voluntary euthanasia would challenge the precept of living in an ordered society? Would allowing mass voluntary euthanasia disrupt society? In addition, one could also consider each of the precepts in conjunction with an understanding of how correct reasoning is applied and also use of the moral virtues. In conclusion, the application of Natural Law, in light of its complexity – let alone the complexity of the issues surrounding both abortion and voluntary euthanasia – could mean that any attempt to apply it may not always be considered to be the definitive model.

Key quote

Casuistry typically uses general principles in reasoning analogically from clear-cut cases, called paradigms, to vexing cases. Similar cases are treated similarly. In this way, casuistry resembles legal reasoning. Casuistry may also use authoritative writings relevant to a particular case. (*Encyclopaedia Britannica*)

AO1 Activity

An **acrostic** is a form of writing in which the first letter of each line spells out a word. Using the words 'Natural Law', aim to write out **ten** points which you feel you could use in an answer on Natural Law and voluntary euthanasia.

Study tip

There are many examples of specialist language and vocabulary in this topic. Make sure that you don't get confused by the different terms which are used to describe the key words associated with euthanasia. Your ability to use the terms accurately in an examination answer would distinguish a high level answer from one that is simply a general response.

Key skills

Knowledge involves:

Selection of a range of (thorough) accurate and relevant information that is directly related to the specific demands of the question.

This means you choose the correct information relevant to the question set NOT the topic area. You will have to think and focus on selecting key information and NOT writing everything you know about the topic area.

Understanding involves:

Explanation that is extensive, demonstrating depth and/or breadth with excellent use of evidence and examples including (where appropriate) thorough and accurate supporting use of sacred texts, sources of wisdom and specialist language.

This means that you demonstrate that you understand something by being able to illustrate and expand your points through examples/supporting evidence in a personal way and NOT repeat chunks from a text book (known as rote learning).

Further application of skills:

Go through the topic areas in this section and create some bullet lists of key points from key areas. For each one, provide further elaboration and explanation through the use of evidence and examples.

AO1 Developing skills

It is now time to reflect upon the information that has been covered so far. It is also important to consider how what you have learned can be focused and used for examination-style answers by practising the skills associated with AO1.

Assessment objective 1 (AO1) involves demonstrating knowledge and understanding. The terms 'knowledge' and 'understanding' are obvious but it is crucial to be familiar with how certain skills demonstrate these terms, and also, how the performance of these skills is measured (see generic band descriptors Band 5 for AS AO1).

▶ **Your new task is this:** below is a fairly strong answer, although not perfect, that has been written in response to a question requiring an examination of the application of Natural Law to abortion. Using the band level descriptors you can compare this with the relevant higher bands and the descriptions inside those bands. It is obviously a fairly strong answer and so would not be in bands 5, 1 or 2. In order to do this it will be useful to consider what is both strong and weak about the answer and therefore what needs developing.

In analysing the answer, in a group, identify three ways to make this answer a better one. You may have more than three observations and indeed suggestions to make it a perfect answer!

Answer

Natural Law has its origins in Aristotle and there has been a significant development of this with Thomas Aquinas to make it a religious system for ethics. Natural Law is absolutist in the sense that there is great focus on the primary precepts in line with the view that God created everything for a purpose.

Natural Law stresses the importance of using human reason to establish what the precepts are but it does not end there. Reason is also then used to apply these precepts to moral issues. It is here where people sometimes disagree.

As Natural Law supports the sanctity of life and the Roman Catholic view about when life begins tends to be ensoulment, then, the conclusion is that personhood and a right to life is applied at this stage in the development of the foetus. Therefore, when the primary precepts are applied to abortion, the act of abortion is considered wrong as it goes against the primary precept of protection of the life of the innocent but also the precept of reproduction.

However, there is also the principle of double effect that would justify abortion under certain conditions, such as when two of the precepts conflict. Some have suggested that this principle is unsound and also has inconsistencies.

Some may argue that Natural Law also should consider the virtues when approaching the issue of abortion; however, what is clear is that Natural Law would not consider the people involved or their emotions because they would feel that in doing so they are not able to make a clear and rational response.

Issues for analysis and evaluation

The effectiveness of Natural Law in dealing with ethical issues

This section covers AO2 content and skills

Specification content
The effectiveness of Natural Law in dealing with ethical issues.

The main argument that would be presented here in supporting Natural Law in dealing with ethical issues is that it is viewed by its proponents as universally applicable. For the followers of Natural Law, the rules apply to all people at all times and in all places and so therefore is an effective way of dealing with ethical issues.

For example, followers of Natural Law would argue that it provides clear-cut rules when approaching ethical issues, such as the view that abortion is wrong as it breaks the primary precept to reproduce. Nothing could be more straightforward.

Another strength of Natural Law in dealing with ethical issues is that it can be deduced by reason alone and does not rely on unpredictable consequences or emotions. This is very much in line with the way the human law operates so that it is rational and not emotionally driven in order to promote overall justice and order in society, another of the primary precepts.

For a religious person, the theory of Natural Law creates a link between the creator, the creation and our purpose as human beings. This brings an ethical system that is coherent and consistent overall.

However, it is not as simple as the above arguments may suggest and some would say that Natural Law, in dealing with ethical issues, is ineffective and is no longer of use today in the light of social and ethical changes and an appreciation of the complexity of both contemporary ethical issues, and, in the face of refined and progressive human laws. In short they would suggest that Natural Law is outdated as society has changed.

The first point in case would be issues of human rights. Discrimination against sexual orientation is not allowed in law. This is clearly not the case with Natural Law on a range of specific issues to do with sexuality.

Natural Law also fails to consider the situation people find themselves in when applying the primary precepts. For example, it does not allow abortion even in the case of rape. Even Roman Catholic thinkers such as Kainz have argued that the principle of double effect is at best unstable and at worst contradictory and inconsistent.

It could be argued that Natural Law, in dealing with ethical issues, is inflexible and fails to consider the consequences of so called 'right' actions. Euthanasia is not allowed, but this could lead to greater pain for the person involved and their family. On its own terms, a consideration of real and apparent goods in relation to intentions needs to be tested against the cold application of a single ruling.

Finally, some would argue that basing decisions is not necessarily a bad thing if that emotion is based in love and concern for others, as these principles can often guide ethical decisions. For example, a mother would not act rationally, but often emotionally, when dealing with an incident involving her child.

In conclusion, there is much debate about the effectiveness of Natural Law in dealing with ethical issues; however, although final agreement on the statement will never be universal, this does not mean that it cannot be effective. To be more effective, however, perhaps a more critical and systematic analysis of its principles and application needs to be considered?

AO2 Activity *Possible lines of argument*

Listed below are some conclusions that could be drawn from the AO2 reasoning in the accompanying text:

1. Natural Law, in dealing with ethical issues, is ineffective and is no longer of use today in the light of social and ethical changes.
2. Natural Law, in dealing with ethical issues, is ineffective as it does not account for the complexities of modern law or ethical issues.
3. Natural Law, in dealing with ethical issues, is effective because it is clear and consistent.
4. Natural Law, in dealing with ethical issues, is effective on the whole, although there are times when it needs applying very carefully.
5. Natural Law, in dealing with ethical issues, is ineffective because it is itself inconsistent.

Consider each of the conclusions drawn above and collect evidence and examples to support each argument from the AO1 and AO2 material studied in this section. Select one conclusion that you think is most convincing and explain why it is so. Now contrast this with the weakest conclusion in the list, justifying your argument with clear reasoning and evidence.

The extent to which Natural Law is meaningless without a belief in a creator God

Aquinas embraced the principles established by Aristotle and clearly developed them into a coherent religious philosophy. For Aquinas, God made the world and established within it a sense of order and purpose which reflects God's will. The idea of an overall creator, then, for Aquinas is integral to Natural Law. His theory rests upon this and develops from it.

For example, it is believed that it should be the goal of every human to return to God and gain eternal life, the beatific vision. In terms of ethical behaviour and human laws, God creates all that exists, including eternal law, which is revealed in divine law found in religious scriptures and teachings. These revelations are then used to shape ethical behaviour and human laws. For example, there are examples of these in the absolutist laws contained within scriptures such as in the Ten Commandments. Again, the primary precepts reflect the main purposes for humankind as outlined in religious scriptures, and the ideas of real and apparent goods, together with an encouragement of virtuous behaviour, are clearly consistent with the teachings of Jesus.

As it is the basis of Roman Catholic theology then religious believers would agree that Natural Law is meaningless without a belief in a creator God.

There is always a counter-argument, however, and many would disagree totally with Aquinas and the Roman Catholic Church.

Two key points that could be put forward to challenge the view that Natural Law is meaningless without a belief in a creator God can be presented by looking at two key figures in the history of Natural Law theory. The first is Aristotle, whose system may be seen to be in line with the idea of a creator God; however, the idea of Prime Mover is so distant from the idea of a creator God found in Christianity that it is sufficient to challenge the statement. Aristotle's Prime Mover is a philosophical principle as opposed to the active, interventionist God found in Christianity. The second individual is John Finnis, who himself is a Roman Catholic and yet Finnis has shown that a Natural Law system can be totally independent of God as humans make their own decisions and the law is autonomous and independent of religion. In such a way is can be argued that it is not true that Natural Law is meaningless without a belief in a creator God.

In conclusion, it appears that Natural Law can operate as a system independent of a creator God and can be meaningful. However, it all really depends upon perspective as some religious believers would disagree. Nonetheless, it could be suggested that even if it were dependent on a creator God, then, it will still have meaning without God because Natural Law applies at all levels, from eternal to human, and in this life, as Aquinas himself said, we could not achieve perfection here on earth. So Natural Law, even from a religious perspective could never be meaningless in itself. Nonetheless, the real issue is whether or not it has deeper meaning or more meaning with a creator God and for religious followers of Natural Law this is clearly the case.

Listed below are some conclusions that could be drawn from the AO2 reasoning in the accompanying text:

1. Natural Law is meaningless without a belief in a creator God as Aquinas' version completes the theory.

2. Natural Law can be meaningful without a belief in a creator God because it is based on philosophical principles, as with Aristotle, rather than religious belief.

3. Natural Law is more meaningful with the belief in a creator God.

4. Natural Law is never meaningless because it can operate with or without a creator God.

5. Natural Law is not meaningless without a belief in a creator God as John Finnis, a Roman Catholic himself, has demonstrated, but this does not mean that it cannot be linked to a creator God.

Consider each of the conclusions drawn above and collect evidence and examples to support each argument from the AO1 and AO2 material studied in this section. Select one conclusion that you think is most convincing and explain why it is so. Now contrast this with the weakest conclusion in the list, justifying your argument with clear reasoning and evidence.

AO2 Developing skills

It is now time to reflect upon the information that has been covered so far. It is also important to consider how what you have learned can be focused and used for examination-style answers by practising the skills associated with AO2.

Assessment objective 2 (AO2) involves 'analysis' and 'evaluation'. The terms may be obvious but it is crucial to be familiar with how certain skills demonstrate these terms, and also, how the performance of these skills is measured (see generic band descriptors Band 5 for AS AO2).

Obviously an answer is placed within an appropriate band descriptor depending upon how well the answer performs, ranging from excellent, good, satisfactory, basic/limited to very limited.

▶ **Your task is this:** below is a reasonable answer, although not perfect, that has been written in response to a question requiring an evaluation of the effectiveness of Natural Law in its application to abortion. Using the band level descriptors you can compare this with the relevant higher bands and the descriptions inside those bands. It is obviously a reasonable answer and so would not be in bands 5, 1 or 2. In order to do this it will be useful to consider what is both strong and weak about the answer and therefore what needs developing.

In analysing the answer, in a group, identify three ways to make this answer a better one. You may have more than three observations and indeed suggestions to make it a perfect answer!

Key skills

Analysis involves identifying issues raised by the materials in the AO1, together with those identified in the AO2 section, and presents sustained and clear views, either of scholars or from a personal perspective ready for evaluation.

This means that it picks out key things to debate and the lines of argument presented by others or a personal point of view.

Evaluation involves considering the various implications of the issues raised based upon the evidence gleaned from analysis and provides an extensive detailed argument with a clear conclusion.

This means that the answer weighs up the various and different lines of argument analysed through individual commentary and response and arrives at a conclusion through a clear process of reasoning.

Answer

On the one hand, those who accept Aquinas' doctrine of Natural Law and seek to apply this to the issue of abortion, believe that the key primary precept involved here is that of preserving innocent life. Therefore the act of abortion is seen as wrong because of the intentional killing of an innocent human being. For others, this is far too absolutist and simplistic an application and does not consider all circumstances.

Then there is the exception of double effect in Natural Law. The doctrine of double-effect does permit the death of the foetus, but only as a by-product of another act. This means that the intention was not to kill the foetus.

There is another approach; for example, a professor of ethics has argued that in the case of abortion, two other precepts are perhaps even more relevant to the issue of abortion, that of procreation and nurturing offspring. He argues if you defend the right of the woman if her life is in danger for abortion, then, in the same way if every woman has a right to conceive and procreate, rape violates this right and so maybe abortion can be justified in the case of rape. In other words, if one uses a principle of exception for the first precept, then you have to be consistent in applying it to other precepts. Not all Roman Catholics may accept this but critics of Natural Law would agree with the apparent inconsistency.

Overall, I think there are problems in applying Natural Law to abortion but this does not mean it is ineffective. It does, however, question how far Natural Law is consistent.

Situation Ethics – a religious approach to ethics

T3

Specification content

Fletcher's rejection of other approaches within ethics: legalism, antinomianism and the role of conscience; Fletcher's rationale for using the religious concept of 'agape' (selfless love) as the 'middle way' between the extremes of legalism and antinomianism.

quickfire

3.1 What were the two extremes to ethics for Fletcher?

quickfire

3.2 Was the approach of situationism entirely new?

Key quote

There is an old joke which serves our purposes. A rich man asked a lovely young woman if she would sleep the night with him. She said 'No.' He then asked if she would do it for $100,000? She said, 'Yes!' He then asked $10,000?' She replied, 'Well, yes, I would.' His next question was, 'How about $500?' Her indignant, 'What do you think I am?' was met by the answer, 'We have already established that. Now we are haggling over the price.' (Fletcher)

A: Joseph Fletcher's Situation Ethics: his rejection of other forms of ethics and his acceptance of agape as the basis of morality

Fletcher's rejection of other approaches within ethics and his rationale for using the religious concept of 'agape' (selfless love) as the 'middle way' between the extremes of legalism and antinomianism

In 1966 an American moral theologian Joseph Fletcher published a book entitled *Situation Ethics: The New Morality*.

In it, Fletcher advocated a 'new' approach to Christian ethics and moral decision making which promoted a compromise between the two extremes of legalism and antinomianism.

Key quote

Situation Ethics was, as are most books, a product of its times. If we distinguish ethics from morality, the method of Situation Ethics had such widespread appeal partly because of its close fit with the 'new morality' that had emerged or was emerging. The 'new morality' provided a fertile ground for the book and helped to make it a bestseller. Fletcher tapped into powerful social and cultural undercurrents that were becoming more and more evident. (Childress)

This approach, labelled 'situationism,' was a theological way of meeting a practical need in light of the radical changes of the 20th century. Bishop John A.T. Robinson, author of the equally popular *Honest to God*, saw Fletcher's book as the only ethic for 'man come of age', a phrase that was to become very pertinent to the whole debate that surrounded Situation Ethics.

Situation Ethics was simply one concise and well-publicised statement of a trend in Christian ethics that had been growing for decades. It was not something entirely new.

The 'liberal era' of the 1960s was certainly part of the reason for the popularity of Situation Ethics (post-Second World War feminism, Vietnam, civil rights, teenager and hippy culture, sexual liberation and rejection of traditional sources of authority), but this was definitely not the reason for its emergence. The theological origins of Situation Ethics are much more complex than its popular social context may suggest.

The changing moralities and questioning of authority that are usually associated with Situation Ethics had their origins much earlier in theological circles. Situation Ethics found a niche in the growing dissatisfaction of religious followers with the inflexible nature of tradition.

There were some key landmarks in the development of Situation Ethics that had an influence on Joseph Fletcher and ones that he responded to:

1. 1928 Durant Drake, published *The New Morality*, calling for a pragmatic approach to ethics.
2. 1932 Emil Brunner published his *Divine Imperative*, an influence on Fletcher.
3. 1932 Reinhold Niebuhr published *Moral Man and Immoral Society*, another influence on Fletcher.
4. 1959 Fletcher himself published a seminal paper on Situation Ethics in the *Harvard Divinity Bulletin* promoting the 'new morality'.
5. 1963 H. Richard Niebuhr published *The Responsible Self*.
6. 1963 Paul Lehmann's *Ethics in a Christian Context* and John Robinson's *Honest to God* were published.

1966 therefore saw a systematic statement of this growing trend when Fletcher published his book *Situation Ethics*.

Fletcher's main argument in his book *Situation Ethics* proposes the idea that the moral principles held to so dearly by the Church for so long cannot be used as moral absolutes because they are problematic and do not work in real situations where an ethical decision needs to be made. For example, 'Do not kill' is 'wrong' only in given circumstances. What about war? Self-defence? Meat-eating? The list is endless.

Joseph Fletcher argued that to make a meaningful ethical decision, the situation needed to be considered first before anything else. Then, when each situation has been considered, deciding to do what is 'right' depends upon the practical application of Christian love (agape) and not by referring back to set moral principles. This is because the 'right' decision in one circumstance, Fletcher argued, cannot become the blueprint for all other circumstances. Each situation should be considered independently.

Fletcher still held to the principle of using reason to make an ethical decision, in line with Natural Law theory, 'while rejecting the notion that the good is "given" in the nature of things'. He also accepted scripture as crucial, accepting revelation 'as the source of the norm' but rejecting all "revealed" laws except for 'to love God in the neighbour'.

Fletcher's conclusion was that the use of absolute ethical principles in applying them to real-life situations was simply not Christian. There were too many problems, inconsistencies and contradictions.

Key quote

The simple-minded use of the notions of 'right and wrong' is one of the chief obstacles to the progress of understanding. (**Whitehead**)

Key person

Joseph Fletcher (1905–1991): was an American professor who formalised the theory known as Situation Ethics in his book *Situation Ethics: The New Morality (1966)*. He was a leading academic involved in topics ranging from abortion to cloning. He was ordained as a priest, but later identified himself as a humanist. He stated that we should always use the principle of love or agape (selfless love) and apply it to each unique situation.

Key quote

The Sabbath was made for man, not man for the Sabbath. (**Mark 2:27**)

The best way to understand Fletcher's work is to cite two anecdotes:

- Fletcher quotes a conversation with a taxi driver, wherein the taxi driver states: 'there are times when a man has to push his principles aside and do the right thing'.
- Fletcher also quotes from Nash's play the Rainmaker in which a father says to his son: 'Noah, you're so full of what's right that you can't see what's good'.

The common thread here is that absolute principles of right and good are not really absolute, and there are times when principles are inappropriate to apply to the real world. The author Arthur Miller referred to the strict application of moral principles (legalism) as 'the immorality of morality'.

Fletcher pointed out two things about his new method of moral decision making:

(1) That his 'new morality' (as it was known) was not really new.

(2) The roots of 'new morality' can be found in 'classical' Christianity.

quickfire

3.3 What principle did Fletcher accept from Natural Law?

AO1 Activity

Create a quick magazine entry entitled: 'The emergence of Situation Ethics' and identify the influences on Fletcher and Fletcher's own reasons for rejecting the two extremes of legalism and antinomianism.

Study tip

In an answer on Situation Ethics remember to focus on the question. Background information is useful for your understanding of Situation Ethics but not always relevant to the question set.

As Robinson writes: 'The 'new morality is, of course, none other than the old morality, just as the new commandment is the old, yet ever fresh, commandment of love.'

In beginning his work, Fletcher argued that there are three possible options for making a moral decision:

1. The legalistic approach – apply set principles rigidly and without consideration of context.

2. Antinomian approach that tended to champion the freedom of the individual without reference to any rules.

3. The situational approach – to consider each situation on its merits before applying the Christian 'principle' of love (agape).

Despite rejecting both legalism and antinomianism as approaches to ethics, he was more dismissive of the former. Professor James Childress wrote in the Introduction to Fletcher's book: 'Even though Fletcher rejects both, he appears to fear the tyranny of legalism more than the anarchy of antinomianism.'

Fletcher's theory does appear to be more in line with 'freedom' from rules and laws that are seen to be artificial, rather than in trying to redefine a flexible legalistic approach. For Fletcher, freedom to reason was crucial and he rejected outright the constraints of any form of legalism.

Fletcher described legalistic approach to ethics taken by the Church as using 'a whole apparatus of prefabricated rules and regulations' as 'directives' rather than as 'guidelines or maxims to illuminate the situation'. Such an approach was too rigid, according to Fletcher who writes, 'What can be worse, no casuistry at all may reveal a punishing and sadistic use of law to hurt people instead of helping them.'

Key quote

What can be worse, no casuistry at all may reveal a punishing and sadistic use of law to hurt people instead of helping them. (Fletcher)

Key quote

The Christian ethicist agrees with Bertrand Russell and his implied judgment, 'To this day Christians think an adulterer more wicked than a politician who takes bribes, although the latter probably does a thousand times as much harm.' (Fletcher)

Many did accuse Fletcher of an antinomian approach but it is clear from his writings that he saw his own approach as grounded, not in **existentialism**, but in a more virtuous 'strategy of love'. Fletcher accused fellow academic thinkers and the Roman Catholic Church, who saw his approach as antinomian, as misunderstanding the term situational and making it synonymous with the term existential. For Fletcher, antinomians had no strategy as he saw it as 'the approach with which one enters into the decision-making situation armed with no principles or maxims whatsoever, to say nothing of rules'. Fletcher likened the antinomian approach to the misunderstanding Paul faced when writing to the church in Corinth.

Fletcher's middle way between the two extremes of legalism and antinomianism is what he called a 'principled relativism' because, although rejecting absolutes, he did not embrace the total autonomy of antinomianism. Fletcher saw laws as 'illuminators' and not 'directors' and he preferred, therefore, to see love (agape) as the only true 'principle' that was constant to which one, as a Christian, had obligation: 'Christian Situation Ethics has only one norm or principle or law (call it what you will) that is binding and unexceptionable, always good and right regardless of the circumstances. That is "love" – the agape of the summary commandment to love God and the neighbour'.

The role of conscience

Fletcher's understanding of **conscience** is different from traditional views; he sees it as a 'function, not as a faculty'. He is not so much interested in what it 'is' as he is in 'what it does'. He writes, 'The traditional error lies in thinking about conscience as a noun instead of a verb'. In other words, it was not something that exists inside us that directs us, for Fletcher it was more a description of the process by which we respond to ethical issues.

Fletcher rejects what he identifies as the four traditional ideas about conscience, i.e. that it is:

1. 'An innate, radar-like, built-in faculty – intuition.'
2. 'Inspiration from outside the decision maker – guidance by the Holy Spirit.'
3. 'The internalised value system of the culture and society.'
4. 'Reason making moral judgments or value choices.'

Fletcher's conclusion is that, 'There is no conscience; conscience is merely a word for our attempts to make decisions creatively, constructively, fittingly.'

Fletcher's understanding of the function of conscience is not one of reviewing past actions or apportioning guilt and shame; according to Fletcher, the way conscience functions is by looking forward towards prospective application, that is, the moral problems to solve.

Fletcher rejects the idea of morality as a manual for the conscience. In other words, morality is not something that is set in stone and dictates how the conscience is to react in a given situation. The Church has made this mistake.

Traditionally, the Church has devised moral principles in abstract, systematised them and then applied them in actual cases (casuistry) to give prescriptions and directives. For example, the principle that to have an abortion is wrong is derived from the ruling found in the Ten Commandments 'do not kill'. When a person considers abortion, then, their conscience is dictated to by this directive.

This is not how Fletcher sees the role of conscience, as this approach to morality is not life-centred nor person-orientated because it only considers an abstract principle. In contrast, Situation Ethics calls for the practical application of Christian love to a given situation. The situation and context come first and principles are put aside.

Key quote

Legalists make an idol of the *sophia*, antinomians repudiate it, situationists *use* it. (**Fletcher**)

Key terms

Conscience: traditionally an internal, intuitive guide to good or bad; Fletcher reinterpreted this notion as a description of ethical action

Existentialism: a philosophy that proposes the individual is free and responsible to determine their own development

quickfire

3.4 Why is love not a noun for Fletcher?

Key quote

The moral precepts of Jesus are not intended to be understood legalistically, as prescribing what all Christians must do, whatever the circumstances, and pronouncing certain courses of action universally right and others universally wrong. They are not legislation laying down what love always demands of every one: they are illustrations of what love may at any moment require of anyone. (Robinson)

Key quote

There is only one ultimate and invariable duty, and its formula is, 'Thou shalt love thy neighbor as thyself.' How to do this is another question, but this is the whole of moral duty. (Temple)

Key quote

The law of love is the ultimate law because it is the negation of law; it is absolute because it concerns everything. (Tillich)

Jesus told the Parable of the Good Samaritan

In essence, Situation Ethics is practical and the emphasis is on action and not theory, on doing and not just debating, on being alive and responsive to the context and not just adhering to a set of rules.

The roots of 'new morality' can be found in 'classical' Christianity. Fletcher saw his approach to ethics as grounded in the Christian gospel. Fletcher sees love as an active principle – it is a doing thing rather than as a noun or thing in itself. 'Love is the only universal. But love is not something we have or are, it is something we do.' Agape is the word used in the New Testament for pure, unconditional Christian love. It is love which is disinterested and seeks only the benefit of the one who is loved.

AO1 Activity

Try and list some reasons why Fletcher may have rejected traditional ideas about conscience and preferred his own definition. Try to link the questions to his relativist approach and the extreme of legalism.

The biblical evidence used to support this approach: the teachings of Jesus (Luke 10:25–37) and St Paul (1 Corinthians 13)

Fletcher himself used a variety of references to scripture but his main focus was on the use of the word agape, the Greek word for Christian love. As seen in the Natural Law section of this book, the word agape expresses pure, unconditional love to set it apart from other Greek words describing different aspects of love.

The main focus of the word was the use of it in the parable of the Good Samaritan, where the 'strategy of love' is clearly outlined, and in Paul's letter to the Corinthians (1 Corinthians 13) where the meaning of agape is elaborated.

The Parable of the Good Samaritan reads:

'On one occasion an expert in the law stood up to test Jesus. "Teacher," he asked, "what must I do to inherit eternal life?" "What is written in the Law?" he replied. "How do you read it?" He answered, "Love the Lord your God with all your heart and with all your soul and with all your strength and with all your mind"; and, "Love your neighbour as yourself".

"You have answered correctly," Jesus replied. "Do this and you will live."

But he wanted to justify himself, so he asked Jesus, "And who is my neighbour?"

In reply Jesus said: "A man was going down from Jerusalem to Jericho, when he was attacked by robbers. They stripped him of his clothes, beat him and went away, leaving him half dead. A priest happened to be going down the same road, and when he saw the man, he passed by on the other side. So too, a Levite, when he came to the place and saw him, passed by on the other side. But a Samaritan, as he travelled, came where the man was; and when he saw him, he took pity on him. He went to him and bandaged his wounds, pouring on oil and wine. Then he put the man on his own donkey, brought him to an inn and took care of him. The next day he took out two denarii and gave them to the innkeeper. "Look after him," he said, "and when I return, I will reimburse you for any extra expense you may have."

Jesus then asked which person fulfilled the role of neighbour to the injured man and it was acknowledged that it was the 'one who had mercy'. Jesus then instructed the questioner to 'do likewise', applying the universal principle of neighbourly love to all. This parable influenced Fletcher's understanding of agape. Luke uses the Greek word αγαπήσεις (agapeis) the future command 'you will love...' from the verb αγαπώ (agapo) 'to love'.

Although charity is the word often used in translation, it is derived from the Greek word for 'love' used by Paul in 1 Corinthians chapter 13, ἀγάπη (agape), which is often understood as pure, unconditional love as opposed to sexual, empathetic (usually associated with family love), and, affection (usually associated with friendship) which are different Greek words but also translated as 'love'.

1 Corinthians reads:

'If I speak in the tongues of men or of angels, but do not have love, I am only a resounding gong or a clanging cymbal. If I have the gift of prophecy and can fathom all mysteries and all knowledge, and if I have a faith that can move mountains, but do not have love, I am nothing. If I give all I possess to the poor and give over my body to hardship that I may boast, but do not have love, I gain nothing.

Love is patient, love is kind. It does not envy, it does not boast, it is not proud. It does not dishonour others, it is not self-seeking, it is not easily angered, it keeps no record of wrongs. Love does not delight in evil but rejoices with the truth. It always protects, always trusts, always hopes, always perseveres.

Love never fails. But where there are prophecies, they will cease; where there are tongues, they will be stilled; where there is knowledge, it will pass away. For we know in part and we prophesy in part, but when completeness comes, what is in part disappears. When I was a child, I talked like a child, I thought like a child, I reasoned like a child. When I became a man, I put the ways of childhood behind me. For now we see only a reflection as in a mirror; then we shall see face to face. Now I know in part; then I shall know fully, even as I am fully known.

And now these three remain: faith, hope and love. But the greatest of these is love.'

It can clearly be seen the impact and influence of Paul's words on the history of Christian ethics, from Augustine and Aquinas through to Joseph Fletcher, all of whom bestow upon 'love' the highest status.

Study tip

It is important to know the scriptural texts on which the principle of agape is based but it is not necessary to re-write them in an answer. Be selective and pick out key points to quote.

Key quote

He answered, 'Love the Lord your God with all your heart and with all your soul and with all your strength and with all your mind'; and, 'Love your neighbour as yourself.' (Luke 10:26)

Key quote

And now these three remain: faith, hope and love. But the greatest of these is love. (1 Corinthians 13:13)

quickfire

3.5 What did Fletcher see as the biblical basis for Situation Ethics?

The Apostle Paul was the author of 1 Corinthians 13

Specification content

Situation Ethics as a form of moral relativism, a consequentialist and teleological theory.

Situation Ethics as a form of moral relativism, a consequentialist and teleological theory

We have already seen that Fletcher referred to his system of ethics as a 'principled relativism'. Situation Ethics is relativistic because it recognises no universal moral norms or rules and proposes that each situation has to be looked at independently because each situation is different.

The only grey area here is with Fletcher's insistence on, and recognition of, the principle of agape which he referred to as the one true binding factor: Christian Situation Ethics has only one norm or principle or law (call it what you will) that is binding and unexceptionable, always good and right regardless of the circumstances. That is 'love' – the agape of the summary commandment to love God and the neighbour'.

It must be remembered, however, that in recognising a principle, Fletcher made sure that it was understood as a practical tool of application that responded to the needs of each situation and not an absolute principle that directed each situation uniformly. In other words, the principle of agape remains constant but at the same time responds differently according to the needs of the situation. In this sense it is truly relativist as an ethical theory according to Fletcher.

Fletcher's Situation Ethics is also consequentialist in that the situation is considered and with application of conscience through agape and in doing so is looking forward towards prospective application. Situation Ethics, then, makes moral judgements based on the outcome or the consequences of an action.

In this way Situation Ethics is also teleological. It is concerned with the end purpose (telos) or goal of any proposed action. For Fletcher, the end should always be that which asserts the triumph of Christian love.

Key quote

There can be no 'system' of Situation Ethics, but only a 'method' of situational or contextual decision making. (Childress)

Key quote

The situation ethic, unlike some other kinds, is an ethic of decision – of making decisions rather than 'looking them up' in a manual of prefab rules. (Fletcher)

AO1 Activity

The recognition of Situation Ethics as a form of moral relativism, a consequentialist and teleological theory can be supported with reference to examples from the four working principles and the six fundamental principles which are the subject of the next section. In preparation for this, create the following table:

Form	Examples from from the four working principles and the six fundamental principles
Moral relativism	
Consequentialist theory	
Teleological theory	

You can then use this table as a way of developing your explanation of the ways in which Situation Ethics may be categorised as such a theory.

AO1 Developing skills

It is now time to reflect upon the information that has been covered so far. It is also important to consider how what you have learned can be focused and used for examination-style answers by practising the skills associated with AO1.

Assessment objective 1 (AO1) involves demonstrating knowledge and understanding. The terms 'knowledge' and 'understanding' are obvious but it is crucial to be familiar with how certain skills demonstrate these terms, and also, how the performance of these skills is measured (see generic band descriptors Band 5 for AS AO1).

▶ **Your new task is this:** below is a below average answer that has been written in response to a question requiring an examination of why Situation Ethics rejects the extremes of legalism and antinomianism. It is obviously a below average answer and so would be about band 2. It will be useful, initially, to consider what is missing from the answer and what is inaccurate. The accompanying list gives you some possible observations to assist you. Be aware, as not all points may be relevant! In analysing the answer's weaknesses, in a group, choose five points from the list that you would use to improve the answer in order to make it stronger. Then write out your additions, each one in a clear paragraph, remembering the principles of explaining with evidence and/ or examples. You may add more of your own suggestions, but try to negotiate as a group and prioritise the most important things to add.

Answer

Joseph Fletcher was a moral theologian in the 1960s who wrote about Situation Ethics. This means that instead of following set rules you just look at each situation separately and then decide what to do.

He didn't like legalism because this was all about rules and just doing as you were told. This didn't help people because there are times when things are difficult and it just gets confusing. Rules don't always apply to every situation, for example, like war when killing is good.

He didn't like antinomianism because it allowed you to do anything. Antinomianists promote immoral behaviour because they do not follow rules. If everyone lived like this then people would only love themselves and not their neighbours as Joseph Fletcher argued.

Observations

1. An introduction needs to include much more biographical information.
2. The introduction needs to address the question set straight away.
3. Needs to explain what legalism is accurately
4. Needs to explain what antinomianism is accurately.
5. Include a relevant quotation from Fletcher.
6. Needs to explain about agape.
7. Reference to conscience may help improve the answer.
8. Needs to include the story of the 'Good Samaritan'.
9. Explain how legalism is not adequate by using an example.
10. Explain how antinomianism is not adequate by using an example.
11. Could explain why Situation Ethics is not antinomian.
12. Needs a summary at the end that relates to the question.

Specification content

The degree to which agape is the
only intrinsic good.

Issues for analysis and evaluation

The degree to which agape is the only intrinsic good

Some would argue that laws sent by God are intrinsically good because they are
part of God's nature and will; for example, Divine Command theory suggests this.
They would continue to express that following the will of God is vital in developing
good character.

Jesus himself, in the Beatitudes, praises many virtues as good; for example, 'blessed
are the peacemakers' and 'blessed are the meek'. Surely it cannot be one thing that
is just classed as good? Also one could argue that agape is the not the only intrinsic
good because if it directs everything else then surely they become good like agape?

The main problems with seeing love as the only intrinsic good it is that it means
that morality is very narrow and that any other virtues are ignored and not
developed, such as Aquinas' courage and justice. It also ignores the fact that 'good'
is always a relative term and has no consistent value in that it is like a variable.

In addition, there is much biblical evidence to suggest that good is used many
times to describe a variety of things. For example, God saw that creation was
good; the 'Good Samaritan' did the right thing according to the story; it is 'good'
to give praise to God. In Matthew 19:17 it states, 'Why do you ask me about what
is good?' Jesus replied. 'There is only One who is good. If you want to enter life,
keep the commandments.' Again in, Mark 10:18 it states, 'Why do you call me
good?' Jesus answered. 'No one is good except God alone.' This all seems to suggest
various applications and designations for what is good.

William Barclay was uncomfortable with Fletcher's view that nothing is intrinsically
good or bad in itself. He allowed that some actions can be seen as morally right
given an extraordinary situation; but this does not necessarily follow that the thing
involved is in itself morally good. He went even further to suggest that there are
some actions that can never be seen to be morally right; for instance, to encourage
a young person to experiment and experience drugs for themselves knowing that it
could lead to addiction. 'The right and the wrong are not so easily eliminated.'

However, in Fletcher's defence it could be argued that we need to define what
he meant carefully. Fletcher, denies that it is some kind of 'thing' as in a 'noun',
rather, it is an action and argues that 'Only in the divine being, only in God, is love
substantive. With men it is a formal principle, a predicate. Only with God is it a
property. This is because God *is* love. Men, who are finite, only *do* love.' This would
be in agreement with Jesus' answer in Mark. This gives us a clue as to what Fletcher
really means in that to do good one must always act lovingly or develop the quality
of love.

Even Aquinas recognised this in agreement with Paul that 'love' was the greatest
of the three revealed virtues and that this superlative was the basis of every other
virtue. In this sense it can be seen that there is a case for seeing agape is the only
intrinsic good.

In conclusion, it could be argued that to take Fletcher's proposition out of context
means that it can be misunderstood and challenged. When it is considered
carefully and in line with Natural Law and virtue theory it can be seen to be
consistent with the idea that both Jesus and Paul propose that in intrinsic terms
agape is the only thing that is good because it is, for want of a better phrase, 'godly'
or 'god-like'.

AO2 Activity *Possible lines of argument*

Listed below are some conclusions
that could be drawn from the AO2
reasoning in the accompanying text:

1. Agape is the only intrinsic good
    and is the foundation of Fletcher's
    ethical argument.

2. Agape is the only intrinsic good
    but this has to be qualified by
    careful explanation as to what is
    meant by this.

3. Agape is the not the only
    intrinsic good because if it directs
    everything else then surely they
    become good?

4. Agape is the only intrinsic good is
    too simplistic to accept.

5. Agape is the not the only intrinsic
    good because good is a relative
    term.

Consider each of the conclusions
drawn above and collect evidence and
examples to support each argument
from the AO1 and AO2 material
studied in this section. Select one
conclusion that you think is most
convincing and explain why it is so.
Now contrast this with the weakest
conclusion in the list, justifying
your argument with clear reasoning
and evidence.

Whether Situation Ethics promotes immoral behaviour

Specification content
Whether Situation Ethics promotes
immoral behaviour.

It can be seen that this has arisen from the accusation of antinomianism that Fletcher was so keen to avoid.

Some have argued that it promotes immoral behaviour because someone could claim to be acting out of love and could perform such acts as murder or adultery whilst really acting in a selfish, unfair and unjust way (on those who suffer as a result). Relativism gives too much freedom to the individual to decide what action to take. Humans are prone to making mistakes or being influenced by personal gain rather than love – this could lead to unjust and immoral behaviour.

William Barclay in his book '*Ethics in a Permissive Society*' wrote, 'If love is perfect then freedom is a good thing. But if there is no love, or if there is not enough love, then freedom can become licence, freedom can become selfishness and even cruelty.' The problem, according to Barclay, is one of human nature. Barclay referred to Robinson's description of Situation Ethics as 'the only ethic for man come of age' and responded by arguing: 'This is probably true – but man has not yet come of age'. In other words, humanity as a whole is not mature enough for such a sophisticated philosophy.

Religious believers could argue that all people should follow divine law as God is the ultimate source of moral authority. They cannot rely on principles devised by sinful mankind.

Some Christians may also argue that God should decide what is fair and just, God is the ultimate source of authority and not humans who often make wrong decisions. For example, consequences may not always be loving or predictable and although the intention may have been to act in a loving, fair and just way, the outcome is not one that reflects goodness or right moral behaviour. People cannot accurately predict the consequences of their actions. Therefore they do not know if the desired goal of love will be achieved.

Fletcher's response would be that Situation Ethics avoids immorality because it is based in love and would quote Paul and Jesus in their recognition that love is the greatest commandment. To follow anything other than love is to make the mistake of legalism and fall into what Miller called 'the immorality of morality'. Remember, 'The Sabbath was made for man and not man for the Sabbath'.

Like virtue theory, Situation Ethics promotes responsibility of the individual but most of all it is grounded in a loving concern for neighbour. As Fletcher comments, 'What a difference it makes when love, understood agapeically, is boss; when love is the only norm. How free and therefore responsible we are!'

In conclusion, it is clear that Situation Ethics, through the principle of agape, is not intended to promote immoral behaviour but in practice the question still remains, 'Can an individual always be trusted to be accurately applying the principle of agape?'

Indeed, this has long been the crucial problem for the practical application of Situation Ethics in that it rests entirely upon, not just the single notion of a universal understanding of agapeic love, but more importantly upon the ability of human beings to relate this accurately to many complex ethical problems. This was indicated by Barclay's argument against Robinson who argued that Situation Ethics was the 'only ethic for man come of age' and the question of human ability to do this remains the central question in this debate.

AO2 Activity *Possible lines of argument*

Listed below are some conclusions that could be drawn from the AO2 reasoning in the accompanying text:

1. It is inevitable that Situation Ethics promotes immoral behaviour because of the imperfection of human beings.
2. Situation Ethics promotes moral behaviour and nothing else because it is guided by the ultimate principle of love.
3. Situation Ethics can promote immoral behaviour if it is not applied correctly but that is the same for any ethical theory.
4. Situation Ethics promotes immoral behaviour because it gives too much freedom to the individual.
5. Situation Ethics promotes immoral behaviour because it challenges laws that have been established through reason and experience and that are right.

Consider each of the conclusions drawn above and collect evidence and examples to support each argument from the AO1 and AO2 material studied in this section. Select one conclusion that you think is most convincing and explain why it is so. Now contrast this with the weakest conclusion in the list, justifying your argument with clear reasoning and evidence.

Key skills

Analysis involves identifying issues raised by the materials in the AO1, together with those identified in the AO2 section, and presents sustained and clear views, either of scholars or from a personal perspective ready for evaluation.

This means that it picks out key things to debate and the lines of argument presented by others or a personal point of view.

Evaluation involves considering the various implications of the issues raised based upon the evidence gleaned from analysis and provides an extensive detailed argument with a clear conclusion.

This means that the answer weighs up the various and different lines of argument analysed through individual commentary and response and arrives at a conclusion through a clear process of reasoning.

AO2 Developing skills

It is now time to reflect upon the information that has been covered so far. It is also important to consider how what you have learned can be focused and used for examination-style answers by practising the skills associated with AO2.

Assessment objective 2 (AO2) involves 'analysis' and 'evaluation'. The terms may be obvious but it is crucial to be familiar with how certain skills demonstrate these terms, and also, how the performance of these skills is measured (see generic band descriptors Band 5 for AS AO2).

Obviously an answer is placed within an appropriate band descriptor depending upon how well the answer performs, ranging from excellent, good, satisfactory, basic/limited to very limited.

▶ **Your new task is this:** below is a below average answer that has been written in response to a question requiring an evaluation of whether or not Situation Ethics can be accused of being antinomian. It is obviously a below average answer and so would be about lower band 2. It will be useful, initially, to consider what is missing from the answer and what is inaccurate. The accompanying list gives you some possible observations to assist you. Be aware, as not all points may be relevant! In analysing the answer's weaknesses, in a group, choose five points from the list that you would use to improve the answer in order to make it stronger. Then write out your additions, each one in a clear paragraph. Remember, it is how you use the points that is the most important factor. Apply the principles of evaluation by making sure that you: identify issues clearly; present accurate views of others making sure that you comment on the views presented; reach an overall personal judgement. You may add more of your own suggestions, but try to negotiate as a group and prioritise the most important things to add.

Answer

Fletcher wished to avoid antinomianism because he argued that if you are not guided by anything then the world would be chaotic and it would be an immoral place to live.

Barclay criticised Fletcher because he argued that even if it is not meant to be antinomian it cannot be avoided because we as humans are not capable of applying love to every single situation.

In conclusion, it can be seen that there are clear arguments for and against but I think it is good because it is based in concern for someone else and so cannot ever be selfish or accused of being antiniomian.

Observations

1. An introduction needs to include much more biographical information.

2. The introduction needs to address the question set straightaway.

3. Needs to explain why Fletcher's theory was accused of being antinomian.

4. Needs to explain what Fletcher said about antinomianism and why his theory was different.

5. Include relevant quotes from Fletcher.

6. Needs to present Fletcher's argument about agape being the middle way between two extremes.

7. Reference to conscience may help improve the answer.

8. Needs to include an explanation of Paul's chapter on love.

9. Explain what antinomianism is and use William Barclay's argument that suggests it cannot be avoided.

10. Could explain why Situation Ethics is not antinomian.

11. Need to evaluate examples of how Situation Ethics may fail and become antinomian.

12. Needs a conclusion at the end that relates to the question.

B: Fletcher's Situation Ethics: the principles as a means of assessing morality

Specification content

The boss principle of Situation Ethics (following the concept of agape).

The boss principle of Situation Ethics (following the concept of agape)

The Old Testament is written in Hebrew and the word used for the loving relationship between God and God's people is 'chesed'. This word describes a 'love' that is faithful, strong, consistently present and kind. It is often translated as 'loving kindness' or 'steadfast love' and incorporates the ideal of commitment and of an already existing bond and a deliberate choice of affection and kindness. The Hebrew people were often reminded to consider or remember this love of God in terms of the action it produced in history when God intervened on their behalf, for example the Exodus.

The word used in Leviticus 19:18, the verse that is referred to in the parable of the Good Samaritan, however, is 'aheb', which is more descriptive of a spontaneous and impulsive love on behalf of humans towards God and fellow human beings. It is also used as a sense of delight by God in righteousness or righteous individuals. Aheb is universal in application and not exclusive to God's loving relationship with the Hebrew people. It is outward looking and embraces all. It is this sense of love that is the origins of agape.

In the New Testament we have Jesus' recognition of the greatest commandment to 'love God and your neighbour as yourself' quoted from Leviticus. The word used in Greek is agape, as we have already seen, and it is this idea of pure, unconditional, sacrificial love that was epitomised in the character and work of Jesus.

This love is a virtuous love, identified and developed by Augustine, and later Aquinas through Natural Law, that is the ultimate, superlative virtue. Fletcher comments, 'Augustine was right to make love the source principle, the hinge principle upon which all other "virtues" hang, whether "cardinal" (natural) or "theological" (revealed).'

It is within this context that Fletcher describes agape as the 'boss' principle of Situation Ethics. As Fletcher comments, 'What a difference it makes when love, understood agapeically, is boss; when love is the only norm. How free and therefore responsible we are!'

Key terms

Aheb: Hebrew word for love that is seen to be similar to the idea of agape

Chesed: Hebrew word that describes an exclusive kind of love in a particular relationship

Key quote

Situation Ethics is more Biblical and verb-thinking than Greek and noun-thinking. It does not ask what is good but how to do good for whom; not what is love but how to do the most loving thing possible in the situation. It focuses upon pragma (doing), not upon dogma (some tenet). (Fletcher)

Key quote

Love alone, because, as it were, it has a built in moral compass, enabling it to 'home' in intuitively upon the deepest need of the other, can allow itself to be directed completely by the situation. (Robinson)

Key quote

This is the radical simplicity of the Gospel's ethic, even though it can lead situationally to the most complicated, headaching, heartbreaking calculations and gray rather than black or white decisions. (Fletcher)

Specification content

The four working principles
(pragmatism, relativism, positivism
and personalism).

quickfire

3.6 Why is aheb significant in relation to agape?

Key quote

To ignore the ethical significance of success is to betray … a defective sense of responsibility. (Bonhoeffer)

Key quote

There must be an absolute or norm of some kind if there is to be any true relativity. (Fletcher)

Key quote

Thus Christian ethics 'posits' faith in God and *reasons* out what obedience to his commandment to love requires in any situation. (Bonhoeffer)

quickfire

3.7 What are the four working principles?

Key quote

Situation Ethics puts people at the center of concern, not things. Obligation is to persons, not to things; to subjects, not objects. The legalist is a *what* asker (What does the law say?); the situationist is a *who* asker (Who is to be helped?). (Fletcher)

Key quote

A basic maxim is that the disciple is commanded to love people, not principles or laws or objects or any other *thing*. (Fletcher)

The four working principles

Fletcher's next task in his book *Situation Ethics*, once the principle of agape was established, was to clarify how this was to work in practice when approaching ethical decision making. In doing this he identifies four key working principles.

1. Pragmatism

The solution to any ethical dilemma first and foremost has to be practical. This idea was influenced by the philosopher and psychologist William James. Fletcher wrote: 'All are agreed: the good is what works, what is expedient, what gives satisfaction.' In other words, it is no good suggesting a solution to a problem because it is a good solution on rational, philosophical grounds if that solution falls flat in practice. The key measure of the success of an ethical solution lay not in its thought but in its application. This does not mean that reason is not important, but simply put, as Fletcher suggests, it is the ethical question, that is, the pragmatic posture that is 'in the chair, at the head of the conference table'.

Key quote

Pragmatism is, to be plainspoken, a *practical* or *success* posture. (Fletcher)

2. Relativism

Again, influenced by earlier theologians, this is the idea that 'the situationist avoids words like "never" and "perfect" and "always" and "complete" as he avoids the plague, as he avoids "absolutely".' However, to be relative there has to be an object to be relative to, a kind of measurement of its true relativity. Fletcher declared this to be 'agapeic love': 'It relativises the absolute, it does not absolute the relative'. In other words, although every situation is unique that does not mean, for Fletcher, a response that is antinomian and typically 'random, unpredictable, unjudgeable, meaningless, amoral' as this would make it anarchic. Rather, the situation is always relative, not to its own circumstance, but to agape.

3. Positivism

This is the view that statements of faith are accepted voluntarily and reason is then used to work within, or work out, one's faith. This is in opposition to the view that reason should be the basis of faith; in terms of Christian ethics this means the voluntary acceptance of the principle of agape. Faith comes first as Fletcher argues, 'The Christian does not understand God in terms of love; he understands love in terms of God as seen in Christ.'

4. Personalism

This is the basic understanding that ethics deals primarily with people; it is a concern for people rather than things. It is a concern for the subject rather than the object; the disciple is given the command to love people and not laws or principles.

AO1 Activity

Make some flash cards with the key principle on one side and a quote from Fletcher with an explanation on the other side.

Study tip

Fletcher uses technical and precise definitions for his working principles. Make sure that you learn them and do not confuse them with each other.

The six fundamental principles (love is the only good, love is the ruling norm of Christianity, love equals justice, love for all, loving ends justify the means and love decides situationally)

Specification content

The six fundamental principles (love is the only good, love is the ruling norm of Christianity, love equals justice, love for all, loving ends justify the means and love decides situationally).

Fletcher identifies six statements on which his 'one "general" proposition' is based, that is, the commandment to 'love God through the neighbour'. In other words, the fundamental principles are there to help elucidate the nature of agape.

1. Only one 'thing' is intrinsically good; namely, love: nothing else at all

Fletcher calls this the New Testaments 'law of love'. Despite love being always 'intrinsically good regardless of the context', Fletcher denies that it is some kind of 'thing' as in a 'noun', rather, it is an action. Argues that 'Only in the divine being, only in God, is love substantive. With men it is a formal principle, a predicate. Only with God is it a property. This is because God *is* love. Men, who are finite, only *do* love.'

He prefers to see love as an active principle – it is a 'doing thing', as he writes, 'Love is the only universal. But love is not something we have or are, it is something we do.' For Fletcher, 'love is a way of relating to persons, and of using things'.

2. The ruling norm of Christian decisions is love: nothing else

Fletcher argues that religious and moral laws have been given artificial status and understanding. He uses the response of Jesus when accused of breaking Sabbath rules: 'the Sabbath was made for man and not man for the Sabbath (Mark 2:27–28)'. In other words, for Fletcher, the purpose of the laws has been totally misunderstood and become dictator to the person, whereas Jesus recognised that laws were there to serve a person.

Fletcher's argument is that love is the new covenant; it replaces the old laws and he refers to the teaching of both Jesus and Paul for justification: 'They redeemed law from the letter that kills and brought it back to the spirit that gives it life'.

Fletcher does not disrespect the law, but argues that the situationist recognises the law for what it is – a 'distillation' of the spirit of love rather than a 'compendium' of the legalistic rules.

3. Love and justice are the same, for justice is love distributed, nothing else

So what is this love? As we have seen already, Fletcher distinguishes agape from other Greek words for love. It is 'giving love'.

Given justice is to apportion a human being that to which he or she is entitled, Fletcher asks what this means in Christian terms? The answer is: 'For what is it that is due to our neighbours? It is love that is due – only love ("Owe no man anything except to love"). Love is justice, justice is love.'

> **Key terms**
>
> **Compendium:** a thorough collection of material
>
> **Distillation:** a process of extracting key, quality material

> **Key quote**
>
> Christian Situation Ethics assert firmly and definitely: Value, worth, ethical quality, goodness or badness, right or wrong – *these things are only predicates, they are not properties. They are not 'given' or 'objectively' real or self-existent.* There is only one thing that is always good and right, intrinsically good regardless of the context, and that one thing is love. **(Fletcher)**

> **Key quote**
>
> To love Christianly is a matter of attitude, not of feeling. Love is discerning and critical; it is not sentimental. **(Fletcher)**

> **Key quote**
>
> Jesus and Paul replaced the precepts of Torah with the living principle of *agape* – agape being goodwill at work in partnership with reason. **(Fletcher)**

> **Key quote**
>
> Justice is the many-sidedness of love. **(Fletcher)**

> **Key quote**
>
> Justice is Christian love using its head … Justice is love coping with situations where distribution is called for. **(Fletcher)**

> **Key ideas**
>
> The six propositions:
>
> 1. Only one 'thing' is intrinsically good; namely, love: nothing else at all.
> 2. The ruling norm of Christian decisions is love: nothing else.
> 3. Love and justice are the same, for justice is love distributed, nothing else.
> 4. Love wills the neighbour's good whether we like him or not.
> 5. Only the end justifies the means, nothing else.
> 6. Love's decisions are made situationally, not prescriptively.

Key term

Kenotic: from a Greek word meaning to empty or make oneself completely receptive to something

Key quote

Disinterested love can only mean impartial love, inclusive love, indiscriminate love, is love for Tom, Dick and Harry. (Fletcher)

Key quote

Unless some purpose or end is in view, to justify or sanctify it, any action we take is literally meaningless. (Fletcher)

quickfire

3.8 Why is the word kenotic important for love?

quickfire

3.9 What is justice the same as according to Fletcher?

4. Love wills the neighbour's good whether we like him or not

Jesus urged everyone to 'love your enemies'. This is a classical statement of the substance and fibre of Christian love leading to a 'radical obligation'. Love then becomes, according to Fletcher, 'kenotic or self-emptying'.

Pure love, then, according to Fletcher is indiscriminate in its application.

5. Only the end justifies the means, nothing else

Fletcher rejects the idea that the end should not be used to justify the means (found in traditional Christian thinking) as an 'absurd abstraction'. Ethics is, in principle, teleological.

In other words, Fletcher saw any system that proposes that means are intrinsically good, and therefore absolute, as fundamentally flawed. For instance, in practice, there is 'an unlovely lip service paid to a maxim that the practices in question all obviously contradict'. For example, whilst on the one hand upholding these as infallible blueprints, the same society can justify war, corporal and capital punishments, surgical mutilations, espionage and 'a whole host of things'.

In this light, there are, according to Fletcher, four factors of judging a situation in ethics:

1. What is the desired end?
2. What should be the means to achieve it?
3. What is the motive in achieving it?
4. What would be the consequences?

The clear contradiction in making 'flexible' the 'inflexible maxims' clearly shows that it is the ends that dictate moral behaviour and ethical decisions.

6. Love's decisions are made situationally, not prescriptively

Fletcher sees it as part of our heritage that we have sought for laws to become slaves to; however, once again this only leads to failure as the principles fail to unfold in practice:

'Nothing in the world causes so much conflict of conscience as the continual, conventional payment of lip service to moral "laws" that are constantly flouted in practice because they are too petty or too rigid to fit the facts of life.'

He calls for an end to the ideology that proposes absurdities: 'For real decision making, freedom is required, an open-ended approach to situations. Imagine the plight of an obstetrician who believed he must always respirate every baby he delivered, no matter how monstrously deformed.'

Fletcher's clear conclusion is that all ethical decisions must be situation based (led, of course, by agape) and not law based.

AO1 Activity

Try and think of a practical example for each fundamental principle that illustrates how it might work in practice.

Study tip

Fletcher uses technical and precise phrases for his fundamental principles that are quite lengthy. Try making a mnemonic to help you remember them and be able to explain them in your own words. Make sure that you learn them and do not confuse them with each other.

AO1 Developing skills

It is now time to reflect upon the information that has been covered so far. It is also important to consider how what you have learned can be focused and used for examination-style answers by practising the skills associated with AO1.

Assessment objective 1 (AO1) involves demonstrating knowledge and understanding. The terms 'knowledge' and 'understanding' are obvious but it is crucial to be familiar with how certain skills demonstrate these terms, and also, how the performance of these skills is measured (see generic band descriptors Band 5 for AS AO1).

▶ **Your new task is this:** below is a below average answer that has been written in response to a question requiring an examination of Fletcher's four working principles. It is obviously a below average answer and so would be about band 2. It will be useful, initially, to consider what is missing from the answer and what is inaccurate. This time there is no accompanying list to assist you. In analysing the answer's weaknesses, in a group, decide upon five points that you would use to improve the answer in order to make it stronger. Then write out your additions, each one in a clear paragraph, remembering the principles of explaining with evidence and/or examples.

Answer

Fletcher made four statements about how his theory would work in practice.

First, it had to be a good solution. For example, no good suggesting to someone who has lost something to buy another if they have no money.

Secondly, the solution all depends on your faith and not on an action. It is what you believe that matters.

Thirdly, it is always relative which means that your decision will always depend upon the situation and not on a rule.

Finally, it makes sure that the most important thing is the person or people involved.

Key skills

Knowledge involves:

Selection of a range of (thorough) accurate and relevant information that is directly related to the specific demands of the question.

This means you choose the correct information relevant to the question set NOT the topic area. You will have to think and focus on selecting key information and NOT writing everything you know about the topic area.

Understanding involves:

Explanation that is extensive, demonstrating depth and/or breadth with excellent use of evidence and examples including (where appropriate) thorough and accurate supporting use of sacred texts, sources of wisdom and specialist language.

This means that you demonstrate that you understand something by being able to illustrate and expand your points through examples/supporting evidence in a personal way and NOT repeat chunks from a text book (known as rote learning).

Further application of skills:

Go through the topic areas in this section and create some bullet lists of key points from key areas. For each one, provide further elaboration and explanation through the use of evidence and examples.

This section covers AO2
content and skills

Specification content

The extent to which Situation Ethics
promotes justice.

AO2 Activity *Possible lines of argument*

Listed below are some conclusions
that could be drawn from the AO2
reasoning in the accompanying text:

1. Situation Ethics promotes justice
   as it is flexible.

2. Situation Ethics promotes justice
   as it is the same as love according
   to Fletcher.

3. Situation Ethics does not promote
   justice because it is too dependent
   on the individual and not focused
   on society.

4. Situation Ethics does not promote
   justice because no-one will agree
   on the most loving course of
   action.

5. Situation Ethics can promote
   justice but it has to be applied very
   carefully and thoughtfully to work.

Consider each of the conclusions
drawn above and collect evidence and
examples to support each argument
from the AO1 and AO2 material
studied in this section. Select one
conclusion that you think is most
convincing and explain why it is so.
Now contrast this with the weakest
conclusion in the list, justifying
your argument with clear reasoning
and evidence.

Issues for analysis and evaluation

The extent to which Situation Ethics promotes justice

In promoting justice some would argue that as each situation is considered
differently in Situation Ethics, unlike in absolutist theories where a person has
to follow rules, this promotes greater justice in society overall. For example, an
abortion may be allowed according to Situation Ethics if the abortion was an act
of selfless love whereas in Natural Law this would not be allowed as it goes against
the primary precept of reproduction and some would see this as unjust.

In addition, it could be argued that the use of Situation Ethics would encourage
people to act selflessly and put other people first. This would make a more just
society overall. Fletcher would also argue that acting is such a way would ensure
justice as one of the six fundamental principles states 'love is justice distributed'.

As Situation Ethics is a consequential theory, we must consider any possible
consequences before acting. Therefore some would argue that this makes us
consider carefully the impact of our actions on others before taking them and can
only promote a just end.

Another argument is that if people used Situation Ethics as a basis for moral
decision making then everyone should act in a loving way to all as one of the six fundamental
principles states 'love wills the good of others, regardless of feelings'. There would be
no room for prejudice or discrimination. This means that people would in effect treat
a stranger in the same way as they treat a member of their family.

However, an alternative line of reasoning could be that without absolute moral
rules many people would fear that there would be chaos and no overall control
over peoples' actions. Adopting a relativistic approach to ethics means what is
'right' then changes all the time and consequently many people are unsure what
the 'right' thing to do is. It will therefore just promote confusion and is a sure
recipe for injustices.

Many would also consider the idea of 'love' as subjective since what one person
considers to be a selflessly loving act another person may not. For example, some
people may argue that euthanasia is an act of selfless love whilst other might argue
it is the opposite and that 'mercy' killing is not mercy at all.

Another point in opposition to Situation Ethics is that people cannot accurately
predict consequences. What we think might end in loving consequences might
actually lead to unloving consequences. In a book published in 1971, *Ethics in a
Permissive Society*, Barclay presented concerns over the theory of Situation Ethics.
Barclay was in no doubt of the sensitive and intelligent nature of agape; 'Obviously,
when we define love like this, love is a highly intelligent thing'; however, it was
Barclay's view there will always be a dispute as to what actually is the most loving
thing to do and actually what this means in practice.

It is also highly unlikely that we would act in the same way and show the same
amount of 'love' to a stranger as we would to our own spouse or children, despite
Situation Ethics suggesting the contrary. There are clear emotional bonds and
duties which link us to our relatives and friends more than to strangers and these
will undoubtedly influence the decisions we make.

In conclusion, there are clearly times when Situation Ethics is very persuasive
and definite examples of where justice might be served. However, there are also
dangers and so no real overall quality control other than a positive in the abilities
and nature of human beings to deliver justice through love. The cynic would say
this is not at all practical and the historian may argue that history shows us it can
never happen. Maybe Situation Ethics is more useful as a personal tool for ethics
more than a blanket social rule?

The effectiveness of Situation Ethics in dealing with ethical issues

Specification content
The effectiveness of Situation Ethics in dealing with ethical issues.

It could be argued that Situation Ethics as a relativistic theory is therefore flexible and practical enough to deal with ethical matters. It takes into account the complexities of human life (the situation) and can take tough decisions where, from a legalistic perspective, all actions seem wrong. It is therefore effective in accommodating the particular as opposed to applying the general.

Another line of argument could be that Situation Ethics allows people the individual freedom and responsibility to make decisions for themselves, which many people nowadays prefer to the prescriptive and legalistic approach. It helps people to see another's perspective and also to grow in moral awareness.

Indeed, the principle of agape involves 'selfless' love, that is, putting others first, which should ensure fairness and justice; in other words, it puts people before laws and this is the essence of ethical concern.

It could also be suggested that it is the consequences of an ethical action that matter; therefore people would have to consider the likely consequences of their actions before they take them, and it is only then that the consequences will be effective for human well-being.

In contrast to this, William Barclay criticised Fletcher's various examples of where an allegedly immoral action prevents further immoralities. He did this on the grounds that such actions were not the only possibilities to prevent further immorality and would certainly not guarantee the end intended. Once again, the abnormal or extraordinary appears to be the basis of Fletcher's theory of ethics.

Despite this, without absolute rules there could be potential for moral chaos for many reasons; for example, by using relativism, it is understood that ideas about what action is 'right' changes all the time. When things change they usually start with small numbers and then spread out to influence the population. This will means several ideas of what is 'right' co-existing and conflicting.

A strong criticism of Situation Ethics is that relativism gives too much freedom to the individual to decide what action to take. Humans are prone to making mistakes or being influenced by personal gain rather than love. When applied to ethical issues, it is not necessarily the case that a personal viewpoint is always the best. Ethical issues need less emotive influence and involvement, and more rational thought.

In summary, Barclay recognises the value of a situationist approach in its reminder for people to be more flexible in applying moral rules and laws; however, 'we do well still to remember that there are laws which we break at our peril'. A great lesson, however, from Situation Ethics, according to Barclay, is that it teaches and encourages sympathy and discourages self-righteousness in approaching ethical dilemmas but this in no way means it should replace established teachings and rules.

Overall, Barclay's was a scathing critique of the new morality. His view was that Fletcher's morality was too dangerous for society as a whole. According to Barclay, there are certain moral principles that are absolute and always morally good. However, Barclay did concede that some absolute principles were not always absolute in their application, especially in extreme circumstances. Such circumstances, nonetheless, are 'so rare as to never justify questioning the whole fabric of the law'.

In conclusion, Situation Ethics can be effective in dealing with moral issues but this does not mean we should follow it entirely. Barclay makes a valid point in indicating what we can learn from Situation Ethics and maybe the way forward is for deontological systems to reflect upon this and try to adapt accordingly?

AO2 Activity *Possible lines of argument*

Listed below are some conclusions that could be drawn from the AO2 reasoning in the accompanying text:

1. Situation Ethics is effective in dealing with ethical issues and can be used in its fullest sense.
2. Situation Ethics is effective in dealing with ethical issues but not in replacing the law or religious teachings that have stood the test of time.
3. Situation Ethics is effective in helping other ethical systems in dealing with ethical issues in its emphasis on empathy.
4. Situation Ethics is not effective in dealing with ethical issues because it is too subjective.
5. Situation Ethics is not effective in dealing with ethical issues because it promotes chaos and anarchy.

Consider each of the conclusions drawn above and collect evidence and examples to support each argument from the AO1 and AO2 material studied in this section. Select one conclusion that you think is most convincing and explain why it is so. Now contrast this with the weakest conclusion in the list, justifying your argument with clear reasoning and evidence.

Key skills

Analysis involves identifying issues raised by the materials in the AO1, together with those identified in the AO2 section, and presents sustained and clear views, either of scholars or from a personal perspective ready for evaluation.

This means that it picks out key things to debate and the lines of argument presented by others or a personal point of view.

Evaluation involves considering the various implications of the issues raised based upon the evidence gleaned from analysis and provides an extensive detailed argument with a clear conclusion.

This means that the answer weighs up the various and different lines of argument analysed through individual commentary and response and arrives at a conclusion through a clear process of reasoning.

AO2 Developing skills

It is now time to reflect upon the information that has been covered so far. It is also important to consider how what you have learned can be focused and used for examination-style answers by practising the skills associated with AO2.

Assessment objective 2 (AO2) involves 'analysis' and 'evaluation'. The terms may be obvious but it is crucial to be familiar with how certain skills demonstrate these terms, and also, how the performance of these skills is measured (see generic band descriptors Band 5 for AS AO2).

Obviously, an answer is placed within an appropriate band descriptor depending upon how well the answer performs, ranging from excellent, good, satisfactory, basic/limited to very limited.

▶ **Your new task is this:** below is a below average answer that has been written in response to a question requiring an evaluation of whether Situation Ethics promotes justice. It is obviously a below average answer and so would be about band 2. It will be useful, initially, to consider what is missing from the answer and what is inaccurate. This time there is no accompanying list to assist you. In analysing the answer's weaknesses, in a group, decide upon five points that you would use to improve the answer in order to make it stronger. Then write out your additions, each one in a clear paragraph. Remember, it is how you use the points that is the most important factor. Apply the principles of evaluation by making sure that you: identify issues clearly; present accurate views of others, making sure that you comment on the views presented; reach an overall personal judgement. You may add more of your own suggestions, but try to negotiate as a group and prioritise the most important things to add.

Answer

Situation Ethics does promote justice according to some people because it is compassionate and thinks of other people.

It also allows for differences of opinion and respects the views of others. This leads to people being more tolerant and not argue with each other because you really do your own thing.

Some people don't like it as a system, however, because it appears too slack and allows anything, including moral behaviour and injustice. Such people argue that people are wicked and need controlling and not let loose on society.

C: Fletcher's Situation Ethics: application of the theory

The application of Fletcher's Situation Ethics to homosexual relationships and polyamorous relationships

This section covers AO1
content and skills

Specification content

The application of Fletcher's Situation
Ethics to homosexual relationships
and polyamorous relationships.

Fletcher on homosexuality and sexual relationships

Fletcher was not only a religious commentator, he was also involved in issues of social injustice and wrote at a time when homosexuality was illegal. In 1960 he wrote an academic paper entitled 'Sex offenses: an ethical view' in which he stated: 'Some forms of sexual activity are historically and conventionally related to criminal law, such as ... homosexuality.' Fletcher was unhappy with the inconsistent approach by the government, which had so long been influenced by the Church in matters such as morality. He was also unhappy with the Church in their approach to issues involving sexuality and sex in general. He argued: 'The Anglo-American policy has been a very confused and inconsistent one, tending to dead-letter laws and hypocrisy. In England, law reformers find it something of a puzzle that adultery, fornication and prostitution are not criminal offenses; nor is homosexuality between females an offense, although between males it is.'

He argued that human laws and attitudes towards sex and homosexuality were outdated, inconsistent, hypocritical but more importantly unjust. Although he did not quote from the Bible, or refer to Situation Ethics, he made it quite clear that to treat people with prejudice and discrimination on account of their sexuality was not a proper legal approach, let alone not a Christian one, and needed reform.

Fletcher pointed out himself that the Wolfenden report was concerned with laws as regarding public and private behaviour and made no judgement according to morality. The Wolfenden report states: 'It should not be the duty of the law to concern itself with matters immorality as such ... it should confine itself to those activities which offend against public order and decency or expose the ordinary citizens to what is offensive or injurious.'

Fletcher argued that any law based upon the presupposition of apparent 'sin' is unreliable and controversial. It was here where he cited his well-known tenet of Situation Ethics, namely, concern for neighbour: 'There is no idea here that ethics, whether religious or not is to be separated from society, and social practice; on the contrary, ethics always limit individual or private freedom by subordinating it to the social or public interest – to neighbour-concern.' It was also a mistake, he argued, to let a particular religious or philosophical stance, based upon what it regards as wrongdoing or 'sin', dictate and shape the law: 'Sin is already divorced from crime in our pluralistic culture and the only real sanction for criminal law is the common interest, public order, or the collective good.'

Although Fletcher acknowledged, and accepted to some extent, that the distinction between personal taste through freedom, and public actions that impact upon this freedom of others, is blurred, he did argue that this should be legally determined, not determined by religious matters. This leaves some scope for personal choice and freedom: 'There is some boundary between personal existence and the social membership. There is some range for private choice and personal taste.'

Fletcher's conclusion was to propose that sex laws should be restricted by three criteria: the age of consent; infringement of public decency; acts involving assault, violence, duress or fraud.

Key terms

Homosexual: being sexually
attracted to people of one's own sex

Wolfenden report: a government-
initiated investigation to explore
the problems of prostitution and
homosexuality, finally published
in 1957

Key quote

The range and complexity of sex laws at present 'on the books' is a monument to the tongue-in-cheek legislation and to the 'prohibitionist' fallacy. (Fletcher)

Key quote

Only may an ideologically free and pluralistic society base frame its moral principles or judgements as to right and wrong and enforce its standards by legal weapons. Society has a right to protect itself from danger within and without, and not to force a monistic and monopoly standard of personal (in the sense of private) conduct. (Fletcher)

quickfire

3.10 Was Fletcher just interested in religious issues?

quicKfire

3.11 Why did Fletcher object to the
Church's approach to sexual ethics?

> **Key term**
>
> Polyamorous: having a (loving)
> sexual relationship with more than
> one individual with the knowledge and
> consent of all partners

Key quote

We can only see a short distance
ahead, but we can see plenty there
that needs to be done. (Turing)

quicKfire

3.12 Why is the story of Alan Turing
significant?

Alan Turing

We begin our consideration of homosexuality and polyamorous relationships
with an account of social injustice. Alan Turing was was prosecuted for
homosexuality under the law at that time, which in retrospect the governing
authority has now recognised as absurd.

Alan Turing 1912–1954

The film 'The Imitation Game'
released in 2014 tells the story of
Alan Turing (1912–1954). Turing
was an incredibly intelligent man,
a brilliant mathematician, and also
widely recognised to be the father
of theoretical computer science and
artificial intelligence. During World
War 2 Turing worked at Britain's
codebreaking centre at Bletchley
Park, enlisted by the government to
break German ciphers. Turing was
successful in creating a machine
that cracked codes generated by
the Enigma machines and it has
been estimated that as a result of
his work the war in Europe was
shortened by up to four years,
saving thousands of lives.

After the war in 1952, whilst
working at Manchester University,
Turing was arrested and prosecuted
for homosexual acts. At that time,
homosexual acts were deemed
criminal acts. Turing evaded
a lengthy prison sentence by
accepting medical treatment that
in effect was equivalent to chemical
castration, widely held to be a 'cure'
for homosexuality. In poor health
due to the effects of the treatment, both mentally and physically, Turing died two
years later from cyanide poisoning. Although determined as suicide by an inquest,
it has also been demonstrated that evidence could suggest accidental poisoning.

It was not until 2009, despite homosexual acts being legal since 1967 and despite
Turing's heroic past, that Gordon Brown, the Prime Minister apologised publically
for 'the appalling way he was treated'. In 2013, Queen Elizabeth II granted Alan
Turing a posthumous pardon.

> **AO1 Activity**
>
> Imagine that you are Joseph Fletcher. Compose a letter to the Prime
> Minister indicating why it is justified that Alan Turing should receive a
> public posthumous apology.

Study tip

When answering a question on applied ethics any background material should
be used carefully and selectively to illustrate a point you are making in focusing
on the question. Do not slip into 'narrative mode'.

Considering that both homosexuality and polyamorous relationships, whether heterosexual or homosexual, have existed as far back in history as we can delve, it is surprising that the laws for treatment of homosexuals have only been liberalised in the western legal system relatively recently.

During the 1950s a committee was established to investigate the issues and 'social problems' associated with prostitution and homosexuality; the committee included a judge, a psychiatrist, an academic and various theologians. Their findings, The Wolfenden Report, was published in 1957.

The main conclusion of the report concerning homosexuality was that it would be wrong for criminal law to intervene in what they did in the privacy of their own homes and, therefore, consenting adults should be given the freedom to explore their sexuality.

The report stated: '... unless a deliberate attempt be made by society through the agency of the law to equate the sphere of crime with that of sin, there must remain a realm of private life that is in brief, not the law's business.'

However, it was not until ten years later, under a more liberal-thinking government, that the recommendations actually came into force on 28 July 1967. This was the result of great pressure from several areas of public influence, who felt that homosexual men, in particular, were already the object of ridicule and derision.

Gay Pride demonstration in London

Even so, it was still widely held to be a disability or condition that carried with it a burden of shame. Since this breakthrough in public and government acknowledgement of the rights of homosexuals there have been several developments in the law:

1. 1967: the age of consent set for homosexual males was 21.
2. 1994: the Criminal Justice and Public Order Act reduces the age of consent to 18.
3. 2000: the Parliament Act was invoked to ensure the passage of the Sexual Offences (Amendment) Act 2000, which made the age of consent 16 (17 in Northern Ireland for girls) for both homosexuals and heterosexuals.
4. 2003: The Sexual Offences Act completely overhauled the outdated procedures for dealing with sexual offences, including making gross indecency between men, buggery and sexual activity between more than two men no longer crimes in the United Kingdom.
5. 2013: Legislation for same-sex marriage came into force on 13 March.

In summary, the privacy law that was initially seen to be a right and a breakthrough, was later seen to have become an admission of disagreement. In order fully to acknowledge the rights of homosexuals, the freedom of expression in public, within the laws of common decency and inoffensiveness afforded to all subjects, needed to be acknowledged. Hopefully we are not far from achieving that now as a society.

Polyamorous relationships

The notion of polyamorous relationships has been around since Greek times and yet still today there is a general tendency to see it as an abnormal ethical deviation rather than one of alternative acceptable practice. Its popularity is growing, and some would argue re-defining sexuality. Polyamorous relationships cover many possible scenarios and can be informal, short term and uncommitted or can be long term.

Key quote

... it is pointless condemning someone for being homosexual: it is a condition that is not arrived at by choice .... the homosexual, whether he or she indulges in homosexual acts or not, is a person loved by God and for whom Christ died. (Shannon)

Key quote

As we live in such a monogamy-centred society, it makes sense that many people can only conceive of non-monogamy in what ultimately still amounts to monogamous terms. There is also a common misconception that will define a polyamorous relationship as no different from an open-relationship agreement: one committed couple, with some light-hearted fun on the side. (polyamorousdefinition.com)

Key quote

The controversial philosopher Michael Foucault (1926–1984) even argued that the idea of 'sexuality' is a modern invention designed to exercise political power over different members of society. (Wilcockson)

Key quote

Queer theory suggests that there can be no hard and fast boundaries about what is or is not a legitimate sexual relationship and no institution has the right to impose its views on others; being queer is the freedom to define oneself according to one's nature, whatever that may be. (Wilcockson)

Key quote

Increasingly, people claim that they embark on a sexual relationship as part of the quest for personal fulfilment …. Sex is seen in that context – as a pleasure in itself, but also as a way of becoming intimate with the partner, sharing in a way that has an effect on the relationship as a whole. (Thompson)

The problem with any definition is that it sets parameters and restraints. It is ironic that this is what polyamory is trying to avoid, that is, being classified and pigeon-holed into a particular set of rules in terms of sex and relationships!

Polyamory is a minefield to comprehend and in some ways it is easier to say what it is not than what it is! For instance, psychology.com rejects 'cheating', 'swinging' and 'polygamy' because there is less emphasis on consent and love, and more focus on dishonesty and sex. Most polyamorous websites try to define their actions and explain them relative to honesty, respect, consent and a loving relationship, and endeavour to distance themselves from what they would consider just sexually driven encounters such as casual sex, prostitution, adultery and forms of dominated hierarchical sexual relationships.

In contrast, sites such as Wikipedia identify many forms of polyamorous relationships that extend beyond the above recommendations.

Until a consensus is reached there will be no real fixed definition and all we can recognise at the time of writing is that through debate many are 'working towards' clarification. For the purpose of our studies, we will assume that the refined understanding of polyamorous is the one that is defined primarily by love and not sex.

It has been proposed that there are values ascribed to polyamory, although this is debated in terms of whether all values are shared by all forms of polyamory. For example, Wikipedia suggests several areas but there are five that are pertinent to what polyamorous websites state:

1. Fidelity and loyalty not as sexual exclusivity, but as faithfulness to the promises and agreements made about a relationship.

2. Communication and negotiation because there is no 'standard model' for polyamorous relationships and so negotiating with all involved to establish the terms of their relationships is required.

3. Trust, honesty, dignity, and respect at all times.

4. Gender equality and the removal of traditional boundaries associated with gender roles that sometimes determine one's behaviour.

5. Non-possessiveness, although it is recognised that jealousy and possessiveness do happen and sometimes cannot be avoided, but they should be explored, understood, and resolved within each individual, with compersion (the sharing of common joy and the opposite of jealousy) as a goal.

Key quote

In our outer world culture, sexual, romantic love is a well-defined box that every human being is supposed to be seeking. We are bombarded with the idea that we can only find romantic sexual love with one person, our soul-mate …. For polyamorous folks, we have, or are trying to discard this narrative. In letting go of the narrative we also let go of the narrow definition of romantic love. Suddenly all is not so clearly defined. You can love in different ways, different intensity and experience an array of romantic and or sexual love. We can experience a partner who we love, spend romantic time with but we are not sexual with them. We can meet wonderful lovers we move in and share our daily lives with, and some we may see just twice a year. We love them, they are romantic or love partners but they do not fit the box of the eternal soul-mate we forsake all others for. (lovemore.com)

AO1 Activity

Write out a contract for a polyamorous relationship.

Applying Fletcher's principles to homosexuality and polyamorous relationships

We can see from Fletcher's writings that it is clear that Fletcher held a view that sexual relationships were a matter of personal individual freedom governed by the rule of concern for neighbour. This is in line with his view that ethics should not be driven by an absolutist, legalistic approach. This is what he called the agapeic approach, the boss principle.

Before considering any other aspects of Situation Ethics it should be recognised that the practices of homosexuality and polyamory should have the same treatment as, say for example, a monogamous relationship in that what applies to them should also be the case for another relationship. This is not legalistic, however, but rather as Fletcher would argue, the agapeic principle that is the one constant and sets Situation Ethics apart from antinomianism.

For instance, the principle of agape would support the law as long as what is done in private or public does not contravene the law or human rights and also that it does not offend public decency. Although there is a grey area with the latter point, this is for a judge and jury to decide and not strictly speaking a moral agent. Therefore, if a relationship is considered honestly, with consent and lovingly then there is no reason why, according to the agapeic principle, that this cannot be considered to be against the principles of Christianity according to Fletcher's Situation Ethics.

For Fletcher's Situation Ethics, it was a matter of applying the principle of agape in line with the four working principles and the six fundamental principles. Again, such a response would be in accordance with the relativity of the law and the genuine act; it would be a practical (pragmatic) solution that addresses the people (personable) involved and not be dictated by any prefabricated moral assumptions; finally, it approaches the situation with the belief in agape as its basis and any reasoning follows from this and does not precede it.

This response therefore ensures that it supports the basis of agapeic concern for 'neighbour' as outlined in the six prepositions: love is the only good, love is the ruling norm of Christianity, love equals justice, love for all, loving ends justify the means and love decides situationally. They key here is that the loving acceptance of the end justifies the means and that justice triumphs in this situation.

It would be very difficult to see Situation Ethics as regarding homosexuality and polyamory as ethically wrong, unless, of course, the law and human rights are infringed upon, but this would be the very same for a monogamous relationship or any other relationship in that case! Indeed, both issues of homosexuality and polyamorous relationships are related specifically to the idea of love. In this sense the only true assessment of the validity of such relationships, then, according to Fletcher's Situation Ethics, would be that they are acceptable if, by partaking in such relationships, the love involved was sincere and that the ideal of agape was upheld.

quickfire

3.13 When was homosexuality decriminalised?

Key quote

Whether any form of sex (hetero, homo or auto) is good or evil depends on whether love is fully served. (Fletcher)

Key quote

What sex probably needs more than anything is a good airing, demythologizing it and getting rid of its mystique-laden and occult accretions, which come from romanticism on the one hand and puritanism on the other. (Fletcher)

Key skills

Knowledge involves:

Selection of a range of (thorough) accurate and relevant information that is directly related to the specific demands of the question.

This means you choose the correct information relevant to the question set NOT the topic area. You will have to think and focus on selecting key information and NOT writing everything you know about the topic area.

Understanding involves:

Explanation that is extensive, demonstrating depth and/or breadth with excellent use of evidence and examples including (where appropriate) thorough and accurate supporting use of sacred texts, sources of wisdom and specialist language.

This means that you demonstrate that you understand something by being able to illustrate and expand your points through examples/supporting evidence in a personal way and NOT repeat chunks from a text book (known as rote learning).

Further application of skills:

Go through the topic areas in this section and create some bullet lists of key points from key areas. For each one, provide further elaboration and explanation through the use of evidence and examples.

AO1 Developing skills

It is now time to reflect upon the information that has been covered so far. It is also important to consider how what you have learned can be focused and used for examination-style answers by practising the skills associated with AO1.

Assessment objective 1 (AO1) involves demonstrating knowledge and understanding. The terms 'knowledge' and 'understanding' are obvious but it is crucial to be familiar with how certain skills demonstrate these terms, and also, how the performance of these skills is measured (see generic band descriptors Band 5 for AS AO1).

▶ **Your new task is this:** below is a list of several key points in response to a question that has been written requiring an examination of the application of Situation Ethics to homosexual relationships. It is obviously a very full list. It will be useful, initially, to consider what you think are the most important points to use in planning an answer. This exercise, in essence, is like writing your own set of possible answers that are listed in a typical mark scheme as indicative content. In a group, select the most important points you feel should be included in a list of indicative content for this question. You will need to decide upon two things: which points to select; and then, in which order to put them in an answer.

List of indicative content:

- Key dates as background include:
  - 1967 the age of consent set for homosexual males was 21;
  - 1994 the Criminal Justice and Public Order Act reduces the age of consent to 18;
  - 2000 the Parliament Act was invoked to ensure the passage of the Sexual Offences (Amendment) Act 2000;
  - 2003 The Sexual Offences Act completely overhauled the outdated procedures for dealing with sexual offences;
  - 2013 Legislation for same-sex marriage came into force on 13 March.
- Fletcher involved in issues of social injustice and wrote at a time when homosexuality was illegal. 1960 wrote an academic paper entitled 'Sex offenses: an ethical view' in which he criticised legislation.
- Fletcher was unhappy with the inconsistent approach by the government and also the Church, to issues involving sexuality and sex in general.
- He argued that human laws and attitudes towards sex and homosexuality were outdated, inconsistent, hypocritical but more importantly unjust.
- Fletcher supported the Wolfenden report.
- Fletcher argued that any law based upon the presupposition of apparent 'sin' is unreliable and controversial.
- It was also a mistake, he argued, to let a particular religious or philosophical stance, based upon what it regards as wrongdoing or 'sin', dictate and shape the law.
- Fletcher argued that issues of privacy and public indecency should be legally determined, not determined by religious matters.
- Fletcher's conclusion was to propose that sex laws should be restricted by three criteria: the age of consent; infringement of public decency; acts involving assault, violence, duress or fraud.
- Fletcher held a view that sexual relationships were a matter of personal individual freedom governed by the rule of concern for neighbour.
- This is in line with his view that ethics should not be driven by an absolutist, legalistic approach.
- This is what he called the agapeic approach, the boss principle.

Issues for analysis and evaluation

Whether agape should replace religious rules

Specification content
Whether agape should replace
religious rules.

Some would argue that Situation Ethics is modelled on altruistic love, which is a major feature of many religions. Fletcher himself was a Christian moral theologian at the time and advocated the principle of agape as found in the Bible in the teachings of Jesus and Paul. He was also influenced by other Christian theologians who argued the same.

Indeed, the idea of putting people first (personalism) is in keeping with the actions of many world religious leaders but especially in the life and work of Jesus. Jesus always put people before religious principles such as when he healed on the Sabbath and declared, when criticised, that 'Sabbath was made for man not man for the Sabbath'. This would suggest that agape should supersede religious rules even if it does not replace them.

The idea of love has been a major feature of the teachings of several religious leaders especially in the history of Christianity such as Augustine and Aquinas who both held that agape was the superlative virtue.

However, the approach of Situation Ethics has been condemned by some religious leaders, for example the leaders of the Roman Catholic Church, as it puts too much emphasis on the benefits of relativism as opposed to the adherence to God's will. They argue that it also fails to consider the traditions within various denominations; for example, sex before marriage is allowed according to this theory if it is an act of selfless love whereas in some denominations it is held that sex is for marriage alone.

Christianity, along with other religions would also claim that love should not be the only desirable quality because other teachings and qualities are as important, for example justice, equality, and discipline through self-control.

The final line of argument in defending religious rules, teachings and traditions was that presented by William Barclay in his book 'Ethics in a Permissive Society'. In response to Fletcher's attack on legalistic religious rules, Barclay clarifies the nature and function of the law as 'the distillation of experience' that society has found to be beneficial. If this is so 'to discard law is to discard experience' and with it the valuable wisdom and insight it may bring. He also argued that religious rules are actually 'the rule of reason applied to existing circumstances' and therefore a valuable tool for defining approval and punishment. Religious rules, for Barclay, serve to work together with human law for the protection of society but he also pointed out that 'there are many things which are immoral, but which are not illegal' indicating that religious rules also serve to maintain morality. Barclay pointed out that Fletcher's view of true morality existing with the freedom to choose does not really consider the fact that that freedom also involves the freedom not to choose a course of action as well!

In conclusion there are religious rules that are outdated that the Church recognises as such but maintains those which it deems necessary for both religious and moral living. Fletcher's challenge did not necessarily mean that religious rules need replacing but more that they need guiding by the principle of love and sometimes, where necessary, adapting. Barclay was a harsh critic but some would say that although religious rules are valuable, history has shown us that they can be contextual whereas the principle of love is not.

AO2 Activity *Possible lines
of argument*

Listed below are some conclusions that could be drawn from the AO2 reasoning in the accompanying text:

1. Agape should replace religious rules as it is more flexible.

2. Agape should replace religious rules as it is an important biblical principle.

3. Agape should not replace religious rules but be guided by them.

4. Agape should not replace religious rules as it is too vague and subjective and open to misuse.

5. Agape should not replace religious rules as the religious rules that remain have stood the test of time.

Consider each of the conclusions drawn above and collect evidence and examples to support each argument from the AO1 and AO2 material studied in this section. Select one conclusion that you think is most convincing and explain why it is so. Now contrast this with the weakest conclusion in the list, justifying your argument with clear reasoning and evidence.

Specification content

The extent to which Situation Ethics provides a practical basis for making moral decisions for both religious believers and non-believers.

AO2 Activity *Possible lines of argument*

Listed below are some conclusions that could be drawn from the AO2 reasoning in the accompanying text:

1. Situation Ethics provides a practical basis for making moral decisions for religious believers because it is flexible and reflects the complexity of modern ethical debates.

2. Situation Ethics provides a practical basis for making moral decisions for religious believers because it is based in the universal religious principle of love for one's neighbour.

3. Situation Ethics does not provide a practical basis for making moral decisions for religious believers because it is too dangerous for religious society as a whole.

4. Situation Ethics does not provide a practical basis for making moral decisions for religious believers because it is itself inconsistent.

5. Situation Ethics can provide a practical basis for making moral decisions for religious believers but only in conjunction with other religious teachings and ethical theories.

Consider each of the conclusions drawn above and collect evidence and examples to support each argument from the AO1 and AO2 material studied in this section. Select one conclusion that you think is most convincing and explain why it is so. Now contrast this with the weakest conclusion in the list, justifying your argument with clear reasoning and evidence.

The extent to which Situation Ethics provides a practical basis for making moral decisions for religious believers

Much of the AO2 so far has dealt with society (i.e. secular notion that incorporates non-believers) so it makes sense to focus on religious believers in this evaluation although bear in mind the Specification does identify the term 'non-believers' for which other appropriate evaluations, much of which you have read so far, can be used.

For Christians, Situation Ethics fits in with the whole 'philosophy' and practical ethics of Jesus in the New Testament. Jesus broke religious rules and dealt with everyone as an individual and according to the circumstances, for example healing on the Sabbath, and declared 'Sabbath was made for man and not man for the Sabbath'.

Situation Ethics is flexible in that it gives personal freedom to people to decide what is the most loving action and still remains consistent with the actions and teachings of Jesus. Indeed, like Jesus, Situation Ethics does not reject laws but sees them as useful tools which are not absolutely binding.

It could be argued that the 'situationism' of Fletcher has been instrumental in, for example, the Church of England (among others) recognising areas of possible injustice, such as the issues of equality, the role of women in the Church, and slavery. This means that it can provide, and has provided, a basis for religious ethical decisions.

Again some would argue that there can only be a Christian basis of morality if agape love is seen as central to morality. There will always be a dispute as to what really is the most loving thing to do, and what this actually means in practice but that is no different to difficulties when applying rules.

However, some see Fletcher's views as not necessarily accurately reflecting New Testament views on morality; for example, the New Testament appears to have clear moral views on theft and adultery. Indeed, the examples Fletcher uses to justify Situation Ethics are so extreme that they account for very few real instances in life. For example, how often does a woman need to commit adultery and get pregnant to escape a captor? This is the point made by William Barclay who argued that the cases are too extreme as to justify changing religious or moral rules.

William Barclay has argued that if law is 'the distillation of experience' that society has found to be beneficial, then 'to discard law is to discard experience' and the valuable wisdom and insight it may bring. Barclay was particularly critical of Situation Ethics. Barclay firmly believed that the law and absolutes are there for the protection of society and a product of past reasoning and experience. This is the reason they exist.

Finally, Situation Ethics seems to deconstruct itself because we need an idea of what outcome is most valued, best or right before we can decide upon which acts are needed to bring about that right!

In conclusion, there are strong arguments against Situation Ethics as a practical basis for making moral decisions for religious believers, most pertinently, those put forward by William Barclay. However, to reject it outright, as Barclay himself pointed out, would be a mistake. Even Barclay said that religious believers could learn something from it when approaching ethical issues. It must be pointed out, nonetheless, that Fletcher's examples of the application of Situation Ethics in practice, using extreme cases, was never with the intention of demonstrating Situation Ethics at its best; rather it was with the intention of pointing out the inadequacy of deontological, absolute systems of ethics and this must be recognised in any objective evaluation.

AO2 Developing skills

It is now time to reflect upon the information that has been covered so far. It is also important to consider how what you have learned can be focused and used for examination-style answers by practising the skills associated with AO2.

Assessment objective 2 (AO2) involves 'analysis' and 'evaluation'. The terms may be obvious but it is crucial to be familiar with how certain skills demonstrate these terms, and also, how the performance of these skills is measured (see generic band descriptors Band 5 for AS AO2).

Obviously an answer is placed within an appropriate band descriptor depending upon how well the answer performs, ranging from excellent, good, satisfactory, basic/limited to very limited.

▶ **Your new task is this:** below is a list of several key points in response to a question that has been written requiring an evaluation of whether Situation Ethics is compatible with religious teachings. It is obviously a very full list. It will be useful, initially, to consider what you think are the most important points to use in planning an answer. This exercise, in essence, is like writing your own set of possible answers that are listed in a typical mark scheme as indicative content. In a group, select the most important points you feel should be included in a list of indicative content for this question. You will need to decide upon two things: which points to select; and then, in which order to put them in an answer.

List of indicative content:

- Agape makes it compatible with any Christian approach that sees 'love' as the centre of Christianity.
- There is strong biblical evidence to support the priority of love in the writings of Paul, for example, 1 Corinthians 13.
- Jesus himself broke the Sabbath law on work in favour of a person-centred approach when he plucked 'heads of grain to eat' on the Sabbath when he and his disciples were hungry.
- Jesus stated that 'Sabbath was made for man and not man for the Sabbath'.
- The change in views within Christianity on issues such as war, slavery, the death penalty and equality for women indicates recognition that absolutes are not always absolute.
- Christians may follow theories such as Utilitarianism that has some similarities with Situation Ethics and so suggests some compatibility.
- Situation Ethics has a major influence on the Anglican Church.
- In 1956, the study of the situationism approach to ethics (referred to as 'new morality') was banned from all Roman Catholic academies and seminaries on the grounds of its incompatibility with Roman Catholic teaching.
- Barclay's official critique that followed later also supported incompatibility.
- There are clear fundamental laws and absolutes in the bible that many Christians adhere to when making moral decisions.
- Situation Ethics dispenses with a lot of Christian teachings that are seen as valuable, if not definitive.
- Some would say that Situation Ethics is too antinomian to be compatible with Christianity.
- Natural Law is compatible with Christianity and only elements of Situation Ethics are compatible.

Key skills

Analysis involves identifying issues raised by the materials in the AO1, together with those identified in the AO2 section, and presents sustained and clear views, either of scholars or from a personal perspective ready for evaluation.

This means that it picks out key things to debate and the lines of argument presented by others or a personal point of view.

Evaluation involves considering the various implications of the issues raised based upon the evidence gleaned from analysis and provides an extensive detailed argument with a clear conclusion.

This means that the answer weighs up the various and different lines of argument analysed through individual commentary and response and arrives at a conclusion through a clear process of reasoning.

This section covers AO1 content and skills

Specification content

Bentham's theory of 'utility' or 'usefulness'; ultimate aim is to pursue pleasure and avoid pain; principle of utility ('the greatest happiness for the greatest number').

Key terms

Greatest happiness principle: a calculation used in utilitarian theory to assess the best course of action to take

Utilitarianism: an ethical theory that maintains that an action is right if it produces the greatest happiness for the greatest number – the ethical nature of actions is therefore based on consequences for human happiness

Key quote

We must, therefore, pursue the things that make for happiness, seeing that when happiness is present, we have everything; but when it is absent, we do everything to possess it. (**Epicurus**)

Key quote

Happiness is a very pretty thing to feel, but very dry to talk about. (**Bentham**)

quickfire

4.1 Why is 'happiness' important for Utilitarianism?

quickfire

4.2 According to Utilitarianism, what are the best actions?

A: Classical Utilitarianism – Jeremy Bentham's Act Utilitarianism: happiness as the basis of morality

Bentham's theory of 'utility'

The term '**Utilitarianism**' comes from the word 'utility', which means 'usefulness'. In particular it concerns itself with working out how 'useful' an action is, based upon assessing its end result. Utilitarianism is not new or even recent. Like most philosophies it can be traced back to ancient Greece. Utilitarians argue that everyone should do the thing that produces the most 'useful' end.

They apply the following reasoning:

1. The most useful end is seen as that which brings the maximum levels of 'happiness or pleasure'.

2. Therefore actions that produce the most happiness for all are seen as the best course of action (i.e. good moral actions).

3. This way of assessing which course of action is the best one to take is known as 'the **greatest happiness principle**'.

Therefore, utilitarians argue that everyone should do the most useful thing. The most useful thing is seen as action or actions that result in maximum levels of happiness or pleasure. Therefore, actions that produce the most happiness are seen as good and right actions or moral actions that produce happiness for all. Since Utilitarianism is concerned about the outcome (or end) of an action, it is therefore a teleological ethical theory.

We have to be careful with explaining the greatest happiness principle, as it can be slightly misleading, since the greatest happiness did not necessarily involve the greatest number of people. The emphasis is more on the action that produces the greatest amount of happiness overall. In other words, what is right is what maximises happiness. This is a very important point to remember.

Jeremy Bentham is usually accepted as the originator of Utilitarianism. He was a social reformer and sought to develop an ethical theory that promoted actions that would benefit the majority of people. As a barrister and expert in the law, Bentham became aware of widespread social injustice. This prompted him to become concerned with issues of public morality. He was instrumental in reforming prisons and advocated that the penalties imposed for crimes should be sufficient to deter but not cause unnecessary suffering. He also advocated such things as censorship and laws governing sexual activity in an attempt to improve public morality. His guiding principle for public policy was 'the greatest happiness for the greatest number'. He then developed this into a moral philosophy. In 1826, Bentham founded University College. Rather strangely, his embalmed body, wearing his usual clothes, sits in the entrance hall in a glass case! Only his head was replaced by a wax model.

For Bentham, happiness was the supreme ethical value or what he called the 'sovereign good'. Happiness is useful, because it is good for people to be happy. Bentham argued that we are motivated by pleasure and pain so that we pursue pleasure and avoid pain. This view of happiness being linked to pleasure owes something to an earlier ethical theory called **hedonism**. In hedonism, the only thing that is right is pleasure.

Study tip

When answering a question, remain focused on the title of the question. Often candidates are drawn into digression by writing biographical details or information that is not directly relevant to the focus of the question, e.g. some interesting information about Jeremy Bentham's childhood!

Although Utilitarianism is a teleological ethical theory, there is a rule or guiding principle underpinning this approach. This guiding principle, known as the **principle of utility**, states that people should act to bring about a balance of good over evil. Bentham saw this as measuring whether or not an act would promote pleasure or pain. Bentham wrote, 'By the principle of utility is meant that principle which approves of every action whatsoever, according to the tendency which it appears to have to augment or diminish the happiness of the party whose interest is in question.' Every action, then, can be measured by this principle.

AO1 Activity

Write a dictionary definition for 'Jeremy Bentham and the principle of utility' that is 200 words long. Try to include key points such as Utilitarianism, hedonism, an explanation of the principle and Bentham's reasons for proposing the principle.

Jeremy Bentham 1748–1832

Key terms

Hedonism: an ethical theory that defines what is right in terms of pleasure

Principle of utility: an action is right if it promotes and maximises happiness

Key quote

Nature has placed mankind under the governance of two sovereign masters, pain and pleasure. It is for them alone to point out what we ought to do, as well as to determine what we shall do. **(Bentham)**

quickfire

4.3 What was Bentham's trained profession?

Specification content

The hedonic calculus as a means of measuring pleasure in each unique moral situation; by considering seven factors: intensity, duration, certainty, remoteness, fecundity, purity and extent.

Key quote

Create all the happiness you are able to create; remove all the misery you are able to remove. Every day will allow you, – will invite you to add something to the pleasure of others, – or to diminish something of their pains. (Bentham)

The hedonic calculus

Having established that the measure of happiness is the criterion for a right act, there arises the problem of how to calculate that measurement. For Bentham, happiness consisted of pleasure minus pain.

The principle of utility centred on the act delivering the greatest amount of pleasure and the least amount of pain. Bentham's solution to measuring this balance was his hedonic calculus, also called the pleasure calculus.

He thought there were seven different elements that should be taken into account when calculating the amount of happiness. Each word used has a specific meaning in relation to a pleasure experience and the resulting happiness produced.

Element of pleasure	Meaning
Intensity	The stronger, the better, meaning that those pleasures that give an acute and extremely potent rush of pleasure bring instant happiness.
Duration	The longer-lasting, the better, meaning that inevitably the enduring nature of the experience of happiness is a key factor in assessing the quality of the pleasure.
Certainty	The more sure that pleasure will result, the better. This is a true 'calculation' of the implications of the pleasure being consistent and, in some cases, more reliable than an alternative. As Driver writes, 'all things being equal, we should go for the more certain than less certain pleasures'.
Extent	The more people who experience it the better, as shared pleasures enhance the impact of happiness beyond oneself in true keeping with the happiness principle.
Propinquity	The nearer the pleasure is to you, the better, meaning the present as opposed to those we are looking forward to in the distant future.
Richness or fecundity	The more chance the pleasure will be repeated or will result in other pleasures, the better. This considers the additional occurrences of the same pleasure or pleasures, or, alternatively subsequent and dependent sub-pleasures that may result.
Purity	The least amount of pain it involves, the better. Some experiences may not be pure happiness but may involve a 'roller coaster ride' of ups and downs. For Bentham, a consistent experience of pleasure that is as far distanced from 'pain' or negative feelings is superior.

Study tip

A mnemonic to help you remember the initial letters of the hedonic calculus is 'In Dark Corners Edward Ponders Radical Propaganda'.

Bentham, in his work, *Principles of Morals and Legislation* wrote a poem to help remember they key principles of the hedonic calculus:

'Intense, long, certain, speedy, fruitful, pure –

Such marks in pleasure and pains endure.

Such pleasures seek, if private be thy end:

If it be public, wide let them extend.

Such pains avoid, whichever be thy view,

If pains must come, let them extend to a few.'

Using these criteria, Bentham argued that it was possible to work out the right course of action in any situation. The balance of pain and pleasure created by one choice of action could be compared with those created by other available choices.

Bentham was concerned with maximising the quantity of happiness; he was not concerned about prioritising which forms of happiness were superior to others. Bentham wrote in *The Rationale of Reward* that, 'Prejudice apart, the game of push-pin is of equal value with the arts and sciences of music and poetry'. Bentham's position was that all pleasures are of equal value.

Utilitarianism measures the balance between pain and pleasure

Key quote

...the rarest of all human qualities is consistency. (Bentham)

quickfire

4.4 State two principles of the hedonic calculus.

AO1 Activity

Create a flow diagram that explains the hedonic calculus with some practical examples to help you explain it.

Study tip

The important thing about Bentham's hedonic calculus is that you understand how it is applied. It is better to remember three elements and explain how they work than to list all seven and not relate them to his theory or an issue.

Key quote

The quantity of pleasure being equal, push-pin is as good as poetry. (Bentham)

Act Utilitarianism

Teleological thinking considers the consequences of a particular action or the 'end' result, and it is the assessment of this 'end' that determines whether or not the action is morally good. In this case the goal should always be 'happiness'.

As it considers consequences it is also known as a **consequentialist** theory. This means that ethical decisions and judgements, whether something is right or wrong, should be based on the outcome or the consequences of an action. In this case does it lead to the 'greatest happiness for the greatest number'?

The term **Act Utilitarianism** is usually associated with the Utilitarianism of Bentham and use of his hedonic calculus. Bentham thought that previous experiences did not always help us make moral choices and that each situation was different, and so had to be calculated afresh. For Act Utilitarianism in its strong form, in each situation the calculus should be applied, regardless of previous experiences in decision making. Jeremy Bentham's theory is therefore considered to be a **relativistic** theory. This means there are no universal moral norms or rules and that each situation has to be looked at independently because each situation is different. Act Utilitarianism appears to favour the individual situations more than the cases for the majority.

Although Bentham is said to be an act utilitarian, he did not claim that it was necessary to calculate the rightness and wrongness of every act from the hedonic calculus, just that this was generally the case.

Specification content

Act Utilitarianism as a form of moral relativism, a consequentialist and teleological theory.

Key terms

Act Utilitarianism: a form of Utilitarianism associated with Bentham that treats each moral situation as unique and applies the hedonic calculus to each 'act' to see if it fulfils the 'principle of utility'. Any action is right if it produces 'the greatest happiness for the greatest number

Consequentialist: people should make moral judgements based on the outcome or the consequences of an action

Relativistic: this means there are no universal moral norms or rules and that each situation has to be looked at independently because each situation is different

quickfire

4.5 Explain why Utilitarianism is a relativist theory of ethics.

Key skills

Knowledge involves:

Selection of a range of (thorough) accurate and relevant information that is directly related to the specific demands of the question.

This means you choose the correct information relevant to the question set NOT the topic area. You will have to think and focus on selecting key information and NOT writing everything you know about the topic area.

Understanding involves:

Explanation that is extensive, demonstrating depth and/or breadth with excellent use of evidence and examples including (where appropriate) thorough and accurate supporting use of sacred texts, sources of wisdom and specialist language.

This means that you demonstrate that you understand something by being able to illustrate and expand your points through examples/supporting evidence in a personal way and NOT repeat chunks from a text book (known as rote learning).

Further application of skills:

Go through the topic areas in this section and create some bullet lists of key points from key areas. For each one, provide further elaboration and explanation through the use of evidence and examples.

AO1 Developing skills

It is now time to reflect upon the information that has been covered so far. It is also important to consider how what you have learned can be focused and used for examination-style answers by practising the skills associated with AO1.

Assessment objective 1 (AO1) involves demonstrating knowledge and understanding. The terms 'knowledge' and 'understanding' are obvious but it is crucial to be familiar with how certain skills demonstrate these terms, and also, how the performance of these skills is measured (see generic band descriptors Band 5 for AS AO1).

▶ **Your new task is this:** below is a list of indicative content that could be used in response to a question requiring an examination of Bentham's hedonic calculus. The problem is that it is not a very full list and needs completing! It will be useful, as a group, to consider what is missing from the list. You will need to add at least five points that you would use to improve the list and/or give more detail to each point that is already in the list. Then, as a group, agree on your final list and write out your new list of indicative content, remembering the principles of explaining with evidence and/or examples.

If you then put this list in order of how you would present the information in an essay you will have your own plan for an ideal answer.

List of indicative content:

- Purity of experience is important.
- Bentham wrote a poem to help remember them.
- They are used to work out the impact and quality of the happiness experience produced.
- Extent of the pleasure is important.
- Intensity of the pleasure is important.
- *Your added content*
- *Your added content*
- Etc.

Issues for analysis and evaluation

The degree to which pleasure can be seen as the sole intrinsic good

**This section covers AO2
content and skills**

Specification content
The degree to which pleasure can be
seen as the sole intrinsic good.

The main issue here is with the vagueness of 'pleasure' and its subjective nature. For example, not everyone may have the same amount of pleasure from the same experience. However, Bentham would argue that if we use the hedonic calculus correctly then this would be accounted for; one person would not choose a scary ride at a theme park but another person would choose it because it was 'thrilling' and not 'scary'.

The most obvious challenge to the idea of pleasure as the sole intrinsic good is once again linked to the idea of subjectivity. Just because a pleasure may produce happiness does that mean it is the same as 'good' in terms of ethics?

The idea of pursuing happiness as a goal has been called into question. Mill later developed Bentham's system and refined the definition of pleasure and 'happiness' into a nobler idea more akin to Aristotle's eudaimonia. Some would argue that the pursuit of eudaimonia is superior because it embraces a more holistic view of an individual's overall well-being.

There are surely some pleasures that are nobler than others. Although Bentham's calculus goes some way towards identifying these through the applications of key principles, it is still left to individual interpretation of these. For example, some may see spiritual and intellectual happiness as superior to sensual satisfaction whilst others may disagree.

However, it is clear that pleasures that produce happiness are vital for complete mental health and quality of life, although one could argue that there is an obsessive compulsion to seek out constant pleasure that may be implicit in the hedonic calculus. Some would argue that life is better as a 'roller coaster' as the ups and downs help us learn and grow as individuals. Indeed, does not the extent of the pleasure grow when we know what pain is? However, despite this it is clear to many that life is to be enjoyed and not 'suffered' and all noble religious and non-religious ideals seek some form of individual satisfaction.

The real question seems to be 'is happiness or pleasure a valid aim?' when compared to more spiritual goals such as salvation. The problem also is that there is no capacity for self-sacrifice or discipline in the ideal of pleasure as the sole intrinsic good. Sometimes we cannot compute what impact an experience may have and can have the tendency to not see how good something may be because it appears too difficult or uncomfortable for us. Are there not instances where pain is good for you? What about pains associated with hard work or exercise?

In conclusion it appears that the answer depends upon the nature of the happiness involved in relation to the pleasure and in Bentham's calculus maybe there ought to be some priority, say for example, the extent and fecundity which have more chance of including more than one person. This leaves us with the lingering doubt that pleasure as the sole intrinsic good does seem rather self-indulgent.

AO2 Activity *Possible lines of argument*

Listed below are some conclusions that could be drawn from the AO2 reasoning in the accompanying text:

1. Pleasure can be seen as the sole intrinsic good because it is the only way to create happiness.

2. Pleasure can be seen as the sole intrinsic good if it is guided carefully by Bentham's hedonic calculus.

3. Pleasure cannot be seen as the sole intrinsic good because it is too subjective.

4. Pleasure cannot be seen as the sole intrinsic good because it is too narrow a view of the life experience.

5. Pleasure cannot be seen as the sole intrinsic good because it does not take into account differences in the quality or overall value of the happiness produced.

Consider each of the conclusions drawn above and collect evidence and examples to support each argument from the AO1 and AO2 material studied in this section. Select one conclusion that you think is most convincing and explain why it is so. Now contrast this with the weakest conclusion in the list, justifying your argument with clear reasoning and evidence.

Specification content

The extent to which Utilitarianism
works in contemporary society.

The extent to which Utilitarianism works in contemporary society

Many people would see the fact that Utilitarianism as a teleological theory aims for the goal of happiness as being realistic as this is what many people claim is their aim in life and for society as a whole in providing 'the greatest happiness for the greatest number'.

Whilst Act Utilitarianism does have a number of weaknesses, the fact that it forms the basis of modern political democracy shows that it must still be useful in contemporary society. Utilitarianism has aims that are attractive in that happiness is desired and the avoidance of pain seem reasonable goals. It does seem that we are motivated by pleasure and motivated to avoid pain. It also seems straightforward to apply to most situations and concurs with common sense. For example, it takes into account consequences of our actions, whereas simply looking at intentions with no regard to their consequences seems impersonal. This is important in establishing social laws.

Utilitarianism also considers others and not just the individual. It is concerned with the common good. It takes into account all who are affected by the action. In short, Act Utilitarianism is pragmatic and concentrates on the situation a person is in and the effects of an action. In addition, another strength of the theory is that it treats everyone the same and no individual gets special treatment. This is consistent with the ideals of contemporary society.

Overall, Utilitarianism allows people the autonomy to make decisions for themselves; for example, in Act Utilitarianism each act is considered individually so it is not prescriptive and restrictive. Ultimately, for many people 'happiness' is an important aspect of decision making as it is their main aim in life and Utilitarianism can provide a clear guidance on what leads to the 'greatest happiness for the greatest number'.

However, Utilitarianism does have a number of key weaknesses as an ethical theory. Although it is essentially concerned with fulfilling the 'greatest happiness for the greatest number' it can, as a result, allow a minority to suffer, for example, leading to the justification of acts such as slavery or torture. This would not be allowed in contemporary society.

It seems to ignore intentions and an individual's motive which conveys that the means by which the greatest good is achieved seems incidental and of no moral relevance. In other words, injustice could be seen as right action, which seems contrary to common sense. Justice is the foundation of contemporary society.

In deciding whether an action is morally right, it requires the outcomes of the action to be known. However, outcomes may not be accurately predictable. This is certainly true in the case of a war. It is also true with some forms of genetic engineering. To decide what action will produce the greatest good, the alternative actions also have to be considered and their possible outcomes predicted. This seems an impossible task. In this way one could argue that Utilitarianism seems too demanding, since we ought always to do that which gives greatest good for the greatest number, but there may always be an act, other than what we choose, that would give greater good.

Another criticism of Utilitarianism fails to consider that we have certain duties or obligations towards others; for example, a mother's duty to protect her child. This is part of human nature and another aspect to this is that people are not infallible and they often can make errors of judgement, specifically in relation to what they think will lead to happiness may not in the end produce it.

There is also the argument that it cannot really be applied consistently: happiness is subjective and people have different ideas about what constitutes 'pleasure'. What is one person's pleasure is another person's idea of pain. How would this work in society?

Finally, a religious believer would argue that the rules for society should be based on God's will not on the pursuit of happiness. Indeed, they would indicate that some of the rules of society are not consistent with the pursuit of an individual's pleasure or 'the greatest happiness for the greatest number'.

In conclusion, it can be seen that aspects of utilitarian theory do work in society but it is clear that using it as a basis for all our laws would be questionable.

AO2 Activity *Possible lines of argument*

Listed below are some conclusions that could be drawn from the AO2 reasoning in the accompanying text:

1. Utilitarianism works in contemporary society as its basis is 'the greatest happiness for the greatest number'.

2. Utilitarianism works in contemporary society as it still influences our political system today.

3. Utilitarianism works in contemporary society as it is the goal of each individual to be happy.

4. Utilitarianism cannot work in contemporary society as a theory on its own.

5. Utilitarianism cannot work in contemporary society because there are too many weaknesses.

Consider each of the conclusions drawn above and collect evidence and examples to support each argument from the AO1 and AO2 material studied in this section. Select one conclusion that you think is most convincing and explain why it is so. Now contrast this with the weakest conclusion in the list, justifying your argument with clear reasoning and evidence.

Utilitarianism forms the basis of modern politics

Key skills

Analysis involves identifying issues raised by the materials in the AO1, together with those identified in the AO2 section, and presents sustained and clear views, either of scholars or from a personal perspective ready for evaluation.

This means that it picks out key things to debate and the lines of argument presented by others or a personal point of view.

Evaluation involves considering the various implications of the issues raised based upon the evidence gleaned from analysis and provides an extensive detailed argument with a clear conclusion.

This means that the answer weighs up the various and different lines of argument analysed through individual commentary and response and arrives at a conclusion through a clear process of reasoning.

AO2 Developing skills

It is now time to reflect upon the information that has been covered so far. It is also important to consider how what you have learned can be focused and used for examination-style answers by practising the skills associated with AO2.

Assessment objective 2 (AO2) involves 'analysis' and 'evaluation'. The terms may be obvious but it is crucial to be familiar with how certain skills demonstrate these terms, and also, how the performance of these skills is measured (see generic band descriptors Band 5 for AS AO2).

Obviously an answer is placed within an appropriate band descriptor depending upon how well the answer performs, ranging from excellent, good, satisfactory, basic/limited to very limited.

▶ **Your new task is this:** below is a list of indicative content that could be used in response to a question requiring an evaluation of the effectiveness of Act Utilitarianism for ethical decision making. The problem is that it is not a very full list and needs completing! It will be useful, as a group, to consider what is missing from the list. You will need to add at least six points (three in support and three against) that you would use to improve the list and/or give more detail to each point that is already in the list. Remember, it is how you use the points that is the most important factor. Apply the principles of evaluation by making sure that you: identify issues clearly; present accurate views of others, making sure that you comment on the views presented; reach an overall personal judgement. You may add more of your own suggestions, but try to negotiate as a group and prioritise the most important things to add. Then, as a group, agree on your final list and write out your new list of indicative content, remembering the principles of explaining with evidence and/or examples.

If you then put this list in order of how you would present the information in an essay you will have your own plan for an ideal answer.

List of indicative content:

In support
- Hedonic calculus is useful as a guide.
- It considers the rights of the individual.
- *Your added content*
- *Your added content*
- Etc.

Against
- Act Utilitarianism is too subjective.
- Act Utilitarianism cannot be consistent.
- *Your added content*
- *Your added content*
- Etc.

B: John Stuart Mill's development of Utilitarianism

Mill's idea that not all pleasure is the same

The ethical theory of Utilitarianism proposed by Bentham soon started to raise some strong criticisms. Not least amongst the critics was his former pupil, John Stuart Mill.

The main criticism against Bentham was that he tried to measure pleasure in quantitative terms. It appeared to allow for some actions to be called right and good when they seemed, to others, to be wrong. For instance, Bentham's approach appeared to conclude that a gang rape would be a right action if the pleasure gained by the group of rapists exceeded that of the pain experienced by the person raped.

This also raised questions about the exact nature of 'pleasure'. It is important to remember that it is in the context of such criticisms of Bentham that Mill developed utilitarian theory.

This equating of happiness with good is a view that can be found in the writings of Aristotle. He referred to it as eudaimonia. Aristotle argued that pleasure was not mere gratification but rather includes the idea of well-being, living well, being fulfilled. This is much closer to the view that Mill took.

Higher and lower pleasures

As a result of the flaw identified in Bentham's definition of defining happiness in quantitative terms, Mill shifted the focus in his version of Utilitarianism from the quantity of happiness and pleasure to the quality of the happiness and pleasure. He recognised that some pleasures were superior to others and developed a system of 'higher' and 'lower' pleasures.

Mill distinguished between pleasure that stimulated the mind, which he called higher pleasure, and pleasure that was merely physical or lower pleasure. He claimed that human beings alone could achieve the higher pleasure and it was the higher pleasure that was more satisfying. However, Mill was aware that often people did not choose the higher pleasure in preference to the lower pleasure. He felt that this was because they had not experienced both. Had they done so, they would have known that higher pleasure was more satisfying than the lower pleasures.

According to Mill, therefore, intellectual pleasures, that is, pleasures of the intellect or mind, are higher and superior. For example, reading philosophy or poetry is far superior to gorging oneself on a feast! Such pleasures help humans to develop their intellect. Albert Einstein became famous for scientific discoveries and so is a classic example of aspiring to higher pleasures by using his intellect.

Lower pleasures, then, are inferior pleasures of the body, that is, physical pleasures such as sex and eating. They are lower because they do not enrich or enhance the intellect or develop the quality of an individual. Eating fish and chips fulfils a lower pleasure by satisfying hunger, but it only serves to meet basic bodily needs.

This section covers AO1 content and skills

Specification content

Mill's idea that not all pleasure is the same – 'higher pleasures' (intellectual) are superior to 'lower pleasures' (basic physical pleasure). Development of the 'harm principle': the actions of individuals should be limited to prevent harm to other individuals.

Key person

John Stuart Mill 1806–1873: was a British philosopher, political economist, civil servant and Member of Parliament. Bentham was his mentor and a close family friend. He was an influential liberal thinker and developed Bentham's version of Utilitarianism. He focused more on the 'quality' of pleasure rather than the 'quantity' of pleasure. Retrospectively some scholars have credited him as introducing Rule Utilitarianism.

J.S. Mill 1806–1873

quickfire

4.6 State one way in which Mill disagreed with Bentham.

Key quote

Over himself, over his own body and mind, the individual is sovereign. **(Mill)**

Key quote

It is better to be a human being dissatisfied than a pig satisfied; better to be Socrates dissatisfied than a fool satisfied. (Mill)

Key quote

No pleasure is a bad thing in itself, but the things which produce certain pleasures entail disturbances many times greater than the pleasures themselves. (Epicurus)

quickfire

4.7 Give an example of a 'higher pleasure'.

quickfire

4.8 Give an example of a 'lower pleasure'.

quickfire

4.9 Why is the 'harm principle' so important for Utilitarianism?

For society to be happy, individuals collectively need to be happy also

Key quote

The only purpose for which power can be rightfully exercised over any member of a civilised community, against his will, is to prevent harm to others. (Mill)

Mill did, however, recognise that people must satisfy the lower pleasures, that is, they do need to eat and sleep. This is a basic requirement. However, it was not good to focus solely upon the lower pleasures and the greatest aim in life was to aspire to achieving the higher pleasures.

By making a distinction between higher and lower pleasures, Mill moved the calculation of pleasure away from quantity towards quality. No longer was it simply how much pleasure an action caused. Now it was also a matter of the quality of the pleasure.

Mill's Utilitarianism, then, was not concerned entirely with the quantity of the happiness that an act produced but argued that this should be weighed against the quality of happiness produced by such an act.

Universalisability and the harm principle

As a political economist, civil servant and Member of Parliament Mill was very interested in social reform and looking at how society worked and what was best for people in general. Perhaps the most important contribution by Mill, then, was his introduction of the idea of universalisability. Similar to Bentham's principle of utility, Mill wanted to show that what is right and wrong for one person in a situation is right or wrong for all. He argued that:

1. Happiness is desirable since we all desire it.

2. Happiness is the only thing desirable as an end, since things are only desirable because they bring about happiness.

3. Therefore, everyone ought to aim at the happiness of everyone, as increasing the general happiness will increase my happiness.

This argument supports the idea that people should put the interests of the group before their own interests. Bentham's principle of utility had focused much more on individual situations and had no concept of protecting the common good universally. However, it is always the identification of the greatest happiness in terms of quality that drives this decision. In essence, as society is made up of individuals, for society to be happy, individuals collectively need to be happy also. It is therefore the 'duty' or 'rule' for society that it should protect the happiness of its subjects.

It was this thinking that led to Mill developing what has been called the 'harm principle'. In his book '*On Liberty*' Mill wrote,

'That principle is, that the sole end for which mankind are warranted, individually or collectively, in interfering with the liberty of action of any of their number, is self-protection. That the only purpose for which power can be rightfully exercised over any member of a civilised community, against his will, is to prevent harm to others. His own good, either physical or moral, is not a sufficient warrant. He cannot rightfully be compelled to do or forbear because it will be better for him to do so, because it will make him happier, because, in the opinion of others, to do so would be wise, or even right .... The only part of the conduct of anyone, for which he is amenable to society, is that which concerns others. In the part which merely concerns himself, his independence is, of right, absolute. Over himself, over his own body and mind, the individual is sovereign.'

AO1 Activity

Write down the key principles of Utilitarianism and colour code them according to (1) what is common to both Bentham and Mill (2) Bentham and (3) Mill.

Study tip

Always remember to point out the historical context and development of Utilitarianism in relation to the different versions presented.

Development of Rule Utilitarianism

Mill thought previous experiences did help us make decisions. Indeed, human beings have already developed some rules that help them make decisions more quickly. These rules are universal in nature, and if applied in any situation, they would lead to the greatest happiness of the greatest number (i.e. they would maximise happiness). In **Rule Utilitarianism**, moral actions are those which conform to the rules that lead to the greatest good. For example, we do not need to use the hedonic calculus to work out that giving money to the poor is right because it is a well-worked rule of Utilitarianism.

In its strong form, **Strong Rule Utilitarianism** claims that an action is right if, and only if, it follows the rules: the rules should never be disobeyed. These rules are universal in nature and, if applied in any situation, would lead to the greatest happiness for the greatest number. They would maximise happiness. The rule utilitarian would notice the similarities between the present case and the previous ones and draw on those previous calculations.

A strong rule utilitarian, on the one hand, believes that any rules created using the principle of utility should never be broken. This is because the rules were made in order to promote happiness. However, on the other hand, in its weaker form known as **Weak Rule Utilitarianism**, a person tries to allow for the fact that in extreme cases the rule created using the principle of utility needs to be broken in order to achieve the greatest happiness. For example, the rule 'do not kill' might have be broken by someone during World War II if they had the opportunity to kill Hitler, as this would have fulfilled the principle of utility.

Mill is said to be a rule utilitarian; however, it is doubtful whether he advocated the strong form. He viewed the rules more as helpful guidance than obligatory. They were necessary as a means of saving time. This view, known as Weak Rule Utilitarianism, states that on certain occasions the rules can be disobeyed if a greater amount of happiness will result. In this latter sense, Mill's theory is often seen as a deontological and teleological hybrid; that is, it is a mixture of the application of rules that have been established through the experience of applying Utilitarianism, but also at times through the consideration of the end goal of his specific form of Utilitarianism without reference to past experience.

AO1 Activity

Design a diagram that links the different elements of Bentham's version of Utilitarianism. Begin with the hedonic calculus but remember, place the ideas of the seven elements within the context of Bentham's ideas as a whole.

Study tip

In the exam, write a brief bullet list by way of a plan for each question that you attempt to answer. Your bullet list should use key words, e.g. for a question on Mill: refinement of Bentham, higher/lower, quality, eudaimonia, universalisability.

Specification content

Every action does not need to be assessed and actions are right if they conform to an historical rule that has demonstrated that it fulfils the principle of utility (now known as 'Rule' Utilitarianism). Mill's Utilitarianism as a teleological and deontological hybrid.

Key quote

There is no case of moral obligation in which some secondary principle is not involved. (Mill)

Key quote

All action is for the sake of some end, and rules of action, it seems natural to suppose, must take their whole character and colour from the end to which they are subservient. (Mill)

Key terms

Rule Utilitarianism: a view associated with John Stuart Mill. Rule utilitarians believe that by using the 'principle of utility', that is, the greatest happiness for the greatest number, one can draw up general rules, based on past experiences, which would help to keep this principle

Strong Rule Utilitarianism: a strong rule utilitarian believes that any rules formulated and established through the application of the 'principle of utility' should never be broken as they guarantee happiness for society

Weak Rule Utilitarianism: a weak rule utilitarian tries to allow for the fact that in some situations breaking a rule originally created because it generally fulfils the principle of utility may be the right course of action, because in this particular situation, breaking the rule is more likely to fulfil the principle of utility than keeping the rule

quickfire

4.10 Explain the difference between Strong Rule Utilitarianism and Weak Rule Utilitarianism.

Key skills

Knowledge involves:

Selection of a range of (thorough) accurate and relevant information that is directly related to the specific demands of the question.

This means you choose the correct information relevant to the question set NOT the topic area. You will have to think and focus on selecting key information and NOT writing everything you know about the topic area.

Understanding involves:

Explanation that is extensive, demonstrating depth and/or breadth with excellent use of evidence and examples including (where appropriate) thorough and accurate supporting use of sacred texts, sources of wisdom and specialist language.

This means that you demonstrate that you understand something by being able to illustrate and expand your points through examples/supporting evidence in a personal way and NOT repeat chunks from a text book (known as rote learning).

Further application of skills:

Go through the topic areas in this section and create some bullet lists of key points from key areas. For each one, provide further elaboration and explanation through the use of evidence and examples.

AO1 Developing skills

It is now time to reflect upon the information that has been covered so far. It is also important to consider how what you have learned can be focused and used for examination-style answers by practising the skills associated with AO1.

Assessment objective 1 (AO1) involves demonstrating knowledge and understanding. The terms 'knowledge' and 'understanding' are obvious but it is crucial to be familiar with how certain skills demonstrate these terms, and also, how the performance of these skills is measured (see generic band descriptors Band 5 for AS AO1).

You are now nearing the end of this section of the course. From now on the task will have only instructions with no examples; however, using the skills you have developed in completing the earlier tasks, you should be able to apply what you have learned to do and complete this successfully.

▶ **Your new task is this:** you will have to write a response under timed conditions to a question requiring an examination of how Mill developed Bentham's Utilitarianism. You will need to focus for this and apply the skills that you have developed so far:

1. **Begin with a list of indicative content. Perhaps discuss this as a group. It does not need to be in any order.**

2. **Develop the list using examples.**

3. **Now consider in which order you would like to explain the information.**

4. **Then write out your plan, under timed conditions, remembering the principles of explaining with evidence and/ or examples.**

Use this technique as revision for each of the topic areas that you have studied. The basic technique of planning answers helps even when time is short and you cannot complete every essay.

Issues for analysis and evaluation

The extent to which Rule Utilitarianism provides a better basis for making moral decisions than Act Utilitarianism

In terms of Bentham's Act Utilitarianism, a great strength is that it has a clear method in its application of the hedonic calculus. Indeed, one could go as far as to argue that the hedonic calculus is thorough in its consideration of measuring aspects of pleasure. Act Utilitarianism is also a morally democratic approach that seeks the fairest result through application of the happiness principle.

There are, however, specific weaknesses of Bentham and Act Utilitarianism. Firstly, it is not clear how the hedonic calculus resolves the problem of assessing the quantity of pleasure. For instance, how is it possible to quantify and compare intensity of pleasure with duration of pleasure? Listing elements of pleasure does not resolve the problem of quantifying the pleasure. Secondly, the hedonic calculus does not prioritise or rank aspects of pleasure and so can lead to further confusion. If applied clumsily the hedonic calculus is open to abuse; for example, it appears to justify gang rape. Finally, Bentham's hedonic calculus criteria seem to be geared towards the individual in its application, that is, more to the principle of utility in general, rather than a consideration of its wider implications of the happiness principle advocated by Utilitarianism.

Mills Rule Utilitarianism has specific strengths, the first of which is that it is arguably a more intelligent and thoughtful approach than Bentham's theory. It clearly addresses the quantitative aspect of pleasure by qualifying it and refining it with the qualitative analysis. Some would therefore say that it avoids the pitfalls of Bentham's basic calculus and comes across as a more refined and nobler system of thought.

However, was Mill right when he argued that higher pleasures are better than lower pleasures? Who is it that decides this? In addition, with the introduction of new variables it could be argued to be too complex a system to calculate and therefore due to its complexity be of no practical use.

Nonetheless, Rule Utilitarianism has the great strength of being directed in the main at society and has a basis of tried and tested experiences on which to act, and not, as in the case of Act Utilitarianism, advocating an unpredictable fresh calculation for each decision. This is useful to help people and guide them rather than to over complicate the theory and confuse people. In Mill's harm principle we appear to be working towards safeguarding against the possibly inconsistencies that Act Utilitarianism could potentially create.

In conclusion, I suppose it all depends upon what the theory is being used for. It would appear that Act Utilitarianism is more pertinent to the individual and allows for more freedom in application whereas Strong Rule Utilitarianism could be seen as possibly too inflexible for society as a whole and not accounting for that freedom. Maybe a happy compromise is to say that overall, a Weak Rule is the most superior approach to ethics because it does allow the individuality of Act Utilitarianism and the guidance of Rule Utilitarianism?

Specification content

The extent to which Rule Utilitarianism provides a better basis for making moral decisions than Act Utilitarianism.

AO2 Activity *Possible lines of argument*

Listed below are some conclusions that could be drawn from the AO2 reasoning in the accompanying text:

1. Rule Utilitarianism provides a better basis for making moral decisions than Act Utilitarianism as it is a more refined system.

2. Rule Utilitarianism provides a better basis for making moral decisions than Act Utilitarianism at is better to apply to society as a whole.

3. Both Rule Utilitarianism and Act Utilitarianism can be a basis for making moral decisions.

4. Weak Rule Utilitarianism provides a better basis for making moral decisions than both Strong Rule Utilitarianism and Act Utilitarianism.

5. A combination of the various aspects of all types of Utilitarianism is the best way for making moral decisions.

Consider each of the conclusions drawn above and collect evidence and examples to support each argument from the AO1 and AO2 material studied in this section. Select one conclusion that you think is most convincing and explain why it is so. Now contrast this with the weakest conclusion in the list, justifying your argument with clear reasoning and evidence.

Specification content

Whether Utilitarianism promotes immoral behaviour.

Whether Utilitarianism promotes immoral behaviour

There is a great deal of emphasis on principles of reason and individual judgements. This is where the main criticisms of Utilitarianism arise and opens it up to accusations of immoral behaviour.

Religious believers, on the whole, would argue that God's rule and teachings are universally applicable, objective and ensure overall justice. This is more reliable than a secular theory developed by humans and applied inconsistently. The latter will only lead inevitably to instances of immoral behaviour.

Another line of argument would be that, according to Utilitarianism, happiness is subjective and that two similar situations could be treated differently as people have different ideas of what happiness is. This could lead to injustice for those involved.

Despite this, however, Utilitarianism, especially that proposed by Mill, is based on a democratic and fair philosophy as it promotes the 'greatest happiness for the greatest number' and Mill's harm principle defends against misuse and immorality. Indeed, even with Bentham's proposals, if the hedonic calculus is used and considered as a whole, it ensures that everyone's happiness is considered when making an ethical decision. In this sense it promotes justice and not immoral behaviour. Indeed, in considering the consequences of each action, Utilitarianism makes people consider how their actions affect others and is another safeguard against immoral actions.

Another challenge to the statement would be that Act Utilitarianism takes the situation into account when making an ethical decision and therefore is more just than absolutist theories, which simply prevent people from performing certain actions. The danger with absolute systems is that they could, according to Arthur Miller, promote the 'the immorality of morality'.

In this way the use of the hedonic calculus ensures that everyone's happiness is considered when making an ethical decision, so it is just. In Weak Rule Utilitarianism, for example, the rules that have been formulated ensure that similar actions are treated in the same way, for example do not lie, but are also considered with the flexibility that legalism or Strong Rule Utilitarianism cannot offer.

Act Utilitarianism, however, can be accused of allowing a minority to suffer as long as the majority are happy. It could justify acts such as the torture or death of an innocent person as long as it fulfilled 'the greatest happiness for the greatest number'. Ultimately, it allows many people put their own happiness before the happiness of others so this will lead to injustice. It is in the very nature of Utilitarianism as a consequentialist theory the intended outcome is not guaranteed and so people may end up being treated unfairly.

In conclusion, it not the case that any particular system of ethical theory ever intends immoral behaviour or promotes it for that matter. Even religious systems can be accused of immorality in practice, for instance intolerance and discrimination but it would be wrong to say that this was intended or promoted. It is how they are applied that matters and it is this application, possibly unwisely, that appears to be the root of immorality and not the theory itself.

AO2 Activity Possible lines of argument

Listed below are some conclusions that could be drawn from the AO2 reasoning in the accompanying text:

1. Utilitarianism promotes immoral behaviour because it is focused on individual human reason.

2. Utilitarianism promotes immoral behaviour because there is no overall objective standard.

3. Utilitarianism does not and never intends to promote immoral behaviour.

4. Utilitarianism does not promote immoral behaviour but there are potential areas in which possible applications of it can lead to injustice and immorality.

5. If it is argued that Utilitarianism promotes immoral behaviour then the same can be said of every other ethical theory.

Consider each of the conclusions drawn above and collect evidence and examples to support each argument from the AO1 and AO2 material studied in this section. Select one conclusion that you think is most convincing and explain why it is so. Now contrast this with the weakest conclusion in the list, justifying your argument with clear reasoning and evidence.

AO2 Developing skills

It is now time to reflect upon the information that has been covered so far. It is also important to consider how what you have learned can be focused and used for examination-style answers by practising the skills associated with AO2.

Assessment objective 2 (AO2) involves 'analysis' and 'evaluation'. The terms may be obvious but it is crucial to be familiar with how certain skills demonstrate these terms, and also, how the performance of these skills are measured (see generic band descriptors Band 5 for AS AO2).

Obviously an answer is placed within an appropriate band descriptor depending upon how well the answer performs, ranging from excellent, good, satisfactory, basic/limited to very limited.

You are now nearing the end of this section of the course. From now on the task will have only instructions with no examples; however, using the skills you have developed in completing the earlier tasks, you should be able to apply what you have learned to do and complete this successfully.

▶ **Your new task is this:** you will have to write a response under timed conditions to a question requiring an evaluation of the effectiveness of Mill's Rule Utilitarianism. You will need to focus for this and apply the skills that you have developed so far:

> **1. Begin with a list of indicative content. Perhaps discuss this as a group. It does not need to be in any order. Remember, this is evaluation, so you need different lines of argument. The easiest way is to use the 'support' and 'against' headings.**

> **2. Develop the list using examples.**

> **3. Now consider in which order you would like to explain the information.**

> **4. Then write out your plan, under timed conditions, remembering to apply the principles of evaluation by making sure that you: identify issues clearly; present accurate views of others making sure that you comment on the views presented; reach an overall personal judgement.**

Use this technique as revision for each of the topic areas that you have studied. The basic technique of planning answers helps even when time is short and you cannot complete every essay.

Specification content

The application of Bentham's
Act Utilitarianism and Mill's Rule
Utilitarianism to both of the issues
listed below:
1. Animal experimentation for
   medical research.
2. The use of nuclear weapons as a
   deterrent.

Key terms

Dissection: the action of dissecting a
body or plant to study its internal parts

Vivisection: the practice of
performing operations on live animals
for the purpose of experimentation or
scientific research

Key person

Claudius Galen: was a Greek physician
who went to Rome and revived the ideas
of Hippocrates and other Greek doctors.
He put great emphasis on clinical
observation – examining a patient very
thoroughly and noting their symptoms.
He compiled much of the knowledge
obtained by previous writers, and
furthered the inquiry into the function
of organs by performing vivisection
on animals, for example extending his
knowledge of anatomy by dissecting
pigs and apes and studying their bone
structure and muscles.

Key person

William Harvey: was born in
Folkestone, Kent on 1 April 1578. His
father was a merchant. Harvey was
educated at King's College, Canterbury
and Cambridge University. He then
studied medicine at the University of
Padua in Italy, where the scientist and
surgeon Hieronymus Fabricius tutored
him. Harvey was an English physician
who was the first to describe accurately
how blood was pumped around the
body by the heart. By a long series of
dissections (from dogs and pigs down
to slugs and oysters), and by a process
of logical argument, Harvey was able
to prove that the body contains only a
single supply of blood; and that the heart
is a muscle pumping it round a circuit.

C: Utilitarianism: application of the theories (Act and Rule)

The application of Bentham's Act Utilitarianism and Mill's Rule Utilitarianism to animal experimentation for medical research

The history of medicine has a long association with the use of animals for medical research through **dissection** and **vivisection**, from the time of Ancient Greece and Rome, with the work of Claudius Galen in particular through to the 16th century and the pioneering work of William Harvey on blood circulation based upon analysis of a dissected pig.

Claudius Galen 130–210

William Harvey 1578–1657

Today animal dissection and vivisection are widespread and still legal for medical research. However, the attitude of people towards animals and the treatment of animals has become the subject of much debate in recent history.

One issue concerns the different views held on the relationship that human beings have to animals today and how this works in practice. Here is summary of some approaches and their legal status:

Term	Definition
Animal use (legal)	The view that supports the idea that humans are supreme species. Animals are to be used for food and pleasure (sports).
Animal protection (legal)	Establishes laws and regulations to control animal experiments and to ensure animals are treated with dignity.
Animal welfare (legal)	Supports the rights of animals to be free from abuse and to be looked after, e.g. RSPCA.
Animal reform (legal)	People who fight for a change in the laws of animal experiments, animal ownership, animal-based clothing and animals sports.
Animal liberation (illegal)	An anonymous group that has used acts of terrorism to free animals from abuse.
Animal control (illegal)	The view that supports the use of animals in extreme sports such as dog fighting or fox hunting, believing that animals are here for our use or pleasure (even if it means they suffer).

The use of animals for medical research is a very specific area of animal research and is hotly debated. The problem with applying any ethical theory to any issue is that we need first to be aware of some facts about the issue. With some issues facts can be straightforward but with other issues the information may be disputed. Unfortunately, with animal experimentation for medical research there are disputed facts.

The area of dispute is focused directly on whether or not animal experimentation is useful for medical research.

Pressure groups such as **Animal Aid** contest its usefulness. Founded in 1977 'the society campaigns against all animal abuse but particularly the use of animals in experiments and the cruel treatment of farm animals'. Animal Aid campaigns by all peaceful and non-violent means and so is legal. It is interesting to note that one of their foundational policies is that they reject current human attitudes towards animals that states that humans are higher intellectual beings, based upon a quotation by Jeremy Bentham: 'The question is not, can they reason? Nor, can they talk? But can they suffer?'

Animal Aid rejects all forms of psychology experiments such as electric shocks, starvation, deprivation, and tormenting techniques that are used just to observe the reactions of animals, and they quote David Helton, Editor of BBC Wildlife in 1984 to demonstrate their stance: 'it takes two to make an experiment – the monkey and the man – and the best way of judging behaviour is not by looking at the monkey'.

The link between diabetes and a damaged pancreas was made in the 18th century by studying human autopsies. However, because scientists for a long time were

quickfire

4.11 Why are Galen and Harvey significant for the use of animals in medical research?

Key term

Animal Aid: a charity that promotes animal welfare and argues against the use of animals for medical research

quickfire

4.12 What is animal welfare?

quickfire

4.13 What is animal protection?

Key quote

To discriminate against beings solely on account of their species is a form of prejudice. (Singer)

Key quote

That which is morally wrong cannot be scientifically right. To seek one's own advantage regardless of the cost to other sentient beings is to renounce humanity. **(Kingford)**

Key quote

During my medical education at Basle I found vivisection horrible, barbarous and above all unnecessary. **(Jung)**

quickfire

4.14 Why is Gill Langley concerned about the uncertainties in the use of animal experimentation in medical research?

Key quote

The value of animal models is constrained by evolution-determined species differences and by inevitable dissimilarities between the conditions created in animals and the human disorders being researched. **(Langley)**

Key term

Understanding Animal Research: a Mutual Society (not-for-profit organisation) that explains why animals are used in medical and scientific research

quickfire

4.15 What is UAR?

unable to cause diabetes in laboratory animals by damaging the pancreas the theory lost favour for many years.

Animal Aid has much to say about the historical results of medical research using animal experimentation. They argue:

1. Much medical research, including into diseases like cancer, is repetitive and pointless.
2. We have enough drugs (only 200 are necessary to human health and yet there are thousands available through marketing and retail competition).
3. Animal experiments are unreliable, for example penicillin is useful for humans but kills guinea pigs and hamsters and chloroform kills dogs and anaesthetises humans.
4. It has been known for drugs passed on in animals to have caused human deaths.
5. Many cancers are preventable and so we should focus on eliminating causes and not searching for cures.

Dr Gill Langley has long been associated as campaigning against the use of animal experimentation in medical research and argues that medical history shows time and again that an understanding of health and disease has been set back due to animal research and experimentation. In addition, she points out that many vital discoveries have been made without animal experiments.

For Langley there are two major uncertainties with animal research and experimentation:

1. There are significant species differences in anatomy, metabolism, physiology or pharmacology caused by underlying genetic variations and these variations between species can, and do, regularly confound the translation of laboratory animal results to humans.

For example, mice are the most commonly used species in medical research. Langley observes, 'There are at least 67 known discrepancies in immunological functions between mice and humans – hardly surprising, since our species diverged between 65 and 75 million years ago.'

2. Human illnesses are researched in animals because there is a lack of knowledge and the causes and progression of a human condition are unknown. However, an animal model is usually developed on the basis of a narrow range of human symptoms, and based upon an ignorance of the distinction between causes and outcomes of illness.

Langley compares Parkinson's disease and the contrasting symptoms in humans and marmosets and argues, 'The marmoset model is simplistic compared to the human condition, involving a more limited number and type of brain cells ... marmosets do not develop the pathological hallmark of Parkinson's disease, the clumps of abnormal protein called Lewy bodies that develop in cells of the brain.'

Langley argues that the poor performance of animal models in medical research should prompt a serious appraisal of the potential of alternative, non-animal models which include human cell and tissue studies (in the 'test tube'), molecular approaches, clinical research, population studies and computer simulations.

The obvious strengths of these research approaches is that they are more relevant to humans and often allow a better understanding of underlying disease mechanisms. She argues that a dependence on 'surrogates' to formulate and test medical hypotheses is 'seriously flawed'.

Despite the strong argument, there is a counter-argument typified by the response of such groups as Understanding Animal Research (UAR). UAR states that it 'supports the humane use of animals in biomedical research, and believes that animal research is a vital part of the scientific process'.

Like Animal Aid and Langley, UAR present some persuasive arguments based on facts:

1. Animal research has played a vital part in nearly every medical breakthrough over the last decade.

2. We share 95% of our genes with a mouse, and animals suffer from similar diseases to humans including cancers, TB, flu and asthma.

3. All veterinary research has relied on the use of animal research.

4. Non-animal methods cannot replace all use of animals.

5. As a result of medical experimentation on animals there have been many breakthroughs, in discovering, developing or perfecting the following: modern anaesthetics; tetanus vaccine; penicillin; insulin; hip replacement surgery; kidney transplants; heart transplants; blood transfusions; herceptin (a humanised mouse protein) increasing the survival rate of those with breast cancer; the development of Highly Active Anti-Retroviral Therapies (HAART), to ensure that AIDS is no longer terminal; asthma inhalers; modern vaccines including those against Polio, TB, meningitis and papillomavirus; and, smallpox has been eradicated from earth thanks to research in animals.

They also argue that:

1. Dogs, cats and primates altogether account for less than 0.2% of research animals and 97% of research in the UK is done on mice, rats, fish and birds.

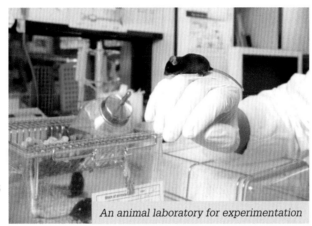

An animal laboratory for experimentation

2. The UK has some of the highest standards of laboratory animal welfare in the world.

3. All research in the UK must be approved by the Home Office, furthermore, the researchers and the institutions doing the research must be licensed by the Home Office.

4. Ethics committees exist to ensure that the potential benefits of research outweigh any suffering to the animals. Animal welfare is underpinned by the 3Rs – there is a legal requirement to replace animals with alternatives, refine experimental techniques and reduce the numbers of animals used in research.

Indeed, Albert Sabin, who developed the Polio vaccine has stated, 'Without animal research, polio would still be claiming thousands of lives each year' and the former CEO of the Medical Research Council, Prof Colin Blakemore, argued that '[primates] are used only when no other species and no alternative approach can provide the answers to questions about such conditions as Alzheimer's, stroke, Parkinson's, spinal injury, hormone disorders, and vaccines for HIV.'

AO1 Activity

Create a small leaflet that outlines the two sides of the debate for the use of animal experimentation in medical research.

Study tip

Make sure that you have a good grasp of key arguments for and against the use of animal experimentation in medical research.

Key quote

For over 150 years research using animals has advanced scientific understanding of human and animal health and the impact of the environment on wildlife. This research should never be undertaken lightly and animals should only be used when there is no alternative method available. **(Understanding Animal Research)**

Key quote

Experiments on animals have contributed greatly to scientific advances. **(House of Lords Select Committee)**

Key quote

Producing a new medicine is a lengthy and complex process … Tests on animals play a vital role. **(The Nuffield Council on Bioethics)**

Key quote

What else is it that should trace the insuperable line? Is it the faculty of reason or perhaps the faculty of discourse? But a full-grown horse or dog, is beyond comparison a more rational, as well as a more conversable animal, than an infant of a day or a week or even a month, old. But suppose the case were otherwise, what would it avail? The question is not, can they reason? nor, can they talk? but, can they suffer? Why should the law refuse its protection to any sensitive being? The time will come when humanity will extend its mantle over everything which breathes …
(Bentham)

Key quote

Even if some individual experiments may be justified, this does not mean that the institutional practice of experimenting on animals is justified. Given the suffering that this routinely inflicts on millions of animals, and that probably very few of the experiments will be of significant benefit to humans or to other animals, it is better to put our resources into other methods of doing research that do not involve harming animals. (Singer)

The focus now needs to be on what the different forms of Utilitarianism would conclude.

In applying Utilitarianism it may be best to look at different aspects of the theory, but also bear in mind that due to the complexity of the issues and the complex nature of the theory itself, there are different ways of applying it. As Bass writes, 'however good the utilitarian case against animal research in general, it will be possible in principle to find cases in which it seems justified'.

Regarding the use of the utilitarian principle that aims for the 'greatest happiness for the greatest number'. On the one hand, it clearly projects the happiness of many human lives than animals if we consider lives already saved and potential human disaster by not controlling epidemics. On the other hand, in the use of animal experimentation for medical research, it would appear that if facts are correct and there are many uncertainties and discrepancies then the greatest happiness for humans is not guaranteed in relation to suffering of animals.

Concerning the principle of utility that 'promotes pleasure and avoids pain', there is pleasure in that it benefits humans that may potentially suffer, but it brings suffering for animals – which outweighs the other? Is it a matter of the numbers involved? For Bentham it may be that the quantity matters most, for Mill it is about the quality of pleasure, which means, reluctantly, a utilitarian would have to support some forms of animal experimentation for medical research.

Bentham himself is considered a pioneer of animal rights. Bentham did not argue that humans and nonhumans had equal moral significance, but argued that the latter's interests should be taken into account. Bentham changed the views of many people towards animals; rather than regarding them as inferior to human beings because of their inability to reason, Bentham applied ethical Utilitarianism to animals as his famous quotation affirms, 'The question is not, can they reason? Nor, can they talk? But can they suffer?' Bentham's 'insuperable line' as he called it, was that it was the ability to suffer rather than the ability to reason that provided the framework and standard of how we treat other animals. Bentham may well have disagreed with animal experimentation for medical research; as Julia Driver notes, 'What struck many as lacking in Bentham's value theory was a special place for the rational capacities that mark a difference between persons and animals'.

Bentham's hedonic calculus suggests that the whole of the calculus should be used in dealing with both human beings and animals. The only satisfactory way of dealing with this is to consider the principle of 'extent' and look long term to when the suffering of animals in the present leads to less suffering for both animals and humans in the future overall.

Mill, however, is quite clear that animal pleasures and pains do not equate to their human counterparts in terms of value. Animals do not appreciate the higher pleasures and cannot, therefore operate as utilitarian beings. This does not mean they do not need protecting and treating well. As Julia Driver comments, 'This distinction between higher and lower pleasures allows Mill to hold that while animals do have moral standing in virtue of their sentience – that is, in virtue of their capacity to feel pleasure and pain, and thus to have both positive and negative experiences – their moral standing is not the same as that of persons who have higher moral standing in virtue of their capacity to experience higher pleasures.'

Mill's harm principle is aimed chiefly at society and humans so that society benefits; however, it would insist on the stringent application of rules to minimise suffering rather than be against it totally.

In response to animal experimentation for medical research, Strong Rule Utilitarianism would most probably advocate a reasonable argument in support based mainly upon the principles outlined in Mill's views above.

Weak Rule Utilitarianism, however, may be more flexible, as Mill also argued that 'reasons for legal intervention in favour of children, apply not less strongly to … the lower animals', and that intervention should be based on 'the intrinsic merits of the case', rather than upon 'incidental consequences … to the interests of human beings'. Therefore, a weak rule utilitarian would not consider the variants but work with the underlying principles as advocated by the distinction between higher and lower pleasures. Elsewhere, Mill is clear that animal pleasures and pains do not equate to their human counterparts in terms of value. Therefore, there would be no absolute response to the issue, which is problematic, not for the utilitarian, but for making a policy regarding animal experimentation for medical research.

The application of Bentham's Act Utilitarianism and Mill's Rule Utilitarianism to the use of nuclear weapons as a deterrent

It is with great sadness that our history recalls the end of World War II when the **atomic bomb** was used by the USA against Japan and devastated the cities of Hiroshima and Nagasaki. Their use has long been debated and both justified and rebuked using utilitarian principles. The problem with nuclear weapons is that there can never really be any justification for their use per se. If used in a war today, many see an eventual end to the world's population due to the devastating impact such a war would have on the rest of the planet. No ethical theory would sit comfortably with this outcome. As a consequentialist theory, Utilitarianism could see only pain and suffering and not even a long-term happiness. In short, there is no pleasure in war. This debate, however, does not concern the actual use of nuclear weapons but their use as a **deterrent**.

However, many argue that the purpose of nuclear weapons is to serve as a deterrent, ironically with the intention that the scenario above will not happen. Others see them as a waste of resources when people are starving and see the potential use of finances spent wisely elsewhere.

CND (The Campaign for Nuclear Disarmament) has long put forward the arguments for nuclear disarmament. In short, they propose:

1. Each nuclear missile today is 8 times the power of the nuclear bomb that was dropped on Hiroshima in 1945, killing an estimated 240,000 people from blast and radiation.

2. Nuclear weapons have no legitimate purpose and their use would be illegal under virtually every conceivable circumstance as civilian casualties would be unavoidable.

3. They are genocidal and completely immoral.

4. When confronted with any of today's real security threats nuclear weapons are irrelevant: they cannot address the actual threats of terrorism, cyber warfare and climate change.

5. If Trident was used, not only would it kill indiscriminately but the radioactive fallout from the detonation means that its effects would know no geographical boundaries.

6. Immediate survivors in the vicinity of any exchange of nuclear weapons would face devastating long-term ill effects or death.

7. Recent research shows that even a so-called 'small exchange' of 50 nuclear weapons could cause 'the largest climate change in recorded human history' and potentially could kill more people than were killed in the whole of the Second World War.

quickfire

4.16 Why does Bentham think animals should be protected?

Specification content
The application of Bentham's Act Utilitarianism and Mill's Rule Utilitarianism to the use of nuclear weapons as a deterrent.

Key quote
So, let us be alert in a twofold sense: Since Auschwitz we know what man is capable of. And since Hiroshima we know what is at stake. **(Frankl)**

Key quote
Japan knows the horror of war and has suffered as no other nation under the cloud of nuclear disaster. Certainly Japan can stand strong for a world of peace. **(Martin Luther King)**

Key terms
Atomic bomb: a bomb which derives its destructive power from the rapid release of nuclear energy

CND: a pressure group calling themselves 'The Campaign for Nuclear Disarmament'

Deterrent: a thing that discourages or is intended to discourage someone from doing something

The case for the use of nuclear weapons as a deterrent, as outlined by our government, indicates the following:

1. Our retention of an independent centre of nuclear decision making makes clear to any adversary that the costs of an attack on UK vital interests will outweigh any benefits.

2. Decision making and use of the system remains entirely sovereign to the UK; only the Prime Minister can authorise the launch of nuclear weapons, which ensures that political control is maintained at all times.

3. The instruction to fire would be transmitted to the submarine using only UK codes and UK equipment; all the command and control procedures are fully independent.

4. We are committed to maintaining the minimum amount of destructive power needed to deter any aggressor.

5. Our preference is for an invulnerable and undetectable system, which allows us to maintain it at a minimum level of scale and readiness, but we believe that it should also be capable of being held at high readiness for extended periods of time.

6. Invulnerability and security of capability are key components of the credibility of our deterrent and contribute to overall stability.

Michael Fallon, in March 2016, set out the full rationale for nuclear weapons as a deterrent in a speech given to **The Ministry of Defence**:

(www.gov.uk/government/speeches/the-case-for-the-retention-of-the-uks-independent-nuclear-deterrent).

He outlines much of his argument based upon the use of a deterrent as a protection for society and argues, 'Deterrence means convincing any potential aggressor that the benefits of an attack are far outweighed by its consequences'. This consequentialist approach is in line with utilitarian principles in that it could be argued to support the harm principle; however, the dilemma for us is that the arguments proposed by CND also do the same!

Ministry of Defence HQ

Key quote

To abandon our deterrent now would be an act of supreme irresponsibility. (Fallon)

Key term

Ministry of Defence: the British government department responsible for implementing the defence policy for the UK

Key quote

So let me say in conclusion … before nuclear weapons, major powers embarked on two of the most destructive wars imaginable. Many millions died, millions more suffered. Yet, for all the conventional conflicts since, and there have been many of them, there hasn't been major conflict between nuclear armed states. The devastating possibilities of nuclear war have helped maintain strategic stability. (Fallon)

quickfire

4.17 What does CND do?

In applying Utilitarianism it may be best to look at different aspects of the theory, but also bear in mind that due to the complexity of the issues and the complex nature of the theory itself, there are different ways of applying it.

As with most moral issues, the outcomes are difficult to predict with any certainty. This is definitely true of nuclear war. The greatest happiness for the greatest number is the criterion used by utilitarians in general; however, the calculation of happiness seems an impossible task where a possible nuclear war is involved.

One of the key considerations would be 'does the end justify the means?' The idea of a just war may be applicable as it is concerned with just causes but the likelihood of success is questionable. Bentham's basic ideas of the calculus and Mill's developments could be applied to two main areas: the extent of suffering and the future prospect of peace and prosperity.

It would appear that the act utilitarian would not be constrained by Mill's refinement of higher and lower pleasures and his harm principle and so would be free to advocate an argument either for or against using nuclear weapons as a deterrent. Mill's refinement and harm principle could possibly outweigh any arguments for anti-deterrent as the protection of society is crucial and a deterrent not only protects but at the same time any worries of attack subside. The rule utilitarian would be bound more by this.

Regarding the use of the happiness principle that aims to assess which course of action is the best one to take based upon happiness, and the principle of utility that 'promotes pleasure and avoids pain', it would all depend upon how one classifies happiness, pleasure and pain. Both sides of the debate propose very positive scenarios. On the one hand, the use of money could be better spent and yet, on the other hand, the safety and protection is an invaluable investment and insurance for others. Alternatively, there could be great pain and suffering if we are not protected and yet the same could be said if no deterrent were present and it would trigger attacks. Admittedly, unless the attack were of a nuclear nature then the consequences could be seen to be less serious if nuclear arms were abandoned.

AO1 Activity

Write down a dialogue between a utilitarian who uses the hedonic calculus and a rule utilitarian over the issue of the use of nuclear weapons as a deterrent.

Study tip

Do not spend too much time on the background materials in exam answers, remain focused on the question.

quickfire

4.18 How does the consequentialist approach of the Ministry of Defence fit in with utilitarian principles?

Key quote

The end may justify the means as long as there is something that justifies the end. (Trotsky)

Key quote

Is it possible for a man to move the earth? Yes; but he must first find out another earth to stand upon. (Bentham)

Key skills

Knowledge involves:

Selection of a range of (thorough) accurate and relevant information that is directly related to the specific demands of the question.

This means you choose the correct information relevant to the question set NOT the topic area. You will have to think and focus on selecting key information and NOT writing everything you know about the topic area.

Understanding involves:

Explanation that is extensive, demonstrating depth and/or breadth with excellent use of evidence and examples including (where appropriate) thorough and accurate supporting use of sacred texts, sources of wisdom and specialist language.

This means that you demonstrate that you understand something by being able to illustrate and expand your points through examples/supporting evidence in a personal way and NOT repeat chunks from a text book (known as rote learning).

Further application of skills:

Go through the topic areas in this section and create some bullet lists of key points from key areas. For each one, provide further elaboration and explanation through the use of evidence and examples.

AO1 Developing skills

It is now time to reflect upon the information that has been covered so far. It is also important to consider how what you have learned can be focused and used for examination-style answers by practising the skills associated with AO1.

Assessment objective 1 (AO1) involves demonstrating knowledge and understanding. The terms 'knowledge' and 'understanding' are obvious but it is crucial to be familiar with how certain skills demonstrate these terms, and also, how the performance of these skills is measured (see generic band descriptors Band 5 for AS AO1).

You are now nearing the end of this section of the course. From now on the task will have only instructions with no examples; however, using the skills you have developed in completing the earlier tasks, you should be able to apply what you have learned to do and complete this successfully.

▶ **Your new task is this:** you will have to write another response under timed conditions to a question requiring an examination of the application of utilitarian theory to the ethical issue of animal rights. You will need to do the same as your last AO1 Developing Skills task but with some further development. This time there is a fifth point to help you improve the quality of your answers.

1. **Begin with a list of indicative content. Perhaps discuss this as a group. It does not need to be in any order.**

2. **Develop the list using examples.**

3. **Now consider in which order you would like to explain the information.**

4. **Then write out your plan, under timed conditions, remembering the principles of explaining with evidence and/or examples.**

5. **Use the band descriptors to mark your own answer, considering carefully the descriptors. Then ask someone else to read your answer and see if they can help you improve it in any way.**

Use this technique as revision for each of the topic areas that you have studied. Swap and compare answers to improve your own.

Issues for analysis and evaluation

The extent to which Utilitarianism promotes justice

This section covers AO2 content and skills

Specification content

The extent to which Utilitarianism promotes justice.

We have seen that as a political economist, civil servant and Member of Parliament, Mill was very interested in social reform and looking at how society worked and what was best for people in general. Mill wanted to show that what is right or wrong for one person in a situation is right or wrong for all and this has major implications for society and social justice.

Mill argued that people should put the interests of the group before their own interests. He pointed out that as society is made up of individuals, for society to be happy, individuals collectively need to be happy also. It is therefore the 'duty' or 'rule' for society that it should protect the happiness of its subjects and maintain justice throughout.

Mill also introduced his 'harm principle' based upon the principle of protection. In his book '*On Liberty*' Mill wrote, 'That principle is ... that the only purpose for which power can be rightfully exercised over any member of a civilised community, against his will, is to prevent harm to others.' He further stated, 'The only part of the conduct of anyone, for which he is amenable to society, is that which concerns others.' This clearly gives Utilitarianism its focus of justice for society as a whole and not just the individual. This then has been clearly established.

However, there is a potential problem with utilitarian theory as regards justice when we consider whether it is more important to work towards reducing pain and suffering or to increase pleasure and happiness? This is a key issue for Utilitarianism. Clearly the focus is to promote happiness by avoiding pain, but sometimes it may be necessary to focus on the pains and sufferings in order for this to be achieved.

Firstly, there is the priority to decide upon. Is it more important to end someone's pain or to satisfy someone's pleasure? In addition, in some moral dilemmas there are no alternatives but those that bring pain and suffering. For example, the lesser of evils situations have no 'happiness' or 'pleasures', say for instance, in the case of war or a just war. In addition, there are also the usual problems associated with ethical systems that only measure morality according to the consequence of an action, such as 'who makes the decision?' and based upon 'what perspective?' since one person's idea of pleasure and pain, and therefore justice and injustice, may differ from another.

A key argument that sets out this challenge is if one is already content, why increase contentment at the expense of suffering? This is morally wrong. For example, just because many people are well fed does not mean we should continue to leave the beggar to starve. This is certainly unjust. Nonetheless, it is here that Mill's harm principle can be applied effectively and it is this that is the key safeguard against just focusing solely on happiness. Mill's principle identified the fact that sometimes injustice needed rectifying and that this was also the task of utilitarian theory to bring about justice in the long term.

In conclusion, it appears to be the case that even though Utilitarianism focuses on pleasure that produces and maximises happiness, it is with Mill's work that we see an awareness of social injustice and a 'duty' for the utilitarian thinker to address this. If it were left up to the utilitarian theory of Bentham alone, however, the answer may be different.

AO2 Activity *Possible lines of argument*

Listed below are some conclusions that could be drawn from the AO2 reasoning in the accompanying text:

1. Utilitarianism promotes justice because it is happiness for the greatest number.

2. Utilitarianism does not promote justice because it is too concerned with the happiness of the individual.

3. Utilitarianism promotes justice because the work of Mill demonstrates it is focused on eradicating social injustice.

4. Utilitarianism does not promote justice because it has completely the wrong focus on ensuring happiness and does not really consider the pains of the few.

5. Utilitarianism promotes justice only if applied from the perspective of Mill rather than that of Bentham.

Consider each of the conclusions drawn above and collect evidence and examples to support each argument from the AO1 and AO2 material studied in this section. Select one conclusion that you think is most convincing and explain why it is so. Now contrast this with the weakest conclusion in the list, justifying your argument with clear reasoning and evidence.

Specification content

The extent to which Utilitarianism provides a practical basis for making moral decisions for both religious believers and non-believers.

AO2 Activity *Possible lines of argument*

Listed below are some conclusions that could be drawn from the AO2 reasoning in the accompanying text:

1. Utilitarianism provides a practical basis for making moral decisions for religious believers because it has a clear concern for the happiness of others.

2. Utilitarianism provides a practical basis for making moral decisions for religious believers as Mill himself saw the similarity in concern for one's neighbour.

3. Utilitarianism provides a practical basis for making moral decisions for religious believers because its goal is pursuit of happiness.

4. Utilitarianism does not provide a practical basis for making moral decisions for religious believers because it is secular in nature and does not recognise the sovereignty of God.

5. Utilitarianism does not provide a practical basis for making moral decisions for Christians because happiness for the greatest number excludes minorities and the parable of the lost sheep encourages the care for every individual.

Consider each of the conclusions drawn above and collect evidence and examples to support each argument from the AO1 and AO2 material studied in this section. Select one conclusion that you think is most convincing and explain why it is so. Now contrast this with the weakest conclusion in the list, justifying your argument with clear reasoning and evidence.

The extent to which Utilitarianism provides a practical basis for making moral decisions for religious believers

Much of the AO2 so far has dealt with society (i.e. secular notion that incorporates non-believers) so it makes sense to focus on religious believers in this evaluation although bear in mind the Specification does identify the term 'non-believers' for which other appropriate evaluations, much of which you have read so far, can be used.

Some Christians could argue that Jesus' death on the cross and his subsequent resurrection is a clear example of the principle of utility. This is because Christians believe that Jesus died to give others happiness through eternal life. The act of self-sacrifice enabled the greatest number to achieve the greatest happiness. This is the foundational belief of Christianity.

In the same way as a utilitarian would claim that the ultimate goal is happiness, Christians would agree in that 'to love thy neighbour' is a basic principle and will bring universal happiness to all if practised. Mill himself believed that his utilitarian ethic had caught the very spirit of the Christian Golden Rule (to treat others as we would want them to treat us) which is also prevalent in other religions. Many claim that religion is based upon making people happy, such as eradicating suffering in Buddhism or serving the poor in Sikhism and Islam.

In addition, Utilitarianism and religious believers may agree on certain issues, for example, if one partner in a married couple commits adultery, then for the other partner's sake and for their children it may be better (less painful) for all concerned if they divorce. Religious believers also keep rules such as 'do not steal' and Strong Rule Utilitarianism would also keep this rule because it would fulfil the principle of utility.

Nonetheless, for some religious believers God's rules and teachings ensure justice, not a secular theory developed by man. They are divinely revealed, consistent and universal and not subject to change; in essence, it is not up to individuals to decide what happiness should be.

It is an integral feature of many teachings in religions, and certainly in Christianity, that through experiencing pain and suffering, which utilitarians avoid, people gain spiritually and become better human beings. People can then identify with the pain and suffering of others and focus on this instead of their own happiness. Following on from this, religions see spiritual goals as far superior to Mill's lower and higher pleasures.

Many religious people believe in moral absolutes such as 'do not kill' and other rules given by God, whereas Act Utilitarianism does not and looks at the consequences of each act to determine whether the act is good or bad. In addition, religious believers would state that rules such as 'do not steal' should only be followed as they are given by God and not because they promote the principle of utility.

Utilitarianism is against the idea of divinely ordained moral codes and the idea of 'means to an end', when it involves people, can challenge beliefs about the sanctity of human life. In the same way, the 'means to an end' principle can be seen to be lacking in compassion; for example, what about the religious teachings that concern support of the weak?

The most striking difference between Utilitarianism can be seen in Jesus' parable of the lost sheep, which delivers a contrasting message, the total opposite of utilitarian thought, namely, that the individual counts just as much as the community.

Overall, there are obvious areas where Utilitarianism shares beliefs and applications that are similar to religious teachings and practices but there are also clear areas where they are very different.

AO2 Developing skills

It is now time to reflect upon the information that has been covered so far. It is also important to consider how what you have learned can be focused and used for examination-style answers by practising the skills associated with AO2.

Assessment objective 2 (AO2) involves 'analysis' and 'evaluation'. The terms may be obvious but it is crucial to be familiar with how certain skills demonstrate these terms, and also, how the performance of these skills is measured (see generic band descriptors Band 5 for AS AO2).

Obviously an answer is placed within an appropriate band descriptor depending upon how well the answer performs, ranging from excellent, good, satisfactory, basic/limited to very limited.

You are now nearing the end of this section of the course. From now on the task will have only instructions with no examples; however, using the skills you have developed in completing the earlier tasks, you should be able to apply what you have learned to do and complete this successfully.

▶ **Your new task is this:** you will have to write another response under timed conditions to a question requiring an evaluation of the usefulness of Utilitarianism in considering nuclear weapons as a deterrent. You will need to do the same as your last AO2 Developing skills task but with some further development. This time there is a fifth point to help you improve the quality of your answers.

> 1. **Begin with a list of indicative content. Perhaps discuss this as a group. It does not need to be in any order. Remember, this is evaluation, so you need different lines of argument. The easiest way is to use the 'support' and 'against' headings.**

> 2. **Develop the list using examples.**

> 3. **Now consider in which order you would like to explain the information.**

> 4. **Then write out your plan, under timed conditions, remembering to apply the principles of evaluation by making sure that you: identify issues clearly; present accurate views of others making sure that you comment on the views presented; reach an overall personal judgement.**

> 5. **Use the band descriptors to mark your own answer, considering carefully the descriptors. Then ask someone else to read your answer and see if they can help you improve it in any way.**

Use this technique as revision for each of the topic areas that you have studied. Swap and compare answers to improve your own.

Key skills

Analysis involves identifying issues raised by the materials in the AO1, together with those identified in the AO2 section, and presents sustained and clear views, either of scholars or from a personal perspective ready for evaluation.

This means that it picks out key things to debate and the lines of argument presented by others or a personal point of view.

Evaluation involves considering the various implications of the issues raised based upon the evidence gleaned from analysis and provides an extensive detailed argument with a clear conclusion.

This means that the answer weighs up the various and different lines of argument analysed through individual commentary and response and arrives at a conclusion through a clear process of reasoning.

Questions and answers

Philosophy Theme 1

AO1 question area: *An explanation of the teleological argument*

A strong answer

The teleological argument originally started by Plato and Aristotle, is used to question design in the universe, based on observation. **1**

Aquinas argued design qua regularity and believed 'natural bodies' could not act in a regular fashion to accomplish their end without an intelligent force behind them. He developed the famous analogy of the arrow and the archer; the arrow being an item of no intelligence it needs the force of the intelligent archer, to move it towards the target (its end). This was the fifth of his five ways '*From The Governance of Things*', and when he used his analogy to refer back to the universe he said that God was the intelligent being behind the 'natural bodies' and the universe. **2**

Following Aquinas, Paley wrote '*Natural Theology*' where he argued both sides of the argument. His first point was made by his famous analogy of the watch; if you were to stumble across a stone on a heath you would disregard it as normal, but if you were to find a watch you would question where it came from and how it was made. Paley looked at the complexity and specific purpose of the watch and said it must have been designed that way by an intelligent watch maker. He then looked at the universe and concluded that it too must have an intelligent designer due to its complexity; 'This being we call God'. **3**

The second part of Paley's argument was design qua purpose and to demonstrate this he used the human eye and its complex function, Newton's law of motion and even the simplest things like why birds have wings. He used these examples to state that surely, design is more probable than chance. **4**

In later years, as a more recent development, F.R. Tennant developed the 'anthropic principle', showing that this world is specific to our needs, that even if one molecule was different, things would be chaotic but they aren't. He developed three natural types of evidence; firstly, that the world can be analysed in a rational manner. Secondly, that the inorganic world contains the basic necessities to sustain life. Finally, the theory of natural selection, that we can progress and develop. **5**

F.R. Tennant, then also developed the 'aesthetic argument' that God wanted us to enjoy our lives by the simple fact that humans possess the ability to enjoy music, art and literature. **6**

Commentary

1 A simple introduction, the answer highlights the origins of the argument but does no more than reference Plato and Aristotle.

2 This section deals very well with Aquinas's Fifth Way and very confidently and clearly explains how Aquinas saw God as the designer of the universe. The analogy of the archer and arrow is fully linked to Aquinas' argument.

3 A concise explanation of Paley and referring to both of his 'qua' arguments (regularity and purpose). Linking Paley's watchmaker to the universe's designer is an important part of this argument and one that many candidates fail to do. It is pleasing to see it done correctly here.

4 Explaining the 'qua purpose' argument in detail demonstrates the answer's clear understanding of Paley's contribution to the design argument. Reference to Newton is also apt.

5 The answer then progresses to discuss Tennant's contribution to the anthropic principle. This is accurately done and demonstrates that key facts have been presented with accuracy and relevance.

6 Again, the answer skims over Tennant's aesthetic principle. Concepts of benevolent designer are missed here.

Summative comment

The student clearly understands the subject and has written an essay demonstrating this. Some parts are explained well but this is not always balanced. Better explanation of Tennant's aesthetic principle would have allowed the answer to access additional marks and raise the overall standard of the answer.

AO2 question area: *Teleological argument*

A weak answer to an assessment of 'Scientific evidence strongly supports the teleological argument.'

Most philosophers would disagree with this because a lot of scientists believe in the big bang as well as the theory of evolution. Richard Dawkins is a philosopher who would disagree with this statement as he followed Charles Darwin who came up with natural selection. Dawkins thinks its non-scientific to believe in a designing God. [1]

David Hume argued against the teleological argument as he believed humans have no experience of the universe being designed so we cannot believe the teleological argument. Some weaknesses are the leaky bucket theory no matter how many buckets you have if they all have a hole in it won't carry water. [2]

There are also strong points to the argument like it's a logical explanation, its part of the cumulative case and it's a posteriori. In conclusion there are many strengths and also many weaknesses but they both are supported by views and have reasons/ evidence to back it up. [3]

Commentary

1 A limited attempt to demonstrate how scientists have disagreed with the design argument is presented here. Names and ideas are, however, accurate although these ideas are not developed.

2 Hume's argument and the leaky buckets argument are presented, again in a limited way. These ideas really need to be developed for the answer to gain a higher mark for AO2.

3 The final paragraph attempts to deal with the counter-arguments but unfortunately the points listed do not really address the question relating to scientific evidence. There is no clear conclusion presented in this part of the essay. For AO2 it is essential that a conclusion is always offered.

Summative comment

The student has made a limited attempt at responding to the argument but, with no conclusion and minimal evidence to support his views.

Philosophy Theme 2

AO1 question area: *An explanation of Descartes' ontological argument*

A weak answer

Descartes lived in 17th-century France and was famous for his phrase 'I think therefore I am' [1] . He argued for God's existence using an argument that resembled that by Anselm. God was the greatest thing conceivable. [2] Existence was part of perfection, so God being perfect must exist. [3] He likened this argument to a triangle and three angles. [4] The argument is deductive and is therefore proof that God exists. [5] Kant criticised the argument on the grounds that existence is not a real predicate and got rid of the triangle altogether which I think is a very good point and that Descartes has been shown as wrong. [6]

Commentary

1 Material about Descartes needs to relate to the focus of the question. Biographical detail about philosophers is usually irrelevant and wastes time. For every minute spent on writing an irrelevancy, there is a minute wasted instead of writing something relevant.

2 The wrong definition. Students often get confused between the Anselm's and Descartes' arguments. The correct definition needs explaining.

3 The argument needs setting out as a formal argument with premise and conclusion. It also needs to be explained.

4 The illustration needs explaining and linking back to Descartes' ontological argument.

5 It is only proof if it is a sound and valid argument. The type of argument does not demonstrate its truth value.

6 This is a challenge and also evaluative and the question only asked to explain the argument (AO1). For this question, no marks would be awarded for any critical evaluation (AO2).

Summative comment

The answer is very limited. Not only is it brief but it has inaccuracies and does not always focus on the correct assessment objective.

AO2 question area: *Ontological argument*

A strong answer to the assessment of the claim that the ontological argument is not a valid proof for the existence of God.

In response to the question of whether or not the ontological argument is a valid proof for the existence of God then we need to look at the strengths and weaknesses. [1]

First of all, it has been established that the argument is one of logical, deductive reasoning. Once the premise is accepted it is difficult to argue against. In addition, it has stood the test of time – some philosophers still accept a developed aspect of it such as Norman Malcolm. Finally, philosophically, it has made an argument for the existence of God credible according to Plantinga, and therefore for many this means that it is serious enough to consider as a proof for God's existence. [2]

However, Kant has demonstrated that the whole argument can be rejected. It is clear that there is a difference between proving something is the case theoretically and proving it is the case in reality. Kant accepted Descartes illustration of the triangle in theory but in reality he responded that this does not mean it exists and rejected it. **3**

Another problem is that it deals with concepts and then makes a sudden shift to 'reality' like a magician suddenly pulling a rabbit from a hat; it is clearly apparent that the rabbit came from the hat but you know that something is wrong and involves some kind of trickery. **4**

In considering the idea of valid proof we have to be clear about what we mean by proof. The argument is deductive and so should be necessarily true and beyond all doubt. However, we have seen that some philosophers have been able to criticise and reject these 'truths' or 'proofs'. It seems to me that there is a difference between accepting something as true and a proof on one level (rationally, conceptually, in theory) but then accepting that this then relates to reality is another matter altogether. This is the real area for debate amongst philosophers regarding the ontological argument and I think that Plantinga is correct in his observation that the argument's successes can be found in the fact that it establishes 'not the truth of theism, but its rational acceptability'. It is here where the Ontological argument has value and this should not be underestimated or devalued. **5**

The ontological argument is an intriguing area of philosophy, but maybe the answer as to its value is best reflected by the fact that it was built from a context of faith. Anselm clearly operates from the stance of a believer. In this way one could argue that the premise is loaded, or alternatively – if one is more sceptical – one could say that the whole argument is invalid because of its obvious bias. Some would go as far as to say that you need faith before the argument begins. Then again, is there ever any argument presented that does not have its own interests or hidden agendas from which to operate? If this is the case, can we ever really establish any type of 'proof' in relation to God? **6**

Commentary

1 Although the introduction is brief and there need not always be an introduction, it does direct the examiner to the answer that follows and links to the second and third paragraphs.

2 A good summary of the strengths in evaluative style, contrasting with paragraph 3.

3 Weaknesses are explained well.

4 This is good evaluation, using an analogy to try to give the sense of how the ontological seems to work and 'feel'. It is a follow up to paragraph 3.

5 An excellent evaluative paragraph using a correct explanation of the nature of deductive proof and then indicating the difference between concept and empirical reality. A good use of a Plantinga quote to establish the point that 'proof' and 'rational acceptability' are two different things.

6 A great conclusion with some personal observations that are clearly linked to the evaluation as a whole. There are even some interesting questions raised. A very mature response.

Summative comment

Overall this is a very mature response and one that would be suitable for A Level. Those studying for AS can learn from this as well as those who are studying for A Level. With the greater emphasis on AO2 at A Level, this is the sort of depth needed for an answer.

Philosophy Theme 3

AO1 question area: *An explanation of the problem of evil*

A strong answer

'The problem of evil' is a problem put forward by non-believers to the believers of 'The Classical God of Theism' questioning why evil exists if the qualities they believe their God to have, (omnipotence – all-powerful, omnibenevolence – all-loving and omniscience – all-knowing) has. **1**

When discussing evil, we must define what we mean and here I am going to define evil as anything that causes suffering. We must also distinguish between natural and moral evil; 'Natural evil', is an evil outside of our free will and control, an example being 'Hurricane Katrina' or the 'Lisbon earthquake'. 'Moral evil', is an evil that an individual or group chooses by exercising their free-will, for example, the 'Holocaust' or the 'Kidnapping of Madeline McCann'. **2**

The inconsistent triad looks at each aspect. The triangle contains three statements of proposals: omnibenevolent, omnipotence and evil, only two of which can ever be true, according to Epicurus, developed by Hume. **3**

If we take away evil, we are left with the fact that God is all loving and all knowing. Due to the world that surrounds us it is evident that evil does exist, although some argue that evil is just an illusion and perspective and that what we see as evil God does not. Non-believers argue that if God was all loving and all knowing, his creation would not suffer, even for 'temporary evil'. **4**

Therefore, either: God is all loving but not omnipotent and evil exists. That means he wants to take away the evil and suffering that we face but he lacks the power to do it. This is a problem for believers as it contradicts what they believe God is. Or, God is all powerful, not all loving and evil exists. This would mean that whilst God has the power to remove evil he chooses not to because he doesn't care enough, or, even worse, he may enjoy watching us suffer. Once again this poses the same problem of contradiction. **5**

As Epicurus concluded, 'Either God wants us to abolish evil and cannot, or he can but does not want to. If he wants to but cannot he is impotent. If he can, but does not want to he is wicked.' **6**

Non-believers also raise the argument of the amount of suffering needed; why didn't two million die in the holocaust as opposed to six million? The very fact that so many people died is appalling and this immense suffering seems to go against what believers think about God. They also argue why should animals suffer abuse? They cannot learn and develop; therefore, their suffering has no meaning. If, as some religions (e.g. Christianity) teach, animals have no souls – how can suffering be useful or 'soul-making' likewise as animals are not descended from Adam and Eve, why should they suffer as humans do? It makes no sense. There is also the problem of innocent suffering, such as the children starving in the developing world. They are not improving their souls, they are slowly and painfully dying and this cannot be justified. Even if evil is temporary it is not compatible with a loving God who wouldn't want innocents in his creation to suffer. **7**

As Hume stated, 'The gravity of suffering is too much.' **8**

Commentary

1 A good introduction which sums up why there is a problem of evil – defining the God of Classical Theism's characteristics demonstrates clear understanding on the answer's part.

2 The answer then develops by defining evil and the types of evil, with examples. Setting up the parameters of why there is a debate in the first place shows good understanding of the subject material and allows the main part of the argument to be developed upon a platform of agreed-upon definitions.

3 Reference to the inconsistent triad is important to any essay of this type; however, more could have been done here to develop how the inconsistent triad came about and the nature of such a philosophical device.

4 The explanation of the illusion/problem of perspective of evil is apt and explained clearly. The answer continues its explanation by showing how this is an insufficient justification in trying to solve the problem of evil.

5 This demonstrates a very competent unpacking of the removal of the omnipotent/omnibenevolent characteristics and, again, shows why each of these 'solutions' is ultimately inadequate. This, again, shows evidence of good understanding. The key facts and ideas related to the inconsistent triad are presented with accuracy.

6 Using Epicurus' dilemma to underline the point made by the inconsistent triad is an intelligent application of a philosopher's viewpoint to support the reasoning of the essay answer.

7 The answer here deals with the particular problems raised by animal, immense and innocent suffering. All examples are apt and serve to illustrate the point being made.

8 Again, using a philosopher's viewpoint to underline the points made in the previous paragraph demonstrates not only clear understanding but also the ability to organise the material in a clear and coherent way.

Summative comment

The student has produced a fairly full answer in the time available for the question set. The information is relevant and, whilst information is not always presented thoroughly, the presentation of material is sufficient to fully meet a high level of response.

AO2 question area: *The problem of evil*

A weak answer to an assessment of 'Religious solutions to the problem of evil fail to convince anyone.'

Religious solutions to the problem of evil do not always convince. Many people will question why God, if there is even a God at all, would let suffering become so extreme and not put a stop to it. For example, immense suffering such as what the Nazis did to the Jews in the Holocaust is one of the biggest types of evil that has occurred. Why would an all loving God let millions of people die? **1**

Innocent suffering such as the children and families in Africa, who struggle for survival in their everyday life. Would an all-powerful God not want to use his power to give them better quality of life? Also animals suffer because they have less authority and are smaller than humans, is this fair? **2**

Religious solutions such as Irenaeus' and Augustine's theodicy are convincing arguments to prove God's existence in the problem of evil. It is our choice as humans to disobey our God who made a world free from flaws. And this is why he designed Heaven and Hell, for the good and the bad to go to. Also, evil is not a substance and therefore it cannot be claimed that God created it. **3**

In my opinion, I think that religious solutions are unconvincing. I feel that there are far too many errors in the argument for the problem of evil and if God created the world and everything in it, then I feel that it is wrong to say that God the designer did not also design the evil that we have to face. The main critique is for the God of Classical Theism as it seems impossible to say that he or any other God can be all knowing, loving and powerful, if evil still exists in the universe. [4]

Commentary

[1] The introduction starts well but then just uses information which is AO1 in nature. An opportunity to make this more evaluative is missed and it is important that, as an introduction to an evaluation, such an opportunity should be grasped.

[2] Again, similarly to [1], the answer is restating information that it has already used in AO1. So far the question set has not been answered.

[3] Augustine's and Irenaeus' theodicies are skimmed over and a superficial analysis of what they state is given. This is limited and would need to be expanded on significantly to contribute adequately to the evaluation.

[4] The concluding paragraph (it's always essential to have one in an AO2 response) provides a personal point of view, based on evidence, but is limited in scope. The inconsistent triad is restated but, overall, reasoning is simplistic and basic.

Summative comment

This answer demonstrates that the issues were only partly appreciated and the analysis was limited. Evidence provided to support the reasoning was minimal and therefore this response would not get a high mark.

Philosophy Theme 4

AO1 question area: *Religious experience: an explanation of mysticism*

A weak answer

Mysticism is an experience of the divine. Bauderschmidt described it as an 'altered state of consciousness' that results in 'unity with the divine'. Mystical experiences cannot be physically measured which leads many to question whether they are authentic. [1]

Firstly, philosopher William James who outlines four characteristics of mystical experiences shows how some question whether they are authentic. James first characteristic is ineffability; this is that the recipient cannot explain what has happened to them. Mystic Rabbi Israel Tov stated he 'couldn't authenticate' his experience. Immediately people question whether mystical experiences are authentic as how can something which cannot be described be real. Equally some suggest that if God is omnipotent, all-powerful, then why can't he show himself to everyone and not just a select few. [2]

Secondly, some people question whether mystical experiences are authentic as they can be deceptive. Psychologists Carl Jung and Sigmund Freud note how these religious images can be merely things conjured up through our lives. This leaves the question are they authentic. Equally the 'miracle of the sun' in which thousands of people in Fatima, Portugal, declared they saw God when looking at the sun has been explained by scientists that looking at the sun for prolonged amounts of time can result in hallucinogenic conceits. This can question authenticity. Finally, scholar Walter Stace believes some people can have extroversive mystical experiences in which the divine is transgressed physically. An example of this is the 1994 evangelical Christian neo-charismatic group Toronto Blessings. Characteristics include laughing hysterically and weeping uncontrollably. They state it is the physical manifestation of the Holy Spirit. Yet many believe these people are secretly drunk and are emphasising these experiences for show. This also questions the authenticity. [3]

In conclusion, it appears that other explanations can explain mystical experiences which is why some people question whether they are authentic. [4]

Commentary

[1] A good, clear and focused introduction to the subject with a scholarly quote to support the introduction. This is good practice and sets the stage for the rest of the response.

[2] Reference to William James and Rabbi Israel Tov are usefully inserted to support the points of view that the very nature of mysticism makes it difficult to authenticate.

[3] A number of relevant examples are now given in the next section of the response. These are highly relevant although the answer needs to explain precisely how they challenge authenticity rather than just writing the sentence 'This questions the authenticity' which only shows partial understanding. A missed opportunity to impress the examiner with his subject knowledge.

[4] The 'conclusion' is unnecessary for AO1; it is only in AO2 where conclusions are required.

Summative comment

The answer presents information that is mainly accurate. It clearly has an understanding of the topic but here it is only basic and occasionally patchy. It would need to extend explanations in order to improve the overall mark.

AO2 question area: *Religious experience: mysticism*

A strong answer to an assessment of 'A mystical experience should not be devalued by the challenge of authenticity.'

Some Christians and mystics argue against the idea that 'authenticity' should devalue the worth of an experience, certainly. For example, F C Happold, one of the prime defenders of mysticism, claimed that 'mysticism exists in a different sphere of experience to science altogether', thus implying that scientific evidence against the existence of authentic mystical experiences should not detract from the sense of religious authenticity the recipient might attribute to his or her experience. [1]

Some, however, have argued against this view of the value of mysticism, such as A F King, and have instead posited that, if one considered any experience valid based simply on the fact that the recipient underwent it in their own mind in a non-scientific 'sphere of thought' then the views of mentally ill people and hallucinatory drug users would have to start to be taken seriously alongside defenders of mysticism – after all, such people also have experiences and visions which seem real to them but are scientifically dubious, and are locked away in hospitals or prisons, not listened to and praised by the Church for having encountered God first-hand. [2]

This argument can be refuted, however, by defenders of mysticism fairly easily via the idea that mental patients and those who have hallucinations are often the recipients of such negative experiences – one of the reasons mystical visitations are considered valuable is because they are not irrational, but serve to heighten the recipient's well-being and impart useful spiritual knowledge onto him or her (James' 'noetic quality'). Indeed, William James further defends mysticism against the aforementioned argument by stating that the transience of an experience – its ability to stay with the recipient and change his/her life despite its fleeting nature – is the quality which proves it is of worth and distinguishes it from the hallucinations by mental patients, who normally forget. [3]

Commentary

1. The use of scholarly names adds support to the answer's opening argument. Supporting the claim in the question, the answer provides appropriate critical analysis and comment.

2. The next paragraph sees a direct response to the answer's first argument and, again, uses scholarly evidence to promote the point being made.

3. The final paragraph counters the counter argument and provides a more sympathetic approach to the issue.

The final sentences imply a conclusion but this is not directly focused on the original question. It is often good practice to refer to the question in the final conclusion so as to demonstrate to the examiner that the issue has been fully understood and responded to.

Summative comment

The answer makes an intelligent response to the question but does not develop the answer sufficiently. The implied conclusion is not directly relevant to the question and this weakens the evaluation as a whole. As such, the answer is fairly strong but to get a higher mark the answer needed to add to arguments with additional material and provide a clear and focused conclusion.

Ethics Theme 1

Meta-ethical theory

AO1 question area: *Divine Command theory.*

A weak answer

Followers of the Divine Command theory accept that there is an overall standard for morality but that the standard is part of God. They believe God decides what is good and what is bad. [1]

Robert Adams argued that morality is grounded in the character of God, who is perfectly good and so therefore his commands are good as well and so God knows what is the best for us. [2]

If whatever God thinks and does is simply by definition good, regardless of what it is, then does it make sense to worship God for his goodness? [3]

If God commands things because they are good, then God is not really in control and cannot be creator. This may mean that God is not really there. [4]

Commentary

1. The first part of the paragraph starts well but then the word 'overall' would be better replaced with 'objective'. The second point needs to be related to the idea of God willing or commanding something as good.

2. This is not really the best explanation of Robert Adams' development. It should make clear it is a development of Divine Command theory and explain why.

3. This is a good question but there needs to be more elaboration and relate it to the Euthyphro dilemma. Really this could have been the first paragraph if developed and then linked to the theory of Divine Command. At present there is really no link.

4 This is really moving away from the focus of the question area as the issue is not really one of power but of the nature of good and God's goodness. The issues that 'God is not really in control and cannot be creator' and it 'may mean that God is not really there' are not explained at all and so are irrelevant.

Summative comment

Although the basics are there, they are really basic and there is just a glimpse of understanding of the Divine Command theory.

AO2 question area: *Evaluating whether virtues are consistent with Christianity.*

A strong answer

There is a long history teaching about virtues in the Christian tradition, and this can be traced back to the Old Testament, for example in the book of Ecclesiastes. Christianity and its teachings are usually associated with rules and commandments but in the Sermon on the Mount, Jesus clearly promotes specific inward qualities or virtues. It is for this reason that virtues are consistent with Christianity. **1**

Each virtue is considered 'blessed' and has a corresponding spiritual reward. Jesus' blessing is praise and affirmation in recognition of the virtuous quality demonstrated. The virtues identified by Jesus are: poor in spirit; mourning; meek; a hunger and thirst for righteousness; mercy; purity of heart; peacemakers; and, the persecuted for the sake of righteousness. **2**

One example of consistency with Christianity is that the term poor in spirit is often interpreted as an understanding of poverty in relation to the whole person; that is, physical, mental and spiritual. For example, people who may have their rights taken from them or are oppressed in some way. They have an awareness of their own insignificance, hopelessness and helplessness before God. This is consistent with religious teaching. **3**

Another example of consistency is those who hunger and thirst for righteousness. This is often understood as a desire for the virtuous outcome of justice in life in relation to the kingdom of God. It is often understood as depicting the virtue of seeking righteousness or justice on a personal, spiritual, social and global sense and can be applied to the actions of the Church worldwide in fighting against poverty and injustice. **4**

Finally, those who display the virtue of mercy are certainly consistent with Christianity. Through humility and an awareness of God's mercy Christians are encouraged to display mercy towards others, not because it brings the reward of God's mercy, but because it is a virtuous disposition in itself, for example in giving to the poor or in the act of forgiveness. **5**

The virtues have been the subject of much scholarly discussion; for example, some scholars see a similarity with Isaiah 61:1–3 because of the references to freedom from poverty, declaring hope for the righteous, who are in despair, and mentioning comfort for those who mourn. Other scholars see it as describing the opposite characteristics to those in Proverbs 6:16–19 which detail vices. Overall, it can be seen that virtues clearly have a basis in the Christian religion, there is no doubt about this. However, the real question is how important are they in relation to the rules and teachings in Christianity? Are they more important? Do they work together with the rules of religion or is there a priority when it comes to application of them to moral issues? This is the real debate for Christians. **6**

Commentary

1 A good introduction that sets out Christianity's connection with virtues and also indicates how the evaluation may go. It is one-sided but not totally, as the final paragraph demonstrates.

2 A good summary of the Beatitudes.

3 The answer selects a particular virtue and explains why and how it is consistent with Christianity.

4 The answer selects another virtue and again explains why and how it is consistent with Christianity.

5 A final virtue is selected and the answer again explains why and how it is consistent with Christianity. Note that only three virtues are selected but the depth of the answer allows this and clearly relates each to the evaluation, rather than an answer that just lists them.

6 The answer relates back to other references in the Bible by making reference to the work of scholars. The conclusion is drawn that is inevitably one-sided but the candidate then acknowledges that inconsistencies may arise not when considering whether the virtues are Christian but in their application to moral issues.

Summative comment

This is a very good answer because it has a clear line of argument. Whilst there is the acknowledgement of inconsistencies when compared to application of other religious teachings – and this could have been the basis of the counter argument – the answer demonstrates how a response can be more one-sided and still be able to perform well.

Ethics Theme 2
Natural Law

AO1 question area: *Examining Aquinas' Natural Law.*

A strong answer

The theology of the Roman Catholic Church follows the strict rules and guidelines set out by Aquinas' Natura Law theory. Natural Law states that all moral decisions can be made using our God-given reason. Aquinas developed Aristotelian ideas that everything has a purpose described this as our 'telos'. Aquinas, unlike Aristotle, believed this purpose was given by God. Our 'telos' is to reach fellowship with God through the decisions we make using our ability to reason. Any action that does not bring about causality or fulfil its final purpose is wrong. Aquinas' basic argument was that through reason we can identify ways to behave that apply to all human beings without exception. They are good acts because they lead us towards the main human purpose or goal. The most fundamental one that underpins them all is 'act in such a way as to achieve good and avoid evil'. **1**

Aquinas determined that Natural Law has five primary precepts for action – worship God, self-preservation and preservation of the innocent, live in an ordered society, to learn, continuation of the species through reproduction and to defend the defenceless. He then explained the secondary precepts, which demonstrate the primary precepts in action. For example, in order to live in an ordered society, we need the secondary precept 'do not kill'. Many Roman Catholics still accept the use of Natural Law because it gives them a clear set of rules by which to lead their lives. Aquinas' theory in work can be seen when we look at the Roman Catholic Church and ethical issues. For example, the Roman Catholic Church upholds the precept of 'an ordered society' by maintaining an absolutist approach to issues such as abortion and euthanasia, which would break this precept. Aquinas' primary precepts are also supported by the Bible, for example in Genesis it states the one of our main purposes is reproduction. **2**

Aquinas made a distinction between the intention of an act and the act itself. For those looking on, it may well be judged that an action was good. However, if the onlooker knew the real motive or intention, then it may well be seen rather differently. Likewise, it is not acceptable to do a bad act intentionally even if the aim is to bring about good outcomes. Many practising Roman Catholics still accept his ideas and believe that doing the right action for the right reasons will improve oneself and enable humans to get closer to God. **3**

One way that correct reasoning can be developed is through the cultivation of certain virtues. Aquinas identified three theological virtues (revealed in the Bible) that are known as the three revealed virtues; he actually referred to them as 'articles of faith'. They are faith, hope and love. For Aquinas, these are the superlative virtues that define and direct all other virtues. As they are the absolute and superlative they are perfect. Although they cannot be *fully* achieved in this world, being far above the capacity of a human being, they should be aimed for. Aquinas also encourages the development of cardinal virtues such as inner strength-fortitude or temperance (everything in moderation). For Aquinas, these were the main framework for moral behaviour that helped human beings become more God-like in their application. Scholars such as Peter Vardy agree that the idea of improving the self and soul is very appealing to religious believers who aim to get closer to God. **4**

Aquinas believed that the main purpose of sex was reproduction as outlined in the primary precepts. Any sexual activity that frustrates this final cause, such as homosexual sex, is therefore wrong. This is why many Roman Catholics hold the view that homosexual sex is not permissible because it does not lead to the fulfilment of the 'telos' of sex, i.e. reproduction. **5**

Commentary

1 Although the answer has been approached by addressing the Roman Catholic Church, it clearly explains why throughout and relates this example to Natural Law. It has carefully selected accurate and relevant information. Specialist vocabulary is also used accurately.

2 The answer has clearly linked the primary and secondary precepts here, not only to each other, but also to Roman Catholic teachings and to Biblical evidence.

3 The answer has clearly defined interior and exterior acts here and explained why these concepts are important to religious believers.

4 In addition to this, the response has identified both the revealed and the cardinal virtues and their link to a human's personal development. The answer has supported the point it makes with a scholarly opinion.

5 Here the answer has clearly identified why Roman Catholics would support Natural Law's view on homosexual acts.

Summative comment

This is a very comprehensive summary indeed covering all the key aspects of Aquinas' Natural Law theory with some good examples used. The answer has also shown a thorough understanding of the issues raised by Natural Law in the application of them.

AO2 question area: *Evaluating whether or not Natural Law is effective in dealing with ethical issues.*

A weak answer

Some would argue against this statement as how can we be sure that the 'telos' or purpose of a particular object or action as defined by Natural Law is correct. For example, Natural Law says the main purpose of sex is reproduction, but what if it's main purpose is pleasure? [1]

Also Natural Law is based on the belief that God created a world and everything within it for a purpose, but many people would challenge this idea. An atheist would have no reason to follow this theory as they don't believe in God. [2]

Aquinas believed that all of mankind has the same universal nature, but is there such a thing as a universal human nature? For example, Eskimos think it is acceptable to allow elderly relatives to die in the cold to stop them becoming a burden on their family. [3]

Commentary

1. Whilst the point raised here is valid, it could have been explained more clearly. Why is the concept of the 'telos' so important within Natural Law? God designed everything with a purpose and therefore fulfilling its intended design is good. The answer could have pointed out a way in which it could not be effective, for example homosexual relationships. Opportunity missed.

2. A valid point partially supported by reasoning.

3. The candidate needs to explain why Aquinas believed there was a 'universal human nature'. He could have introduced the idea of wrong reasoning and real and apparent goods but instead focuses on a criticism without first fully explaining the idea. The example of Eskimos is relevant and good but loses its impact without proper debate.

Summative comment

Although the answer shows some grasp of the main issues here, the analysis or comment is limited and any points made are really undeveloped. The arguments given are only partially supported and lack deeper evaluation or analysis. The answer also lacks any argument which support the 'agree' viewpoint and a conclusion.

Ethics Theme 3

Situation Ethics

AO1 question area: *Examining Fletcher's reasons for rejecting the two extremes of legalism and antinomianism.*

A weak answer

Fletcher believed in agape, which means that you should love everyone and not just follow rules unless the rules are loving. Legalism follows rules without love so he rejected it as rules should be loving. [1]

Antinomianists were people who said that you could do whatever you wanted and rebelled against rules. They would not love other people but only themselves. This is why Fletcher rejected them because they did not follow the rules. [2]

Fletcher's way of agape is the middle way between the two extremes. Christianity follows legalism and that is why he rejected it and became an atheist. Many people followed him. [3]

Commentary

1. This is not an accurate description of agape. It lacks a depth of understanding and is too simplistic. It also misunderstands how Situation Ethics views rules.

2. This is partially accurate but not at all well explained.

3. The legalism of Christianity was not the reason Fletcher lost his faith but the first bit is accurate, although again, not developed enough.

Summative comment

The answer demonstrates very weak understanding of Fletcher's reasons and it lacks detail and depth to even consider it as scraping into the A Level standard!

AO2 question area: *Evaluating whether Situation Ethics provides an adequate basis for making ethical decisions.*

A strong answer

Some would argue that Situation Ethics as a relativistic theory is flexible and practical. It takes into account the complexities of human life and helps people make tough decisions, whereas from a legalistic perspective all actions seem to be wrong. [1]

Situation Ethics allows people the individual freedom to make decisions for themselves and to consider the situation they are in before acting. Many people nowadays prefer the prescriptive legalistic approach, which gives you no choice about what to do. Also people can consider if the desired end goal (in this case love) is likely to be achieved before taking action. This is a major strength because it means, just as with the legal system, there are other factors to consider before making a judgement. **2**

As a relativistic theory, Situation Ethics allows you to make a choice between the 'lesser of two evils', whereas a legalistic approach would not allow you to do this. For example, a legalistic approach would face difficulties in that there is a conflict of principles. This is clearly seen in the cases of double effect in Natural Law. **3**

However, others may argue that relativism gives too much freedom to the individual to decide what action to take. It has been seen that time and time again humans are prone to making mistakes or being influenced by personal gain rather than love. Clearly this could lead to unfair and immoral behaviour and is a major weakness because the freedom Situation Ethics has does not bring with it a quality control beyond the individual and so it can be open to abuse at worst or vague misuse. **4**

In addition, many religious believers would claim that the moral standards within society have declined since people have rejected absolutist religious principles in favour of more relativistic and teleological systems, although you could argue that this is not a strong criticism as its basis is a personal view on what standards should be. Nonetheless, there is the problem that people cannot accurately predict the consequences of their actions. Therefore, they do not know if the desired goal of love will be achieved. How will this be measured? **5**

Finally, religious believers would argue that all people should follow divine law as God is the ultimate source of moral authority. They cannot rely on principles devised by sinful mankind.

In conclusion, there are both strengths and weaknesses in considering Situation Ethics as an adequate basis for making ethical decisions. What is clear, however, is that a legalistic approach and a situationist approach both have their issues and so the weaknesses of Situation Ethics does not mean it is inferior to a legalistic approach. **6**

Commentary

1 A good introduction and explanation of why Situation Ethics is seen positively.

2 Relates the argument to contemporary society with effective explanation.

3 This is a good point, although the example from double effect could have been developed more.

4 Notice the personal reflections interjected in response to a point made. A good evaluative skill.

5 Again more evaluation is included in response to the issue raised.

6 A very good conclusion that is balanced and also has the strength of warning us that just because a system has problems does not mean it fails or is inferior to another. Very clever.

Summative comment

A very mature, reflective and evaluative response that focuses more on a range of views than developing specific ones, but the interjected evaluation and clever conclusion demonstrate its quality.

Ethics Theme 4

Utilitarianism

AO1 question area: *Examining Bentham's hedonic calculus.*

A strong answer

Bentham stated in his book *An Introduction to the Principles of Morals and Legislation* that 'Nature had placed mankind under the governance of two sovereign masters, pleasure and pain.' Bentham believed that humans are aim to seek pleasure and avoid pain. This is the idea on which he based his principle of 'utility' or 'usefulness' – to aim for the 'the greatest happiness for the greatness number'. He developed the relativistic and teleological theory known as Act Utilitarianism. It was called 'Act Utilitarianism' because it treats each situation as being unique and believed that consequences of an action are what make our actions right or wrong. **1**

However, he realised that it was hard for an individual to work out what the happiest consequences might be, so he devised the Hedonic Calculus to help people discover this. The calculus consisted of seven criteria which would be used to judge whether an action was right or wrong. The first of these seven criteria was intensity and refers to how intense the happiness will be. The second is duration and this means how long the happiness will last. The third criterion is certainty, how sure are you that what you are going to do will lead to happiness? The fourth is propinquity or remoteness, meaning how far your happiness will reach. The fifth criterion is fecundity, which means how likely is your original action, which initially leads to happiness, to lead to further happiness. The sixth is purity, which means how free from pain is this action likely to be? The seventh criterion is extent and refers to how many people will receive happiness. **2**

To give an example, imagine there was a burning house and trapped inside were a scientist who has the cure for cancer and your elderly father? Who do you save? Bentham would say you should save the scientist because saving her will bring strong happiness to the millions of people suffering from cancer (intensity and extent). It would also allow the cancer suffers to live longer – the duration of their combined happiness would last longer than the happiness of your elderly father. Saving the scientist would definitely lead (certainty) to pleasure, as millions of people would be happy to be saved from a previously terminal disease. The initial happiness from saving the scientist and therefore the cancer suffers will lead to further happiness for their friends and family (fecundity). The action would not be completely free from pain (purity) as your father will die, but the happiness will be far reaching and many people will experience the happiness if you save the scientist (extent). **3**

Commentary

1 The answer has started well by accurately quoting from Bentham's book. It then successfully defines the principle of 'utility' and uses key terminology such as 'hedonist' and 'consequentialist' accurately. The terms 'relativistic' and 'teleological', although correctly related to Bentham's form of Utilitarianism, could have been more clearly defined here.

2 The answer has clearly defined the purpose of the hedonic calculus but could, however, have stated why it is called the 'hedonic' calculus and explained that the term 'hedone' is the Greek work for 'pleasure'. The answer has also been able to list the seven criteria it contains and to accurately define five out of the seven criteria, which is enough. 'Intensity' is not correctly defined and means how strong the happiness is. In addition to this, propinquity or remoteness actually means how close in time is the happiness? These are not major issues overall but it highlights the importance of using technical terminology correctly.

3 In this paragraph the answer has demonstrated a clear understanding of how Act Utilitarianism can be applied to a particular situation using six out of the seven criteria. The answer has also actually shown an understanding of 'intensity' here even though the definition in the previous paragraph was not clear. The only criterion that has not been successfully applied here is 'remoteness'.

Summative comment

Although not perfect, this answer is of a good standard. There are obviously areas for improvement for it to gain anywhere near to full marks but it is clear that the candidate will do well.

AO2 question area: *Evaluating whether or not Utilitarianism is too weak to work in contemporary society.*

A weak answer

Utilitarianism as an ethical theory has many flaws. For example, when you fulfil 'the greatest happiness for the greatest number' principle, a minority are allowed to suffer. Also this principle allows the justification of any act which goes against religious teachings. Many people would argue that Act Utilitarianism's lack of rules would lead to moral chaos. In addition to this, many people have different ideas of what happiness is, so how can you make a judgement on this basis? Utilitarianism as a consequential theory asks us to predict consequences, which is impossible. **1**

On the other hand, Utilitarianism is fairly successful as most people want to aim for happiness. Hospitals and medical practices make decisions using the Utilitarian principles. Using Utilitarianism could help to promote a community spirit through the pursuit of the common goal of happiness. **2**

Commentary

1 An attempt has been made to construct an argument here, but the points raised are only partially supported by reasoning or evidence. For example, the argument about a minority being allowed to suffer is correct, but there is no evidence or further reasoning to support this or any of the other arguments given here.

2 Whilst there is recognition of more than one view here the points raised continue to be only partially supported by reasoning or evidence. For example, how do hospitals make decisions using the principles outlined by Utilitarianism? How does Utilitarianism promote a community spirit through happiness?

Summative comment

Overall, this answer shows some grasp of the main issues but the analysis or comment is limited. The arguments given are only partially supported and lack deeper evaluation or analysis. It is clearly not a strong answer and there are many areas for improvement.

Quickfire Answers

Philosophy Theme 1

1.1 Evidence or experience.

1.2 God.

1.3 i. Marble, statue and sculptor

ii. Wood, burning wood, fire.

1.4 In the world of sense.

1.5 It is necessary to admit a first efficient cause that is itself uncaused – this can only be (according to Aquinas) God.

1.6 The universe and all things within it.

1.7 Something that must exist and cannot not exist.

1.8 That it has a cause of its existence.

1.9 Something that has no beginning and no end.

1.10 The fundamentalist Christian churches of America.

1.11 Things without intelligence did not have the ability to direct themselves towards an end – they required a guiding intelligence to do this.

1.12 The stone was a natural object with no apparent purpose, whereas the watch was a complex machine that had a specific purpose.

1.13 The world provides the things necessary for life; the world can be rationally analysed; evolution led to the development of intelligent human life.

1.14 The designer wanted his creation to enjoy existence not just survive.

1.15 That just because everything in the universe has a cause does not mean that the universe itself had a cause (what is true of the parts is not necessarily true of the whole).

1.16 Analogy only works where two similar things are compared – this was not possible with the universe as the universe was unique.

1.17 That life on earth developed and changed according to the external stimuli of the environment.

Philosophy Theme 2

2.1 Deductive proof makes use of logic rather than evidence.

2.2 To deepen the understanding of faith.

2.3 That something (in this case God) cannot not exist.

2.4 The triangle and the mountain/valley analogies.

2.5 If it were self-contradictory or logically absurd.

2.6 He did not believe it was possible to define things (including God) into existence.

2.7 Existence was not a defining predicate.

Philosophy Theme 3

3.1 Moral evil and natural evil.

3.2 Any suitable response according to stated definitions – e.g. murder and earthquakes.

3.3 The God that possesses the characteristics of omnipotence, omniscience and omnibenevolence. Also the God worshipped by the three main western religions of Christianity, Islam and Judaism.

3.4 The incompatibility of an omnipotent and omnibenevolent God allowing evil to exist.

3.5 Where the three statements: God is omnipotent; God is omnibenevolent and Evil exists cannot co-exist without a logical contradiction.

3.6 The account of The Fall in Genesis, chapter 3.

3.7 The lack or absence of something that should be present in normal circumstances.

3.8 It allowed God to send Jesus into the world to atone for humankind's sin and to provide a way back to perfect harmony with God.

3.9 How can a perfect world go wrong?

3.10 It contradicts the idea that humankind was originally created perfect.

3.11 Genesis 1:26 – 'Let us make man in our image after our likeness'.

3.12 To allow humankind to grow into God's likeness by understanding that all actions have consequences – both positive and negative.

3.13 It takes no account of animal suffering; the immensity of suffering or the unfair distribution of suffering; neither does it encourage individuals to choose to do good in the here and now if all people will eventually end up in Heaven.

Philosophy Theme 4

4.1 Corporeal; imaginary and intellectual.

4.2 That those who convert demonstrate this by a change in the way in which they live their life – this can quite often be a significant change that is externally apparent or it may be an internal change that is evidenced through the beliefs and subsequent actions of the converted.

4.3 The suspension of the exterior senses.

4.4 A watered garden.

4.5 Ineffability; noetic quality; transiency and passivity.

4.6 A state of intense awe experienced by the individual or group.

4.7 Description-related; subject-related and object-related challenges.

4.8 It may still have meaning for the individual and make a difference to both their life and the lives of those they come into contact with.

Ethics Theme 1

1.1 The nature of ethics, for example 'why do we act like we do?'

1.2 Reference to a person and their behaviour in ethics.

1.3 One that has set moral rules that cannot change.

1.4 Teleology.

1.5 Omnibenevolence.

1.6 The Euthyphro dilemma.

1.7 Character of a person.

1.8 Focuses on the ethical virtues developed in a person.

1.9 It was used by Aristotle to describe the perfect virtuous state of happiness.

1.10 Nicomachean Ethics.

1.11 Moral virtues are to do with behaviour, intellectual virtues are to do with the mind.

1.12 Justice is a collective outcome of virtuous behaviour.

1.13 Ecclesiastes.

1.14 Psychological egoism points out that we always act out of self-interest whereas ethical egoism says that we should act out of self-interest.

1.15 An action for the benefit of others.

1.16 He thought we were always bound to some system of duty.

1.17 When we embrace our ownness and recognise our unique nature.

Ethics Theme 2

2.1 Happiness, eudaimonia.

2.2 God was seen as the source of the Natural Law.

2.3 Deontological because what should be done is seen as being determined by fundamental principles that are not based on consequences.

2.4 The fact that the term casuistry comes from the word 'case' suggests that a given context and 'end' results are considered and so the teleological aspect of Natural Law is often accepted.

2.5 Casuistry is essential: it involves the careful use of thought in applying general principles to particular circumstances.

2.6 There are different words for love in the Greek language.

2.7 Prudence is sound judgment; temperance is moderation or balance; courage is endurance; and, justice is guidance.

2.8 Aquinas made a distinction between the intention of an act and the act itself.

2.9 Real good is in line with Natural Law with intention and apparent good is an act that appears good but leads to bad. An example of an apparent good would be following our desires for something that seems good at the time but not in line with our good overall in relation to Natural Law such as eating as much as possible because the food tastes good.

2.10 24 weeks.

2.11 1967.

2.12 (1) A woman's physical health is threatened by having the baby / any existing children would be harmed mentally or physically by the woman proceeding to have the baby. (2) There is a high risk the baby would be handicapped.

2.13 Birth, consciousness, ensoulment, viability, etc.

2.14 One person kills another with intention or allows another's death at their request.

2.15 1961.

Ethics Theme 3

3.1 Two extremes of legalism and antinomianism.

3.2 Not entirely, it was simply one concise and well-publicised statement of a trend in Christian ethics that had been growing for decades.

3.3 The use of reason.

3.4 It is not some 'thing' but something we 'do'.

3.5 Agape in Jesus' teachings and Paul's writings.

3.6 The Hebrew word closest to its meaning.

3.7 Pragmatism, relativism, positivism and personalism.

3.8 It means 'self-emptying' and signifies agape.

3.9 Love.

3.10 No, also in social justice.

3.11 He argued that human laws and attitudes towards sex and homosexuality that were influenced by the Church were outdated, inconsistent and hypocritical.

3.12 An example of intolerance and injustice against homosexuals.

3.13 1967.

Ethics Theme 4

4.1 The end, telos.

4.2 Those that bring the greatest good for the greatest number.

4.3 Barrister.

4.4 Intensity, duration, extent, etc.

4.5 Utilitarianism is considered to be a relativistic theory as it means there are no universal moral norms or rules and that each situation has to be looked at independently because each situation is different.

4.6 Mill argued that there were higher and lower pleasures (not all pleasure was the same) and pleasure should be measured by quality not just quantity.

4.7 Reading philosophy.

4.8 Eating.

4.9 It protects all individuals in society.

4.10 A strong rule utilitarian believes that any rules formulated and established through the application of the 'principle of utility' should never be broken as they guarantee happiness for society. A weak rule utilitarian tries to allow for the fact that in some situations breaking a rule originally created because it generally fulfils the principle of utility may be the right course of action, because in this particular situation breaking the rule is more likely to fulfil the principle of utility than keeping the rule.

4.11 Early examples of the productive nature in medical research of dissection and vivisection.

4.12 An approach to animals that supports the rights of animals to be free from abuse and to be looked after, e.g. RSPCA.

4.13 An approach to animals that establishes laws and regulations to control animal experiments and to ensure animals are treated with dignity.

4.14 Langley argues that there is evidence of poor performance of animal models in medical research.

4.15 Understanding Animal Research (UAR). UAR states that it 'supports the humane use of animals in biomedical research, and believes that animal research is a vital part of the scientific process'.

4.16 Bentham's 'insuperable line' as he called it, was that it was the ability to suffer rather than the ability to reason that provided the framework and standard of how we treat other animals.

4.17 It is a pressure group calling themselves 'The Campaign for Nuclear Disarmament' that argue against having nuclear weapons.

4.18 Because Fallon stated, 'Deterrence means convincing any potential aggressor that the benefits of an attack are far outweighed by its consequences.' This consequentialist approach is in line with utilitarian principles in that it could be argued to support the harm principle.

Glossary

Absolutist: an ethical system that believes there exists a standard of right and wrong that is fully and totally binding on all human beings

Actual infinite: something that is actually infinite in extent or in extent of the operations performed – it literally has no beginning and no end

Actuality: when something is in its fully realised state

Act Utilitarianism: a form of Utilitarianism associated with Bentham that treats each moral situation as unique and applies the hedonic calculus to each 'act' to see if it fulfils the 'principle of utility'. Any action is right if it produces 'the greatest happiness for the greatest number.

Aesthetic: related to the concept and appreciation of beauty

Agape: Greek word for pure, unconditional love

Aheb: Hebrew word for love that is seen to be similar to the idea of agape

Akrasia: incontinent, that is, lacking self-restraint and uncontrolled

Akrates: one who is weak-willed and overcome by vices

Altruism: selfless concern for the well-being of others

Animal Aid: a charity that promotes animal welfare and argues against the use of animals for medical research

Anthropic: related to being human

Anthropology: the study of human beings, their culture and social development

Antinomianism: a theory of ethics that does not recognise the authority of but promotes freedom from external rules, from the Greek word meaning lawless

Apologist: an individual who writes or speaks in defence of a particular cause or belief

A posteriori: a statement that is based on actual observation, evidence, experimental data or experience – relates to inductive reasoning

Apparent good: apparent good is a vice or sin that takes us further away from the ideal human nature that God had planned for us

Applied ethics: the debates that arise when ethical *issues* are considered

A priori: without or prior to evidence or experience

Arete: a Greek word meaning virtue

Atomic bomb: a bomb which derives its destructive power from the rapid release of nuclear energy

Attribute: a descriptive characteristic that someone or something possesses

Beatific vison: the state of perfect happiness through supernatural union with God

Beatitude: blessing given by Jesus for certain personal virtues

Bigotry: intolerance and narrow-mindedness

Birth: the point at which the child is separated from the mother and becomes a separate entity

Blastocyst: a group of multiplying cells

Casuistry: the art of applying key principles to an ethical case

Chesed: Hebrew word that describes an exclusive kind of love in a particular relationship

CND: a pressure group calling themselves 'The Campaign for Nuclear Disarmament'

Community ethos: the character or spirit of a community

Compendium: a thorough collection of material

Conscience: traditionally an internal, intuitive guide to good or bad; Fletcher reinterpreted this notion as a description of ethical action

Consciousness: awareness of self

Consequentialism: an ethical theory based on considering consequences

Consequentialist: people should make moral judgements based on the outcome or the consequences of an action

Contingent: anything that depends on something else (in the case of a contingent being – it is contingent upon another being for its existence, e.g. a child is contingent upon its parent)

Conversion: in the religious context the change of state from one form of life to another

Corporeal: of a material nature, physical

Cosmological and teleological arguments: two examples of inductive arguments that use the evidence of, and within, the universe to attempt to prove the existence of the God of Classical Theism

Courage: a cardinal virtue involving physical, moral or spiritual endurance and strength of character

Deductive proof: a proof in which, if the premises are true, then the conclusion must be true

Deontological: a theory that explores obligation or duty

Deterrent: a thing that discourages or is intended to discourage someone from doing something

Dissection: the action of dissecting a body or plant to study its internal parts

Distillation: a process of extracting key, quality material

Dreams: in terms of visions, the unconscious state where knowledge or understanding is gained through a series of images or a dream-narrative, that would not normally be available to the individual in the conscious state

Ecstatic: an overwhelming feeling of bliss or peace

Efficient cause: the 'third party' that moves potentiality to actuality

Eigenheit: ownness, the idea of mastering oneself

Einzig: uniqueness, the freedom from all impositions leaving pure individuality

Einzige: ego

Embryo: an animal in the early stage of development before birth; in humans, the embryo stage is the first three months after conception

Empirically: using knowledge gained through the experiences of any of the five senses

Enkrates: one who is tempted, but strong, and lives in the mean

Ensoulment: the point when the soul enters the body

Epistemic distance: a distance measured in terms of knowledge rather than space or time

Ethical egoism: the normative view that holds that all action ought to be motivated by self-interest

Ethics: from the Greek 'ethike' meaning habit or behaviour and closely related to the word ethos, it is a study of the framework of guiding principles that direct an action

Ethos: a Greek word used by Aristotle for character of a person

Eudaimonia: a Greek word used by Aristotle to define the end purpose of human life to be happiness, flourishing or fulfilment

Euthanasia: literally meaning a gentle or easy death, it is the controversial and, in some cases, illegal action of allowing a terminally ill person to die with dignity, avoiding pain and suffering

Evil: anything that causes pain or suffering

Evolutionary theory: scientific theory, originally proposed in the 19th century that posited that life developed from simpler to more complex life forms via a process of natural selection and genetic mutation

Existentialism: a philosophy that proposes the individual is free and responsible to determine their own development

External act: an action that is seen to be good or bad but one that does not correlate with, nor is consistent with, the intention behind it

Faith: a strong belief or trust in something or someone

Fallacy of composition: philosophical notion that what is true of the parts is not necessarily true of the whole (i.e. atoms are colourless but this does not mean that a cat, which is made of atoms, is colourless)

Foetus: the unborn baby from the end of the eighth week after conception (when the major structures have formed) until birth

Free will: the theological and philosophical concept that states that humans have the ability to choose freely between good and evil

Geological: the science relating to how the earth was formed

God of Classical Theism: the God that is generally associated with the Western monotheistic religions of Christianity, Islam and Judaism

Greatest happiness principle: a calculation used in utilitarian theory to assess the best course of action to take

Hedonism: an ethical theory that defines what is right in terms of pleasure

Hexis: a Greek word used by Aristotle for a person's manner of behaviour

Homosexual: being sexually attracted to people of one's own sex

Inductive proof: argument constructed on evidence and/or experience that puts forward a possible conclusion based on these

Ineffable: that being of which a person cannot speak as no words can describe the experience

Intellectual: in terms of visions, that which brings the recipient(s) knowledge and understanding

Intermediate cause: this refers to a cause that relies on something else to have triggered it (remember the 2nd domino in the line!)

Internal act: an action that is consistent with intention whether good or bad

Intrinsic maximum: a term often associated in the context of the ontological argument with English philosopher, Charles Dunbar Broad, to refer to the necessary properties of God – in that they must all possess this intrinsic maximum in order for the definition of God as the greatest possible being to be accurate

Justice: a cardinal virtue involving guidance in how we act towards others

Kenotic: from a Greek word meaning to empty or make oneself completely receptive to something

Legalism: an approach to ethics that accepts the absolute nature of established rules or principles

Literalist: interpreting the text of the bible in a literal sense – that is, every word should be taken at face value; interpretation is not required

Medical abortion: abortion by means of the abortion pill

Meta-ethics: the debates that arise when the *nature* of ethics is considered

Ministry of Defence: the British government department responsible for implementing the defence policy for the UK

Moral: a term used to describe ethical behaviour

Moral evil: evil caused as a result of the actions of a free-will agent

Mysticism: a religious experience where union with God or the absolute reality is sought or experienced

Natural evil: evil caused by the means of a force outside of the control of free-will agents – usually referred to as 'nature'

Naturalism: that which arises from real life or the world of nature

Natural world: the world of nature, comprising of all objects, organic and inorganic

Necessary being: Aquinas' contention that a non-contingent being is necessary for contingent beings to exist. It is this necessary being that is the source of all existence for all other contingent beings

Noetic: knowledge gained through mystical experience that would otherwise not be available to the recipient through ordinary means

Normative ethics: the debates that arise when ethical *theories* are considered

Objective: a theory that is independent of personal view

Omnibenevolence: God's all-loving nature

Omnibenevolent: all-loving

Omnipotent: all-powerful

Ontological argument: argument for the existence of God based on the concept of the nature of being

Passive: in this context, where the mystical experience is 'done to' the recipient – it is not instigated by the individual or group but is instead due to some kind of external force or influence

Perfection: the complete absence of flaws also the ultimate state of a positive trait

Polyamorous: having a (loving) sexual relationship with more than one individual with the knowledge and consent of all partners

Posit: to put forward, or state, a fact or belief, usually as the basis for an argument or conclusion

Potential: the possibility, at conception, of becoming a human person

Potential infinite: the potential infinite is something that could continue on, were effort to be applied. E.g. it would be possible to always continue a number line if we wanted to, or we could always come up with a bigger number

Potentiality: the ability to be able to become something else

Prayer: in simple terms, communication with the divine

Predicate: a defining characteristic or attribute

Premise: a statement or proposition used to construct an argument

Principle of utility: an action is right if it promotes and maximises happiness

Privation: the absence or loss of something that is normally present (i.e. a privation of health means that a person is ill and not healthy)

Pro-choice: supporting women's rights to have abortions

Pro-life: against abortion

Proslogion: a work written by Anselm, used as a meditation, but including within it the classical form of the ontological argument

Prudence: a cardinal virtue involving sound judgement

Psychological egoism: the descriptive view that all human action is motivated by self-interest

Quickening: traditionally, when the child is first felt to move inside the mother

Real good: real good is a characteristic that will help people to become closer to the ideal human nature that God had planned for us

Reason: the use of logic in thought processes or putting forward an argument

Redemption: the act of saving something or someone. In the Christian context it refers to Jesus saving humanity from evil and sin

Reductio ad absurdum: an argument that shows a statement to be false or absurd if its logical conclusions were to be accepted

Relational factors: different interpretations of the same words or terms, depending on the viewpoint of the observer

Relativist: an ethical system that believes there is no absolute right or wrong

Relativistic: this means there are no universal moral norms or rules and that each situation has to be looked at independently because each situation is different

Rule Utilitarianism: a view associated with John Stuart Mill. Rule utilitarians believe that by using the 'principle of utility', that is, the greatest happiness for the greatest number, one can draw up general rules, based on past experiences, which would help to keep this principle.

Sanctity of life: the belief that life is sacred or holy, given by God

Sensory: a vision where external objects/sounds or figures convey knowledge and understanding to the recipient

Situation Ethics: a relativist theory of ethics made famous by Joseph Fletcher

Sophron: one who effortlessly lives according to the mean

Soul-making: a process where the soul is developing towards spiritual perfection by gaining the wisdom to always make the correct moral choices when faced with the ambiguities of life as a human being

Strong Rule Utilitarianism: a strong rule utilitarian believes that any rules formulated and established through the application of the 'principle of utility' should never be broken as they guarantee happiness for society.

Subjective: a theory that is dependent on a personal view

Surgical abortion: abortion by means of the suction method

Teleological: a theory concerned with the end purpose or goal of an action

Telos: the term can have a number of meanings but generally refers to the 'end' (as in final destination); 'goal' or 'purpose' of something – the term is frequently found in Aristotle's philosophy

Temperance: a cardinal virtue involving balance and restraint

Temporal: things relating to time

Thaler: currency used in 18th-century Prussia

The Fall: the events of Genesis chapter 3, where Adam and Eve face God's punishment for disobeying his divine command not to eat of the fruit from the tree of knowledge of Good and Evil

Transcendent: that which lies beyond the everyday realm of the physical senses

Transient: an experience that is short lived yet has far-reaching and/or long-lasting consequences

Ultimate cause: in the sense of Aquinas' writings, this is the end cause in the sequence that could not have occurred had there not been preceding efficient and intermediate causes (think about this as the penultimate domino in the line to fall)

Understanding Animal Research: a Mutual Society (not-for-profit organisation) that explains why animals are used in medical and scientific research

Unitive: the feeling of complete oneness with the divine

Utilitarianism: an ethical theory that maintains that an action is right if it produces the greatest happiness for the greatest number – the ethical nature of actions is therefore based on consequences for human happiness

Viability: the ability to grow and develop into an adult, especially the ability of the child to exist without dependence on the mother

Visions: the ability to 'see' something beyond normal experiences – e.g. the vision of an angel; such visions usually convey information or insight concerning a specific religious tradition

Vivisection: the practice of performing operations on live animals for the purpose of experimentation or scientific research

Weak Rule Utilitarianism: weak rule utilitarian tries to allow for the fact that in some situations breaking a rule originally created because it generally fulfils the principle of utility may be the right course of action, because in this particular situation, breaking the rule is more likely to fulfil the principle of utility than keeping the rule.

Wolfenden report: a government-initiated investigation to explore the problems of prostitution and homosexuality, finally published in 1957

Zygote: a cell formed by the union of a male sex cell (a sperm) and a female sex cell (an ovum), which develops into the embryo according to information encoded in its genetic material

Index